W9-AOX-518

368-3
12

RL
1-7

THE BETRAYAL OF THE NEGRO

The Betrayal of the Negro

from Rutherford B. Hayes to Woodrow Wilson

BY

RAYFORD W. LOGAN

PROFESSOR OF HISTORY
HOWARD UNIVERSITY

Originally published as
The Negro in American Life and Thought:
The Nadir, 1877–1901

NEW, ENLARGED EDITION

LIBRARY
BRYAN COLLEGE
DAYTON, TENN. 37321

COLLIER BOOKS

COLLIER-MACMILLAN LTD., LONDON

71852

Copyright 1954 by Rayford W. Logan
Copyright © 1965 by Rayford W. Logan
All rights reserved. No part of this book may
be reproduced or transmitted in any form or
by any means, electronic or mechanical, including photocopying, recording or by any information storage and retrieval system, without permission in writing from the Publisher.

Library of Congress Catalog Card Number: 65:23835
First Collier Books Edition 1965

The Betrayal of the Negro originally appeared as *The Negro in
American Life and Thought: The Nadir, 1877–1901*

This edition, revised for Collier Books, is published by arrangement
with the author.

"O Black and Unknown Bards" by James Weldon Johnson. Copyright, 1909, by The Century Company. Reprinted by permission
of Appleton-Century-Crofts.

Fifth Printing 1970

The Macmillan Company
866 Third Avenue, New York, N.Y. 10022
Collier-Macmillan Canada Ltd., Toronto, Ontario
Printed in the United States of America

To my wife

Contents

PART III

Preface

AMERICAN NEGROES have made notable progress toward first-class citizenship in recent years. But foreign critics—not all of them Communists—point with great effectiveness at many inequalities from which Negroes still suffer. Some of the sincere criticism is based, in large part, upon ignorance of greater inequalities during earlier periods in our history, especially that from the end of Reconstruction to the end of the nineteenth century. This ignorance is understandable in view of the fact that it is one of the neglected periods in American history. This book, for example, is the first attempt at a comprehensive analysis of the Negro in American life and thought during the last quarter of the century.

Among the most valuable sources previously unexplored for this subject were the *Congressional Record*, the *Messages and Papers of the Presidents* and the platforms of the two major parties. Even more revealing—and at times shocking—were some of the most representative Northern newspapers and literary magazines. Southern newspapers were analyzed for the period immediately before and after Booker T. Washington's famous speech at Atlanta, Georgia, in 1895. They do not entirely justify his assertion that the Southern white man was the Negro's best friend.

At the beginning of the twentieth century, what is now called second-class citizenship for Negroes was accepted by Presidents, the Supreme Court, Congress, organized labor, the General Federation of Women's Clubs—indeed, by the vast majority of Americans, North and South, and by the "leader" of the Negro race. One is tempted to refer to this quarter of a century as "The Dark Ages of Recent American History." Barely visible were "The Roots of Recovery"—the forces that were to gain such strength in our times that today the future of the American Negro is as bright as it was gloomy fifty years ago. The contrast should make the faint-hearted in the United States and the honest critics abroad give an eventual affirmative answer to the question that Frederick Douglass posed in 1889, namely, whether "American justice, American liberty, American civilization, American law, and American Christianity could be made to include and protect

9

alike and forever all American citizens in the rights which have been guaranteed to them by the organic and fundamental laws of the land."

The author is happy to record his thanks to Dr. John Hope Franklin, Professor of History at Howard University, for his many valuable suggestions on the entire manuscript; to Dean George Johnson and Professor Dorsey Lane of the Howard University Law School for their most helpful criticism of Chapter 6; to Mrs. Elvena S. Bage for much of the most important research; to those graduate students whose master's theses provided the raw material for more complete analyses of the newspapers and magazines; and to Miss Marie V. Wood and Mr. Armand Labat for typing most of the manuscript. The author absolves all of them from any responsibility for any mistakes that may have eluded them. He is also grateful to the staffs of the Library of Congress and the Moorland Room, Founders Library of Howard University, especially its supervisor, Mrs. Dorothy B. Porter, for their unfailing assistance.

Rayford W. Logan

October 29, 1953

Preface to the New Edition

THE publication in 1954 of *The Negro in American Life and Thought: The Nadir, 1877–1901* has provoked discussion as to whether 1901 or a later date marked the lowest point in the quest for equal rights. For example, Henry Arthur Callis, a physician who was born in 1886 and who until recently was still active in the quest, has termed the first decade of the twentieth century "a low, rugged plateau." John Hope Franklin, now Professor of History at the University of Chicago, who was born in 1915, stated in the Sidney Hillman Lectures at Howard University, 1961, that "The Long Dark Night" continued until 1923.

Even before the publication of the first edition of this volume, there was a lack of consensus as to when the take-off began. William Edward Burghardt Du Bois and William Monroe Trotter declared in the "Declaration of Principles" in 1905, the first year of the Niagara Movement, that the preceding decade had shown "undoubted evidences of progress." But in 1944 Du Bois stated: "For the American Negro, the last decade of the nineteenth and the first part of the twentieth centuries were more critical than the Reconstruction years of 1868 to 1876." In retrospect, some writers view the founding of the National Association for the Advancement of Colored People in 1909 and of the National Urban League in 1911 as the beginning of a new era. The death of Booker T. Washington in 1915 has been called the end of his "Era of Compromise," but evidence which this writer has found in the Booker T. Washington Papers in the Library of Congress clearly reveals his outspoken disillusionment several years before his death. Marcus Garvey, who arrived in New York about a year after the death of Washington, owed much of his early meteoric career to the frustrations and bitterness of American Negroes during World War I.

Part III of this new edition presents information—much of which has not been previously published—and interpretations which will probably arouse more discussion than did the first edition, about the lowest point in the American Negro's struggle for equal rights. This discussion and further studies would be more valuable than agreement or disagreement.

The author is indebted particularly to Dr. Callis and Professor Franklin for their incisive analyses of *The Nadir*. He again expresses his gratitude, also, to many of his students whose master's theses provided valuable raw material. One of the most valuable was Sidney T. Tobin's "Debates on Negro Problems in Congress, 1907–1921," which made extensive use of the *Congressional Record*, of The Archibald H. Grimké Papers in the Negro Collection of Howard University, and of the Booker T. Washington Papers. Mrs. Dorothy Porter, Supervisor of the Negro Collection, has once more suggested valuable leads; and the staff of the Library of Congress has, as usual, given its wholehearted cooperation. Colonel Campbell C. Johnson, the author's life-long friend, has provided much useful information and helped the author to check some of his own reminiscences. Miss Dorothy Butler, the author's senior research assistant, checked or supervised the checking of some references, typed and proofread the manuscript. Mr. William Scott, junior research assistant, aided the checking of references. The investigation by Mr. Michael R. Winston, Instructor of History, Howard University, of many newspapers provided the basis upon which the selection of headlines appearing on the cover of this book was made.

The author's wife has accepted with her usual equanimity the inconveniences which accompany the writing of a book.

Finally, sincere thanks are expressed to Mr. Carl Morse, Editor, Collier Books, for many valuable suggestions in the final revision and for the new title.

If, despite this helpful cooperation by many persons, a few errors have gone undetected, the author must accept the responsibility.

Rayford W. Logan

April 15, 1965

Part I

Problem of how to assimilate
        freedmen — factors affecting

① Sectionalism

② no data or research on how other
nations found solutions to
assimilation of Negroes

③ North & South not interested in
protecting Negroes economic or
social rights.

④ Fact that Negroes were of different
race and culture complicated readjust
ment. Looked on as inferior

⑤ ~~Fear~~, esp in South, that Negro voters
could control elections

⑥ U.S. not prodded by foreign criticism
for lack of civil rights program.
Europe busy in wars.

⑦ South more embittered after Recon.
than after Civil War.

ONE

The Problem

THE problem of determining the place that Negroes should occupy in American life was the most difficult of the "racial" problems that confronted the American government and people after the Civil War. The Chinese Exclusion Act of 1882 virtually stopped an immigration that might have provoked an increase of violent disorders. Five years later, the Dawes Act attempted to improve the plight of some 260,000 Indians living on reservations. European immigrants rushed to the United States in such vast numbers that by the end of the century passionate demands were voiced for severe curtailment of their numbers, and even for a complete halt. But, since these Europeans were of the same racial stocks as most other Americans, they could be more easily fused into the melting pot than could Negroes. The Negro population—of four million ex-slaves and of a half million who had been free prior to the Civil War—doubled by the end of the century. Their number was too large for either deportation or reservation to be a practical solution.

The question that the architects and engineers of human relations had to answer was trenchantly posed by Frederick Douglass—the ex-slave who had become the most eminent Negro spokesman during the struggle for abolition and throughout the Civil War. In 1889 he queried whether "American justice, American liberty, American civilization, American law, and American Christianity could be made to include and protect alike and forever all American citizens in the rights which have been guaranteed to them by the organic and fundamental laws of the land."[1] The question is equally pertinent today.

The task confronting the United States was more formidable than that which European nations had to face when they freed their slaves. Only a few Negroes, slave and free, had lived in England, and even fewer in France and Holland. The considerable number of Negroes in Portugal and Spain had been largely absorbed by, and assimilated to, other elements in the population. For England, France, and Holland emancipation involved primarily slaves in far-distant colonies.

Europe had no problem of assimilating freed slaves. werent many

Largely for this reason the debates over abolition were less acrimonious than those in the United States. Emancipation was achieved in the Spanish and Portuguese colonies after they had become independent nations. Of the former Spanish American colonies which had gained independence, only Venezuela, Colombia and the Dominican Republic had considerable numbers of slave and free Negroes. When Brazil completed emancipation in 1888, most of its slaves had already been freed.

In the United States alone had slavery been a direct and immediate cause of a civil war on its own soil that resulted in the emancipation of slaves. That war increased a spirit of sectionalism, arising out of the question of slavery or emancipation, that had not harassed the other countries. Since most of the American Civil War had been fought on Southern soil, large portions of the South were devastated, and the entire region was impoverished. The uncompensated emancipation of the slaves added to the humiliation, bitterness and impoverishment of the former slaveholders who had constituted a closely-knit ruling class. The North, on the other hand, tremendously expanded its industrial potential, and thereby increased its pre-war economic superiority over the South. The subordination of the South to the North would become even greater, most Southerners believed, if the black peasantry had to be paid a living wage out of the depleted resources of the defeated, devastated and impoverished former slave states.

Despite the differences between the conditions and circumstances in the United States and those elsewhere, the task might have been facilitated if scientific studies of the progress of emancipation had been available. But most of the literature on the British West Indian colonies and on Haiti was propaganda, designed to support the arguments of either abolitionists or slaveholders. Haiti especially—where the only large-scale distribution of land to the former slaves had been carried out—was held up as the illustration par excellence of the inability of Negroes to progress in a free society. The decline of sugar production, particularly in the British West Indies, was widely attributed to the perverseness of the freedmen, without allowance for the effects of the development of beet sugar in Europe. A rebellion in Jamaica, in 1865, gave Britain an opportunity to reduce the limited participation of freedmen in the insular government. Americans knew little about conditions in the French and Danish West Indies, and slavery in the Dutch West Indies was abolished at about the same time as in the United States. It may be doubted that even a score of the architects of Reconstruction in the United States were familiar with economic and social conditions in Central and South America.

The existence of such studies would not, however, have helped materially in the drafting of plans for improving the economic and social plight of the freedmen. Since even the concept of economic and social rights on any level—federal, state or local—was virtually non-existent, the enumeration, definition and protection of such rights would have involved an exploration into virgin territory. Some idea of the difficulty of this aspect of the problem can be gained from a study of the policy of the United States today with respect to the Universal Declaration of Human Rights and the Draft Covenants on Human Rights. The United States led the fight for the adoption, by the General Assembly of the United Nations, of the Declaration—the Declaration includes both political and civil rights on the one hand, and economic and social rights on the other. But the United States has become increasingly reluctant to support the inclusion of specific economic and social rights in a draft covenant[2] which, if ratified by the Senate, would presumably be binding on the people of the United States.

Much of the reluctance of the United States today, to agree to specific economic and social rights in the Draft Covenants, stems from the federal structure of our government. For some of these rights run counter to the limitations that states, especially those in the South, have placed upon the enjoyment of these rights by Negroes. The opposition by Southerners to the federal program of economic and social amelioration of the plight of the freedmen in the last half of the nineteenth century was, of course, even greater than it is today. But not many Northerners were enthusiastic about federal intervention in behalf of the economic and social advancement of the freedmen. It is no mere coincidence that the Fourteenth and Fifteenth Amendments sought to protect only the political, civil and legal rights of Negroes.

The failure to include in the Constitution protection of economic and social rights was also due to the fact that the status of the Negroes had to be determined in an era when

Big Business in the North was beginning the phenomenal growth that has made the United States today the greatest industrial and financial power in the history of mankind. The Gilded Age was hardly the most propitious period for enlightened social engineering. In that age, the egalitarian theories of some Northerners could not long prevail against the increased profits that would result from the re-establishment of friendly relations with the former enemy. Organized labor was neither strong enough to improve the condition of workers in general, nor farsighted enough to integrate the new contingent of black workers into its ranks.

The fact that the Negroes were of a different race and culture further complicated the difficulties of the post-war readjustment. In the pre-Civil War period, not only most Southerners but many Northerners had looked upon Negroes as an inferior and unassimilable race. Some New England colonizationists, supposedly friends of the Negroes, had repeatedly declared: "This is a white man's country."[3] Many Northern states had placed restrictions on the right of free Negroes to vote. Free Negroes had been frequently discriminated against in job opportunities, and they had sometimes been mobbed. Segregation was not uncommon, especially in the churches, even after Northern and Southern church branches had separated over the issue of slavery.

Few Northern Negroes, then, had been fully acculturated. Except for the house slaves in the better Southern homes, the Southern Negro was almost an alien culturally when he was emancipated.[4] Physical differences in many instances heightened the repugnance that many whites, North and South, believed that they felt toward Negroes. This repugnance, real or feigned, flamed into hatred when the former slaves sought to exercise their rights of citizenship. The statement by Senator William Windom of Minnesota in 1879, "the black man does not excite antagonism because he is black, but because he is a *citizen*, and as such may control an election,"[5] was especially accurate when Negroes had voted in large numbers during the period of Reconstruction.

This fear of Negro control had pervaded particularly the states of South Carolina, Mississippi and Louisiana, where Negroes outnumbered whites, and those parts of other Southern states in which the freedmen constituted the majority of the population. Historians will probably continue to disagree as to whether the fear was real or imagined, and as to whether the acts of the freedmen inspired the whites to undertake reprisals. The essential point is that there were areas in which, under normal democratic processes, the numerically superior Negroes might control the elections and the government.

Quite apart from considerations of race and class, the elements in a community that have long exercised exclusive control of government do not generally relinquish that control without a struggle. The contest in the South, however, was inevitably embittered by the difference in race and culture. The sympathies of most Northerners would naturally be on the side of those who were of their own race and blood, especially after the bitterness engendered by the Civil War had subsided.

During the crucial period of Reconstruction, the government and people of the United States were not prodded by any effective foreign criticism. While the Southern states were evolving their post-Civil War Black Codes, Bismarck was maneuvering Austria into the Six Weeks' War. The thunder at Sadowa in 1866, and at Sedan in 1870, left English and Continental statesmen little time to listen to the remote rumblings on the other side of the Atlantic. New alliances and alignments had to be formed. The War Scare of 1875 put Europe on "the razor's edge," on the eve of the end of Reconstruction; and the scramble for Africa began almost immediately thereafter. Leopold II of Belgium organized the International Association for the Exploration and Civilization of Central Africa in 1876, the year of the Hayes-Tilden election. Belgium, Britain, and France, soon followed by Germany and Italy, carried the "blessings" of white civilization to Africa. They were not likely, at the same time, to condemn the restoration of white supremacy in the South. Tsar Alexander II's emancipation of the Russian serfs, 1861–1866, and the subsequent attempts at reform of his vast empire imposed upon him his own problems of reconstruction. The Russian-Turkish War was brewing when Hayes withdrew the federal troops from South Carolina and Louisiana in 1877.

In these critical years, moreover, the United States had not become the "arsenal of democracy" in a world war against Nazism and Fascism or in a cold war against Communism. The place of the Negro in North American society, therefore, was not a vulnerable point of attack in a global ideological conflict. Since laissez-faire "liberalism" dominated the thinking of most Western European governments, "liberals" could not logically denounce the United States for her early abandonment of governmental intervention in behalf of the economic status of Negroes.

Finally, the experiment had to be continued after a period of Reconstruction that left the South even more embittered than had the Civil War. It is with this post-Reconstruction experiment that this book is concerned. A brief summary of Reconstruction will reveal how greatly it complicated the problem of fixing the status of Negroes in American society.

Soon after the ratification of the Thirteenth Amendment, the Southern states revealed in their Black Codes the level at which they would have placed the freedmen. The emancipation of the slaves was conceded, but they were not granted the right to vote. Little provision was made for their education—or, indeed, for the education of whites. The mobility of the freedmen, their freedom to sell their labor, and the protection of their legal rights were so restricted that a modern Southern historian has concluded: "The new laws relegated to a distinct caste all individuals possessing a certain amount of Negro blood, usually one-eighth."[6]

The determination of the South to maintain its own way of life naturally increased when the federal government sought to change it. The Freedmen's Bureau, first created in 1865 as a war measure, was continued in order to provide material relief and aid in economic and social readjustment. The Civil Rights Act of 1866 declared that all persons born in the United States, except untaxed Indians, were citizens of the United States and, as such, entitled to equality of treatment before the law, any "statute to the contrary notwithstanding." In an attempt to prevent any contest over the constitutionality of many of the main features of this law, they were incorporated in the first section of the Fourteenth Amendment, 1868, which also bestowed state citizenship upon all persons born or naturalized in the United States and subject to its jurisdiction. No state was to take any action that would violate the rights that this section sought to protect. The second section, in substance, gave the states the choice between granting suffrage to all adult male citizens or suffering a reduction in the House of Representatives, and in the electoral college, proportionate to the number denied the right to vote. The third section barred from federal and state office many of the most prominent pre-Civil War Southerners. This amendment was adopted when the Southern states were under military rule, established by the "Great" Reconstruction Acts of 1867. In accordance with these laws, Negroes were given the right to vote and to sit in state constitutional conventions— that were to adopt constitutions giving Negroes the right to vote. The Fifteenth Amendment, 1870, declared that the right of citizens of the United States to vote should not be abridged or denied by the United States or any state on account of race, color or previous condition of servitude. Other federal laws sought to protect Negroes from armed attacks. Finally, the Civil Rights Act of 1875 prohibited individuals from discriminating against Negroes in public places and on public carriers.

So determined were most white Southerners to maintain their own way of life, that they resorted to fraud, intimidation and murder, in order to re-establish their own control of the state governments. They found some justification, in their own eyes at least, in the facts that some Negroes undoubtedly intended to "enjoy their freedom" by taking a rest from work, and that the Reconstruction conventions and legislatures were not entirely free from fraud and corruption. Basically, however, the new civil war within the Southern states stemmed from an adamant determination to restore white supremacy. Regulators, Jayhawkers, the Black Horse Cavalry, the Knights of the White Camellia, the Constitutional Union Guards, the Pale Faces, the White Brotherhood, the Council of Safety, the '76 Association, the Rifle Clubs of South Carolina, and, above all, the Ku-Klux Klan terrorized, maimed and killed a large number of Negroes. Not even the presence of federal troops was able to prevent the achievement, by force, of "home rule." In some instances, indeed, Northern soldiers sided with the gangs that terrorized and killed Negroes.

White rule was restored in Tennessee in 1869; in Virginia, North Carolina, and Georgia, in 1870; in Alabama, Arkansas, and Texas, in 1874; and in Mississippi, in 1875. Thus, only South Carolina, Louisiana, and Florida remained to be "redeemed" in 1876. In these three states, and in Mississippi, the coalition of Negroes, Southern whites and Northern whites had exercised a large measure of control during most of the period of Reconstruction. But, in none of them had Negroes alone completely controlled the state governments. Moreover, the great increase of the state debts—which is still cited as indisputable evidence of the "orgy of misrule"— must, in the opinion of Professor Howard K. Beale, be restudied.[7] But this modern conclusion—recall that there were contemporary scandals on a much larger scale in the Grant administration and in New York City—does not alter the fact that it was asserted that the restoration of white rule was necessary for the establishment of honest and efficient government in the South.

Nor did the fact that many of the Southern states had enacted constructive legislation change the conviction of most white Southerners that they had to regain power. The most important general provision, in the judgment of Professor Arthur M. Schlesinger, was the inauguration of a mandatory system of free public schools for both white and colored children.[8] In various Southern states other provisions liberalized the suffrage, enlarged the rights of women, abolished dueling and imprisonment for debt, and instituted reforms in the organization of the courts, in the codes of judicial procedure and in the system of county administration. These Reconstruction governments also abolished the whipping post, the branding iron and the penal stocks. Many of the main features of the state constitutions and laws that do not pertain specifically to Negroes have survived to the present day.[9]

One of the main reasons why the South had opposed abolition had been its realization that it had no plans for free Negroes in Southern society. During the first months after the Civil War, the Southern states had attempted almost overnight to improvise plans. For a few years the federal government had sought to impose its own ideas. In 1877, however, the entire South had regained the right to resume its plans for social engineering, in so far as the federal Constitution and laws and public opinion in the North permitted. During the next quarter of the century, the South sought to have the Constitution interpreted, federal laws repealed or rendered innocuous, and Northern public opinion made amenable to the end that Negroes should become what were later called second-class citizens.

TWO

The "Let Alone" Policy of Hayes

A SUCCESSION of weak Presidents, between 1877 and 1901, facilitated the consolidation of white supremacy in the South, and Northern acceptance of victory for "The Lost Cause." Professor Schlesinger, after polling a number of historians in 1948, rated Hayes, Arthur, Harrison, and McKinley as "average," and Cleveland as "near great."[1] Garfield served for too short a period to permit an evaluation. All these Presidents, except Cleveland, were Republicans. All came from the North. Hayes, Garfield and McKinley were Ohioans; Harrison, elected from Indiana, had been born and educated in Ohio; Arthur and Cleveland came from New York. Hayes, Garfield, and Harrison had been Union generals in the Civil War and McKinley a major. While all the Republicans uttered pious platitudes about the denial to Negroes of rights guaranteed to them by the Constitution and laws of the United States, they did virtually nothing to protect those rights. Cleveland—who undoubtedly deserved the encomium of "near great" in many respects—remained almost completely silent on the rights of Negroes; and he did practically nothing to protect them. This chapter and the following three chapters present the first systematic analysis of the pertinent planks of the two major parties, and the views and policies of the Presidents with respect to the experiment in fixing the status of Negroes.

Rutherford B. Hayes—the principal presidential architect of the consolidation of white supremacy in the South, during the post-Reconstruction period—floundered between devotion to the Constitution and democracy on the one hand, and to the political fortune of the Republican party, pacification of the country and good will toward the South on the other. Only a truly great President *might* have been able to achieve the miracle of reconciling these conflicting aims. Hayes's task was made all the more difficult by the coalition of Northern and Southern businessmen interested in a federal subsidy for the construction of the Texas and Pacific Railroad and other Southern internal improvements.[2] While the importance of this coalition in securing Hayes's election over Tilden has perhaps been overemphasized, this economic basis for the Compromise of 1877 undoubtedly strengthened Hayes's determination to prevent a possible renewal of civil war. Since the consummate political skill of Franklin D. Roosevelt and the stubbornness of President Truman were unable to overcome a similar coalition of Republicans and Southern Democrats, it is not to be expected that a weaker president would have succeeded even if he had so desired.

Hayes's floundering was evident prior to the campaign of 1876. In 1867, while running for governor of Ohio, he had publicly declared: "The plain and monstrous inconsistency and injustice of excluding one-seventh of our population from all participation in a Government founded on the consent of the governed in this land of free discussion is simply impossible." But, in 1875, he had written to Guy M. Bryan, a college classmate from Texas: "As to Southern affairs, 'the let alone policy' seems now to be the true course." He further assured Bryan that he felt "nothing but good will" toward the South.[3]

The inherent conflict between these two views was clearly revealed in the Republican platform of 1876, and in Hayes's public pronouncements, private observations, and policies as President. The platform committed the party to the complete pacification of the country and to "the complete protection of all its citizens in the free enjoyment of all their constitutional rights." Hayes, in his acceptance speech of July 8, 1876, spelled out the ambivalence of these policies more clearly when he stated:

> All parts of the Constitution are sacred and must be sacredly observed—the parts that are new no less than the parts that are old. The moral and material prosperity of the Southern states can be most effectually advanced by a hearty and generous recognition of the rights of all, by all—a recognition without reserve or reservation.

There followed immediately, however, a sentence which indicated an attitude that might nullify the commitment to the recognition by all of the new parts of the Constitution, namely, the Fourteenth and Fifteenth Amendments. For Hayes added: "With such a recognition fully accorded it will be practicable to promote, by the influence of all legitimate agencies of the federal government, the efforts of those States to obtain for themselves the blessings of honest and capable government."[4] It should be noted that this acceptance speech prescribed the political basis for the Compromise of 1877—observance of the Constitution and the restoration of "home rule." Highly significant is the fact that this offer of a political compromise was made more than five months before the railroad lobbyists entered the picture and laid the economic basis for the Compromise.

This acceptance speech also clearly implied that the governments in the Southern states, during Reconstruction, had not been honest and capable; and it appeared to approve the methods that had been used to regain white control. On the very day that Hayes delivered his acceptance speech, the town of Hamburg, South Carolina, was the scene of a bloody riot. Another race riot occurred at nearby Ellenton, September 15–20. Many Southerners and some Northerners justified the resort to force as the only means by which the whites could obtain redress for the wrongs which, they alleged, had been inflicted upon them by a Negro majority. But Grant's attorney-general, Taft, wrote Hayes on September 12 that "it is a fixed and desperate purpose of the Democratic party in the South that the negroes shall not vote, and murder is a common means of intimidation to prevent them."[5]

Hayes seems at first to have inclined toward Taft's view, for he wrote in his diary, at the end of October, 1876, that "bloodshed and civil war must be averted if possible. If forced to fight, I have no fear of failure, from lack of courage and firmness." On the day after the election, when it appeared that he had been defeated, he wrote: "I don't care for myself; and the party, yes, and the country, too, can stand it; but I do care for the poor colored men of the South. . . . The result will be that the Southern people will practically treat the constitutional amendments as nullities, and then the colored man's fate will be worse than when he was in slavery." On the Saturday after the election, when the outcome still seemed in doubt, he confided to his diary the anxiety that he and his wife felt about the South, "about the poor colored people especially." But on December first, he told Colonel W. H. Roberts, managing editor of the New Orleans Times, that he wished to consult with such prominent Southerners as L. Q. C. Lamar of Mississippi, and General Wade Hampton, who claimed the gubernatorial election in South Carolina. Hayes added his conviction that the complaints of the Southern people against the carpetbag governments were justified. He would "require absolute justice and fair play to the negro, but . . . he was convinced that this could be got best and almost surely by trusting the honorable and influential southern whites."[6]

From the end of December until the final count in the disputed presidential election, railroad lobbyists energetically sought to arrange a compromise—by which the election of Hayes would be conceded in return for a federal subsidy for the construction of the Texas and Pacific and other internal improvements. But C. Vann Woodward, whose recent book, *Reunion and Reaction*, has vividly portrayed these negotiations, also leaves no doubt that the terms of the political compromise were constantly in the foreground. Reciprocal promises—of withdrawal of the federal troops from South Carolina and Louisiana, and of protection of Negro rights by Southerners—were repeatedly given between December, 1876 and March 2, 1877. When a newspaper friendly to Hayes appeared to repudiate Hayes's promises, the consternation of the Southern intermediaries was allayed only with great difficulty. These promises were confirmed at the famous Wormley Hotel conference on February 26 and 27. A few days thereafter, a Democratic filibuster in the House of Representatives, to prevent a vote on the selection of a President, was broken when one of the participants in the hotel conference announced that he had received "solemn, earnest, and, I believe, truthful assurance" of a policy of conciliation toward the South and the abandonment of the use of federal troops.[7] A few hours later, early in the morning of March 2, it was announced that Hayes had been elected president.

Professor Woodward has declared that the explanation of the Compromise of 1877 in political terms is "inadequate." It should be noted, however, that Congress did not pass the federal subsidy bill; and the Texas and Pacific had to be constructed by private funds. Thus, the Compromise of 1877 rested upon two hopes: one that Hayes would withdraw the federal troops and pursue a conciliatory policy toward the South; the other that a federal subsidy would be provided by Congress. Since both the political and the economic bases for the Compromise rested upon hope, it is difficult to see how one could have been a more adequate explanation than the other. In any event, the South did not get its federal subsidy, but it did get the fulfillment of Hayes's political promises.

More important than this question is the fact that Hayes was quite complaisant about the failure of the South to live up to its part of the bargain. It is true that Southerners, with the aid of a Democratic majority in the House, made it virtually impossible for Hayes to renege on his promise to withdraw the troops from South Carolina and Louisiana. The House, in the closing days of the session, attached a rider to the Army appropriation bill forbidding the use of troops to support the claims of any state government in the South until it had been approved by Congress. Since the Democrats would have a majority in the new House also, they could prevent the recognition of any Southern state government objectionable to them. The Republican Senate rejected the bill, and Congress adjourned without making any appropriation for the army.

It may be doubted, however, that Hayes's complaisance toward the South was dictated wholly by fear of using unpaid troops to protect Negroes. Whether he sincerely believed that this protection could be entrusted to the "honorable and influential southern whites" is debatable. It can hardly be doubted, on the other hand, that he was fully committed to leaving that protection to them. He had probably concluded that his paramount duty was to restore peace between the North and the South.

In his inaugural address of March 5, 1877, Hayes demanded a government that would guard the interests of both races "carefully and equally." He specifically recognized a "moral obligation" of the federal government to employ its constitutional powers and influence to establish and protect the rights of Negroes. But, he then officially proclaimed his intention of living up to his part of the bargain when he prescribed "honest and efficient *local** government as the true resources of these [i.e., Southern] states for the promotion of the contentment and prosperity of their citizens." Since he had previously expressed his private fear that the Southern people would practically nullify the constitutional amendments, this prescription must be interpreted as indicating his

* My italics.—R.W.L.

approval of the curtailment of the rights of Negroes by the resurgent South. A cynic would probably even accuse Hayes of suggesting to the South the method by which some Southern states later were "legally" to disfranchise practically all Negroes. For he laid down the principle that, since universal suffrage rested upon universal education, the state governments should make liberal and permanent provision for the support of public schools. He then made the first recommendation by a President for "legitimate aid" to public schools by the federal government.[8] It may be doubted that Hayes was as Machiavellian as a cynic might suggest, but it is undeniable that some Southern states did later use educational qualifications as a means of disfranchising many Negroes. In any case, it is probable that the linking of federal aid for public education with the right to vote doomed his proposal to defeat.

Shortly after Hayes took office, he received further evidence that the withdrawal of the troops would result in the curtailment of the constitutional rights of Southern Negroes. In a letter from New Orleans, at the end of March, 1877, W. G. Eliot—who gave the names of Carl Schurz and General Sherman as references—criticized the "Radical" Packard government, and expressed his doubt that the property holders and educated people would accept such a government even if it were *legally* elected. The withdrawal of the federal troops would most certainly result in a government under the Democrat, Nicholls. Eliot then candidly stated that, under Democratic rule, he feared that the spirit, and even more the letter, of the Fifteenth Amendment would not be upheld for several years to come. The situation in Louisiana would be similar to that in Alabama and Mississippi, "and when the blacks are in the majority or approximating it, they will be 'discouraged' from voting, with whatever degrees of moral or physical force may be necessary to secure the end." Eliot expressed the belief, however, that the freedmen would be "entirely free" to vote the Democratic ticket; that their condition would further improve as they advanced in thrift and intelligence, and as new social and political issues arose. But, like Hayes, Eliot was clearly prepared to accept, temporarily at least, widespread disfranchisement of the freedmen. For Eliot asserted that, if an education or property qualification test for voting could be secured by amendment, there could be reasonable hope for permanent peace.[9] Since there was little evidence that Negroes in the states that had relatively small numbers of Negroes were being encouraged to vote the Democratic ticket, there was little likelihood that they would be "entirely free" to do so in a state like Louisiana, where the population was almost equally divided. It may be doubted, also, that Hayes would have been willing to procure the recognition of the constitutional rights of the freedmen by sacrificing their vote to the Democratic party. In consequence, withdrawal meant in Louisiana, as in South Carolina, the virtual disfranchisement of the freedmen.

It should be emphasized that the Northern press, in general, supported Hayes in his determination to withdraw the federal troops from the two states regardless of the effect of the withdrawal on the rights of the Negroes. The Boston *Evening Transcript* declared editorially that the people of the United States "want the South Carolina and Louisiana difficulties adjusted, so that real peace may ensue in these States, and the reign of corrupt politicians come to an end." Boston merchants and business men wanted "cordial relations" between North and South. The paper denounced the "Radical" Governor Chamberlain for asserting that the federal government had abandoned the freedmen of South Carolina; it lauded Hayes for his determination not to interfere with the experiment of local authority, that was capable of enforcing its decrees, and that based its "support upon the intelligent and more reputable portions of the community." The rabidly Democratic Cincinnati *Enquirer* interpreted the withdrawal from Louisiana as "an eloquent tribute to the power of the people, a recognition of the omnipotence of the popular will in a free land." The more restrained Washington *Evening Star* also expressed its approval, provided that peace was really restored. "After sixteen years," an editorial pointed out, "the end of the war of the rebellion has been reached—that is if Hampton and Nicholls are able to keep their promises of maintaining the peace in the absence of federal troops." *Harper's Weekly* and the *Nation* joined the chorus of acceptance and satisfaction. The staunchly Republican Chicago *Tribune* asserted that the withdrawal of the troops would not only give the people of Louisiana local self-government, but that such a government, without the aid of federal troops, would have the power and will to support the rights of all classes of people.[10]

The New York *Times*—which under Henry J. Raymond had been Lincoln's strongest supporter, and which remained Republican until George Jones backed Cleveland in 1884—was at first more skeptical than the other papers and magazines cited. An editorial, on March 29, 1877, criticized the conduct of Wade Hampton while he was en route to Washington for a conference that he and Chamberlain—rival claimants for the governorship of South Carolina—were to have with Hayes. The editorial quoted Hampton as having declared that he would "demand his rights, nothing less, and so help him God, to take nothing less." Another editorial, three days later, again referred to the "arrogance" of Hampton, and doubted the wisdom of withdrawal, but expressed a willingness to suspend judgment. But another editorial, on April 5, commented upon the general weariness in the North with the Southern question. Then, on April 7, the *Times* expressed its complete acceptance of Hampton's own assurances. "They are emphatic and to the point," the editor declared. "Inconsistent as some of them are with the methods employed by his supporters in the canvass, we are not disposed to doubt his sincerity in making them or his ability to give effect to them within the limits of his personal influence." The *Times* recognized, however, that complete fulfillment was contingent upon circumstances which Hampton might not be able entirely to control. But his "moral responsibility" extended no further than his personal following.[11]

The New England Conference of the Methodist Episcopal Church, on the other hand, roundly condemned Hayes for yielding to the Southern "Redeemers." Its resolution on April 4 declared:

We protest earnestly against the action of the new Administration in making terms with the chief KuKlux instigator of the Hamburg massacre, M. C. Butler; and still more earnestly do we protest against the official recognition by the Administration of that archenemy of the Republic, who long since ought to have been hanged for treason—Wade Hampton of South Carolina—and who now, by threats and intimidation, under the very roof of the White House, as well as on the railroad platforms and in other public places defies the power of the Government and bullies the President into compliance with his traitorous and wicked usurpation.[12]

As not infrequently happens, a person who doubts the wisdom of an action prior to his decision to take a course finds his doubts revived after the die has been cast. Hayes had steeled himself to go through with the withdrawal. The troops in South Carolina—34 officers and 316 enlisted men—were withdrawn on April 10, 1877. On April 20, the 22 officers and 271 enlisted men stationed in New Orleans were withdrawn.[13] Although these numbers were small, they had symbolized the power, and perhaps the determination, of the federal government to support the constitutional rights of the freedmen. Two days later on April 22, Hayes made certain that posterity would still know the doubts in his mind. His diary states that, since the troops had been ordered away, he could hope for "peace, and what is equally important, security and prosperity for the colored people." Apparently not fully satisfied by the previous promises of the Southerners, he planned to get from Southern governors, legislators, press, and people pledges that the Thirteenth, Fourteenth and Fifteenth Amendments would be "faithfully" observed; "that the colored people shall have equal rights to labor, to education, and to the privileges of citizenship." He was confident that he was engaged in a good work. But at the end of this entry in the diary, he added: "Time will tell."[14]

If Hayes read the Washington *Evening Star* the next day, April 23, he found evidence that some Northerners were convinced that he had not done a good work. William Lloyd Garrison and Wendell Phillips, two of the most ardent of the abolitionists, and Senator Blaine of Maine, an aspirant to the presidency, declared that Hayes had betrayed the trust to which the Republicans were pledged. Senator Wade of Ohio, a "Radical" Republican, stated that the failure to protect Negroes after they had been emancipated was a crime as infamous as had been enslavement itself. He added that Hayes had proved faithless to the very men who had risked their lives to vote for him, although without their vote he would "never have had the power to do this injustice."[15]

These discordant notes were not powerful enough to disturb the harmony of perfervid orations, in which some of the most rabid of the former Southern and Northern fire-eaters rivaled one another in recanting their bitterness and expressing the highest regard for the former enemy. Wade Hampton's address, June, 1877, in Auburn, New York—the home for most of his life of Lincoln's Secretary of State, Seward, and the adopted home of Harriet Tubman, famous Negro worker on the underground railroad—was typical of many such orations. Hampton declared:

> I come to do honor to my distinguished friend, General Shields. He wore the blue and I wore the gray, but we can let the curtain drop over these years, and go back to the time when that flag borne by him waved alike over the men of the South and the men of the North, and we can look beyond to the future, when through all time that flag shall float over a free and prosperous and reunited country.

Hampton also gave assurance of future protection of the Negro.[16]

Encouraged by the general acceptance of his policy of reconciliation and of desire for surcease from sectional strife and discord, Hayes made a "good-will" tour of the South, in September, 1877. Perhaps he believed that enough time had elapsed for him to discover for himself whether he could get from Southern governors, legislatures, the press, and people assurances that they would live up to their pledges to observe faithfully the Thirteenth, Fourteenth and Fifteenth Amendments.

Despite the importance of this trip, no historian has deemed it worthy of complete coverage. The tour really began with a visit to his home state, Ohio. In a speech at Marietta, on September 7, 1877, Hayes sounded both keynotes of his Southern policy: fraternal union, peace and harmony between the North and the South; and adherence to the Constitution with all its amendments. But he stressed particularly the theme of peace and harmony. On September 11, in an otherwise unpublished interview, Hayes revealed— perhaps more clearly than at any other time—why he placed peace and harmony above adherence to the Constitution with all its amendments. En route to his home in Fremont, he was asked by a reporter of the Cincinnati *Evening Times* how he had come to construct his Southern policy, which was "seemingly at variance with his views" while on the stump in his last gubernatorial campaign. After replying that his views had begun to take form in his letter of acceptance, Hayes revealed clearly his desire for peace:

I considered the situation of things in the South; how impossible it seemed to restore order and peace and harmony; saw the violence and bloodshed at their elections; how white Republicans as well as black, were shot down during their political contests, and I asked myself why is it, and how long must this continue. Those men down South— *the white educated citizens*—are as good men as you or I; they are Christians; not thieves, nor cutthroats; nor bandits, yet they see these things and tacitly approve them, if they do not take part in them. Why is it, and how long will they continue? . . . That one word [war] solved in my mind the problem of the South.

He added that, in fact, the people in the South were at war. But let the causes of war be removed and there would be peace, and ultimately harmony and prosperity.

When the reporter observed that "we do not see much disposition in the South to manifest a loving temper toward us of the North," Hayes chided him for his lack of accurate information on the subject. The President thought that most of the people, North and South, were more disposed to encourage fraternal, harmonious, social and business relations than "the extremists who, unfortunately, too often get control of newspapers." Even they, or most of them, would come around in time.[17] Except for the implication in the question about remarks that Hayes had made when he was running for governor, no mention was made of "the poor colored people of the South," other than the fact that they, like white Republicans, had been shot down in cold blood.

Whether Wade Hampton read the interview, which had been reprinted in the Louisville *Courier-Journal,* is not known. But he seems to have grasped clearly, if he had not previously done so, Hayes's horror of "war." On September 14, in a speech at Chicago, Hampton no longer stressed the "Blue and the Gray" theme. He lauded Hayes as the first President in twelve years who had done his duty. But—serving notice perhaps to the President that he was still on trial—Hampton added: "While he performs his Constitutional duty, I think it is our duty to say to him that we will sustain his policy, whether he be Democratic or Republican." In a speech in Louisville the next day, Hampton regretted that he had worn out his voice talking to "those 'suckers' of Illinois." But he had strength enough to repeat, in the same words that he had used in Chicago, his praise of the President and his veiled threat. At the close of the speech, a band played "Dixie," "Yankee Doodle," and "Home Sweet Home." When he was serenaded that night, following a reception in his honor, he expressed his pleasure that he could take back to South Carolina the assurance that his Louisville friends had sympathized cordially and heartily with the people of South Carolina "in their trials." The people of Louisville could not realize how difficult it had been for South Carolinians to restrain themselves. They had done so simply because "they knew, they felt, that bloodshed in South Carolina meant civil war in America." Since South Carolina was at last free, "she intends honestly, truly, bravely and, in the best acceptation of the term, loyally, to fulfill all her duties to the laws and constitution of the country. [Applause]"[18]

There can be little doubt that Hampton had preceded Hayes to Louisville in order to set the tone for the President's speech. At Dayton on September 12, Hayes had again intoned his dual policy. In Louisville he did likewise; and made his first public effort on this tour to get the pledges that had motivated the trip. He dwelt at considerable length on the courage of the soldiers in both the Union and Confederate armies, and the mutual respect for one another of men who had previously been engaged in battle. Since the war was over, why could not all Americans come together? The demonstration in Louisville had convinced him of the happiness and peace that "we are now enjoying in all sections of the Union." It was possible, therefore, to look forward to fraternal union on the basis of the Constitution as it then was with all the new amendments. After this long preliminary, Hayes put the crucial question: "My friends, my Confederate friends, do you intend to obey the whole Constitution and Amendments? [Applause] I thought you would. I believe you will and that removes the last cause of dissension between us." His flowery peroration portraying the beauties of "a vast Confederacy . . . that would contain one people, one language, and one faith, and everywhere a home for freemen, and a refuge for every race and every clime to come together," was greeted with great applause.[19]

A reporter for the New York *Tribune* gave the local color that has more than usual significance. He noted that Hayes's "escort is of Confederate veterans; his greeting is the Rebel yell." The President could hardly have failed to observe, as did the reporter, that the white people were friendly, but that the Negroes were somewhat "less enthusiastic" over the policy "for which their old masters cheer so lustily."[20]

Evidence is lacking as to whether Hayes endeavored to ascertain the sentiments of the colored leaders of Louisville. After a visit to a white school, he went to the Central Colored School where he was greeted by T. H. Sherley, a trustee, and by a colored man, Horace Morris. Morris gave a speech of welcome in the same strain as had the trustee who, in accordance with an old Southern custom, was probably a "discreet" white man—present to make sure that a prearranged program was carried out. After music by the children, the President praised the people of Louisville for their "liberal and just sentiments on the subject of education for all classes."[21]

Crossing by ferry to Jeffersonville, Indiana, the next day, Hayes reiterated his two usual themes; and Postmaster General Key, the only Southerner in the cabinet, remarked that the South was capable of controlling its own affairs loyally since there were no more federal troops stationed there. Returning to Louisville, the party then made a "whistle stop" at Bowling Green, Kentucky, where Hayes made his usual speech without, however, seeking any pledges from the crowd. Hampton also made his usual speech: "We can pledge him that we will do all in our power to hold up his hands while he is sustaining the Constitution of the United States."

At Nashville, the site of Fisk University—one of the schools for Negroes founded by the American Missionary Association—Hayes emphasized education as "precisely the thing which of all others, . . . will do the most to bring about the exact condition we want in this country." Whether it was because of this remark or not, the crowd at that point became so unruly that Hayes expressed fear that what he had to say was not very interesting to the crowd. After prolonged applause for the President, there were insistent shouts for Hampton. Perhaps because the crowd had not been cordial to the President, Hampton—on this occasion, more than any other—praised Hayes for planting himself upon the Constitution, and for declaring that the people of all races and all sections were to be equal. Hampton concluded:

I have tried, honestly, earnestly and faithfully to discharge my pledges that every man, white and black, who was a citizen of that State, should be equal before the laws and Constitution of the State and of the Constitution of the United States. [Applause] We have there now profound peace.[22]

After leaving Nashville en route to Chattanooga, the train made a number of "whistle stops." While the train was on a siding in Murfreesboro, Tennessee, the inevitable note of humor about a Negro was picked up by a reporter for the Nashville *American*. A crowd of both races immediately gathered. Many were introduced to the President who shook hands with them. An old gray-haired colored man gave a peculiar grunt significant of his appreciation of the President's visit. As the train moved from the siding, the old man gave the same guttural sound and peals of laughter followed. On the main tracks, Hayes made his familiar speech, and again asked for no pledges. Secretary of State Evarts, Key, and Hampton were introduced; the South Carolina governor was "hailed with vociferous applause." At other stops, in Tullahoma and Decherd, Tennessee, and Stevenson, Alabama, the reporter for the Nashville paper noted the great anxiety of the colored people who flocked to see the President. The great delight manifested by those colored people who succeeded in shaking hands with the President "has been a source of infinite amusement to those who witnessed it." At Stevenson, when the President interpreted the cheers for him as acceptance of the idea of peace based upon equality of all citizens, a voice from the crowd assured him: "You see how we treat these darkies." The President agreed that they seemed "to be entirely at peace with their white friends, and the white people with them, and I think that can be mentioned everywhere in this country. . . . They [the colored people] certainly don't look here as if they were in need of bayonets."[23]

The speech in Chattanooga was notable for the fact that, after Hayes had made a long speech emphasizing his usual themes, an address was made on behalf of the colored people of the city and vicinity by a colored minister, A. P. Melton. The gist of his speech is contained in the sentence: "He [President Hayes] was at first mistaken by some and regarded with disfavor by others; but in the onward approach of the sun, the clouds have disappeared."[24] Negro public school teachers and ministers in the South have generally been relied upon, until very recent years, to say the "right thing."

Hayes's answer expressed great pleasure that the colored people of that part of the United States had given evidence of their satisfaction with the President's policy. Their satisfaction was

> precisely in accord with what I believed would occur when the effort to give to the country complete and permanent pacification was made. . . . Our confidence . . . was perfect that with the bayonets removed from the South, the people of all colors would be safer in every right, in every interest, than they ever were when protected merely by the bayonet.

He hoped for his "colored friends" that their future would be ever brighter, and that they would remember always "that to command respect men must have the virtues to deserve respect. Industry, good conduct and intelligence are good for white and good for colored men."[25]

While Hayes journeyed on to Knoxville to make his usual speech, Hampton went direct to Atlanta, undoubtedly for the purpose of laying the groundwork for the President's reception as he had done in Louisville. On the morning of the day on which Hayes was to speak, an editorial in the Atlanta *Constitution* praised him for adhering to his Southern policy despite the severe criticism in the North. The paper, however, served a warning on the President by stating that it reserved its final decision until after he had spoken. But it was sure that he would benefit from his visit, for

> where he had been led to look for a race of bleeding, starving, oppressed negroes, he will find a host of careless, contented darkies, protected in their legitimate aspirations, and mingling happily with the white people in processions that line his route of travel.

At the meeting which Hayes addressed, a reporter for the *Constitution* observed that at first the "enthusiasm was not of a very marked character, but cordiality was noticeable on all sides." Both Mayor Angier and Governor Colquitt, in their welcoming addresses, stressed the themes of pacification and reconciliation, but neither was reported as having given any pledges about the colored people. Hayes was greeted with immense cheering when he declared: "Here we are, Republicans, Democrats, colored people, white people, Confederate soldiers, and Union soldiers, all of one mind and heart today!" The reporter did not indicate the reaction to the President's question: "What is there to separate us longer?" But the gathering did cheer when he urged: "Let us wipe out in our parties the color line forever." The greatest enthusiasm, and cheering that lasted for several minutes, followed the president's admonition, addressed directly to the colored people in the audience: "I believe that your rights and interests would be safer if this great mass of intelligent white men were let alone by the general government." After the prolonged cheering had died down—the reporter did not state whether the Negroes had joined in the cheering—Hayes continued: "And now, my colored friends, let me say another thing. We have been trying it these six months, and in my opinion, no six months since the war have there been so few outrages and invasions of your rights, nor you so secure in your rights, persons and homes, as in the last six months. [Great cheering]" The editor of the *Constitution*, quite naturally, then praised Hayes without reservation. Only one sour note seems to have been reported: the correspondent for the New York *Tribune* observed that not one of the three or four military companies in the parade carried the Stars and Stripes.[26] Hayes did not ask the people of Atlanta whether they intended to obey the whole Constitution and its amendments. Evidence is lacking, again, that he obtained the pledges privately from Georgia leaders. Hayes, however, had given them abundant assurance that he would continue his hands-off policy to their satisfaction. But, apparently, he made no pledges to the "poor colored people of the South," and no inquiries as to their grievances.

Hampton, evidently concluding that he had accomplished his mission of reminding Hayes constantly of the dire consequences of any lagging in his policy of hands off, left the president at Atlanta. Entering Virginia from Bristol, Tennessee, Hayes again made a number of "whistle stops" before going to Lynchburg. Perhaps the proximity of Monticello led him to recognize room for differences of opinion: "There may be many in both sections not reconciled, but we all know that in the march of progress there are always some stragglers. [Applause]" At Monticello he stressed the equality of all people without distinction of race or color. A short stop at Gordonsville, and he was back in Washington on September 26.[27]

In an interview the President stated that, as far as he had been able to judge the Southern people, they were loyal to the national government. "I believe," he affirmed, "the era of good feeling between the North and the South is permanent." An editorial in the New York *Herald*, after his Atlanta speech, concluded that Hayes was more useful to the South than Tilden would have been.[28] It was, indeed, much more significant for a Republican than for a Democratic President to have believed that peace had been achieved, and that the Constitution with all its amendments would be faithfully observed.

Hayes must not be judged too harshly. He did not go all the way to Canossa; for he generally included in his speeches reference to the Constitution and all its amendments. He was no woebegone, penitent beggar. But he was no knight in shining armor either. His obvious desire to please his Southern friends can not be attributed to Kentucky mint juleps or Southern Comfort, since his abstinence from liquid refreshments is famous. Rather, his subordination of the amendments and the future of "the poor colored people of the South" to peace and prosperity stemmed, primarily, from his obvious fear of a renewal of civil war. Apparently not schooled in the virtue of "bargaining from positions of strength," he candidly revealed his greatest weakness—horror of bloodshed. His principal coadjutor, Hampton, who prepared the way for him in Louisville, accompanied him to Chattanooga, and prepared the way for him in Atlanta, struck repeatedly at this weakest point. Hampton waved a potential Southern "bloody shirt" before Hayes's eyes. Moreover, Hampton, strong-willed, with the arrogance of the ex-slaveholder, had a single objective—the restoration of white supremacy. Hayes, possessed of good intent, but devoid of an iron will, tried to walk a two-forked road. A succession of labor strikes in the summer of 1877 had added to Hayes's concern about peace and prosperity. Few men, and certainly not Hayes, could have, under all these circumstances, ventured into former enemy territory and returned to march firmly along his bifurcated road.

The President was evidently still under the spell of his cordial reception in the South when he sent his first annual message to Congress, December 3, 1877. He asserted that the withdrawal of the troops had been effected "with solicitous care . . . for the protection of the property and persons and every right of all classes of citizens." He reiterated his determination to protect the legal and constitutional rights of the freedmen, "now advanced to full and equal citizenship[!]." But he no longer urged federal aid to public education. One may surmise that some Southerners had shown him the error of his ways, for he left legislation with respect to education and general welfare to the states. Nor did he specify the respective jurisdictions of the federal and state governments, when he urged the punishment of every instance of lawlessness against Negroes and violation of their rights.[29]

While Hayes, on the whole, left the protection of the freedmen in the hands of the states, he made specific recommendations for federal action in behalf of Indians. These included provisions for the purchase of cattle and agricultural instruments, the establishment of schools and, under certain circumstances, admission to the benefits of the Homestead Act, and the privileges of citizenship.[30] No contrast between Hayes's Indian policy and his Negro policy is suggested, since the Indians lived on reservations while the Negroes were already citizens of states to which the Constitution gives reserved rights. It is pertinent to note, however, that Hayes made no effort to have Congress pass a new Southern Homestead Act —the old one had been repealed in July, 1876.

By the end of 1878, it was evident that the President's Southern policy, as far as the protection of the rights of the freedmen was concerned, was a failure. The New York Times, in an editorial on November 14, gave what is perhaps still the most perspicacious analysis of this failure. The editorial doubted a Washington report that Hayes intended to abandon his Southern policy. But what Hayes was bound to change was his estimate of the Southern politicians and, to some extent, of the Southern people. He had believed their promises. But he had discovered that there was bad faith somewhere. It would be hard to determine the extent to which

Southerners as a body were responsible for measures that had resulted in the suppression of the right to vote possessed by three-quarters of a million colored Republican voters. But there could be no mistake about the Democratic politicians, for "the pledges they gave to the President have been broken. Their promises of fair play have been falsified." Even so, there could be no revocation of that policy. The *Times,* however, urged the attorney-general to use such powers as he possessed for the punishment of outrages. Even this proposal had provoked an outcry, by that same Northern Democratic press that had remained silent while Negroes in the South were, through the use of violence, being denied the right to vote.[31]

In the light of overwhelming evidence of bad faith on the part of the Southern politicians and many of the Southern people, Hayes could only express his disillusionment quite candidly, in his second annual message to Congress, December 2, 1878. In some of the Southern states, he observed, the colored people had been unable to vote because of influences not easily measured nor remedied by legal protection. He then specified that in the states of Louisiana and South Carolina at large, and in some Congressional districts outside those states, the records of the elections seemed to compel the conclusion that the rights of the colored voters had been overridden, and their participation in the elections not permitted to be either general or free. Hayes called upon Congress to examine the validity of the claims of certain members to their seats, and upon the federal executive and judicial departments to inquire into, and punish, any violations of the laws of the United States. He repeated his determination to use whatever power he had to obtain these ends; and he urged the government and people of the Southern states to give their assistance toward bringing the offenders to justice, and preventing the repetition of the crimes. He finally quoted the Act of February 28, 1871, which gave the federal government power to enforce the right of citizens to vote.[32]

Acting on Hayes's recommendation, Blaine introduced a resolution on December 2, 1878, for the appointment of a Senate committee to investigate charges of fraud and violence during the 1878 elections. On the basis of investigations in South Carolina, Louisiana and Mississippi, the committee concluded that the governors and legislatures had violated their pledges to uphold the Constitution in securing the rights of all citizens alike. Negroes had been beaten, frightened and killed by armed men who went unpunished for their crimes. The committee concluded that the grave situation warranted protection of Negro citizens in the election of members of the House of Representatives.[33] The House took no steps to remedy this situation until the introduction of the Lodge Bill in 1890.

Hayes had further evidence of the denial of equal rights to Negroes in the South, during the debates on a resolution introduced on January 16, 1879, by Senator Windom of Minnesota. During the winter of 1878–1879, there had begun the so-called Great Exodus (discussed in Chapter 7) of some 40,000 Negroes fleeing into Kansas and other states in order to escape the intolerable conditions in the South. Windom's resolution called for the appointment of a committee to examine the expediency and practicability of encouraging the migration of Negroes to various states and territories of the United States. Somewhat wistfully, Hayes wrote in his diary on May 25, 1879:

> The exodus of colored people from the South still attracts attention. The effect is altogether favorable. The tendency will be to force the better class of Southern people to suppress the violence of the ruffian class, and to protect colored people in their rights. Let the emigrants be scattered throughout the Northwest; let them be encouraged to get homes and settled employment.[34]

But Hayes failed to take action designed to encourage this migration.

While Hayes did not prod Congress into taking action for the protection or for the welfare of Negroes, he vigorously opposed efforts designed to weaken existing federal legislation. When the Democrats, who had a slight majority in both Houses, passed a "rider" to the Army appropriation bill barring the use of the Army to keep peace at the polls, Hayes vetoed the law on April 29, 1879. In his veto message, he pointed out that the rider would prevent the civil authorities of the United States from keeping peace at Congressional elections as provided in Article 1, Section 4 of the Constitution. He also called attention to the Fifteenth Amendment which forbade the United States or any state to deprive any citizen of the right to vote because of race, color or previous condition of servitude. Hayes vetoed eight bills designed to weaken federal protection of the rights of Negroes.[35] Hayes won this fight against Congress. His policy, however, was motivated as much by his refusal to have the executive branch of the government placed under the coercive dictation of a bare majority in the two Houses, and by his opposition to the device of riders, as it was by concern for the colored people of the South.

In the face of this stubborn determination to weaken federal protection of the constitutional rights of Negroes, it is not surprising that Hayes did not recommend the enforcement of the second section of the Fourteenth Amendment. This section provides, in brief, that, when inhabitants of any state are denied the right to vote, except for participation in rebellion or other crime, the representation of that state shall be proportionately reduced in the House of Representatives and in the electoral college. Indeed, this section was almost completely forgotten. James A. Garfield had introduced resolutions in the House in 1869, 1871 and 1875 for the enforcement of the section, but Congress had taken no action on them.[36]

A rather obscure Congressman, Horace F. Page of California, probably inspired by the fact that the Democrats had retained control of the House, announced his intention, on November 27, 1878, to introduce a bill for the enforcement of this section. This proposal by Page is especially noteworthy since it provides one of the earliest evidences of a new coalition—one less well known than that between some Northern Republicans and Southern Democrats—a coalition based on the sympathy that some Westerners entertained for the South because of the increasing Oriental population in California. The raucous Democratic San Francisco *Examiner* pointed out, as soon as Page had made his announcement, that the bill would affect not only the Southern states but also California,[37] presumably because of the disfranchisement of Chinese there. When Page introduced his bill for the enforcement of the Fourteenth and Fifteenth Amendments on December 9, 1878, however, he made no specific reference to the second section of the Fourteenth Amendment. It was referred to the Committee on the Judiciary and buried there.[38]

On the next day the *Examiner* attacked an unidentified "Radical" paper of California for urging the enforcement of the Fourteenth Amendment. The *Examiner* editorial denied that Negroes in the South were intimidated, except in rare instances. On the other hand, the "Radicals" of New England compelled their employees to vote in accordance with the wishes of their employers. The *Examiner* also condemned the New York *Sun* for favoring the admission of Mongolians. The *Sun*, observed the *Examiner* sarcastically, appeared to be willing for Negroes in the South to be disfranchised since many of them were illiterate. But, the *Examiner* continued, the colored people could at least speak English. Shortly thereafter, the *Examiner*, which frequently published excerpts from other papers, printed two that further reveal this paper's opposition to federal intervention in behalf of Negroes. Colonel Pat Donan, editor of the Lexington (Missouri) *Tribune* was quoted as having declared: " 'No simian-souled, sooty-skinned, kink-curled, blubber-lipped, prehensile-heeled, Ethiopian gorilla shall pollute the ballot box with his leprous vote.' " The *Examiner* quoted another article from the Albany (New York) *Argus* which insisted that business men of the North would resent the attempt to organize the Republican party on the basis of hatred for the South.[39] Thus, even before George Hearst became head of the Examiner Publishing Company (1880), the specter of the "Yellow Peril" had already been paraded before the eyes of Californians. Along with it stalked the "Black Peril" in the South.

"The Whiggish alliance of 1877"—to use Woodward's apt expression—seemed, on the other hand, to be threatened by a rising tide of radicalism and agrarianism in the South and West. Readjusters, Independents, Greenbackers and Laborites became forces to be reckoned with in many of the Southern states. In 1879, the Readjusters, pledged to a scaling down of the state debt, which was largely held in the East, carried the state of Virginia. In the face of this new threat to peace and profits, conservatives in the North and South were drawn even closer together than they had been by the railroad lobbyists of 1876–1877. Because of indisputable evidence that the pledges to protect Negro rights, especially in the lower South, were being grossly violated, Hayes refused to give support to attempts to repeal the Reconstruction Acts. On the other hand, he stubbornly refused to join the remnants of the Republican "Radicals" in waving the "bloody shirt." In his annual message to Congress, December 1, 1879, he once more expressed his concern about elections in the South. But, still holding out the olive branch to the South, he hoped that public opinion would override all political prejudices and that intelligence would ensure obedience to the laws aimed at the protection of the rights of suffrage. Vaguely, he urged Congress to supply any defects in the laws that it had power to remedy, and the state governments to cooperate to that end.[40]

In his last message to Congress, December 6, 1880, Hayes continued to the end his habit of calling attention to the violation of the constitutional rights of the Negroes, of expressing the conviction that the South could be depended upon to observe those rights, and of mildly urging Congress to take such action as was necessary to protect them. He again called attention to fraudulent practices in connection with the ballot, with the regulations as to the place and manner of voting for Representatives, and with the counting, returning and canvassing of the votes cast. He mildly admonished: "The disposition to refuse a prompt and hearty obedience to the equal-rights amendments to the Constitution is all that now stands in the way of a complete obliteration of sectional lines and political contests." He was convinced, none the less, that opposition to the Fifteenth Amendment was diminishing in many parts of the nation, and that it might cease completely if firm and well-considered action were taken by Congress. The President also warned again that he had the duty to prosecute all violations of rights guaranteed to Negroes by the Constitution, and he repeated the suggestion in his inaugural address for federal aid to public education.[41]

However well-intentioned Hayes may have been, he had accomplished only one of the two tasks that he had set for himself. He had pacified the country, in so far as a threat of a new civil war between the North and the South was concerned, and he had allayed the bitterness between the two sections. But he had abandoned "the poor colored people of the South" to the "honorable and influential Southern whites." He had kept his part of the bargain, but had been unable to hold the other parties to theirs. White supremacy was more securely entrenched in the South when he left the White House than it had been when he had entered it.

But Hayes, in his own evaluation of his administration,

appeared to believe that he had accomplished both his goals. Reviewing his administration in his diary, December 29, 1881, he wrote that he had found the country "divided and distracted and every interest depressed." His administration had left it "united, harmonious, and prosperous." At the beginning of his administration "the South was solid and the North divided. At its close the North was united and solid and the South was divided[!]." In addition, leaders like Cameron, Blaine and Conkling had "reviled" his Southern policy. "Now," he concluded, "all are silenced by the results. Their president [Arthur] mutters not a word on the subject."[42] The silence of Arthur about the continued violation of the constitutional rights of the Negroes was obviously more convincing than the evidence of the violation.

The principal biographer of Hayes, and editor of his letters and diaries, gave a more accurate evaluation of the President's Southern policy. Writing in 1914 he asserted:

> Every one can see now that the experiment of permitting a newly enfranchised and ignorant servile race, led and dominated by unscrupulous adventurers, to govern American States in defiance of the intelligence, the culture, and the property interests of the Anglo-Saxon inhabitants, was bound to prove a failure. The forces of civilization were sure to assert themselves and gain control. It was Mr. Hayes's merit to see clearer and think straighter than many of the forceful leaders of his party, and to be willing to admit that events had discredited the policy long pursued toward the reconstructed States. . . . The judgment of history will unhesitatingly commend not only the wisdom but the moral courage with which Mr. Hayes answered for all time the obstinate and distracting Southern question.[43]

Much of this frank statement is open to question. It does not make allowance for the fact that Reconstruction was not the unmitigated horror that it portrays. Not all historians will accept the equating of the "forces of civilization" with "the intelligence, the culture, and the property interests of the Anglo-Saxon inhabitants." Moreover, at the time the statement appeared, many of the Southern states were in the hands of demagogues. And, finally, it is no longer true that Hayes's policy "answered for all time the obstinate and distracting Southern question." On the contrary, the question is being answered today, more in terms of Douglass's criteria than it has ever been before. The statement is essentially correct, however, when it points out that Hayes had left the South to work out its own will in fixing the status of the Negro in American society.

THREE

Dead Center Under Cleveland

PRESIDENTS Garfield, Arthur and Cleveland allowed the Southern question to simmer during the next eight years, 1881–1889. Agrarian and "Radical" unrest in parts of the South threatened briefly to forge a coalition between the Negroes and the poorer Southern whites, against the "honorable and influential Southern whites" whose control Hayes had helped to entrench. But the coalition lacked capable leadership and a national organization, and the participation of Negroes in the politics of Reconstruction still aroused fear and hatred. Not until the 1890's was the Populist Revolt to constitute a serious threat of a possible revival of Negro "domination." Meanwhile, however, the South won a victory at least as great as the restoration of white political control. In 1883 the United States Supreme Court declared unconstitutional the Civil Rights Act of 1875, and thereby made possible the segregation of Negroes by individuals in all the states. The South, armed with this legal sanction of the denial of equal "social" rights for Negroes, accelerated by law and custom the separation of the races. This decision also probably encouraged the South to continue the reduction of the use of violence to keep Negroes from the polls, and to increase the use of legal means to effect this end. By 1884, when the first Democrat since the Civil War was elected President, the South might well have concluded that it need no longer fear federal interference with its solution for the experiment in democracy. Cleveland did nothing to alter this conviction.

The virtual abandonment of Southern Negroes by both parties is revealed in their 1880 platforms. The Republican plank asserted:

The dangers of a "Solid South" can only be averted by a faithful performance of every promise which the nation has made to the citizen. . . . A nation can not with safety relegate this duty to the States. The "Solid South" must be divided by the peaceful agencies of the ballot, and all honest opinions must there find free expression. To this end the honest voter must be protected against terrorism, violence or fraud.

The South probably attached no more meaning to this plank than it did to the pronouncement in the Democratic platform: "The right to a free ballot is the right preservative of all rights, and must and shall be maintained in every part of the United States."[1] For sheer disingenuousness this pronouncement is probably the equal of any until the Republican plank of 1892.

Although President Garfield was shot four months after he took office, and died in September, 1881, his brief administration is notable for a definition of the status of the Negro that has been almost entirely overlooked.[2] On many previous occasions he had asserted that Negroes should enjoy full equality after they had been freed. He had been closely allied with Thaddeus Stevens and other "Radicals" who advocated a strong policy in behalf of the freedmen. In 1866, he had declared: "I say here, before this House, that I will never so long as I have any voice in political affairs, rest satisfied until the way is opened by which these colored people, as soon as they are worthy, shall be lifted to the full rights of citizenship." As previously indicated, he was one of the few Congressmen who seemed to have remembered the second section of the Fourteenth Amendment.

It is a neglected passage in his inaugural address, however, that deserves to be rescued from oblivion. In two pungent sentences he declared: "Under our institutions there was no middle ground for the negro between slavery and equal citizenship. There can be no permanent disfranchised peasantry in the United States."

Were these statements as meaningless as the Republican platform? Garfield had been one of the intermediaries in both the political and the economic bargains of 1877. The rest of his inaugural address seems somewhat tortuous in the light of his brave pronouncements. He admitted that the free enjoyment of the suffrage was still in question, for it was "alleged" that in many communities Negroes were virtually denied the right to vote. He acknowledged that the lack of education by the great mass of the Negroes might be the only "palliation" that could be offered for refusing them the freedom of the ballot. Bad local government, resting upon an ignorant electorate, was certainly an evil, but the violation of the freedom and sanctities of the suffrage was more than an evil. There was no standard by which to measure the disaster that might be brought about by ignorance and vice in the citizens, when joined to corruption and fraud in the suffrage. Since the nation was responsible for the extension of the suffrage to a large mass of illiterates, all the constitutional power of the nation, and of the states, and all the volunteer forces of the people should be used to provide for universal education. Garfield did not, however, propose any specific legislation to implement these generalities.[3] While he did not specifically propose federal aid to public education, it is probable that his linking of universal suffrage with education did not predispose many Southerners to a great expansion, by the states, of educational facilities for Negroes.

Little attention was paid, at that time or later, to the two sentences which, one would think today, would have called for considerable comment. The leading magazines—*Harper's Monthly, Nation, Atlantic Monthly, North American Review, Harper's Weekly*—did not mention the rejection of a "middle ground," and of a "permanent disfranchised peasantry." Concerning the address as a whole, Godkin's *Nation* quipped: "Everybody knows that it contains nothing in the nature of a program, either of legislation or administration, which is likely to be carried into effect." Only a few of the leading papers commented on the two sentences. The Richmond *Dispatch*, while not agreeing with the "beneficent" effect of making voters of the Negroes, did concede that "there was no middle ground between slavery and full citizenship." The New Orleans *Times* characterized the entire address as political claptrap, but agreed that there could be no permanent disfranchised peasantry,

provided such class have the facilities for howling or have the ability to induce others to howl for them. This conclusion is totally independent of the right or wrong of the disfranchisement; and as all classes . . . have the means (newspapers) of howling in the Land of the Free . . it appears to be a result inevitable that suffrage must continue to extend until the bladder (the Constitution) which holds the gas bursts. That it will burst is as inevitable as the collapse of the strongest boiler under pressure of too much steam. Our idiotic country-men are almost unanimously agreed in ramming in more fuel without paying the slightest attention to worn rivets and gnawing rust.[4]

Other leading Southern newspapers, while omitting reference to the two forgotten sentences, seized upon Garfield's allusion to the Negro question in the South to voice their objection to his concepts. Watterson's Louisville *Courier-Journal* dismissed the inaugural address as containing no insight into the President's future policy and added: "The talk about the suppressed vote in the South has long since lost its significance and will soon lose its power of irritation." The indignant editors of the Mobile *Daily Register* accused Garfield of violating good taste when he asserted that the South denied Negroes the right to vote. The Atlanta *Constitution* went so far as to disclaim state responsibility for educating Negroes, and asserted that the right to vote would take care of itself if Northern Republicans would accord Negroes the right to hold office. The classic response to criticism of the South, however, was voiced in the Memphis *Commercial Appeal*, which declared that the South would deal with the situation in a just and honorable way if left alone, "free from the intermeddling, propagandistic spirit of fanatics, possessed with a negrophobia."[5]

Northern and Western papers ran the gamut of expressions in stating their reactions to Garfield's inaugural address. The Democratic press was most censorious. George Hearst's San Francisco *Examiner* simply regarded the address as a "partisan stump speech," as did the New Haven *Evening Register*. The Cincinnati *Enquirer* mocked: "It is hardly necessary to call attention of the colored people to the fact that they got a nice word in the Inaugural but no place in the Cabinet." The Republican papers varied in their comments. The Indianapolis *Journal* and the St. Louis *Globe-Democrat* praised it. In Detroit, the Scripps family's *Post and Tribune* agreed that education was needed, but affixed responsibility upon local authorities. The paper pointed out: "The national government cannot open their jaws and force this educational program down the throats of ignorance until the Constitution is changed." The Boston *Evening Transcript* went so far as to interpret Garfield's allusion to education as a sanction for educational tests and payment of a poll tax, as in Massachusetts. Instead of examining these issues as did other dailies, the Pittsburgh *Dispatch*, along with the independent Washington *Star*, registered hope that the address marked the "funeral oration" over sectional strife.[6]

Three Republican papers commented upon the two preg-
nant sentences. Joseph Medill's Chicago *Tribune* interpreted
them to presage a vigorous policy by the new administration.
In like fashion, the Philadelphia *North American,* terming the
propositions "forcible" and "incontrovertible," surmised: "It
is high ground, but it is not higher than a free and enlightened people can occupy." The New York *Times* viewed the
principles as having wider application than to the Negro
alone, since "it is a declaration of the necessity of universal
suffrage as a protection of the subjects of government." That
Negroes were denied the freedom of the ballot was deemed a
truth which had long been "too palpable to admit of honest
denial." Even though universal education might be the ultimate solution, the question remained as to what was to be
done in the meantime. The paper also questioned the manner
in which the President proposed to protect the rights of six
million Negroes unevenly distributed among twice as many
whites in a third of the states. The editorial concluded that,
evidently, Garfield was not ready to define his policy. Notwithstanding, it advised the administration to exercise the
utmost care to free the national government from involve-
ment in defective local conditions.[7]

It is thus evident that the press did not look upon Garfield's
pronouncement as worthy of ranking with Lincoln's "A nation cannot exist half slave and half free." This analysis of
the daily press and of the leading magazines suggests, on the
contrary, that the nation as a whole accepted the possibilities
that there was a middle ground between slavery and freedom,
and that at least a black, permanently disfranchised peasantry
could exist under American institutions. In any case, there
appeared to be little that the federal government could do
about either possibility.

Although there were, apparently, some thirty Negro newspapers published at the time, only two are on file at the
Library of Congress or the Moorland Room of Howard University.* The only issue for the month of March, 1881, was

* Scattered files of more than 250 Negro papers of the nineteenth
and twentieth centuries, a work sponsored by the American Council
of Learned Societies and filmed by the Photoduplication Service of
the Library of Congress, are now available. Adequate research in
these papers, nearly all of which were ephemeral, with local
distribution, would yield probably only minimal results.

that of the New Orleans *Weekly Louisianian*, a paper founded by P. B. S. Pinchback, former lieutenant-governor and former acting governor of Louisiana. Its form, printing, spelling and English usage were defective, but its uncompromising reinforcement of Garfield's principles was clearly evident. This is shown in the following quotation which is given exactly as it appears in the paper:

> The position of the Negro in the South since reconstruction has been a very peculiar one: debarred literally from the rights justly accorded to him in the ammendments to the Constitution, by the coercive power of the State rights, rendering the National Government powerless to protect him as one of its common citizens, and in accordance with the Constitution. President Garfield is the first to announce this brave and patriotic sentiment, that; "Those who resisted the change should remember that there was no middle ground between slavery and equal citizenship," and we trust that in the future it will be so understood. . . .
>
> It is alleged that the danger growing out of the Negro suffrage question owing to his ignorance is a standing menace to local self-government. . . . This reasoning cannot be gainsayed, and it is the shoal upon which the South is likely to be wrecked, unless the National Government come to its aid. The Negro is not the only source of ignorance in the South; but the hoards of white children growing up in utter ignorance and depravity in the South, is a grave question and should be seriously considered by those who are interested in the welfare of this section. . . . The educational facilities of the Negro in this State outside the parish of Orleans, is a farce. In a majority of the parishes, the scholastic year does not embrace two months of actual teaching and in many parishes for the past two years is a luxury unknown. Such is the measures taken by a loyal states government to educate a race and to liberate the franchise of its citizens.[8]

This penetrating, albeit ungrammatical, analysis of conditions in Louisiana in 1881 would have been equally applicable to most parts of the South. It is a fitting commentary upon the result of Hayes's policy, and was perhaps intended to be a warning to the Republicans. It helps us to understand why

Garfield, like Hayes, entertained doubts as to the effectiveness of his future policy; for Garfield had confided to a friend in January, 1881: "Time is the only cure for the Southern difficulties. In what shape it will come, if it come at all, is not clear."[9]

Garfield's death, on September 19, 1881, deprived him of an opportunity of showing what he could do to help time give shape to the experiment in American democracy. The San Francisco *Examiner* of February 23, 1881, reported that more Negroes than whites had bought tickets for his inaugural ball. Colored men, in accordance with established custom, had marched in the inaugural parade. He had appointed Negroes to "Negro" jobs—John M. Langston as minister to Haiti and consul general to the Dominican Republic; Henry Highland Garnet as minister to Liberia; ex-Senator Blanche K. Bruce as register of the treasury; and Frederick Douglass as recorder of deeds of the District of Columbia. Perhaps Garfield's most significant policy was his alliance with the ex-Confederate General, William Mahone of Virginia, leader of the Readjusters in that state.

Hayes, it will be recalled, had pinned his faith on the ex-Confederate Brigadiers, the "rejuvenated Whigs," the "Bourbons," "the honorable and influential Southern white men." These conservatives had almost as much contempt for "poor whites" as they had for Negroes. Indeed, they may have felt an even greater scorn for the former, since they did not offer indubitable proof of the superiority of all white men. The conservatives in the South were eager to restore the credit of their respective states, by regular payments on the state debts, by balancing the state budget through minimum expenses for social legislation. Even though taxes were relatively light, the poorer classes felt that those in power were less concerned with them than with re-establishing the credit of the state in order to attract Northern investors. The most potent protest against these conservatives was led by Mahone, who appealed to "poor whites" and Negroes in particular to aid his efforts to readjust or scale down the state debt, to keep the schools open and pay the teachers, to provide for higher education, to abolish the whipping post, and to remove the insane from jails to well-equipped asylums. The conservative Funders retaliated by accusing Mahone of being a demagogue, and the Negroes of voting for him at the behest of the national Republican party. Mahone, who was elected to the United States Senate in 1880, strengthened their case when he proclaimed himself a Republican, and attempted to build up a Republican party in Virginia composed of liberal whites and Negroes. After Mahoneism had achieved some of its goals— including the establishment of Virginia Normal and Industrial Institute, and a considerable expansion of schools for colored children—John W. Daniel, a conservative leader, declared in 1884: "I am a Democrat because I am a white man and a Virginian." At the same time John M. Langston, minister to Haiti, won large numbers of Negroes to vote for him in his successful campaign for Congress, on the ground that he was a Negro. The old issue of Negro Republicans versus white Democrats was revived, Mahone's regime soon ended, and at the beginning of the twentieth century Virginia disfranchised most Negroes.[10]

President Arthur decided to support Mahone and other Southern anti-Bourbon Democrats, rather than follow Hayes's let-alone policy or revive a carpetbag regime, as some of his advisors advocated. In this alliance with Readjusters, Independents and Greenbackers, Arthur had the support of Secretary of the Navy Chandler of New Hampshire, George S. Boutwell, who had been Grant's secretary of the treasury and senator from Massachusetts, and even Grant himself. In order to prevent criticism of this policy by Negroes, Arthur appointed some of their leaders to fairly important jobs. The most notable of these were Pinchback, surveyor of the port of New Orleans; H. C. C. Astwood (Pinchback's associate editor), consul to Trinidad; ex-Senator Bruce, an assistant United States commissioner-general; and Mifflin W. Gibbs, receiver of monies at Little Rock, Arkansas.

But many Negroes roundly condemned Arthur for his alliance with the Southern anti-Bourbon Democrats. Some of these criticisms were evidently dictated by the failure of editors and others to get jobs for themselves or their friends. Charles Hendley, editor of the Huntsville (Alabama) *Gazette*, for example, complained: "Spit upon in the house of his friends, despised and ignored at feast times, and recognized only when his services are needed—is the lot of the negro." Similar views were expressed by the Washington *Bee* and the Cleveland *Gazette*.

On the other hand, much of the criticism was based upon

Arthur's abandonment of Negro voters in the South. T. Thomas Fortune, the fiery and able editor of the New York *Globe* (later the *Freeman* and still later the *Age*), charged: "the Republican party has eliminated the black man from politics. This is as plain as a nose on a face. The blind alone refuse to see it. It has left the black man to fight his own battles." D. Augustus Straker, professor of common law at Allen University, Columbia, South Carolina, pointed out that since 1877 the Republican party had sacrificed the Negro vote on the altar of reconciliation with Southern Democrats. Negroes, he continued, resented the failure of the Republicans to protect them at the polls and the refusal to recognize their right to hold office equally with whites.

Even Frederick Douglass, at the National Convention of Colored People in Louisville, September, 1883, severely criticized the failure of the Republican party to protect the civil rights of Negroes. The Convention refused to endorse Arthur's administration. The revolt against Arthur's "Southern policy" even prompted demands that Negroes form an independent party.[11]

The rising tide of Negro criticism of Arthur's Southern policy reached its crest after the United States Supreme Court, in 1883, declared unconstitutional the Civil Rights Act of 1875. There is, of course, no evidence that Arthur played any such role as had Buchanan in connection with the Dred Scott case. But the Cleveland *Gazette*, for example, declared that this decision by a "Republican Supreme Court"—a term used by many Democratic dailies—would not aid the Republican party in 1884. T. Thomas Fortune stated that the colored people of the United States felt as if they had been "baptized in ice water." From Maine to Florida, he asserted, public meetings were being held to give expression to the common feeling of disappointment and apprehension for the future. In typical language, Fortune warned: "The Republican party has carried the war into Africa, and Africa is accordingly stirred to its centre." A packed audience at the fashionable Negro Fifteenth Street Presbyterian Church in Washington heard Langston call the decision a "stab in the back."[12]

Arthur's general reticence about the Negro in his public pronouncements added to the growing revolt against the Republicans. He made no references at all to Negroes in his inaugural address; and he devoted more space to Indians than to the freedmen in his first annual message, December 6, 1881. His brief reference to the latter repeated the implications of statements by Hayes and Garfield that, until Negroes became literate, they might justifiably be disfranchised. His suggestion for federal aid to public education was even weaker than that of Hayes. Instead of making a forthright recommendation, Arthur suggested that if any funds were used for that purpose, they might be wisely employed in the different states according to the ratio of illiteracy. In his second annual message, December 4, 1882, he left it to Congress to determine the "momentous" question of the use of federal funds for education. He limited his suggestion to "public primary education" in his last annual message, December 4, 1883, but again left the matter to the discretion of Congress. With reference to the Civil Rights decision, he vaguely promised to give his "unhesitating approval" to any legislation by which Congress might lawfully supplement the Constitutional guaranties for the lawful enjoyment of all rights. Congress was not likely to push legislation so innocuously adumbrated. On January 14, 1884, he transmitted to Congress, without comment, a communication from the secretary of the interior which submitted an estimate of $25,000 for the settlement of certain freedmen in the Oklahoma district of the Indian Territory.[18] The President did not, in any of his official messages, take cognizance of the Eight-Box Ballot Law instituted in South Carolina in 1882. This was the most ingenious of the many devices instituted to make voting by Negroes difficult. This law required a separate box for each office, and the boxes were frequently shuffled about when a Negro endeavored to find the correct box for each ballot.

Similar devices as well as the fear of potential, and in some instances actual, intimidation prevented most Negroes from voting in the South—which again voted solidly, in 1884, for the Democratic candidate. But the revolt of many Northern Negroes against Arthur's Southern policy may have contributed to this first Democratic success after the Civil War. It is true that, as far as platforms were concerned, they had little to choose between, since by this time many must have known that they were meaningless.

The Republican platform declared that it had gained its

strength by quick and faithful response to the demand of the people for the "freedom and equality of all men; for a united nation, assuring the rights of all citizens." The perpetuity of American institutions rested upon the maintenance of "a free ballot, an honest count, and correct returns. We denounce the fraud and violence practiced by the Democracy in Southern States, by which the will of a voter is defeated, as dangerous to the preservation of free institutions." The party extended to the Republicans of the South, regardless of their former party affiliations, its cordial sympathy and pledged its "most earnest efforts to promote the passage of such legislation as will secure to every citizen of whatever race or color, the full and complete recognition, possession, and exercise of all civil and political rights."

The Democratic platform also listed "the equality of all citizens before the law" as one of the bases for the preservation of American liberties. Only fraud had defeated the will of the people in the election of 1876; in 1880 this will had been defeated by the lavish use of money. The "Democracy" pledged itself to restore respect for law, asserted its belief "in a free ballot and a fair count," and expressed its favor of "the diffusion of free education by common schools, so that every child in the land may be taught the rights and duties of citizenship."[14]

The defeat of Blaine in this "vilest political campaign ever waged" has been attributed, too simply, to a remark by one of his supporters which gave the Democrats an opportunity to declare that Blaine looked upon the Democratic party as the party of "Rum, Romanism and Rebellion." Many Catholics voted against Blaine, but charges of corruption against Blaine also lost him many independent votes; he lost the state of New York by a narrow margin. There is no way of knowing how many Negroes in New York and other states voted for Cleveland. Some Negroes, on the other hand, may actually have believed that Cleveland's election would mean a return to slavery.

T. Thomas Fortune has left a graphic picture of the reaction of Negroes and of the attempts to reassure them.[15] An editorial in the *Globe* on July 26, 1884, shortly after Cleveland's nomination, stated: "If Cleveland is elected (and there are ninety chances of his being struck by lightning against one of his being President), it would be a cold afternoon for this country and especially for the Negro and the laboring classes." In October, Fortune sarcastically praised the courage of the Columbus (Ohio) *Afro-American*, for supporting Cleveland when "nearly every other colored paper in the country was for Blaine." After Cleveland's election, Fortune deemed it necessary to assure his readers that there was no cause for alarm. He believed that there was no Democrat in the country more disposed to do justice to the Negro than was Cleveland. By November 22 the alarm had grown to such an extent, however, that Fortune wrote an editorial under the caption, "Colored Men Keep Cool." In order to allay their fears, he printed articles from some of the most influential Southern dailies. The Atlanta *Constitution* had declared:

> "It is both our duty and to our interest to see that he [the Negro] is quickly assured of safety and protection, including, of course, all his war-created rights. If every good citizen will take hold of this matter at once, in a week every darkey will be made happy, and he will go to work to earn a living and to lend a hand toward carrying on the great industries of the South."

The Memphis *Commercial Appeal*—frequently noted for its vigorous and at times vicious articles about Negroes—not only gave similar assurances, but predicted that in two years Negroes would have benefited by the change of government. Fortune even published, with obvious approval, an article from the Raleigh *News*, which referred to the fact that Negroes had been living under Democratic rule in North Carolina for twelve years, as evidence that they need have no fear.[16]

The following week, Fortune summarized the views of Douglass and of ex-Congressman Rainey of South Carolina. Douglass was prepared to give the President-elect a fair trial and credit for whatever good things he might do. Cleveland had done some good things in the state of New York and might do equally well as President. Rainey was much more forthright. He would say to Negroes: " 'Possess your souls in peace, your liberties are not in danger.' " He did not believe that even the "most ultra Democrats" would care to see slavery restored.[17]

Cleveland took cognizance of these fears in his inaugural

address, when he proclaimed his intention of being President of all the American people. He gave the further assurance that "there should be no pretext for anxiety touching the protection of the freedmen in their rights or their security in the enjoyment of their privileges under the Constitution and its amendments." He added that all discussion as to their fitness for the place accorded to them as American citizens was idle and unprofitable, except as it suggested the necessity for their improvement. And, he concluded: "The fact that they are citizens entitles them to all the rights due to that relation and charges them with all its duties, obligations, and responsibilities."[18]

Fortune received these promises with only slight reservations. Cleveland would be taken at his word, and each phase of his policy would be watched. The *Freeman* would condemn him when he departed from his pronounced policies, and praise him when he adhered to them. Like other politicians, Negroes were seeking government positions. Fortune recognized that, because he had supported Blaine, he could not look for an appointment. He advised Douglass, Bruce, Pinchback, John R. Lynch (former Congressman from Mississippi), and all other "knuckle-close" Republicans likewise to forget plums from the new regime.[19]

Cleveland followed the Republican practice of appointing colored men to the "Negro jobs," of ministers to Haiti and Liberia, and recorder of deeds of the District of Columbia.[20] This last appointment resulted in further evidence of Cleveland's courage whenever he considered himself thwarted in a good cause. He nominated James C. Matthews of Albany, New York, to succeed Douglass. When the Senate rejected the nomination, Cleveland gave him a recess appointment and submitted his name a second time, on December 21, 1886. He did so, he declared, because of Matthews' demonstrated fitness for the office, and because of "a desire to cooperate in tendering to our colored fellow-citizens just recognition and the utmost good faith." After a second rejection, Cleveland obtained the confirmation of another colored man, James Monroe Trotter.[21]

Other than these traditional appointments, Cleveland apparently deemed it unnecessary to take any special action with respect to Negroes. After his inaugural address he did not mention them in his messages to Congress, except to urge the payment of the balance due to the depositors in the bankrupt Freedmen's Savings and Trust Company. Like Arthur, he devoted more space to Indians in the United States.[22] On the other hand, he did little to justify the fear that the Union would be subverted by the election of a Democrat. He appointed only two Southerners to his cabinet. He signed a bill granting pensions to all who had served in the Mexican War, and he refused to approve certain pension measures for veterans of the Union army. Since most of those who had served in the Mexican War were Southerners, the net result seemed to be discrimination in their favor. Cleveland was perhaps most bitterly condemned in the North for ordering the return to their respective states of Confederate flags captured by Union troops. But he certainly took no positive steps to return Negroes to slavery.

The New York *Times* was convinced that Cleveland's election and administration was in the best interest of both the Negro and the nation. The mere fact that a Democrat had been elected President, it averred, practically eliminated the sectional issue. The relaxing of party lines aligned the Southern Democrats and Southern Republicans more closely together, and it was no wonder that Northern Republicans had begun again to wave the "bloody shirt." But Southern Republicans had protested, for without that issue, the *Times* agreed, the Republicans had a "fighting chance" to gain control in Virginia, West Virginia, Tennessee, North Carolina and South Carolina. The Cleveland administration had led to a spirit of political tolerance. The Republicans could not deny that fact, and the *Times* urged them to find a live issue upon which to base their party platform in the presidential election of 1888.[23] Cleveland provided the issue when he devoted all of his annual message to Congress, December, 1887, to the question of the tariff.

Meanwhile, it was evident that, so long as the South was left unmolested, the nation had arrived at a dead center with respect to the Negro. It made little difference whether a Republican or a Democrat—at least a Northern Democrat—was President. Party platforms were frankly hypocritical on the constitutional rights of Negroes. Presidents of both parties uttered pious platitudes, but said nothing and did nothing, except to give a few jobs to professional Negro officeholders.

The Reopening Under Harrison

THE last decade of the nineteenth century and the opening of the twentieth century marked the nadir of the Negro's status in American society. The continued decline, in the recognition of his political and legal rights, can not be attributed entirely to the emergence of new issues that shunted the Southern question further into the background. To be sure, the tariff, the free and unlimited coinage of silver, the federal regulation of interstate commerce and of corporations, the "closing of the frontier," the reform of the civil service and of municipal governments—these and other domestic questions diverted attention from the treatment of the Negro. At the turn of the century, the United States "emerged as a world power" with greatly increased responsibilities, especially in the Caribbean and the Far East.

The nadir was reached, however, not because of lack of attention. On the contrary, the plight of the Negro worsened precisely because of the efforts made to improve it. The Republicans, once more in the White House, and with a majority in both Houses for the first time since 1875, introduced two major pieces of legislation: to protect the right to vote, and to provide expanded educational facilities. The resurgent South, supported by old allies in the North and by new allies in the West, not only defeated both these measures, but launched a counterattack that further curtailed the already diminishing rights of Negroes. The questions of the tariff and of free silver served less to divert attention from the deterioration of the Negro's status, especially in the South, than to buttress the deliberate relegation of Negroes to an inferior class. At the turn of the century it seemed, indeed, that they might become a caste.

The revival of Republican interest in the Southern Negro was due in large measure to Cleveland's victory in 1884, and to the subsequent support given by some prominent Negro Republicans to the Democrats—there were proposals for a separate Negro party or for independence in voting. In order to recover the votes of the bolters, the Republicans contrived, in their platform of 1888, the plank that was to be their battle cry for a number of years. More eloquent, pungent, and specific than any previous pronouncement, it reaffirmed the party's "unswerving devotion . . . to the personal rights and liberties of citizens in all the States and Territories of the Union, and especially to the *supreme and sovereign right of every lawful citizen, rich or poor, native or foreign born, white or black, to cast one free ballot in public elections and to have that ballot duly counted.*"* The platform also demanded effective legislation to secure the integrity and purity of elections. It charged that the Democratic majority in Congress owed its existence to the suppression of the ballot by a "criminal nullification" of the Constitution and laws of the United States.[1]

The Democratic platform blandly asserted that, in every branch of the government under Democratic control, "the rights and the welfare of all the people have been guarded and defended, every public interest has been protected, and the equality of all our citizens before the law, without regard to race or color, has been steadfastly maintained."[2] Few Americans today are deluded by promises of what parties proclaim they will do if elected, but few of them would believe, except in the face of incontrovertible evidence, that both major parties have so completely distorted the facts.

Since the principal issue, in the campaign of 1888, had been the tariff, Harrison and the Republican party interpreted his election as a mandate to raise the tariff. For the next twelve years the Republicans made a protective tariff—and the "full dinner pail"—one of their major appeals. Harrison evidently believed that he could persuade the South that freedom of suffrage was necessary in order that the South enjoy the blessings of prosperity which would accrue from a high tariff. He declared, in his inaugural address, that Southern opposition to a protective tariff during slavery had prevented that section from producing as much cotton fabric as had New England. In order to drive his point home, he rather tactlessly inquired: "Shall the prejudices and paralysis of slavery continue to hang upon the skirts of progress?" He then surmised that farmers, as well as businessmen in the mining and manufacturing industries recently established in the South, might find that the free ballot of the workingman, without distinc-

* My italics.—R.W.L.

tion as to race, would be needed for their own defense, as well as for that of the workers. The President also linked the maintenance of law and order with the growth of business in the South. The denial of the rights of citizenship, he asserted, demoralized the violators of the law, and destroyed the faith of their victims in the laws designed to protect them. Moreover, those who lost faith were "naturally the subject of dangerous and uncanny suggestions." He reverted to his *idée maîtresse* when he added that only in those communities where law was the rule of conduct and where courts, not mobs, executed the penalties for violations of the law, would business investments and honest labor find an attractive field.[3]

Harrison was probably as ill-advised in putting into one package a protective tariff, Southern prosperity, and freedom of suffrage for both black and white voters, as Hayes had been in linking federal aid for education with Negro suffrage. The President appears to have believed, however, that the South would have preferred a protective tariff and Negro suffrage to "dangerous and uncanny suggestions" that would appeal to those who had lost faith in the effectiveness of the laws. He probably had in mind the activities of the Farmers' Alliance, and possibly of Socialists. Harrison's appeal provides an interesting forerunner to Booker T. Washington's Atlanta address in 1895, and to recent admonitions that concessions should be made to Negroes to prevent them from heeding the blandishments of Communists.

The President, in his first annual message to Congress, December 3, 1889, continued to woo both the Negroes and the South. He pointed out that the suggestion for a national grant-in-aid of education grew out of the needs of the freedmen and their descendants. He sought further to propitiate the colored vote by a rather lengthy statement, extolling the progress that the race had made since emancipation and the courage and fidelity of the colored regular army regiments. He then softened his criticisms of the South, by a statement of his understanding of the resentment of Southern employers against agents who were encouraging Negroes to leave the South; and he praised Negroes for not leaving the South, despite the fact that they were deprived of their political and many of their civil rights.

But Harrison made it clear that he had little expectation that the South would grant those political and civil rights to

Negroes. It was contended by some, he observed, that local
communities should be permitted to work out their own problems. But "we have a right," he stated flatly, "to ask whether
they are at work upon it. Do they suggest any solution? When
and under what conditions is the black man to have a free
ballot? When is he in fact to have those full civil rights which
have so long been his in law? When is that equality of influence which our government was intended to secure to the
electors to be restored?" The scant degree of reliance that he
placed upon "home rule" is seen in the fact that he invoked
the attention of Congress to the consideration of such measures, within its "well-defined constitutional powers," as would
secure to all the people a free exercise of the right of suffrage
and every other civil right under the Constitution and laws of
the United States. Many constitutional lawyers would challenge his contention that the power to take "the whole direction and control of the election" of members of the House of
Representatives, was "clearly" given to the federal government. He urged, however, the strengthening of existing legislation, rather than the enactment of a new law which would
place all the processes of these elections under federal control.
He further weakened his bold pronouncement by the vagueness of his suggestion that the colored man should be protected in all his relations to the federal government, whether
as litigant, juror, witness, as voter for members of Congress,
or as an interstate traveler.[4]

Despite the milder tone and vagueness at the end, his
views on the treatment of the Negro in the South constituted
the strongest threat to Southern "home rule" since the restoration of white control. The Bourbons were undoubtedly
alarmed, not only by the threat to their denial of political
and civil rights, but also perhaps to the basic pattern of segregation. As will be seen in Chapter Six, the Interstate Commerce
Commission had made three rulings which laid down the
principle of "separate but equal" accommodations for Negroes
engaged in interstate travel. The question was perhaps raised
by alert Southerners as to whether Harrison meant to insist
upon identity, rather than upon equality, of right.

Harrison's message was the catalytic agent that prompted
Mississippi to revise its constitution, in 1890, for the express
purpose of disfranchising most Negroes while permitting most
whites to vote. Fear of enforcement of federal laws for the

protection of Negro suffrage, and other rights, clearly motivated Mississippi's revision; Negroes had already lost most of
their political power in the state. John R. Lynch had been the
last Negro representative from that state to sit in Congress,
1881–1883. Whereas in 1876 there had been 16 Negroes in
the state House of Representatives and 5 in the state Senate,
in 1890 there were only 6 in the Mississippi House and none
in the Senate.

Through the system known as the "fusion principle," white
Democratic leaders in some eight counties of the black belt
permitted a certain number of Negroes, usually Republicans,
to be elected to some of the minor offices—such as assessor,
coroner, supervisor, constable, and justice of the peace. But
the minor white politicians and the mass of white voters objected to even this minimal office holding. Lynch had accepted
"fusion" as the best bargain that could be made at that time.
Some Negroes, however, were voting for the Greenback-labor
candidates—evidence perhaps that they were listening to
"dangerous and uncanny suggestions." It is probable, however, that even without this danger of "Radicalism," the
Bourbons were determined to disfranchise the Negro by state
constitutional action in order to render ineffective federal action. For, it was believed, if the state constitution disfranchised Negro voters, their right to vote could not be protected
by the federal government. Vernon Wharton, who has made
the authoritative study of Mississippi during this period, is
convinced that "the most powerful factor in the desire for a
legal elimination of the Negro voter was the change that had
occurred in Washington."[5]

The significance of that change was evident when the Republicans in Congress began almost immediately to introduce
legislation to implement Harrison's recommendations. Senator
Hoar of Massachusetts—one of the few Republicans who
seemed to have had a genuine interest in the Negro, for he
did not need their vote—prepared a bill for the federal supervision of federal elections. The attack was, in fact, launched
even before the bill was introduced. Pasco of Florida, on
January 20, 1890, attacked Harrison's proposal on the ground
that it was an attempt to restore Republican rule in the South.
Pasco made a plea for the continuation of "home rule," by
alleging that "kindly feelings have been cherished and
strengthened between the races." Chandler, a New Hampshire

Republican, retorted by calling attention to many instances of fraud, intimidation, violence and murder, in Florida particularly. Hoar's measure was laid aside because of the valid argument that a bill dealing with the election of members of the House of Representatives must originate in the House.[6]

Meanwhile, however, the Senate gave a kind of preview of the action that it would take when such a bill would come before it. Senator Blair, Republican from New Hampshire, introduced his bill for federal aid to public education on January 22, two days after Pasco made his attack upon Harrison's proposal for federal supervision of the right to vote. Blair's bill offered a plan for federal assistance during eight years to the public school systems of the various states—the money to be allotted among them on the basis of the proportion of a state's illiterates above the age of ten to the total number of illiterates in the United States. In states that had separate schools, the money was to be allotted on the basis of the proportion of colored, ages ten to twenty-one, to the whites of the same age span. No money was to be appropriated to a state unless the governor filed, with the secretary of the interior, data to show that there was no discrimination between white and colored, in the raising or expenditure of common school funds, and in the provision of educational opportunities for each. (No discrimination did not mean, of course, no segregation.) The secretary of the interior was to investigate charges of misappropriation of funds, and of acts of discrimination, and to make a report to Congress. An additional sum of two million dollars was to be apportioned among the states and the territories, to be known as the "common-school-house-fund," for the construction of schoolhouses in sparsely settled districts.[7]

The debates on this bill revealed considerable difference of opinion as to the need for such aid in the South, and the desire of Southerners for aid. Senator Ingalls, a Republican from Kansas, asserted, for example, that the Negro in the South was advancing rapidly in wealth and education. But the New Orleans *Picayune* was cited by Blair to show that the situation was as bad as it had been twenty-five years previously, and was possibly worse, as proved by figures for illiteracy and assessment rolls. Hugh Thompson, a South Carolina member of the Civil Service Commission, declared that his state was ready and willing, but unable by itself, to reduce the high percentage of illiteracy among the colored people. The state superintendent of public schools in North Carolina, on the other hand, was convinced that a large proportion of the leaders of both political parties were opposed to public education, for either whites or Negroes, in any manner other than by charity.[8]

Census statistics indicate an almost phenomenal rise in the literacy rate of Negroes between 1870 and 1890. It rose from 18.6 per cent in 1870, to 30 per cent in 1880, to 42.9 per cent in 1890. Since these statistics are for Negroes in the nation as a whole, they reflect a probably greater rate of increase in the North than in the former slave states. Since, however, 90.3 per cent of all Negroes lived in the South in 1890, the increase there must have been considerable. How much of this was due to public education and how much to private schools would be difficult, if not impossible, to ascertain. This question is particularly pertinent when one recalls that many of the teachers of the public schools were trained in private schools.[9]

The judgment of an authoritative Southern educator and historian is probably as accurate as any; Edgar W. Knight has stated as his conviction:

> The per-capita expenditure for public education remained pitifully low throughout the period from 1875 to 1900 and provided only the most meagre elementary educational facilities. . . . The schoolhouses . . . were often log or dilapidated buildings without windows, desks, tables, maps, charts, or blackboards. . . . In district or local supervision and direction the school work was also defective. Each little school was left to itself, with no attention from school or county officials. . . . As late as 1900 the public school system of almost every Southern state was defective in these and other respects.[10]

It should be emphasized that Knight was describing schools for white children as well as those for Negro.

It seemed at first that Blair's bill would pass the Senate. The Senate had passed his education bills, in 1884, by a vote of 33 to 11; in 1886, by a vote of 36 to 11; and in 1888, by a vote of 39 to 29. Each time, however, they had been defeated in the House.[11] The Treasury, moreover, had been accumulating, since 1880, an annual surplus of more than one hundred million dollars. But long discussion of the measure had crystallized the arguments of the opponents. They contended that local efforts for self-support would be checked; that an unfortunate precedent would be created for federal largesse; that it was absurd to distribute grants upon the basis of illiteracy without regard to age; that the Supreme Court would declare the bill unconstitutional.[12]

In addition to these general arguments were the basic questions of state rights and education of Negroes. Senator Faulkner, West Virginia Democrat, objected to the provision which authorized the secretary of the interior to ascertain whether the federal funds were being equitably distributed in the states that had separate schools. Coke of Texas denied the right of federal government to levy a tax in order to return the money in the guise of a gift for the public welfare. His colleague, Reagan, voiced the apprehension that once Congress was allowed to appropriate money to support public schools, it might soon seek to prescribe the courses of study, the text books to be used, the duties of teachers and officers, and might even require the mixing of the races in public schools. Jones of Arkansas doubted the value of education for Negroes.

But, in addition to all these objections, the political implications of the bill were openly expressed. Senator Barbour of Virginia, for example, declared that the South should not be made to bear alone the burden of educating the Negroes. He then warned:

> If you proclaim to the negroes of the South that you take no further interest in them; that you care nothing about their education; that you leave them to do the best they can in their blindness—if you take that position, there can be no necessity to send down your Federal officers to protect the purity of the ballot-box. Abandoned by the Federal government, neglected by the State, what interest would they further take in the Government of the country?

Barbour was perhaps sincere in his expression of interest, but he also pointed up the nexus between education and suffrage.

George of Mississippi, on the other hand, wanted it distinctly understood that federal aid to education should not disturb the status quo. When he looked at the condition of the black people of his state, he felt that he had no right to reject the offer. He then laid down the conditions for acceptance:

> If you would keep your intermeddling from outside the state of Mississippi; if you would allow these diverse races, locally intermingled, and yet in all the attributes which distinguish men from one another as far apart as the poles—if you would allow us to work out our own salvation without your external and, I might add, infernal, intermeddling, we might at last work out something.

Senator Hoar inquired whether the plan that George had in mind included protection of the right to vote and equal justice under the law. George's evasive reply made clear that it did not.

Blair kept his bill before the Senate from February 5 to March 20, 1890, engaging in what has been termed a "positive" filibuster. He believed that at last he could obtain passage with the casting vote of the Vice-President. But two senators switched their votes at the last minute, and his bill was defeated, 31 to 37. Blair voted in the negative in order to be able to move reconsideration.[13]

An analysis of the vote reveals that 8 Democrats (all but one of whom were from the South) and 23 Republicans voted in the affirmative. That the Republicans were responsible for the defeat of the bill is evident since 16, not counting Blair, voted in the negative. It is especially worthy of note that Fry and Hale of Maine, Aldrich and Dixon of Rhode Island, voted against the bill; while Colquitt of Georgia, George of Mississippi, Wade Hampton and Woody of South Carolina, Pasco of Florida and Pugh of Alabama, voted for it. On the other hand, most of the 20 Democrats who voted against the measure came from the South.[14] This fact probably accounts for the defection of at least some of the 16 Republicans. The terms "Republicrats" and "Dixiecrats" had not then been coined but already some Republicans and Southerners were voting together. This "Unholy Alliance" was even clearer in the case of the defeat, in the Senate, of the Lodge bill for the federal supervision of federal elections.

Henry Cabot Lodge, a young Republican from Massachusetts, introduced into the House on June 26, 1890, a bill for federal supervision of federal elections. Although opponents of the bill skillfully labeled it a "Force Bill"—a term which some contemporary historians still use without the quotation marks—it clearly did not provide for the use of force. In any election district where a specified number of voters petitioned the federal authorities, federal supervisors representing both parties were to be appointed. These supervisors were to have the power to pass on the qualifications of any voter challenged in a federal election. They also were to be given the power to receive ballots which were wrongfully refused by local officers and to place such ballots in the ballot box.

The acrimonious debates in the House reveal clearly the determination of the Southerners and some Northerners that the white people of the South would continue to handle the Negro question without federal interference. Lodge, in his opening speech, attempted to show that the bill would be applicable to only federal elections. He cited the views of Madison in the Constitutional Convention, decisions of the United States Supreme Court in *Ex parte* Siebold and *Ex parte* Yarbrough as evidence that, under Article I, Section 4, Congress had power to enact the proposed legislation. He contended that many Southern representatives privately, and the Southern press publicly, avowed that Negroes were denied the right to vote; and he presented an imposing array of statistics to show that elections in the South were not representative of the will of the people. Thus, the average vote in thirty designated Southern congressional districts was 4,167 votes each, or 26,673 votes less per district than the average of two hundred four districts in the twenty-two states of the North and West. Thirty Southern districts, with thirty votes in the House, cast and returned a total of 125,015 votes, which was 11,000 votes less than the returned vote of the three districts of Nebraska; 3,000 votes less than the returned vote of the four districts of Maine; nearly 70,000 votes less than the returned vote of the six districts of California. Lodge sarcastically suggested that the population of Georgia, Mississippi, and South Carolina must have decreased considerably: since the ratio of the voting population to the total population was usually accurate, then between 1880 and 1890 the population of Georgia must have decreased by 145,530; that of Mississippi by 123,154 and that of South Carolina by 533,027. He warned that "if we fail as a people to deal with this question rightly, we shall pay for it just as we paid the debt of slavery of which all this is a part."[15]

The first speaker for the opposition was John J. Hemphill of South Carolina. He flatly contradicted Lodge, contending that the real purpose of the bill was to control state and local elections, and even the election of the President. But instead of meeting head-on Lodge's argument that Negroes were deprived of the right to vote in the South, Hemphill dragged out the specter of federal intervention during Reconstruction. Not even Republicans, he declared, would want to live under the kind of regime that South Carolina had suffered during eight years of Reconstruction. What was most needed was a "New North," freed of prejudices about the South. He believed that many Republicans owed "an everlasting debt of gratitude to the darky," for they would never have heard of him had it not been for their support of the black man and their abuse of the white man in the South. To offset Lodge's statistics about the "rotten boroughs" in the South, he contended that in 14 Northern states an average of 27,000 voters were needed to elect a Republican congressman, but 65,000 to elect a Democratic. The South Carolina representative declared that, so far as the law affected only members of Congress,

> we protest against it, but we can shoulder it if the country can, but as to our own State, we know that the honest and intelligent people must either rule it or we must leave it; and for myself, gentlemen, in this presence, and before the people of the United States and before that God who sits upon the circle of the heavens, in all reverence, but in all earnestness, I swear that we will not leave it.

Hemphill believed that the colored men in the South had their rights in full. They had as many rights as he had, but they could not have their rights and his too. The bill was intended to put the black men again in control of the government of the Southern states. He quoted excerpts from a speech made shortly before by the "Radical" ex-Governor Chamberlain of South Carolina, who had returned there and found that the Negro had never known such an era of advancement and prosperity as he had since 1876. Hemphill gave the assurance that Southerners would not resort to fraud or violence, but that they would employ every lawful means consistent with honor to preserve their civilization, prosperity and freedom.[16]

As is frequently the case, the opening speeches presented the core of the opposing arguments. A few additional sidelights, however, show the scope and tenor of the debate. Lehlbach, a Republican from New Jersey, preferred to let the people of the states regulate their own affairs and to let time, the education of the masses, and the advancement of the moral sentiments of the communities bring about the desired result on a more permanent basis. H. St. George Tucker, a Democrat from Virginia, noted the factor of expense which he calculated to be almost $12,000,000 for each biennial election. Tucker also added the plea that the people of the South wanted home rule, just as did the people of Ireland. Covert, a Democrat from New York, was as bitter as was Hemphill or Tucker. The Republican Smyser of Ohio insisted that Hemphill really meant that the Southern white men wanted their own rights and the Negro's too; and that, "by the Eternal, they were not going to have them as long as there was a Republican majority" in the House. Kennedy, another Ohio Republican, devoted a good deal of his time to a demonstration of the reduced vote that certain Southern states would have if the second section of the Fourteenth Amendment were enforced. Using official returns, he calculated that Alabama would have only 5 representatives instead of 8; Georgia, 4 instead of 10; Louisiana, 4 instead of 6; Mississippi, 4 instead of 7; South Carolina, 3 instead of 7. He insisted that unless Congress enforced this second section, it "wantonly" violated the plain language of the Constitution.[17] Evidence is lacking, however, that he introduced a bill to enforce it.

McComas, a Republican from Maryland, quoted Henry W. Watterson of Kentucky as having admitted: " 'I should be entitled to no respect or credit if I pretended that there is either a fair poll or count of the vast overflow of black votes in States where there is a negro majority, or that in the nature of things present there can be.' " McComas retorted that the defalcations during Reconstruction were no worse than those that had occurred in some Southern states since that time. Ewart, a Republican from North Carolina, contended that no Republican in his state, black or white, was denied the right to vote; that more and more Negroes were voting for Democrats, and that the defeat of the Blair education bill by a Senate that had a Republican majority would make even more votes for Democrats. He then charged that the Lodge bill was introduced for the specific purpose of destroying the good feeling that had developed between whites and blacks under the influence of the Farmers' Alliance.[18]

The debate was undoubtedly one of the most acrimonious since the end of Reconstruction. The presiding officer was frequently compelled to restore order on the floor and to admonish the gallery not to applaud. After a great deal of parliamentary maneuvering, a vote was taken on July 2. The bill managed to squeak through by the slim margin of 155 to 149, with 24 not voting. The bill was sent to the Senate on July 7.

An analysis of the vote shows that it was almost along strict party lines. Except for one Independent Union Laborite, all those voting in the affirmative were Republicans. One of them, Henry P. Cheatham of North Carolina, was a Negro. Similarly, those opposing the measure were almost entirely Democrats. Two Republicans, however, Coleman of New York and Lehlbach of New Jersey, joined ranks with the Democrats. Of those in opposition to the measure, 82 were Southerners and 67 Northerners. In view of this almost solid party alignment, it may be doubted that the votes of the 24 who abstained (16 Republicans and 8 Democrats) would have changed the outcome.[19] It is thus more evident than perhaps it had been before that the right of Southern Negroes to vote was a political question rather than a sectional or constitutional one. It was this political alignment that undoubtedly spurred Southern Democrats to take effective action designed to offset federal legislation in support of Negro suffrage.

The Mississippi Constitutional Convention assembled six weeks later, on August 12, 1890. It consisted of 130 Democrats, one "National Republican," one "Conservative," and one Greenbacker. Only one Negro, Isaiah T. Montgomery, a wealthy and conservative businessman, was a member. Since the Negro population of Mississippi in 1890 was 56.9 per cent of the total, the extent of the elimination of Negroes is evident. Montgomery favored, in October, a bill that would disfranchise 123,000 Negroes and 12,000 whites, leaving a total Negro vote of about 66,000 and a white majority of more than 40,000. Montgomery perhaps sincerely believed that relations between the races would thereby be improved and that, as Negroes increased in knowledge and property, they would be allowed to vote. In the opinion of Wharton, who is by no means hostile to Montgomery, the latter must have known, however, that "it was the intention of the Democratic majority to eliminate Negroes with or without education, and to remove no white voters from the rolls."[20]

Montgomery's speech naturally won the approval of the Democratic press in Mississippi and in the nation as a whole. Even Cleveland praised it.[21] The former President seemed to have forgotten the act of Congress, approved February 23, 1870, by which Mississippi had been "readmitted" to the Union. One of the fundamental conditions of readmission—as for other Confederate states—was the pledge that the state constitution should never be "so amended or changed as to deprive any citizen, or class of citizens of the United States, of the right to vote, who are entitled to vote by the constitution [of 1868] herein recognized, except as punishment for such crimes as are now felonious at common law."

Although the intention of the white majority to disfranchise the Negro was clear before the convention met on August 12, Senator Quay of Pennsylvania, on the same day, introduced a resolution postponing consideration of the Lodge bill until the next session and providing that the debate on the Mc-Kinley Tariff bill be limited to the end of August. The purpose of this bill was candidly indicated in a private letter of Senator Orville Platt of Connecticut. On August 18 he wrote:

> With no rule in the senate by which we can limit debate, the Democrats can discuss the Tariff bill till the first day of the next session, and they intend to do it unless we will bargain with them not to take up the Election bill. . . . Quay's resolution which indicates the bargain . . . has I presume Republican votes enough behind it, added to the Democrats, to pass it. . . . It will probably give us a Tariff bill—but acquired at what a sacrifice!

Quay's resolution did not come to a vote, but, by tacit agreement, the Federal Elections bill was sidetracked by the Senate so that the tariff duties could be raised at that session.[22] The tariff had taken the place of federal subsidy to railroads in promoting peace and harmony at the expense of the constitutional rights of the freedmen.

This pussyfooting in Washington probably emboldened the

advocates of white supremacy in Mississippi. On October 22, 1890, the convention adopted a report of the state judiciary committee that it was unnecessary to submit the proposed changes to the people. The convention approved the new constitution on November 1. It imposed a poll tax of two dollars, excluded voters convicted of certain crimes, and barred from voting all those who could not read a section of the state constitution, or understand it when read, or give a reasonable interpretation of it.[23] What answer would the federal government have to this clear intent to nullify the Fifteenth Amendment of the Constitution of the United States?

Harrison's annual message of December 1, 1890, avoided specific reference to his intent. After lauding " 'free and honest' " elections, he expressed his satisfaction that "generally there is a growing and nonpartisan demand for better election laws." But he was probably referring especially to Mississippi and South Carolina when he warned that "against this sign of hope and progress must be set the depressing and undeniable fact that election laws and methods are sometimes cunningly contrived to secure minority control, while violence completes the shortcomings of fraud." The President gave rather vigorous support to a federal law for the protection of voters, although he did not mention specifically the Lodge bill. He probably had it in mind when he pointed out that, if a law that sought to give the advantage to honesty and the control of majorities had a sectional application, that was due to the sectional location of the crimes.[24]

When the second session of the 51st Congress began in December, 1890, it was fully aware of the action taken by Mississippi, and it had before it the President's recommendation. At the opening of the session, chances for the passage of the Lodge bill by the Senate seemed good, despite the bargain struck on the Blair bill in the previous session. Hoar, who had taken the responsibility for securing approval, won a vote of 41 to 30, on December 2, to consider the bill. But this healthy majority at once stirred the Democrats to action. After a party caucus on the following day, a statement was released that Democrats would resist the bill at every point, but that there would be no filibuster. In actual fact, the Democratic filibuster is still famous in the literature on the subject. It was all the easier to engage in a filibuster since there was no Senate rule governing it until 1917.[25]

Limitations of space do not permit a detailed analysis of the debates in which some Southern senators were more virulent than some of the Southern representatives had been. Senator Pugh of Alabama contended, on December 4, that Negroes were illiterate and consequently unable to vote intelligently. He sought to anticipate rebuttal when he argued that the unlettered white voter could acquire much knowledge by observation and association with other members of his own race. Pugh warned that in regions where there were large numbers of Negro voters, no power—no public opinion, state, federal or military force—could stop whites from preventing Negroes from voting. This determined spirit he called a "gift of God." His vow is strikingly similar to that made in 1943 by Mark Ethridge, a leading Southern white liberal of Kentucky, who declared: "There is no power in the world—not even in all the mechanized armies of the earth, Allied and Axis—which could now force the Southern white people to the abandonment of the principle of social segregation."[26]

Berry of Arkansas appealed to Northern businessmen by declaring that passage of the bill would undermine the Southern economy, thereby discouraging investors and settlers from entering the region. Gibson of Louisiana chose as his target the people of property and education who, he asserted, would find themselves opposed by the poor and uneducated. Jones of Arkansas invoked the specter of the rule of whites by blacks in Haiti, in order to frighten the unwary into preventing such a horrible situation in the South. Morgan of Alabama, who had many connections with Northern businessmen, made an impassioned plea for the right of Southern white people to handle their own problem. Coke of Texas argued that great progress in race relations had been made and would be continued if meddlers did not interfere. Bate of Tennessee developed more specifically the theme that the Southern white man was the Negro's best friend.

Senator George of Mississippi, where the amended constitution had been adopted, boldly proclaimed the South's defiance. He warned:

If you will not [stay the passage of the Election bill] then, remembering the history and traditions of our race, we give you notice of your certain and assured failure; it will never come to pass in Mississippi, in Florida, in South

Carolina, or any other State in the South, that the neck of the white race shall be under the foot of the negro, or the Mongolian, or of any created being.

Vest, of the border state of Missouri, was equally categorical. The white race was the dominant race in the world, and the "tiger blood" in its veins could not "be tamed or chained." By contrast, the Negro race was not a governing race and "you may pass all your force bills until millennial glory and we will see the same result." In less flamboyant language, Pasco of Florida promised that "the Anglo-Saxon will be true to his history. In every quarter of the world where he has been placed side by side with people of other races he has ruled." Wade Hampton, who had convinced Hayes of the good faith of the better class of the Southern whites, did not hesitate to proclaim: "In my opinion the voters who in any State represent the best elements, the capital, the intelligence, and the virtue should govern, despite all finespun theories of fraternity and equality, the sacred brotherhood of mankind, and the divine right of universal suffrage."

At least two Republicans talked almost like Southerners. Stewart, of the silver-producing state of Nevada, opposed the bill because he feared it would consolidate Southern whites, bring further misery to the Southern blacks, increase sectional animosities, and renew past discords. When Negroes should have secured education, position and property, their political rights would then be respected. (Here again is evidence that Booker T. Washington did not originate his idea in his 1895 speech.) Stewart was satisfied, in the meanwhile, to entrust the civil and political rights of the Negro to the Southern whites. Wolcott, a silverite Republican of Colorado, took the line that, in view of the existing economic condition of the South and the general ignorance of the colored race, "there are many things more important and vital to the welfare of this nation than that the colored citizens of this nation shall vote."

Not many Republicans rallied to the support of the bill. Hoar, in his opening statement on December 3, referred to his statements during the previous session in support of the constitutionality of the bill, the necessity for it, and the sheer nonsense of calling it a "force bill." He also called attention to Harrison's espousal of the bill in his annual message. In answering Democratic criticisms of the bill, he gave evidence that federal supervision was necessary to prevent fraud in elections. Ingalls of Kansas pointed out that Southern states suppressed the Negro vote but retained, none the less, their full representation in the House. Hiscock of New York ridiculed assertions that the Lodge bill was a "force bill," and insisted that evidence in the *Congressional Record* and newspapers left no doubt that Negroes were denied a free ballot. He conceded the superiority of the Anglo-Saxon over the Negro, but asserted that the former were a just people. He pertinently observed that "as long as those who dominate and deprive the black man of his political rights are united in political faith and interests, agitation will continue, constantly increasing in volume and force, powerfully inspired by economic considerations." Spooner of Wisconsin laid bare the weakest argument of the opposition when he demanded why the new Mississippi constitution did not operate alike on ignorant whites and Negroes. Higgins of Delaware insisted that transparent frauds made federal supervision necessary. Former Secretary of State Evarts—one of the best legal minds in the country—warned that "unless we can keep the suffrage within the regulation of legal obligation and maintain it by authority and obedience to it on the part of the people of the whole country as a working force in our affairs, wider and wider estrangements from these methods will extend themselves among the people." He somewhat sarcastically observed that, while Southerners insisted upon being let alone in regard to the suffrage, they had introduced three bills for federal aid in favor of the expatriation of Negroes.

Two Republicans, while ostensibly in favor of the bill, probably did it more harm than good. Cullom of Illinois, who argued that Negro equality was not involved, insisted that Southerners opposed federal aid to education lest it result in rule by the majority. Blair's long speech leaves doubt as to where he really stood. No suffrage, he declared, was fit to be supported unless it were intelligent and fit to govern. It would be a "logical absurdity" to "kill ourselves almost" in order to pass the Lodge bill, unless at the same time Congress took steps to make the voters sufficiently intelligent to govern. He then queried: "Are we, the Republican party, to make ourselves the allies of a despotic ignorance and impose it upon the South and upon ourselves and at the same time refuse to expend, it may be one-half of the amount that would be required to execute this law, in the education of the suffrage?" He expected to vote for the bill, but he served notice that the American people would condemn Congress if it did not also make the suffrage intelligent. The main point to be considered was not the colored vote in the South, but rather "the uninformed" white suffrage of the South as well as in the North that needed education. "I care much for the negro race," but, he continued, "I care more for my own, and the future of this country is in the hands of the white race. If you permit our white children to be or to become ignorant you simply ordain the ruin of both races." Not until the white voters of the South had intelligence enough to know the meaning of real freedom would they be willing to permit Negroes to vote.[27]

Negroes were themselves divided on the merits of the bill. Morgan of Alabama introduced a petition from a group of colored citizens from his state protesting the passage of the bill. Hoar, on the other hand, presented a petition of the Colored South Carolina Republican Association *of the District of Columbia* denouncing the irregularities in the South Carolina voting system in connection with the eight-box ballot.[28] The Alabama Negroes may have feared that, however much their rights were violated, it was better to go along with the wishes of the dominant race.

Early in 1891 the final defeat of the bill was presaged. On January 5, Stewart, the Nevada silverite who had made a speech opposing passage, moved consideration of currency legislation. A coalition of Democrats and silver Republicans won the day, 34 to 29.[29] But once the silver bill had passed, January 14, the contest on the Elections bill still had to be resolved. Hoar's motion to consider it resulted in a tie vote, 33 to 33, which Vice President Morton broke with an affirmative vote.[30]

There ensued a typical half-hearted attempt by the Republicans to break the filibuster. Unlike some recent filibusters, begun near the end of the session, which have given Democrats an advantage, this session still had more than six weeks before its expiration. It should be borne in mind, on the other hand, that the Senate had no rule governing filibusters.

On January 20, Senator Aldrich, Republican from Rhode

Island, moved for cloture. While the Democrats were seeking frantically to prevent it, Cameron, a Republican from Pennsylvania, and several silver Republicans rescued them. Two days later, the silverite Wolcott moved to consider an apportionment bill. Needless to say, it contained no reference to the second section of the Fourteenth Amendment. On a very close vote, 35 to 34, Wolcott's motion prevailed. All affirmative votes were cast by Republicans. One was that of Cameron, of the manufacturing state of Pennsylvania; one that of Washburn of Minnesota. Four came from the silver states: those of John P. Jones and Stewart of Nevada, Teller and Wolcott of Colorado.[31] The responsibility of the Republicans, and especially those from the silver states, for the laying aside of the Lodge bill is beyond dispute.

One reason for the defection of some Republicans was their hope that the admission of the six new Northwestern states—Idaho, Montana, North Dakota, South Dakota, Washington and Wyoming—would reduce the power of the Solid South. But the New York *Times* had perhaps not been unduly cynical when it charged editorially, on June 19, 1890, that the bill was merely "for the purpose of permitting the Republicans to prove to their constituents that they favored free elections."[32]

Only Fortune in the New York *Age*, of the three colored papers available, unmercifully berated the Republicans for their failure to pass the bill. In November, 1890, he observed that the obligations of the party to manufacturers were considered "more sacred and urgent" than those to 1,500,000 Afro-American members of the party. A month later, he contended that the bill was also opposed by five Republican papers whose tendencies were largely free-trade, namely, the Omaha *Bee*, the St. Paul *Pioneer Press*, the St. Louis *Globe-Democrat*, the Chicago *Tribune* and the Philadelphia *Telegraph*. If the Republicans failed to pass the Lodge bill, as they had failed to pass the Blair bill, they would strike a "death blow at the confidence of those it has deceived." Getting into full stride, Fortune charged on January 3, 1891:

The whole Southern election system is an infamous putrescence, in the nostrils of honest and decent men and the squeal about force and fraud set up by the Democratic and

Mugwump newspapers is one of the most impudent bluffs a paper ever adopted as a shibboleth to astonish and confound its enemy. . . . The Democratic party is the party of force and fraud.

A week later he predicted that the bill was "as dead as a door nit, . . . stabbed to death" by eight Republican Senators. "The treachery of the Hayes Administration has been repeated under the Harrison Administration."[33]

William Calvin Chase, editor of the Washington *Bee*, was considered even by some of his friends as "indiscreet." The *Bee* certainly stung when Chase was aroused. But he was also a persistent office seeker and, at that time, a loyal supporter of Harrison. He therefore failed to exercise his truly extraordinary gift for vitriolic denunciation. On January 24, 1891, he attributed the defeat of the bill to the impeding of the will of the majority by a minority whom he did not identify. On January 31 he quoted a letter from Senator Spooner: " 'We have been shamefully deserted by a sufficient number of Republicans to make our ability to do justice in the matter of Federal Elections doubtful.' " Chase clearly preferred to allow a Republican senator to place the blame on the party, rather than do so himself in his colorful language. Hendley, of the Huntsville (Alabama) *Gazette*, charged that the Democrats would not have opposed the bill if Southern Negroes would only vote the Democratic ticket. He made no comments after the bill was defeated.[34]

The Senate had been aware of not only Mississippi's defiance of the Fifteenth Amendment and the Act of Congress of February 23, 1870, but of an evident determination on the part of Governor Ben Tillman in South Carolina to do likewise. This state, like Mississippi, had a Negro population that exceeded the white population. South Carolina Negroes had participated more fully in Reconstruction than those of any other state. It is not surprising, then, that South Carolina was to be the first to follow in the footsteps of Mississippi. "Pitchfork" Ben Tillman's advent to power is significant, however, since it marked the beginning of the Southern demagogue who rode into power by blasting both "the honorable and influential Southern whites" and the Negroes.

Much of the opposition of the farmers and workers in the South stemmed from the economic forces that had led to

Mahoneism in Virginia and elsewhere in the late 1870's, and that were to flare up with greater vigor in the Populist Revolt of the 1890's. But in South Carolina, Tillman's victory over Wade Hampton was also due to the fact that Wade Hampton had not eliminated the Negro as completely from politics as Tillman and his supporters demanded. The latest biographer of Hampton has insisted that if his middle of the road policy had been followed, South Carolina would have been spared the rule of the Tillmanite extremists. Alrutheus Taylor, Simkins and Woody have asserted, on the other hand, that after 1877 Hampton did not keep his promises to protect the Negro.[35] In any case, Negro participation in the politics of South Carolina had steadily declined from 1876 to 1890, as the following table indicates:[36]

	1877–1878	1879–1880	1880–1881	1882–1883	1884–1885	1886–1887	1888–1889	1890–1891
Senate Republicans	4	3	2	3	1	2	0	0
Senate Democrats	0	0	0	0	1	2	0	0
House Republicans	32	3	4	9	4	4	3	6
House Democrats	3	6	1	3	0	0	2	0
Total	39	12	7	15	6	8	5	6

Thereafter the only Negroes in the legislature were Republicans in the House: three in 1892–1893, and five in 1894–1895. Five were members of the constitutional convention in 1895. There was one Negro member after that, a Republican in the House.

Tillman, in his inaugural address, December 4, 1890, boldly proclaimed the path that he would follow. For the first time in the history of the state, he declared, the people had demanded and obtained the right to elect their own governor. As the leader and exponent of that "revolution," he was prepared to enter upon the discharge of his duties. "Democracy," he continued, "has won a great victory unparalleled. The triumph of Democracy and white supremacy over mongrelism and anarchy is most complete." He left no doubt that the whites had "absolute control of the government" and intended, "at any hazard, to retain it." It was beyond the capacity of most Negroes at that time to exercise an intelligent suffrage. It was not true that all men are created equal. There was, however, "no just reason why the white man and the black man of Carolina should not live together in peace." As further evidence of his friendship for the Negroes, he asked that the governor be given the right to remove from office those sheriffs who failed to prevent mob violence.[87]

Tillman was not able, at first, to push through his program. Bills to remove sheriffs from office for failure to prevent mob violence were defeated in 1890 and 1891, and in the latter year six Negroes were lynched in the state. His request for the separation of the races in railroad coaches was defeated in the state Senate after having passed the House. (In South Carolina, as in many other Southern states, the railroads themselves segregated the two races.) His demand for a constitutional convention to disfranchise the Negro failed to pass the House after getting the necessary two-thirds majority in the Senate. Tillman also failed in his attempt to obtain legislation to gerrymander the state so as to prevent the election of a Negro Congressman. (One had been elected for the 51st Congress, 1889–1891.) He did succeed, however, in obtaining the passage of a law placing a prohibitive tax upon the operations of labor agents who were enticing Negro farm hands to migrate. The fiery leader of the farmers also got the state Democratic executive committee to prescribe that Negroes, who had been allowed to vote in the Democratic primary because of their loyalty to Wade Hampton in 1876, were to be allowed to vote only when they would get ten white men to vouch for their loyalty.[88] But Tillman had to wait until the Populist Revolt assumed larger proportions before he accomplished the disfranchisement and segregation of the Negro by law.

Tillman's inaugural address and the revision of the Mississippi constitution inspired one of the few congressional resolutions designed to enforce the second section of the Fourteenth Amendment. On December 10, 1890, Senator Dolph, a Republican from Oregon, introduced a resolution to direct the Committee on Privileges and Elections to investigate if the right to vote for President, members of the House of Representatives, the executive, legislative and judicial officers of any state were denied to any persons meeting the general requirements stipulated in the Fourteenth and Fifteenth Amendments. He specifically stated that the new Mississippi constitution could not be justified since it violated the second section of the Fourteenth Amendment. Vest of Missouri proclaimed that the South would be willing to lose its proportional representation in Congress if only the Fifteenth Amendment were repealed. Dolph's resolution received no more consideration than had those of Garfield and Page. It was referred to the Committee on Privileges and Elections on December 12, 1890, where it was buried.[39] The resolution is most significant, because it led to one of the first suggestions of a bargain for enforcement of the second section of the Fourteenth Amendment in return for the repeal of the Fifteenth Amendment. This proposal for a bargain was to be frequently repeated.

Harrison and the Republicans virtually abandoned the fight to protect the constitutional rights of Negroes after the defeat of the Lodge bill early in 1891. Harrison perhaps took cognizance, in his third annual address, December 9, 1891, of Tillman's efforts at gerrymandering, when he devoted what amounts to three pages in Richardson's *Messages* to berating the practice everywhere. He followed this attack upon gerrymandering with a reference to the failure of the Federal Elections bill. That failure led him to state pertinently: "It is important to know whether the opposition to such measures is really vested in particular features supposed to be objectionable or includes any proposition to give to the election laws of the United States adequacy to the correction of grave and acknowledged evils." Since the Federal Elections bill had been defeated, he proposed a nonpartisan commission to consider the question of the evils in the election system. He believed that the Constitution permitted the selection of such a commission by the United States Supreme Court.[40] There is no evidence that the commission was appointed.

Further evidence of the unwillingness of the Republicans to seek to protect Negroes is seen in the first proposal for federal action to prevent lynching. The most reliable statistics show the following numbers of persons lynched in the United States. Beginning with 1882 the annual number was 113, 130, 211, 184, 138, 120, 137, 170, 96, and 184 in 1891. Most of them were Negroes living in the South. But Harrison's proposal came as a result of the lynching of 11 Italians and the subsequent demands of the Italian government. This first anti-lynching law, therefore, would have protected only foreign nationals in the United States. But Harrison did not present such a bill to Congress. It remained for the last Negro in Congress during this period to introduce a bill to prevent the lynching of American citizens.

In this third annual message, Harrison also denounced the pogroms against Jews in Russia, the slave trade in Africa, and the tariff in the Congo Free State. Labor troubles in the West Indian island of Navassa, if space devoted to subjects is a valid index, were more important than the status of Negroes in the United States.[41]

The adoption of the new Mississippi constitution, Tillman's evident plan to change similarly South Carolina's constitution, the defeat of the Lodge bill, and Harrison's proposal for the protection of foreign nationals from lynching make the Republican platform of 1892 even more preposterous than its predecessors. It grandiloquently proclaimed:

> We demand that every citizen of the United States shall be allowed to cast one free and unrestricted ballot in all public elections, and that such ballot shall be counted and returned as cast; that such laws shall be enacted and enforced as will secure to every citizen, be he rich or poor, native or foreign born, white or black, this sovereign right, guaranteed by the Constitution. The free and honest ballot, the just and equal representation of all the people, as well as their just and equal protection under the laws, are the foundation of our republican institutions and the party will never relax its efforts until the integrity of the ballot and the purity of elections shall be fully guaranteed and protected in every state.[42]

Since Negroes were almost completely disfranchised in the South, Harrison did not win a single Southern state, and he was defeated in the election of 1892 when dissatisfaction with the McKinley Tariff led to the loss of some Northern states. His last message to Congress, December 6, 1892, has therefore only academic interest. He devoted about the same amount of space to Negro suffrage as he had done in 1891. He called for legislation by Congress to offset the tendency of the legislation in some states to deny equal protection of the franchise. He did not make any specific recommendations on this point, but he did recommend to Congress "repressive legislation" to stop the lynching of Negroes.[43] Thus the first presidential recommendation for Congressional action to stop this crime was made three months before the end of his term. It is not surprising that Congress took no action on his recommendation.

A penetrating analysis of Harrison's administration concludes that "in the spring of 1892 no impartial observer could have maintained that President Harrison had given either the Republican party or the people of the United States the magnetic and responsive leadership that they sought."[44] This general conclusion is especially pertinent as far as protection of the Negro was concerned, and is even more relevant for the spring of 1893 than for the spring of 1892. The attempts made during his administration to reopen the "Southern question" had provoked a counteroffensive from which the South emerged even more triumphant than it had in 1877.

The Nadir Under McKinley

THE Populist Revolt threatened, briefly, to halt the South's triumphant march back to the way of life it had mapped out for the freedmen prior to the federal government's attempt to organize its own program of Reconstruction. Distressed white farmers in the South temporarily laid aside their racial animosities and joined black farmers and workers in order to alleviate their common grievances. But the economic program of the Populists floundered on the shoal of Free Silver, and the racial solidarity concept was overwhelmed by a new tide of demagoguery.

Cleveland's second administration was so beset with national and international problems—the panic of 1893, Free Silver, the Populist Revolt, Hawaii, Venezuela and Cuba—that he had little opportunity to stop the steady deterioration of the Negro's status. He probably concluded that the Southern question was definitely settled, when Booker T. Washington won national acclaim for his Atlanta Compromise Speech, in September, 1895. In the following year, the United States Supreme Court consolidated the triumph of the former slave states when it sanctioned the doctrine of "separate but equal accommodations."

The Spanish American War—followed by the assumption by the United States of the role of trustee for the "little brown brother" in the Philippines; for the white, colored and brown Puerto Ricans; and of the role of protector for the white, colored, brown and black Cubans—diverted attention from additional denials of constitutional rights to colored Americans. The specter of Free Silver was exorcised, the agrarian revolt failed, and Big Business, personified by Marcus A. Hanna, fastened an ever tightening grip on the country. In the words of Vernon Parrington, "America lay fat and contented in the lap of McKinley prosperity."[1] Since the newly acclaimed "leader" of the Negroes had accepted an inferior status for Negroes, and since the opposition of the few who did not was drowned by the praise lavished upon Washington, America seemed at the turn of the century to have resolved to the satisfaction of all the question raised by Douglass. The principles of democracy did not have to be applied alike to all Americans. Douglass was dead and the Road to Reunion was complete.

Cleveland was elected in 1892, on a platform which scathingly denounced the Federal Elections bill. Such a policy was "fraught with the gravest dangers, scarcely less momentous than would result from a revolution practically establishing a monarchy on the ruins of the Republic." This policy struck at the North as well as at the South, and injured the colored citizens even more than the white. In language that was not at all veiled, the platform upheld the right of revolution to overthrow "the self-perpetuating oligarchy of office-holders" who would gain office if a Federal Elections bill were enacted.[2]

While the treatment of the Negro played an infinitesimal role in the election of 1892, Cleveland, elected on such a platform, was hardly likely to urge vigorous action for the protection of Negro rights in the South. It will be recalled that he had praised Isaiah T. Montgomery for accepting a subordinate position for Negro voters in Mississippi. It is not surprising, then, that he remained silent when South Carolina, in 1895, adopted an amendment similar to Mississippi's, and when it became evident that Louisiana was also planning the "legal" disfranchisement of most Negroes. The closest that the President came to condemning such action was his statement in his second inaugural address, March 4, 1893, that the right of equality before the law "follows the badge of citizenship wherever found, and, unimpaired by race or color, it appeals for recognition to American manliness and fairness."

The only other occasion on which Cleveland officially called attention to the presence of Negroes in the United States was a request for an appropriation to relieve the distress of some Alabama Negroes who had returned in a miserable condition to the Texas border after the failure of an attempt to settle in Mexico. In his annual messages, however, he made lengthy statements about Indians, the slave trade in Africa, the Congo Free State, Haiti, Liberia, the lynching of Italians in Colorado, and pogroms against the Jews in Russia.[3]

This vagueness, and almost complete silence on Cleveland's part, concerning one of the most delicate problems in the United States stand out in sharp contrast with his courageous and forthright pronouncements and policies on issues in which he believed that the nation's welfare or his own principles were involved. In the bitter struggle resulting from the increasing demand for Free Silver, he took vigorous steps, despite caustic denunciation, in support of a single standard, gold. His refusal to permit the annexation of Hawaii shows, perhaps better than any other policy, the extent to which, as Professor Nevins has said, he was "a slave to his conscience." On a smaller canvas, Cleveland sought to bring to an end American participation in the tripartite protectorate of Samoa. When the Senate and the House passed a concurrent resolution favoring recognition of the belligerency of the Cuban insurgents, Cleveland ignored it. He went further, and warned that, even if Congress declared war, he would not mobilize the United States army. On the other hand, Cleveland seems to have been willing to risk war with Great Britain because of the latter's refusal to arbitrate with Venezuela the boundary with British Guiana. It is thus evident that, when Cleveland was convinced that vigorous action was necessary, he did not hesitate to take it. He resisted American jingoism in Hawaii, Samoa and Cuba, and encouraged it against Great Britain.

These policies of Cleveland help us to understand why Allan Nevins has used as the subtitle for his authoritative biography of Cleveland *A Study in Courage*. But this very characteristic raises the pertinent question: Why did Cleveland not manifest equal courage in dealing with the problem of the Negro? The most obvious answer is that he had so many other pressing problems that he did not have the time to consider the question of the violation of the constitutional rights of the Negroes. On the other hand, his basic attitude is revealed by his signing, in 1894, bills that removed most of the last vestiges of the Reconstruction legislation from federal statutes. If Cleveland had believed that it was still desirable for the federal government to protect these constitutional rights, he would probably have vetoed the laws which repealed federal protection of them.

In brief, Cleveland undoubtedly believed, with most other Americans, North and South, that the Southern question should be handled by Southerners. He had approved the virtual disfranchisement of the Negro in Mississippi; and he had remained silent while Ben Tillman was vociferously demanding similar disfranchisement in South Carolina. There is little reason to doubt that he subscribed to the Democratic platform of 1892, which had denounced a Federal Elections law. Further light is thrown on his conscience, in respect to the Southern question, by the approval that he gave to Booker T. Washington's Atlanta Compromise Speech of September 18, 1895.

A comprehensive analysis of this speech and of nation-wide reaction to it will be found in Chapter Fourteen. For the time being, it suffices to summarize its salient theses. Washington, principal of Tuskegee Institute, Alabama, renounced "social equality," at least temporarily conceded a subordinate position for Southern Negroes in politics, urged education for the practical end of gaining a livelihood, and emphasized the necessity for Negroes to cooperate with their Southern white friends. In one passage, the importance of which has been grasped by only a few of the many students of this speech, Washington painted a beautiful picture of the loyalty of slaves during the Civil War, opposed foreign immigration and, by clear implication, promised that Negro workers could be depended upon to work "without strikes and labor wars." It was one of the most momentous speeches in American history. Booker T. Washington emerged as the "leader" of his race; he was acclaimed by some of the most prominent Americans, in both the North and the South, as a farseeing statesman. Cleveland's approval was, therefore, in harmony with the general approbation.

A few days after the speech, Cleveland wrote to Washington concerning it:

> The Exposition would be fully justified if it did not do more than furnish the opportunity for its delivery. Your words cannot fail to delight and encourage all who wish well for your race; and if our colored fellow-citizens do not from your utterances gather new hope and form new determinations to gain every valuable advantage offered them by their citizenship, it will be strange indeed.[4]

It would be unfair to Cleveland to conclude that in conscience and in principle he favored a subordinate status for Negroes in American society. Like Washington, he may have believed that it was necessary to accept that subordinate status at that time. Perhaps courage is required to accept the apparently inevitable, despite the obvious violations of the Constitution of the United States—which Cleveland had sworn to uphold. It is clear, however, that Cleveland was in this instance cautious rather than courageous. The higher courage would have demanded at least some effort to stop the descent of the Negro to the lowest and lowliest position that he has occupied since emancipation.

That descent was accelerated by the first United States Supreme Court decision, Plessy v. Ferguson, 1896, which declared constitutional state laws that provided "separate but equal accommodations." This decision conformed to Southern customs of segregation and to the increased number of "Jim Crow" laws following the Civil Rights Decision in 1883. The Interstate Commerce Commission, in three rulings, and lower federal courts had already approved the doctrine of separate but equal accommodations. It is not suggested, then, that this decision was prompted by Cleveland's policies or pronouncements, for even the repeal, in 1894, of the last of the Reconstruction laws was the culmination of efforts continuing over several years.

While the President is absolved of responsibility for the decision, his deserved reputation for conscience and courage raises the question of why he remained silent on this. He did not know what fifty years of application of the doctrine have conclusively proved, namely, that the separate accommodations are rarely, if ever, equal. Nor did he have the benefit of the very recent insistence that the act of separation itself constitutes inequality. Despite all these attenuations of criticism of Cleveland, a truly courageous President, who did not believe in the constitutionality or wisdom of the decision, would have spoken out against it. Lincoln, for example, had told an audience, in 1858, that Americans were prepared to become "fit subjects of the first cunning tyrant who rises among you . . . if the elections shall promise that the next Dred Scott decision and all future decisions shall be acquiesced in by the people." And in his famous question at Freeport, Illinois, in the same year, he presented Stephen A. Douglas with the dilemma of rejecting either the Dred Scott decision or his own principle of "popular sovereignty." But Cleveland clearly had no such reservations about Plessy v. Ferguson as Lincoln had had about the Dred Scott decision. With respect to the Negro, Cleveland accepted the view—prevailing in the South and growing in the North—that the Negro was not entitled to identity of rights with the white man. If Cleveland had shown as much courage in seeking to stop the descent of the Negro toward the nadir as he manifested in his foreign policy and in the "Battle of the Standards," he might have earned the encomium of "great" instead of merely "near great."

While Cleveland accepted what he may have considered the inevitable, William McKinley put his firm stamp of approval upon it. The defeat of Free Silver, the Spanish American War, Hay's Open Door Policy in China, negotiations with Great Britain for the sole right to construct an Isthmian canal, and the return of prosperity have been the principal grist for the historians' mills. Some have included also disfranchisement of Negroes in Louisiana, North Carolina, Alabama and Virginia. But McKinley's callous disregard for the protection of the constitutional rights of Negroes has been almost entirely overlooked.

McKinley has generally been portrayed as the puppet of Marcus A. Hanna of Ohio, the symbol of the plutocracy which dominated the country at the turn of the century. Cartoons of the period usually depicted Hanna dressed in a suit made of dollar signs. William Allen White has left an unforgettable picture of the "economic lechery" of Hanna whom he at one time admired. But this perspicacious newsman was convinced that "McKinley, not Hanna, was dominant in the relationship."[5] It is possible that McKinley dominated Hanna, but the President surely did not dominate all the forces of plutocracy that Hanna typified and that he had led to victory in 1896.

This presidential contest has frequently been termed the first in which the class struggle was the major issue. From the panic of 1873 until 1879, farmers, workers, and debtors in general were being crushed by the high prices they had to pay for manufactured goods and transportation on the one hand, and the relatively low prices they received for their goods and their labor on the other hand. A temporary return to prosperity, after the passage of the Bland-Allison Act in 1878, was attributed, at least in part, to the purchase and coinage of $2,000,000 worth of silver a month. Before the end of 1883, however, new economic difficulties contributed to the first election of Cleveland. Advocates of "cheap money" and of additional government purchase and coinage of silver obtained the passage of the Sherman Silver Purchase Bill, in 1890. Following the panic of 1893, Congress repealed the Sherman Silver Purchase Bill, despite loud cries by the silver followers for "another revolution of 1776" to free the nation from domination by the bankers.

The Populist party, which had been formed in 1891, had entered the campaign of 1892 with a platform that included, among other things, demands for the unlimited coinage of silver, an income tax, public control of trust-dominated railroads, telegraphs, and telephones, direct election of senators, and reforms for labor. The East promptly labeled this "revolt" of farmers and workers in the West and South as "communistic" and "subversive." The Populist candidate for President obtained only twenty-two electoral votes, but the Republicans —who were held largely responsible for the woes of the farmers and the workers—lost the presidency.

After the panic of 1893, the Populists made a better showing in the Congressional and state elections of 1894. Curiously enough, many of these victories in the South were the result of "Fusion" between Populists and Republicans—many of whom were Negroes—against the Democrats who, on the whole, represented conservative business interests. They gained their most notable victory in North Carolina, where they won control of the state legislature, elected the two United States senators, and a majority of the representatives. It was this threat to Democratic and white control that helped Tillman to push through the amendment to South Carolina's constitution that effectively disfranchised most of the Negroes in the state.

In the 1896 campaign, the Populists named Bryan, the Democrat, as their candidate, largely because he advocated Free Silver and was considered the standard bearer of the distressed farmers and workers. In North Carolina, Fusionists won the governorship, and increased their representation considerably in the House and slightly in the Senate. In Georgia, Louisiana and Texas, the Republicans and Fusionists polled 40 per cent of the votes.[6]

Thus, in addition to the class struggle, in the election of 1896 there was the specter of the revival of Negro participation in politics in the South. McKinley and the Republicans were therefore confronted with a dual problem: defeating the "radical" Democrats and Populists in the national elections;

and breaking up the fusion of "radical" Republicans, including Negroes, and Populists in the South. McKinley and the Republicans succeeded in both objectives. Cleveland and the "Gold Democrats" helped defeat Bryan; and white demagogues in the South soon lured white farmers and workers away from the Negroes—the Negroes received practically no support from the Republican national party. The return to prosperity left Southern Negroes worse off, politically, than they had been before.

In the presidential election of 1896, the Negro was almost completely forgotten, except in the South where the specter of a new era of Negro "domination" was invoked to keep the South solidly Democratic. The Democratic platform, in addition to calling for the unlimited coinage of silver, condemned the increasing centralization of government, praised the doctrine of state rights, and demanded legislation for the protection of labor. It did not hesitate to reaffirm its allegiance to the great principles of justice and liberty which the party had advocated from the time of Jefferson—"freedom of speech, freedom of the press, freedom of conscience, the preservation of personal rights, the equality of all citizens before the law, and the faithful observance of Constitutional limitations." It also asserted that the Democratic party had "always been the exponent of political liberty."

The platform did not contain a denunciation of a Federal Elections bill, as had the 1892 platform. Evidently, the Democrats believed that there was little likelihood that such a bill would again be introduced. There was, indeed, nothing in the Republican platform to suggest that it would be.

The Republican platform repeated that part of the 1892 plank which had read: "We demand that every citizen of the United States shall be allowed to cast one free and unrestricted ballot, and that such ballot shall be counted and returned as cast." But this plank did not repeat the demand of 1892 that "such laws shall be enacted and enforced as will secure to every citizen, be he rich or poor, native or foreign born, white or black, this sovereign right, guaranteed by the Constitution." Nor did the plank repeat the 1892 declamation that the free and honest ballot, the just and equal representation of all the people, and their just and equal protection under the laws were the foundation of American republican institutions and that the party would "never relax its efforts until the integrity of the ballot and the purity of elections shall be fully guaranteed and protected in every State." As far as the presidential election of 1896 was concerned, the class struggle did not involve a commitment by either party to introduce legislation for the protection of the political and legal rights of the Negroes, the most submerged class. The Republican platform did, however, assert: "We watch with deep and abiding interest the heroic battle of the Cuban patriots against cruelty and oppression, and our best hopes go out for the full success of their determined contest for liberty." The Republicans also unqualifiedly condemned "the uncivilized and barbarous practice" of lynching, but made no commitment to put an end to the barbarism.[7]

The victory of the propertied classes in the election of 1896 permitted McKinley a smugness that might not have been possible if the "radical," "communistic," "anarchistic," and "subversive" forces had gained the day. McKinley's inaugural address set the keynote for his administration. "These years of glorious history," he proclaimed, "have exalted mankind and advanced the cause of freedom throughout the world and immeasurably strengthened the precious free institutions which we enjoy. Equality of rights must prevail, and our laws be always and everywhere respected and obeyed." Although American citizens might have failed in the full discharge of their duties, it was encouraging that civil liberties and "free and fair elections are dearer and more unreservedly enjoyed today than ever before." Lynching should not be tolerated in the United States; courts, and not mobs, should execute the penalties of the law. He painted a glowing picture of the end of sectional discord: "The recent election not only most fortunately demonstrated the obliteration of sectional or geographical lines, but to some extent also the prejudices which for years have distracted our councils and marred our true greatness as a nation." The North and the South no longer divided on the old lines, but upon principles and policies. In order to leave no doubt as to where he stood, the new President promised:

It will be my constant aim to do nothing, and permit nothing to be done, that will arrest or disturb this growing sentiment of unity and cooperation, this revival of esteem and affiliation which now animates so many thousands in both the old antagonistic sections, but I shall cheerfully do everything possible to promote and increase it.[8]

McKinley kept his promise. His fellow-Ohioan, Hayes, had laid the cornerstone of the monument dedicated to reunion, and McKinley completed it.

In perhaps only one respect did McKinley disturb the peaceful relations between the two sections, namely, by continuing the practice of appointing a few Negroes to federal positions in the South. In North Carolina, for example, between fifteen and twenty-five postmasterships were held by Negroes. John C. Dancy, who had served as collector of customs at Wilmington, North Carolina, was reappointed by McKinley. James E. Shepard was appointed deputy collector of the Bureau of Internal Revenue in 1899. As a consequence of these and similar appointments in other Southern states, McKinley aroused opposition, especially from potential officeholders. In 1901, Jeter G. Pritchard, Fusionist senator from North Carolina, became one of the earliest advocates of a "Lily-white" Republican party. McKinley was assassinated on September 6, 1901, and Theodore Roosevelt had to come to grips with this movement, which had little to do with the right to vote, but rather with the exclusive right of Southern white Republicans to hold federal office.

On the vitally more important question of Negro suffrage, McKinley remained silent, until the party in 1900 made its usual appeal for Negro votes. He had several opportunities to convince the South that he, like Hayes, would keep his promise to leave the South alone.

In 1898, while colored soldiers were helping to liberate Cubans from Spanish "tyranny," Louisiana adopted the so-called "Grandfather Clause." This device set certain qualifications for voting, but exempted whites from meeting those qualifications. It was such a patent violation of the Fifteenth Amendment that the United States Supreme Court, in 1915—in its first decision to put a brake on Southern laws abridging the right of Negroes to vote—declared unconstitutional a similar amendment to the Oklahoma constitution. McKinley took no public notice of the "Grandfather Clause."

In Wilmington, North Carolina, two days after the 1898 election, a race riot resulted in the killing of a score or more of Negroes and a mass flight of the frightened Negroes from the city. As is usual in the case of a riot, the full facts are difficult to establish. But the argument of Negro "domination" can not in this case be logically advanced, since the riot took place after the election which had resulted in a victory for the "white supremacy" campaign.[9] In any case, the Northern press as a whole condemned the riot as an act of barbarism, unjustifiable and needless.[10] As will be seen in Chapters Ten and Eleven, the Northern press generally condoned peaceful methods for maintaining white supremacy. Its general condemnation of the Wilmington race riot makes all the more significant McKinley's failure to take public cognizance of it. When North Carolina, in 1900, adopted a constitutional amendment to disfranchise Negroes, McKinley again remained silent. His only reference to Negroes in his message to Congress during his first administration was an obscure passage in that of December 5, 1899, when he demanded respect for law and obedience to lawfully constituted tribunals. Even then he was probably referring rather to the lynchings of Italians and Mexicans—which had prompted him to send special messages to Congress urging an appropriation for the relatives of the victims.[11]

It is appropriate that the last Negro Congressman of the post-Reconstruction era completed his term at the end of McKinley's first administration. Two Negroes had been members of the House and one of the Senate, 1869–1871; five had been members of the House, 1871–1873 and seven, 1873–1875. The high-water mark had been reached in the 44th Congress, 1875–1877, when there had been seven representatives and one senator. Thereafter the number steadily declined. The senator, B. K. Bruce of Mississippi, completed his full term in 1881. In the previous Congress there had been two colored representatives, but none during Bruce's last two years. From 1881 to 1887 there had been two Negro Congressmen in each session; from 1889 to 1891, three; and from that time to 1901, only one. The last of these, George H. White of North Carolina, had been elected during the Fusionist campaign of 1896, and was returned in the election of 1898 despite the "white supremacy" campaign—which even Josephus Daniels was to regret in his old age.[12]

None of these Negroes had been able to obtain the passage of important legislation in behalf of their own race. During White's two terms, Negroes were subjected to vilification in

Congress the like of which has rarely been equaled, except in the early days of the Nazi struggle for power in Germany, and some recent attacks upon eminent Americans by an irresponsible senator.* In April, 1898, David A. De Armond of Missouri described Negroes as being "almost too ignorant to eat, scarcely wise enough to breathe, mere existing human machines." John Sharp Williams of Mississippi, who was a little more polished than the other demagogues, gave perhaps the classic denunciation of the Negro race when he declared on December 20, 1898:

> You could ship-wreck 10,000 illiterate white Americans on a desert island, and in three weeks they would have a fairly good government, conceived and administered upon fairly democratic lines. You could ship-wreck 10,000 negroes, every one of whom was a graduate of Harvard University, and in less than three years, they would have retrograded governmentally; half of the men would have been killed, and the other half would have two wives apiece.[18]

Other similar diatribes led White to attempt to reply, since his Republican colleagues did not relieve him of the responsibility of being the spokesman for his own people. On January 9, 1898, he pointed out that while he had heard Negroes referred to "as savages, as aliens, as brutes, as vile and vicious and worthless," he had heard little or nothing with reference to their better qualities. He made perhaps his most effective reply on February 23, 1900, when he observed:

> It is easy for these gentlemen to taunt us with our inferiority, at the same time not mentioning the cause of this inferiority. It is rather hard to be accused of shiftlessness and idleness when the accuser closes the avenue of labor and industrial pursuits to us. It is hardly fair to accuse us of ignorance when it was made a crime under the former order of things to learn enough about letters to even read the Word of God.[14]

Ben Tillman, who had become a senator, boldly declared that South Carolina had disfranchised all the colored people it

* In the 1960's, even more vicious attacks were made by the "radical right."

could. "We have done our level best," he added; "we have scratched our heads to find out how we could eliminate the last one of them. We stuffed ballot boxes. We shot them [Negroes]. We ARE NOT ASHAMED OF IT." Congressmen Kitchen of North Carolina, Wilson of South Carolina, and Meyer of Louisiana, during January, 1901, also rang the changes on white supremacy.[15]

On January 20, 1900, White introduced the first bill to make the lynching of American citizens a federal crime. The bill would have had little chance of passage under any circumstances, although 109 persons, of whom 87 were Negroes, had been lynched in 1899. White made defeat of his bill inevitable when it stipulated that any person participating, actively or as an accessory, in a lynching "shall be punished as is now prescribed by law for the punishment of persons convicted of treason against the United States Government." When White delivered his valedictory on January 29, 1901, he lamented that the bill "still sweetly sleeps" in the Judiciary Committee.[16]

Samuel D. Smith, author of The Negro in Congress, 1870–1901, who rarely found Negro members worthy of commendation, paid White a mild tribute when he said that the valedictory "would have been an excellent one had the note of bitterness not been so strong. Always, in White's estimation, the white race was wrong and the Negro, the innocent victim."[17] The speech was a better one than Smith was willing to concede; in view of the plight of the Negro at that time, it was relatively restrained. In his conclusion, White made a prediction that has today been fulfilled:

> This, Mr. Chairman, is perhaps the Negroes' temporary farewell to the American Congress; but let me say, Phoenix-like he will rise up some day and come again. These parting words are in behalf of an outraged, heart-broken, bruised and bleeding, but God-fearing people, faithful, industrious, loyal, rising people—full of potential force.

He added that the only "apology" that he had to make for the earnestness with which he had spoken was that he was "pleading for the life, the liberty, the future happiness, and manhood suffrage for one-eighth of the entire population of the United States."[18]

White was not a candidate for re-election in 1900. Although

the North Carolina constitutional amendment disqualifying virtually all Negro voters was not to become effective until 1902, White realized that the second restoration of white supremacy in North Carolina was complete enough in 1900 to make his chances of re-election negligible. On February 5, 1900, he quoted on the floor of the House a diatribe in Josephus Daniels' Raleigh *News and Observer*; one typical sentence read: "It is bad enough that North Carolina should have the only nigger Congressman." On March 4, 1901, both houses of the North Carolina legislature noted, with speeches of thanksgiving, that White's term in the United States Congress had ended.[19]

McKinley's second inaugural address, on the same day, did not contain a single reference that can be construed as calling attention to the inequalities inflicted upon Negroes. The smugness of McKinley, Hanna, and the Republican party in general had been manifested in its platform for 1900. It began with praise for the prosperity that had been achieved as a result of Republican legislation. It spoke in glowing terms of the victory gained in the Spanish American War, and added: "To ten millions of the human race there was given 'a new birth of freedom' and to the American people a new and noble responsibility." But to the almost nine millions of Negroes in the United States, the Republican party platform gave only the usual platitudes:

It was the plain purpose of the fifteenth amendment to the Constitution to prevent discrimination on account of race or color in regulating the franchise. Devices of State governments, whether by statutory or Constitutional enactment, to avoid the purpose of this amendment are revolutionary, and should be condemned.[20]

Thus, a revolution in Cuba had led to American intervention and "a new birth of freedom." But action by Southern states, which the platform called "revolutionary," called for only a slap on the wrist—it "should be condemned."

The platform also warned that "the American Government must protect the person and property of every citizen wherever they are wrongfully violated or placed in peril." This language unquestionably included lynchings, of which there had been 115 in 1900—an increase of six over the previous year. One can only speculate as to why the word lynching was not used, and why it was not described, as it had been in the 1896 platform, as an "uncivilized and barbarous practice." Perhaps the many articles in the leading magazines—to be analyzed in Chapter Thirteen—which bitterly assailed Negro "rapists" of white women explains the silence. The linking of protection of persons with protection of property was probably due to a growing realization that, if mobs that lynched men and women went unpunished, other mobs would be encouraged to do damage to property.

The Democratic platform made a plea for liberty, for government based upon the consent of the governed. But these principles of the Declaration of Independence were applied to Puerto Rico, Cuba, the Philippines, and to the Boers in the Union of South Africa. Apparently, these principles had no application to Negroes in the United States, for the platform was completely silent about them.[21]

Even more revealing than some Supreme Court decisions, party platforms, and presidential messages at the turn of the century were the debates in the House of Representatives—the House, more than any other branch of the government, generally reflects the climate of opinion of the times. The extent to which these representatives of the people had repudiated, in practice, the Fourteenth and Fifteenth Amendments is clearly revealed in the debates on the reapportionment of the House after the census of 1900.

Bills introduced by Republican representatives Albert J. Hopkins of Illinois, and Edwin C. Burleigh of Maine, in January, 1901, were concerned only with the size of the House. But Republican representatives Marlin E. Olmsted of Pennsylvania, and Edgar D. Crumpacker of Indiana, sought to direct attention to the second section of the Fourteenth Amendment because of the disfranchisement of Negroes in Southern states. Olmsted, on January 3, 1901, introduced a resolution authorizing the appointment by the Committee on Census of a committee to investigate the alleged abridgment in Mississippi, South Carolina and Louisiana. Oscar W. Underwood of Alabama bitterly opposed the resolution. He argued that the Fourteenth Amendment had proved to be a lamentable mistake for both major parties and for both sections of the country. Southerners, he continued, were not trying to oppress the Negro, but were seeking to "protect their homes and property against misgovernment," and at the same time to give to "this inferior race a chance to grow up and acquire their civilization." His most persuasive plea was directed to the mood of reconciliation, for he asked that Northerners allow Southerners to handle their Negro problem and also to "protect the investments that you have brought there among us." If the North would agree to this proposal, Underwood would recommend that Olmsted's resolution be sent back to the Committee on Census to die. Then, if conditions did not change within six or ten years, the Fourteenth and Fifteenth Amendments should be repealed, and a Constitutional Amendment be added that would put representation on a "fair and equitable basis."

John Sharp Williams of Mississippi contended that Olmsted's resolution was sectional, because it was aimed at three Southern states. He also questioned the competence of anyone to find out the number of citizens who did not vote because of educational requirements or of the poll tax. Since the House did not possess this information, Olmsted's resolution was returned to the Committee on Census.

Crumpacker's amendment to Burleigh's bill, January 7, 1901, provided for the loss of three seats each by Mississippi, South Carolina, Louisiana and North Carolina. He insisted that, when the Fourteenth and Fifteenth Amendments had been adopted, it had been thought "both unjust and unwise to allow States representation in the House and the electoral college based upon a population that was given no voice in the politics of the country." If a community were composed of two distinct races, between which the ties of blood and sympathy did not exist, neither race could hope for representation and protection through the other. If Southern states understood that the disfranchisement of the Negro were to result in loss of representation, they would be prompted to educate him for the duties of citizenship. But Crumpacker was not optimistic that the South desired this improvement of the Negro, "since the best thought in the South is persuaded that the Negro is not capable of elevation."

Only three of the 356 members of the House spoke in support of Crumpacker's amendment. Republican representative Charles H. Grosvenor of Ohio feared that disfranchisement would be followed by the denial of educational facilities for Negroes. John F. Fitzgerald, a Massachusetts Democrat, invoked the heroic conduct of the black soldiers at San Juan Hill and at El Caney, in supporting Crumpacker. George H. White, the only Negro in Congress, regretted that only two or three Congressmen had risen to the defense of Negroes. The maligners had asserted that they could "manage" the Negroes. "Can they manage us like oxen?" he queried. Removed from slavery by thirty-five years, Negroes, like other Americans, were men, and as such they claimed "the right of the American citizen and the right to vote."

One of the most effective arguments used by the opposition was the fact that Crumpacker was the only member of the Committee on Census—composed of eight Republicans, three Northern Democrats, and two other Democrats—who favored his amendment. The opposition also harped especially upon the alleged threat to revive sectional animosities. Typical of this opposition was an article from the Washington *Post* that Andrew F. Fox read into the *Record*. On December 29, 1900, the *Post* warned:

As the *Post* has stated in previous discussions of this question, this nation is not going into the new century with a revival of sectional animosity; the second McKinley administration is not going to be a new era of ill feeling between the North and the South. The South will not be further punished for the fateful mistake of the fifteenth amendment.

No vote was taken on Crumpacker's amendment. But, when he moved to recommit Burleigh's bill to the Committee on Census with his amendment included, his motion was rejected, 110 to 130. Since no record vote was taken, it is impossible to determine the political and sectional alignment. Burleigh's bill, however, was passed by a vote of 166 to 102. Eighty-eight Republicans, 74 Democrats and 4 Populists voted yea; 52 Republicans, 49 Democrats and 1 Populist voted nay. On January 11, Republican Senator Thomas H. Carter of Montana obtained unanimous consent for the approval of the Burleigh bill which President McKinley signed on January 16.[22]

Thus, at the beginning of the twentieth century, both major parties had decided that the American principles of justice, liberty and democracy did not have to be applied alike to white men and to Negroes. The United States had emerged as a "world power," but at home it was faithless to its own basic principles as far as nine million black citizens were concerned.

The Supreme Court and the Negro

PRACTICALLY all the relevant decisions of the United States Supreme Court during Reconstruction and to the end of the century nullified or curtailed those rights of Negroes which the Reconstruction "Radicals" thought they had written into laws and into the Constitution. Some of these decisions are still generally accepted—even though two of the most important were decided by a five to four vote. Another, Plessy v. Ferguson which laid down the doctrine of "separate but equal accommodations," is being challenged in the Supreme Court as this book goes to press. The rulings in the jury cases have been largely reversed. This fairly good record of the Supreme Court is, however, somewhat vitiated by expressions of social philosophy in some of the cases.*

The decisions of the Court were largely the handiwork of Northerners and Republicans. The first Southerner appointed to the Court since 1852 was William B. Woods, a Republican from Georgia, in 1880. John Marshall Harlan, appointed in 1881, came from the ex-slave state of Kentucky, but he had fought in the Union Army. The first Democrat after Stephen J. Field of California, appointed in 1862, was Lamar of Mississippi, appointed in 1888. There were thus only two Southerners, both of them Republicans, and one Democrat, from California, on the bench when it handed down the devastating Civil Rights decision in 1883. In 1896 when the Court wrote the more controversial decision, Plessy v. Ferguson, there was only one Southerner, Edward Douglass White of Louisiana (Woods and Lamar had died). There were only two Democrats, Field and White. An Ohio Republican, Morrison R. Waite, was Chief Justice from 1874 to 1888. Chief Justice Melville W. Fuller (1888–1910), was a graduate of Bowdoin College, Maine; he had attended Harvard Law School and practiced law in Illinois. Field, the California Democrat, and Joseph Bradley, the New Jersey Republican—who served

---

* Supreme Court decisions since 1941, the Civil Rights laws of 1957, 1960, 1964, and state laws now give evidence of attempts to apply these basic principles to almost 12 million American Negroes.

from 1863 to 1897 and 1870 to 1892, respectively—were probably the most conservative. The most notable dissenter was the Kentucky Republican Unionist, Harlan, 1877–1911.[1] His dissenting opinions in the Civil Rights Cases and in Plessy v. Ferguson are still cited by lawyers and laymen who reject the validity of these decisions.*

In order to obtain a complete picture of the loopholes that the Supreme Court found in the efforts of the Reconstruction "Radicals" to protect the rights of Negroes, an examination of decisions from 1873 to 1877 is necessary. To some degree, the decisions against Negroes after 1877 followed the general pattern of the reaction against nationalism that had become evident, 1870–1873, under Chief Justice Salmon P. Chase. During the eighty-one years from 1789 to 1869 only four Acts of Congress had been declared invalid, but from 1870 to 1873 six such Acts were held unconstitutional.[2] Since none of these six cases involved the rights of Negroes, it may be argued that subsequent decisions affecting Negro rights merely reflected the continued reaction of the Court against federal power. It can not be gainsaid, however, that some of these subsequent decisions also reflected the changing attitude in the nation at large with respect to the Negro.

It was during this early period of judicial reaction against nationalism that the Supreme Court first interpreted the Fourteenth Amendment. While the Slaughter-House Cases, 1873, did not directly involve the rights of Negroes, the Court frequently referred to these cases in later interpretations of those rights. The legislature of Louisiana had passed a statute which granted a monopoly of the slaughterhouse business within certain parishes of New Orleans in favor of one corporation, and thus deprived over one thousand persons of the right to engage in that business. Opponents of the monopoly contended that this state law created an involuntary servitude, abridged the privileges and immunities of citizens of the United States, denied them equal protection of the laws, and deprived them of their property without due process of law. By a majority of five to four the Court upheld the state law on all counts. The decision scoffed at the idea that the involun-

* The doctrine of "separate but equal" was reversed by the Supreme Court decision of May 17, 1954. This decision stated: "We conclude that in the field of public education the doctrine of 'separate but equal' has no place." Subsequent decisions expanded the thrust of this decision.

tary servitude forbidden by the Thirteenth Amendment could possibly refer to a servitude attached to property. But the real significance of the case involved the interpretation of the Fourteenth Amendment.

The five majority justices pointed out: "We do not deny that no one else but the negro can share in this protection." But, they declared, if the right to be freed from monopoly existed, it was not as a privilege or immunity of a citizen of the United States. The majority opinion did not attempt to give a complete list of the privileges and immunities that inhered in state citizenship. The former, however, could all be comprehended under the following general heads: "protection by the government, with the right to acquire and possess property of every kind, and to pursue and obtain happiness and safety, subject, nevertheless, to such restraints as the government may prescribe for the general good of the whole." Having concluded that the privileges and immunities relied on in the argument belonged to citizens of states, as such, the Court held that it was excused from defining those privileges and immunities of citizens of the United States which no state can abridge, until some case involving those privileges and immunities made it necessary for the Court to define them. The Court, did, none the less, enumerate certain privileges and immunities that inhered in United States citizenship. Among these were the rights secured by the Thirteenth and Fifteenth Amendments and the clauses in the Fourteenth Amendment which the Court then considered.

The due process clause had been a part of the Constitution since the adoption of the Fifth Amendment which placed a restraint upon the federal government. But, under no construction of cases involving that Amendment could the Court find that the butchers in the Slaughter-House Cases had been deprived by Louisiana of their property without due process of law. The history of the Fourteenth Amendment showed clearly that the equal protection clause was clearly designed to forbid laws "which discriminated with gross injustice against them [the newly emancipated Negroes] as a class." The Court doubted whether any action of a state that did not fall within this category would ever be held to come within the purview of the equal protection provision. (In fact, however, between 1890 and 1910 only 19 of the 528 cases before the Court involving the Fourteenth Amendment applied to Negro rights; 288 of these cases referred to corporations which were considered "persons" within the language of the Fourteenth Amendment.)[3] No such case was before the Court in this instance, the majority held.

The four dissenting judges, including Chief Justice Chase, pointed out that the majority opinion rendered the privileges and immunities clause a practical nullity. For, "with privileges and immunities pertaining only to citizens of the United States *as such*, no State ever could have interfered by its laws," and hence no new constituional provision was necessary to prohibit such interference. The dissenting opinions added that, even before the Fourteenth Amendment, the supremacy of the Constitution and laws of the United States always controlled any legislation of that character. The clear purpose of the relevant clause was to prevent states from abridging the privileges and immunities which citizens enjoyed as citizens of states.[4]

One of the most intriguing aspects of this case is the fact that the principal attorney for the plaintiffs argued frequently that the Fourteenth Amendment was intended to secure the rights of the recently emancipated slaves against their former masters. This attorney was John A. Campbell of Alabama, a former member of the United States Supreme Court who had concurred with the majority in the Dred Scott Case and who had resigned when Alabama seceded from the Union. Against a background of frequent references to the purpose of the amendment, he insisted that it "brought the federal government into immediate contact with every person and gave to every citizen a claim upon its protecting power." The Amendment, he continued, placed the privileges and immunities of national citizenship beyond the power of the state government. National citizenship and state citizenship were the same.[5]

Campbell later declared that the decision was "probably best for the country."[6] Had he deliberately portrayed the fulsome potentialities of the Fourteenth Amendment in protecting rights of Negroes in order to evoke a decision curtailing those potentialities? Whatever his purpose may have been, consideration of the privileges and immunities of national citizenship virtually disappeared from constitutional law until a tax case in 1935.[7] A five to four decision nullified the aim of the Reconstruction "Radicals"—if Campbell was right— to protect, through the privileges and immunities clause, the freedmen against hostile state laws. One wonders how Campbell would have voted had he still been a member of the Court.

Three years later, in 1876, the Supreme Court found loopholes in the Civil Rights Enforcement Act of May 31, 1870. In United States v. Reese, the Court held that under the Fifteenth Amendment, congressional action was limited to that which prevented discrimination in the right to vote on account of race, color or previous condition of servitude. Since sections three and four of the Act were not confined to such a limited class of discrimination, those sections were unconstitutional.[8] The sections of the Act of May 31, 1870, dealing with the right to vote were repealed by the Act of Congress of February 8, 1894.*

In the same year the Court held that section six of the Act of May 31, 1870, was constitutional, subject to a vital restriction of its scope. That section forbade two or more persons to "injure, oppress, threaten, or intimidate any citizen with intent to prevent or hinder his free exercise and enjoyment of any right or privilege granted or secured to him by the Constitution or laws of the United States, or because of his having exercised the same." The penalty for violation of this section was a fine of not more than $5,000, imprisonment for not more than ten years, and ineligibility "to any office, or place of honor, or trust created by the Constitution and laws of the United States." The defendants were charged with conspiring to prevent two Negro citizens of the United States from the enjoyment of their rights peaceably to assemble with others, to petition for redress of grievances, to bear arms and to vote. They were further charged with conspiring falsely to imprison and murder the two Negroes and thus to deprive them of their lives and liberty without due process of law. The Court, in United States v. Cruikshank, with one dissenting opinion, rejected all the charges as not having been indictable under any act of Congress.**

* Title I of the Civil Rights Acts of 1957, 1960, and 1964 included provisions designed to protect the rights of Negroes to vote. The language can be construed as being based upon both the Fourteenth and Fifteenth Amendments.
** Section six of the Act of May 31, 1870 became, with immaterial changes, section 5508 of the revised statutes of 1874–1878. This section was repeated without change as section nineteen of

In order for the case to be brought under the operation of the statute, the Court held that it would have to be demonstrated that the right in question was one granted or secured by the Constitution or laws of the United States. Since the rights peaceably to assemble and to bear arms had existed prior to the Constitution, they were therefore not derived from it. If the right to petition Congress had been involved, the case would have come within the statute, and within the scope of the sovereignty of the United States. The offense, as stated in the indictment, would have been established if it had been shown that the object of the conspiracy was to prevent a meeting for *any* lawful purpose. The United States had no more power to punish for a conspiracy falsely to imprison and to murder than to punish for false imprisonment or murder itself. This power was vested in the states. The Court also laid down the doctrine which is generally accepted,[9] namely, that the due process clause in the Fourteenth Amendment did not add anything to the rights of one citizen against another. The due process clause merely furnished an additional procedural guarantee against any encroachment by the states upon the fundamental rights which belong to every citizen as a member of society. The counts in the indictment did not call for the exercise of any of the powers conferred by the due process clause of the Fourteenth Amendment.

The judgment of the Court with respect to equal protection of the laws is especially revealing. The Court pointed out that there was no allegation that the conspiracy under this count was because of the race or color of the persons conspired against. It then gave this interpretation of the meaning of the equal protection clause:

The fourteenth amendment prohibits a State from denying to any person within its jurisdiction the equal protection of the laws; but this provision does not, any more than the one which precedes it, and which we have just considered, add any thing to the rights which one citizen has under the Constitution against another. The equality of the rights of citizens is a principle of republicanism. Every republican government is in duty bound to protect all its citizens in

the Criminal Code of 1909 (35 Stat. 1092). Section 241, United States Code, 1950 ed., repeated the terms of conspiracy, the fine and the imprisonment, but dropped the ineligibility clause.

the enjoyment of this principle, if within its power. That duty was originally assumed by the States; and it still remains there. The only obligation resting upon the United States is to see that the States do not deny the right. This the amendment guarantees, but no more. The power of the national government is limited to the enforcement of this guaranty.[10]

But this unequivocal statement of the responsibility resting upon the federal government did not define the equality of the rights of citizens. When the Court did rule on that question twenty years later, in Plessy v. Ferguson, it declared that equality of right did not prevent segregation.

The Court, meanwhile, invoked the equal protection clause to limit the exclusion of Negroes from jury service, the only cases during this period in which the Court interpreted the Fourteenth Amendment in favor of Negroes. The case of Strauder v. West Virginia established the precedent. West Virginia statutes of 1872–1873 excluded Negroes from grand and petit juries. The Court, in 1880, held that these laws flagrantly violated the equal protection clause and were therefore unconstitutional. In the same decision, the Court held valid that section of the Civil Rights Enforcement Act which authorized the removal of a case into the United States courts when the equal rights of a citizen were denied in a state court. During the same term, the Court ruled, in Ex parte Virginia, that acts by officers and agents of a state constituted state action under the Fourteenth Amendment. A county judge who had excluded Negroes from jury service had therefore violated that amendment.[11]

In both these cases, Justice William Strong, a Pennsylvania Republican, made interesting observations that might be used today by organizations and individuals seeking congressional legislation in behalf of Negroes. In the first case, he expressed his conviction that the true spirit and meaning of the Reconstruction Amendments could not be understood without keeping in view "the history of the times when they were adopted and the objects they plainly sought to accomplish." He repeated this conviction in the second case, and added that the amendments were intended to be and were "limitations of the power of the States and enlargements of the power of Congress." It made no difference that such legislation by Congress was restrictive of what a state might have done before the amendments were adopted. He affirmed:

> The prohibitions of the Fourteenth Amendment are directed to the States, and they are to a degree restrictions of State power. . . . No such enforcement is an invasion of State sovereignty. No law can be, which the people of the United States have, by the Constitution of the United States, empowered Congress to enact.

Justice Harlan was to take an even stronger tone in his dissenting opinion in the Civil Rights Cases, three years later.

The Supreme Court further strengthened the right of Negroes to serve on juries, in Neal v. Delaware, 1880. The Court held that the Fifteenth Amendment *ipso facto* rendered inoperative the constitution and laws of Delaware which, at the time the amendment was adopted, restricted jury service to white persons who were qualified to vote. Since, moreover, the state had not subsequently passed any law in violation of the Fifteenth Amendment, Delaware recognized its binding force. Consequently, there was no denial of equality on that score by the state. Since, however, the facts presented showed that no Negroes had been called to jury service, the discrimination constituted a "prima facie denial . . . of that equal protection which has been secured by the Constitution and laws of the United States."

Two years later, the Court declared void the indictment of a Negro who had been indicted and arraigned for trial under Kentucky laws which excluded Negroes from all jury service. But, in Virginia v. Rives, 1880, the Court had declared that the Fourteenth Amendment was not violated if, when the jury was all white, it could not be shown that Negroes were excluded solely on the ground of race or color.

To the traditional "man from Mars," it would be difficult to justify the ruling, in 1882, that an Alabama statute which provided a more severe punishment in cases of fornication and adultery between Negroes and whites than between members of the same race did not violate the equal protection clause.[12] As will be seen later in this chapter, five other cases involving alleged exclusion of Negroes from juries resulted in decisions against federal intervention and only one in favor of it.

Meanwhile, the Supreme Court had handed down its first decision sanctioning segregation in interstate traffic. This decision, Hall v. De Cuir, 1878—the year after the withdrawal of federal troops from Louisiana and South Carolina —has not been accorded the importance that it deserves.[13] The decision is all the more fascinating against the background of the complex struggle over the federal regulation of interstate commerce.

In the Granger Cases, 1877, the Court had upheld the right of states to regulate railroads. Since most of the traffic was interstate, such regulation was clearly a direct burden on interstate commerce. But, in Hall v. De Cuir, the Court held unconstitutional a Louisiana statute forbidding discrimination on account of race, because the law placed a direct burden on interstate commerce. In order to make clear that this was true, the Court pointed out: "A passenger in the cabin class set apart for the use of whites without the State must, when the boat comes within, share the accommodations of that cabin with such colored passengers as may come on board afterwards, if the law is enforced." The decision, written by Chief Justice Waite, observed that "it was to meet just such a case that the commercial clause in the Constitution was adopted." While this may be doubted, it is none the less true that, as the Court stated, it would be difficult to conduct business if, in one state white and colored passengers were separated by law, and in another were required by law to be put in cabins together. The racial aspects of this burden on interstate commerce were further pointed up when the Court observed:

If this statute can be enforced against those engaged in interstate commerce, it may be as well against those engaged in foreign; and the master of a ship clearing from New Orleans to Liverpool, having passengers on board, would be compelled to carry all, white and colored, in the same cabin during his passage down the river, or be subject to an action for damages, "exemplary as well as actual," by any one who felt himself aggrieved because he had been excluded on account of his color.[14]

If these two cases had stood alone, a logician would have been justified in concluding that state regulation of interstate commerce was less a violation of the Constitution if it dealt with commerce *per se* than if it involved the mingling of the races. But in 1886 the Court ruled, in the Wabash Case, that rates fixed by state law could not be applied to transportation beginning or ending outside the state. Even after this decision the Court found it difficult to fix the exact line of demarcation between a direct and an indirect burden on interstate commerce. One of the most interesting decisions was the Lake Shore Case in 1889, since it required consideration of the De Cuir Case. An Ohio law required some interstate passenger trains to stop at certain points in Ohio in order to let off and receive passengers. Rejecting the appositeness of the De Cuir decision, the Court declared that the Ohio law did not at all interfere with the "management" of trains outside the state and that it applied only to some trains. The Ohio law so manifestly subserved the public convenience, and was "in itself so just and reasonable, as wholly to preclude the idea that it was, as the Louisiana statute was declared to be, a direct burden upon interstate commerce, or a direct interference with its freedom."[15]

It was easier for the Supreme Court to find that laws requiring segregation in intrastate commerce did not violate the interstate commerce clause. In 1890, the Court held that a Mississippi statute requiring separate but equal accommodations did not violate the interstate commerce clause, since the Mississippi Supreme Court had construed the law as applying only to intrastate commerce. At the turn of the century, the Court ruled that a separate coach law applicable only to passengers within the state of Kentucky was valid.[16]

While the Supreme Court was seeking to define the precise line of demarcation between state laws that placed a direct, and those that placed an indirect, burden on interstate commerce, the Court had little trouble in fixing the limits between state action and individual action. The principle that the first section of the Fourteenth Amendment was prohibitory upon states only, and not upon individuals, was first upheld in United States *v.* Harris, 1882. Those sections of the so-called Ku-Klux Act of April 20, 1871, which had laid severe penalties upon anyone conspiring to impede the effects of the Fourteenth and Fifteenth Amendments, were therefore declared unconstitutional.[17] In accordance with this same principle, the Court in 1883 held the Civil Rights Act of 1875 unconstitutional.

The preamble of this law stated that Congress deemed it

essential to just government that "we recognize the equality of all men before the law, and hold it is the duty of government in all its dealings with the people to mete out equal and exact justice to all, of whatever nativity, race, color, or persuasion, religious or political," and that it is "the appropriate object of legislation to enact great fundamental principles into law." The Act provided that all persons within the jurisdiction of the United States should be entitled to "the full and equal enjoyment of the accommodations, facilities, and privileges of inns, public conveyances on land or water, theaters, and other places of public amusement; subject only to the conditions and limitations established by law, and applicable alike to citizens of every race and color, regardless of any previous condition of servitude." The person aggrieved by a violation could recover $500; the offender was guilty of a misdemeanor, and federal courts were given exclusive jurisdiction. This law was the culmination of the various federal laws that were passed to counteract the post-Civil War Black Codes in the Southern states. More than any of the other laws it rankled Southern views on the proper place of the free Negro.

The aversion of white men to personal contacts with Negroes after the Civil War stemmed largely from the new status of Negroes as free men. Masters and mistresses had had personal contacts with their house slaves. Indeed, the not infrequent practice of cohabitation had caused Mrs. Mary Boykin Chesnut, the wife of a rich planter, to pour out in poignant passages her bitterness against the slave system which permitted Southern gentlemen to live "like the patriarchs of old, . . . all in one house with their wives and concubines; and the mulattoes one sees in every family partly resemble the white children."[18] After emancipation personal contacts became social relations. The etiquette of slavery permitted, for example, a slave girl to travel as maid for her mistress on a train. The etiquette of freedom found it intolerable that a colored woman paying her own fare should travel in the same coach with a white woman. The extramarital activities of white men with a free colored woman were considered even more reprehensible than similar infidelities with a slave woman. The myth of the faithful slave was replaced by the legend of the Negro as a rapist. Attempts to give the freedmen political and economic equality threatened the old way of life. Social equality—the mingling of the races in schools, inns, theaters and on public carriers—would encourage black men, it was asserted, to dream of cohabitation with white women. While these fears were most deeply rooted in recollections of the slave system in the South, they prevailed also to some degree in the North where free men had suffered economic, political and social inequality.

The case of the United States *v.* Stanley, and other cases, or the Civil Rights Cases as the decision is better known, involved seven different incidents. These included the denial of hotel accommodations to Negroes in Kansas and Missouri; the denial to a Negro of a seat in the dress circle of a theater in San Francisco; the denial to a person (presumably a Negro) of the full enjoyment of the accommodations of the Grand Opera in New York; the refusal by a conductor on a passenger train to allow a colored woman to travel in the ladies' car of the Memphis and Charleston Railroad Company. Only two of the five cases originated in the South. This fact should not lead to the conclusion that the aversion was greater in the North than in the South, but rather that Negroes in the North had more frequent personal contacts with whites in public places.

The decision was written by Justice Bradley, the "Fifth Judge" of the Electoral Commission which had decided every controversial issue of the Hayes-Tilden election in favor of Hayes. Woodward finds it appropriate that Bradley should have written the decision since it "constituted a sort of validation of the Compromise of 1877."[19] The essential points in the decision are two: the first section of the Fourteenth Amendment is prohibitory upon states only; Congress is authorized by the amendment to adopt only corrective, not general legislation. In brief, the person wronged must look for vindication or redress to the laws of the state. Since the cases considered arose within states, the constitutionality of the act with respect to territories and to the District of Columbia was not presented. As in the Cruikshank Case, the Court held that if state laws were to make any unjust discrimination, Congress would have the power under the Fourteenth Amendment to afford remedy.

Harlan, the Kentucky Unionist, opened his classic dissent by stating that the majority opinion proceeded upon grounds

entirely too narrow and artificial. I cannot resist the conclusion that the substance and spirit of the recent amendments of the Constitution have been sacrificed by a subtle and ingenious verbal criticism. Constitutional provisions, adopted in the interest of liberty, and for the purpose of securing, through national legislation, if need be, rights inhering in a state of freedom, and belonging to American citizenship, have been so construed as to defeat the ends the people desired to accomplish by changes in the fundamental law.[20]

This far-reaching decision thus legalized race distinctions by individuals with respect to enjoyment of facilities in carriers and places of public accommodation and amusement. In addition, it virtually assured the subsequent development of Jim Crow laws, and other forms of race discrimination, and the passivity of the Federal government in the face of this discrimination. The sequel proved that Harlan was correct when he declared in his dissenting opinion: "We shall enter upon an era of constitutional law, when the rights of freedom and American citizenship cannot receive from the nation that efficient protection which heretofore was unhesitatingly accorded to slavery and the rights of the master."

But the nation, as a whole, rejoiced over the decision. It is still the law of the land. Charles Warren, whose book *The Supreme Court in United States History* is considered one of the most authoritative treatises on the subject, commented with respect to the Civil Rights Cases, the Harris Case and others of a similar character:

Viewed in historical perspective now [1922], however, there can be no question that the decisions in these cases were most fortunate. They largely eliminated from national politics the Negro question which had so long embittered Congressional debates; they relegated the burden and the duty of protecting the Negro to the states, to whom they properly belonged; and they served to restore confidence in the national court in the Southern states.[21]

The decision, of course, had the reverse effect on many Negroes. Despite the admonition of the Court that Negroes were not justified in interpreting denials of equal accommodations as a badge of inferiority, they could hardly construe such discrimination otherwise. They found some solace in the fact that fifteen Northern states soon thereafter passed civil rights laws, and three others strengthened existing laws. But the lower courts frequently found loopholes which largely nullified these state laws.[22] Moreover, the vast majority of Negroes still lived in the South where they were increasingly subjected to segregation and discrimination by law and custom.

While the Court upheld the right of individuals to discriminate in public places against Negroes on account of their race, in the following year, it construed the Civil Rights Act of 1870 as a valid exercise of the power granted under the Fifteenth Amendment. In the Cruikshank Case, the Court had dismissed the charge that Negroes had been denied the right to vote, because the allegations did not show that the denial had been based on race or color. But, in *Ex parte* Yarbrough, 1884, the Court ruled that the Fifteenth Amendment "does, *proprio vigore*, substantially confer on the negro the right to vote, and Congress has the power to enforce that right."[23] The ineffectiveness of this 1870 law was so evident that Congress, in 1890, attempted to enact legislation that would give practical effect to the Fifteenth Amendment. That attempt not only failed but led to constitutional amendments by Southern states to "legalize" the disfranchisement of most Negroes.

No case involving the right of Negroes to engage in business came before the Supreme Court. But, in a case involving Chinese laundrymen in California, the Court construed the equal protection clause of the Fourteenth Amendment to the advantage of the Chinese. Chinese who conducted their business in wooden buildings were denied licenses while white persons conducting laundries under similar conditions were left unmolested. The Court vigorously ruled:

> Though the law itself be fair on its face and impartial in appearance, yet, if it is applied and administered by public authority with an evil eye and an unequal hand, so as practically to make unjust and illegal discriminations between persons in similar circumstances, material to their rights, the denial of equal justice is still within the prohibition of the Constitution.[24]

The Court pointed out that it had sanctioned this principle in a number of cases, including *Ex parte* Virginia, and Neal *v.*

Delaware. In neither of these cases, however, did the Court use such strong language as it did in Yick Wo v. Hopkins. Moreover, the decision in this case was unanimous, whereas in the cases involving the right of Negroes to sit on juries, Justice Field of California had dissented in both, Justice Clifford in one and Chief Justice Waite in the other.

Thirteen years after the Supreme Court had sanctioned discrimination by individuals in public places and on public carriers, the Court approved separation of the races by state action. In Plessy v. Ferguson, 1896, the Court for the first time invoked the doctrine of police powers to deny in effect the equal protection which the framers of the Fourteenth Amendment thought they had established. It was this decision by which the Supreme Court accepted the doctrine of "separate but equal accommodations." Between 1882 and 1888, lower federal courts had upheld the principle in four cases. In three cases involving segregation on public carriers, the courts had held that separate cars were a proper exercise of the state's police powers. In the fourth case, dealing with an Ohio statute which authorized school boards to organize separate schools for colored children, the lower federal court ruled: "Equality of right does not mean identity of right and . . . so long as educational opportunities for Negroes were substantially equal to those for whites no denial of protection resulted."[25] Three rulings of the Interstate Commerce Commission, 1887, 1888 and 1889, had approved this doctrine of separate but equal accommodations.[26]

It was not until 1896, however, that the United States Supreme Court upheld this doctrine. A Louisiana law required separate but equal accommodations on public carriers and provided a penalty for passengers who sat in a car or compartment assigned to the other race. The petitioner, an octoroon in whom "Negro blood was not discernible," sat in a white car and was arrested. The Court held that the law was a reasonable exercise of the state police power and was therefore constitutional. Justice Henry B. Brown, a Republican from Michigan, speaking for the Court, made this revealing observation:

The object of the [Fourteenth] Amendment was undoubtedly to enforce the absolute equality of the two races before the law, but in the nature of things it could not have been intended to abolish distinctions based on color, or to enforce social, as distinguished from political equality, or a commingling of the two races upon terms unsatisfactory to either.

The Court added, as it had done in the Civil Rights Case, that laws requiring segregation did not necessarily imply "the inferiority of either race to the other." Moreover, the Court pointed out that separate schools had been held valid in several Northern states by the state courts. Expanding even further the social philosophy which controlled the thinking of the judges, the Court continued:

If the two races are to meet upon terms of social equality, it must be the result of natural affinities, a mutual appreciation of each other's merits and a voluntary consent of individuals. . . . If one race be inferior to the other socially, the Constitution of the United States cannot put them upon the same plane. The distinction between the two races, which was founded in the color of the two races, must always exist so long as white men are distinct from the other color.

Harlan, who had dissented in the Civil Rights Cases, again wrote a scorching dissent. Laws requiring segregation on public carriers, he declared, were unconstitutional, since they interfered with the personal freedom of citizens "under the guise of giving equal accommodations to whites and blacks." They fostered ideas of caste and inferiority and the majority decision would stimulate further aggressions upon the rights of Negroes. Giving his own social interpretation of the Constitution and laws, he insisted: "Our Constitution is blind, and neither knows nor tolerates classes among citizens. . . . The law regards man as man, and takes no regard of his surroundings or his color when his civil rights as guaranteed by the supreme law of the land are invoked."[27]

It is easy enough, then, to understand why one student of the subject has written that "the invocation and application of the police power is nothing more than an appeal to the sociological method of interpreting our Constitution and laws."[28] Justice Harlan prophesied that the decision—which is not mentioned in Warren's authoritative history of the Supreme Court—would prove as pernicious as the Dred Scott decision. The Washington *Post*, in 1949, editorially called Plessy *v.* Ferguson the "worst" decision in the history of the Supreme Court except the Dred Scott decision.[29] But this decision is still the law of the land. In recent years the Supreme Court has sought to enforce "substantial equality" in the separate accommodations, but it has not yet ruled on the constitutionality of segregation itself under the equal protection clause.*

The principle of separate but equal accommodations was not again clearly presented to the Supreme Court during the period under study. The Court found an opportunity to avoid a direct ruling in a case originating in Richmond County, Georgia. Cummings, a Negro taxpayer, complained that the high school for Negroes in that county had been suspended "for economic reasons" while the high school for whites remained open. The constitutionality of all laws providing separate accommodations for whites and Negroes was attacked in the argument of the plaintiff's counsel, but the question was not presented in the record. Harlan, speaking for the Court, declared that the relief asked for was an injunction which would close the school for the whites without furnishing any additional opportunities for Negroes. The trial did not show any abuse of the discretion allowed by law to the County Board of Education. The Court further held that the education of people in schools maintained by state taxation was a matter belonging to the respective states, and interference could not be justified except in a case of "clear and unmistakable disregard of the rights secured by the supreme law of the land."[30]

During the last six years of the century, Negroes found it increasingly difficult to establish that exclusion from juries violated the equal protection clause. In one case, the Court declared that the petitioner had used the wrong method of procedure, since the regular trial of a state court can not be reviewed by *habeas corpus* proceedings. The second case, Gibson *v.* Mississippi, 1895, is more significant, since it revealed a growing insistence by the Court that indisputable evidence be presented of the exclusion from juries because of

* Title II of The Civil Rights Act of 1964 was based upon both the equal protection clause of the Fourteenth Amendment and the interstate commerce clause.

race or color. The petitioner in this case sought removal of his case from a Mississippi state court on the ground that Negroes were excluded from the grand and petit juries in Mississippi. Counsel for the petitioner—this seems to have been the first case in which Negro lawyers appeared before the United States Supreme Court—contended that at the time of selecting jurors in Washington County there were 7,000 colored citizens competent to serve as jurors and only 1,500 whites. Nevertheless, no colored juror had been summoned for a number of years. The Court rejected the petition because no proof had been offered that Negroes were excluded solely because of race or color. In any event, as Justice Harlan pointed out: "It is clear in view of what has been said that these facts, even if they had been proved and accepted, do not show that the rights of the accused were denied by the Constitution and laws of the State." But the Court also declared that evidence of the failure to call Negroes to jury service would be for the consideration of the trial court upon motion by the accused to quash the indictment.[31] The Court thus required the accused to establish proof in the court of a state which had rendered Negroes politically impotent. But in 1899, the Court reversed the decision of a Texas court and remanded the case on the ground that the state court had erred in refusing to receive proof that Negroes were excluded from the grand jury solely because of their race or color. In two other cases, the Court based its rulings on failure to prove that the exclusion was due to discrimination.[32]*

Perhaps the least defensible decision of the United States Supreme Court on the right of Negroes to serve on juries was handed down in the too little known case of Williams v. Mississippi. Cornelius J. Jones, one of the colored lawyers who had appeared in Gibson v. Mississippi, was determined that he would this time give the Court no loopholes. The accused had been indicted for murder by a grand jury of white men. Jones had made a motion to quash the indictment, on the ground that the state constitution required the ability to read and write and understand any section of that constitution for service on a jury. The motion had been denied, and the de-

---

* The Supreme Court ruled in Norris v. Alabama, 1935, that the systematic exclusion of Negroes from juries was *prima-facie* evidence of the denial of equal protection of the laws guaranteed by the Fourteenth Amendment.

fendant had then moved to remove the case to the United States Circuit Court on substantially the same ground. This motion had likewise been denied. The defendant had thereupon been tried by a jury of white men and convicted. When his motion for a new trial had been denied, he had appealed to the United States Supreme Court.

The ruling of the Court was based upon the doctrine that possibility of evil administration of a law was not necessarily proof of the fact that the law itself was evil. This case does not, therefore, offer an exact parallel with Yick Wo v. Hopkins, in which it was clearly demonstrated that Chinese laundrymen had been deprived of their right to conduct a business solely because of their race. But, the Court in this Mississippi case had to fall back upon a decision of the Mississippi Supreme Court for proof that Negroes were not excluded from the jury lists because of their color. The Court observed:

> We gather from the statements of the motion that certain officers are invested with discretion in making up lists of electors, and that this discretion has been exercised against the colored race and that from these lists the jurors are selected. The Supreme Court of Mississippi, however, decided in a case presenting the same question as that at bar that jurors are not selected from or with reference to any lists furnished by such election officers.[33]

By the beginning of the twentieth century, the first section of the Fourteenth Amendment—except the definition of citizenship—had been virtually nullified by decisions of the United States Supreme Court. The Court had ruled that most privileges and immunities of citizens inhered in state, rather than in United States, citizenship. The Fourteenth Amendment placed prohibitions upon states and not individuals. Under the doctrine of police powers the states could, however, do some of the very things which the framers of the Fourteenth Amendment thought they had prevented. Separation of the races, for example, was not a denial of equal protection of the laws, provided that the separate accommodations were substantially equal. Due process of law did not add to the rights of any citizens, but merely strengthened the procedure by which their rights were safeguarded. The only right of Negroes under the Fourteenth Amendment which the Court upheld was the right of Negroes to serve on juries when state laws and state officers clearly violated that right, and proof was presented at the trial that Negroes had been barred because of their race or color. The Supreme Court had further held that state law requiring separation of races was not a direct burden on interstate commerce and was, therefore, constitutional. The Interstate Commerce Commission had also upheld segregation in interstate travel, provided the accommodations were equal. The protection of the Negro was left to the states, which increasingly were relegating Negroes to what is today called second-class citizenship. The decision of the Supreme Court, that the Fifteenth Amendment did substantially confer on the Negro the right to vote, was being increasingly nullified by the revision of state constitutions that disfranchised most Negroes. No cases involving these new constitutions were presented to the Court during this period.

It is not clear whether Douglass meant abstract justice or the interpretation of the Constitution and laws when he listed "American justice" as the first principle which should apply alike to all Americans. Whichever he meant, the Supreme Court had been compelled to rule that, in substance, "Equal Justice under Law" did not guarantee to Negro Americans the same rights that other Americans enjoyed.

SEVEN

The Economic Roots of Second-Class
Citizenship: Agriculture

THE economic basis of second-class citizenship for Negroes was rooted deep in slavery. On the eve of the Civil War almost nine out of ten Negroes in the United States were slaves. The vast majority of these 3,953,760 slaves were field hands and domestic servants. A small number were carpenters, coopers, tailors, shoemakers, bootmakers, cabinet makers, plasterers, seamstresses. Others were employed in salt works, iron and lead mines, on railroad construction, on river boats and on docks. Some worked in textile mills, especially in Florida, Mississippi, Alabama, Georgia, South Carolina and Louisiana. The exigencies of the war, which increased the number of Negroes engaged in non-agricultural pursuits, particularly in iron works, coal mines and salt works, clearly demonstrated that "Negro labor, properly directed, was adaptable to diversified agriculture and to a varied industrial program."[1] But, at the end of the war most Southern Negroes were without capital, without the rudiments of education, and without experience in work except as agricultural field hands and as domestic servants.

Contrary to the Marxist interpretations of Reconstruction, there was little sense of solidarity between white and black workers in the South. Prior to the war, most of the non-slaveholding and landless whites held slavery responsible for their own distress. White urban workers particularly resented the hiring of Negro slave artisans. It was, in fact, the plight of the poor whites that had led forward-looking Southerners like William Gregg to favor industrialism.[2] They had accomplished little, however, except perhaps to increase the gulf between free black workers and white workers and to prepare the way for the almost exclusive employment of whites in the post-war industries.

The 488,000 free Negroes encountered many difficulties in their attempts to gain a livelihood. More than forty per cent of them lived in the South where they, like the non-slaveholding and landless whites, had to compete with slave labor. In addition, many Southern states circumscribed the mobility of Negroes even within the state and prohibited them from engaging in certain occupations. Despite all these handicaps, some of them became skilled artisans. They worked in fifty different occupations in Charleston, and in more than seventy in North Carolina. In the slave state of Maryland, some 2,000 free Negroes of Baltimore engaged in nearly one hundred occupations, including paper-hanging, engraving, quarrying, photography and tailoring. New Orleans had colored jewelers, architects and lithographers. "Almost every community had its free Negro carpenters, barbers, cabinet makers, and brickmasons; many had shopkeepers, salesmen, and clerks, even where it was a violation of the law."[3]

Free Negroes in the North worked not only as artisans but also in the professions. They were engaged in more than 130 skilled occupations in Philadelphia alone. Many of the urban communities had colored ministers, teachers, lawyers and dentists. But free Negroes in the North were often victims of violence that occasionally flared into riots, especially in cities where there were relatively large numbers of Negroes, such as Cincinnati, Philadelphia and New York. But small towns like Utica and Palmyra, New York, also were the scene of riots. Recent investigation reveals two destructive riots against Negroes in Providence, Rhode Island, in 1824 and 1831.[4] Further research may show that there were others.

A few free Negroes had acquired property in larger amounts than is generally known. In New York City they owned more than $1,000,000 worth of property, in Cincinnati more than $500,000, and comparable amounts in such cities as Philadelphia, Baltimore, Washington and Boston. Negro holdings in Providence were estimated at between $35,000 and $50,-000, in 1839. Even more surprising is the amount of property possessed by free Negroes in the South. In Virginia, they owned more than 60,000 acres of farm land, and city real estate valued at $463,000; in North Carolina, more than $1,000,000 in real and personal property. Free Negroes in New Orleans paid taxes on property variously estimated at from $9,000,000 to $15,000,000. A few individual Negroes were wealthy. James Forten, of Philadelphia had accumulated a fortune of more than $100,000 and Thomy Lafon of New Orleans, $500,000. A few Southern Negroes even held slaves.[5]

It is thus inaccurate to assert, as do some orators, that the

Negro started from scratch in 1865. Most free Negroes, none the less, in both North and South eked out a precarious existence. Moreover, the war had in many cases increased the bitterness against Negroes. Many Southern poor whites expressed bitter resentment against a "rich man's war and a poor man's fight." In some parts of the North, whites were equally bitter against the "nigger war." The most extreme manifestation of this attitude in the North erupted in the "Draft Riots" in New York City, July, 1863. For four days the city was in the hands of a mob against which the police were powerless. The mob demolished draft headquarters, chased and beat Negroes, hanged them from trees and lampposts. Much of this violence stemmed not only from aversion to fighting a war in which the whites had little interest, but also, perhaps more so, from the competition of Negroes for jobs.[6]

The economic basis for second-class citizenship for Negroes is found also in the failure of the federal government to accept responsibility for a long-range, comprehensive and intelligent policy of economic habilitation of the emancipated Negroes. Some fifty private organizations wrote a memorable chapter in the history of American philanthropy, by providing substantial relief and inaugurating educational programs for the freedmen in the South. But, obviously, the job was too stupendous for private philanthropy. Either private capital or governmental action, therefore, had to provide the freedmen with economic opportunities to undergird their new political and civil rights. Southern capital could not provide the jobs. Northern capital, especially in the years immediately after the war, found more profitable investments in the East and West than in the South. The Black Codes of the Southern states, 1865–1866, showed clearly the determination to deny the freedmen equal economic opportunity. During the critical period immediately after the war, federal action alone could have provided the freedmen with the economic opportunities without which their new political and civil liberties had little foundation.

The nature and extent of the aid that the federal government should give to freedmen, and the South in general, precipitated in 1863 one of the earliest debates in American history on what is today called the "welfare state." Proponents of governmental aid insisted that private charity was insufficient to alleviate the woeful plight of the freedmen, and that the freedmen could not measurably alleviate it through their own efforts. Opponents declared that governmental aid would be "revolutionary," that it would create a large number of bureaucrats and pave the way for corruption in government. They also contended that governmental aid would curtail the freedmen's initiative and self-reliance. After two years of debate, Congress, on March 3, 1865, finally approved a bill, without a record vote, and Lincoln immediately signed it. It was clearly designed as a war measure, for the Bureau of Refugees, Freedmen and Abandoned Lands was placed under the Secretary of War and it was to continue for only one year after the end of the war. The Secretary of War was to issue necessary provisions, clothing and fuel and, under the direction of the President, the commissioner in charge could set aside, for the freedmen and refugees, tracts of land of not more than forty acres to be leased to tenants. The lessees were to be protected in the use of the land for three years at a low rental, and at the end of the term they could purchase the land at an appraised value.

The "Radical" Republicans who dominated the Congress that met in December, 1865, sought to make the Freedmen's Bureau permanent. But President Johnson vetoed the new bill on February 19, 1866, in a message that summarized the views of the opposition expressed during the previous debates. Johnson, a Tennessee Unionist, had frequently revealed, as a member of Congress and as governor of his state, the hostile attitude of many poor whites toward the Negro.[7] He was also determined that he, not Congress, would formulate Reconstruction policies. His conflict with Congress may have prompted in part his veto, but the persistence of his pre-Civil War and Civil War hostility to Negroes was manifest when he wrote:

It [Congress] has never deemed itself authorized to expend the public money for the rent or purchase of homes for the thousands, not to say millions of the white race who are honestly toiling from day to day for their subsistence. A system for the support of indigent persons in the United States was never contemplated by the authors of the Constitution; nor can any good reason be advanced why, as a permanent establishment, it should be founded for one class or color of our people more than another.

He recognized the need that had existed during the war for the freedmen to receive aid from the government, but "it was never intended that they should thenceforth be fed, clothed, educated and sheltered by the United States." The slaves had been assisted to freedom with the idea that, when they became free, "they would be a self-sustaining population. Any legislation that shall imply that they are not expected to attain a self-sustaining condition must have a tendency injurious alike to their character and their prospects."[8] How the freedmen were to lift themselves by their own bootstraps was not indicated in the veto message.

The "Radicals" had not gained sufficient control of Congress to override this veto. By April, however, they were able to override Johnson's veto of the Civil Rights Bill, and in June to adopt the Fourteenth Amendment for ratification by the states. Then, on July 16, Congress passed, over Johnson's veto, the second Freedmen's Bureau Bill. The overriding of this veto was due not only to the widened breach between the Congress and Johnson, but also to the elimination of some of the more drastic provisions of the February bill. Instead of making the Bureau permanent, the new law limited its duration to two years after its passage, and its jurisdiction to those cases where the deprivation of civil rights was the consequence of the rebellion. Even with these changes, it was necessary for the party to exercise its strictest discipline to defeat the veto. The retreat from the concept of the functions of the welfare state was already evident.

Most Southerners violently opposed the Freedmen's Bureau. They contended that it threatened to intervene between employer and worker. They further accused it of promoting political ambitions on the part of the colored population, and of spreading the belief among the freedmen that they would be given forty acres and a mule. Because of strong Southern opposition and lack of vigorous Northern support, the main work of the Bureau continued only until 1869. Of course, it made mistakes, as did, for example, some of the relief and rehabilitation agencies in European countries devastated by World War II. But, on balance, the Freedmen's Bureau helped the South to get back on its feet. Between 1865 and 1869, the Bureau issued more than 20,000,000 rations, approximately 5,000,000 to whites and 15,000,000 to Negroes. The medical department operated more than forty hospitals and treated some 450,000 cases of illness. The Bureau distributed a small portion of abandoned and confiscated lands to freedmen. It sought to protect them from violence and outrage, from serfdom, and to defend their right to hold property and to enforce contracts. Its most notable work was in the field of education.[9] The limited operations after 1869 ceased in 1872, five years before the withdrawal of the last federal troops from Louisiana and South Carolina. As Du Bois wrote in 1903, a permanent Freedmen's Bureau, with adequate funds, might have provided "a great school of prospective citizenship, and solved in a way we have not yet solved the most perplexing and persistent of the Negro problems."[10]

Until a few years ago, it was popular to make fun of the "naïve" belief encouraged by some agents of the Freedmen's Bureau that the freedmen were going to be given forty acres and a mule by the federal government. The levity decreased somewhat when the Great Depression of the 1930's revealed the plight of white sharecroppers—who outnumbered colored by two to one. Perhaps because federal assistance then included more whites than Negroes, there was less opposition to various agricultural programs, especially after large planters and bankers discovered that they would receive directly and indirectly a great share of the largesse. More recently, the bitter attacks upon these New Deal projects and "socialistic" programs have begun again to influence American historiography. In the meanwhile, however, some historians have stopped sneering and laughing at the "forty acres and a mule" joke. Some of them consider the failure of the federal government to expand and continue the insufficient program of land distribution through the Freedmen's Bureau the greatest blunder of Reconstruction.[11]

The policy of the federal government after the Civil War was all the more fatal to the economic habilitation of the impoverished freedmen because the Southern states had curtailed the right of freedmen to become landowners. The Black Code of Mississippi, for example, stipulated: "Provided, that the provisions of this section shall not be so construed as to allow any freedman, free negro or mulatto to rent or least any lands or tenements except in incorporated cities or towns, in which places the corporate authorities shall control the same." As Wharton has remarked, this part of Mississippi's Black Code was the "hardest of the whole group to

justify. It stood as a direct discouragement to the most industrious and ambitious of the Negroes, and as an almost
insurmountable obstacle to those who hoped to rise from the
status of common laborers." In some other states, on the other
hand, their holdings were limited to the countryside.[12]

Although the Black Codes were repealed by the Reconstruction legislatures, the freedmen encountered great difficulty
in acquiring land for the simple reason that few of them
possessed the means of doing so. Some came into possession
of land in various ways: through the assistance of the federal
government, through a kindly planter who turned over land
to them, or an impoverished or indolent planter who allowed
them to pay the back taxes and thus acquire title. In Florida,
they secured homesteads covering 160,000 acres within a
year after emancipation. By 1874, Georgia Negroes owned
more than 350,000 acres of land. It is not clear how many
had been held by free Negroes prior to the war. Negroes in
Virginia acquired perhaps some 80,000 acres of land in the
late sixties and early seventies.[13] In 1890, 120,738 Negroes
owned farm homes, all of which except 12,253 were unen-
cumbered. By 1900, the number owned had risen to 192,993,
but the number of encumbered had risen from 12,253 to
54,017.[14] The vast majority of these farm owners lived in the
South. If it may be assumed that those who owned farm
homes also owned their farms, they had made commendable
progress. But their number was small, for almost 7,000,000
Negroes lived in the South—which included, according to the
Census, Delaware, Maryland, West Virginia and the District
of Columbia.

These farm owners constituted only one-fourth of Negroes
living on farms. The other three-fourths were tenants who
were greatly exploited, especially by the crop-lien system.
They were compelled to obtain advances from the country
merchants for meal, bacon, molasses, cloth and tobacco, as
well as for tools, farm implements, fertilizer and work ani-
mals. The mark-up for the difference between cash and credit
frequently amounted to from 40 per cent to 100 per cent.
Since the value of the crops was sometimes less than the advances, the tenant started the new year in debt. Since, moreover, the books were kept by the merchants and many of
the debtors could not read, the chances for cheating were
usually not allowed to slip. It has been estimated that in some

portions of the South, nine-tenths of the farmers fell into debt. Many poor whites found escape in the textile mills.[15] Some Negroes sought escape in flight.

As early as the beginning of the eighteenth century, colonization of Negroes outside the United States had been advocated as a partial solution to slavery and the presence of unwanted free Negroes. In 1816, the American Colonization Society was formed for the purpose of settling Negroes in Africa. But perhaps not more than 25,000 had left the United States for Africa, Haiti and elsewhere by the end of the Civil War. Plans for colonizing in Liberia and other places were revived after the war, but the most important proposals for the migration of Negroes envisaged other parts of the United States. The federal government refused to aid any of the plans for migration. This refusal constitutes the third basis for the second-class citizenship of the Southern black farmers and farm workers who numbered almost one-half of all black workers.

The first proposals for federal aid to migration during the post-Reconstruction period resulted from the "Exodus" of 1879. It is no coincidence that the Exodus began less than two years after the withdrawal of the last of the federal troops from the South. The seventeen hundred pages of testimony presented to a senatorial investigating committee naturally contain conflicting evidence. On the one hand, it was contended that the Southern white man was the Negro's best friend; that most Negroes were contented and prosperous; that only a small minority were disgruntled and that they had been stirred up by white agitators from the North. Some Negroes, whom recent authors have called "collaborationists,"[16] supported these assertions. It was argued further that Republicans were luring Negroes to the North in order to assure Republican victories and that transportation companies were enticing Negroes to leave home in order to increase their profits.[17]

There were, however, real grievances. The crop-lien system probably kept more Negroes than whites in debt. Educational opportunities for Negroes were even more inadequate than those for whites. New industries relegated black workers to the lowest paid jobs. "Bulldozing" and other forms of violence prevented Negroes from voting and from becoming "uppity." They were frequently jailed for petty offenses. Most whites treated them with contempt or with a patronizing paternalism. Frederick Douglass gave a detailed summary of the Negroes' grievances in an address at Saratoga Springs before the American Social Science Association on September 12, 1879. He recognized that a speech by Senator Windom a few months earlier had greatly increased the migration from Mississippi and Louisiana, since it had led some Negroes once again to believe that the government was going to give them in the new lands forty acres and a mule. Despite all these rumors, Negroes were "a remarkably home-loving race." The real reasons for the Exodus had been given by the emigrants themselves. Theirs was

a sad story, disgraceful and scandalous to our age and country. . . . They tell us with great unanimity that they are badly treated at the South. The land owners, planters, and the old master-class generally, deal unfairly with them, having had their labor for nothing when they were slaves. These men, now they are free, endeavor by various devices to get it for next to nothing; work as hard, faithfully and constantly as they may, live as plainly and as sparingly as they may, they are no better off at the end of the year than at the beginning. They say that they are the dupes and victims of cunning and fraud in signing contracts which they cannot read and cannot fully understand; that they are compelled to trade at stores owned in whole or in part by their employers, and that they are paid with orders and not with money. They say that they have to pay double the value of nearly everything they buy; that they are compelled to pay a rental of ten dollars a year for an acre of land that will not bring thirty dollars under the hammer; that land owners are in league to prevent land-owning by Negroes; that when they work the land on shares they barely make a living; that outside the towns and cities no provision is made for education, and, ground down as they are, they cannot employ teachers to instruct their children; that they are not only the victims of fraud and cunning, but of violence and intimidation; that from their very poverty the temples of justice are not open to them; that the jury box is virtually closed; that the murder of a black man by a white man is followed by no conviction or punishment.

Crimes for which a white man went free brought severe punishment to a black man. "Wealthy and respectable" white men gave encouragement to midnight raids upon the defenseless. Even the old slave-driver's whip had reappeared, "and the inhuman spectacle of the chain-gang is beginning to be seen." The fleeing Negroes had declared that the government of every Southern state was in the hands of the "old slave oligarchy," and they feared that "both departments" of the federal government would soon be in the same hands. "They believe that when the Government, State and National, shall be in the control of the old masters of the South, they will find means for reducing the freedmen to a condition analogous to slavery. They despair of any change for the better, declaring that everything is waxing worse for the Negro, and that his only means of safety is to leave the South." If only half this statement was true, Douglass added, the explanation for the Exodus was abundantly clear.

But Douglass urged Negroes to stay in the South. As a staunch Republican, he proclaimed his faith in President Hayes's determination to assert his constitutional powers for the protection of Negroes in the South. He was on firmer ground when he pointed out that encouragement of the flight amounted to "an abandonment of the great and paramount principle of protection to person and property in every State of the Union." If it were conceded that the Federal government could not provide this protection in the South, what would be the final stopping-place for the Negro? Where would he go if some sand-lot orator in Kansas or California stirred up a mob as one was doing against the Chinese in California? Negroes should also stay in the South because they had "a monopoly of the labor market" there, and because they had adopted "the careless and improvident habits of the South" which they could not quickly discard in the North. Douglass even doubted that many of these Southern Negroes could stand the more rigorous Northern climate. In what was perhaps the first evocation of the possible dire effects of radical doctrines from Russia, Douglass concluded:

> The cry of "Land and Liberty," the watchword of the
> Nihilistic party in Russia, has a music sweet to the ear of
> all oppressed peoples, and well it shall be for the land-
> holders of the South if they shall learn wisdom in time

and adopt such a course of just treatment towards the landless laborers of the South in the future as shall make this popular watchword uncontagious and unknown among laborers, and further stampede to the North wholly unknown, indescribable and impossible.

Richard T. Greener, the first colored graduate of Harvard College (1870), member of the faculty of the University of South Carolina during Reconstruction, and Dean of the Law School at Howard University (1879–1882) and later United States consul at Bombay and Vladivostok, appeared on the same program in opposition to Douglass. His principal argument held that the western lands were waiting for settlement, and were being rapidly filled up by Swedes, Norwegians, Mennonites, Icelanders and Poles. Six hundred thousand acres of public land had been taken up since June 30, 1878. Irish Catholics and Jews were raising money to help migration from cities to the West. He proposed therefore that Negroes should raise $200,000, organize a National Executive Committee and have agents to buy land, procure cheap transportation and disseminate accurate information.[18] This proposal for self-help was made necessary by the failure of Congress to assist the migrants.

On January 16, 1879, Senator Windom, Republican from Minnesota, had introduced a resolution for the appointment of a committee of seven senators to examine the expediency and practicability of encouraging the partial migration of Negroes to various states and territories of the United States. This resolution was the first gesture, after the abolishment of the Freedmen's Bureau, to provide federal aid for the welfare of the freedmen. It antedated the Blair bill and the Lodge bill by eleven years. But Windom was unable to obtain approval for a resolution that provided merely for the appointment of an investigating committee. Once more, it is evident that federal aid to economic welfare encountered more serious opposition than did federal aid to education, or protection of the right to vote.

The debates on Windom's resolution have been overlooked even more than those on the Blair and Lodge bills. On February 7, 1879, the Republican senator from Minnesota insisted that constitutional amendments and acts of Congress had alike failed to enforce rights "solemnly" guaranteed to the freedmen. The "Southern question" still presented the most difficult problem in American politics. None of the methods that the federal government had adopted to protect the freedmen had proved effective. The Southern white man, he categorically asserted, would "tolerate no conditions but those of domination on one side and subserviency on the other. Centuries of negro slavery have rendered the white men of the South far less competent to deal with colored citizenship than they have the negro to exercise it." Windom was particularly concerned about those sections of the South in which Negroes were in the majority and where, under the constitution and laws, they would probably control the local government. The senator put his finger on one sore spot already mentioned, namely, that when Negroes elected Negroes to office, some white men were out of jobs. Since the federal government would no longer use force to protect Negroes in the right to vote, and since otherwise that right could not be exercised, especially in regions where Negroes were in the majority, the only solution was migration. Migration to Liberia was impracticable for the simple reason that the natural increase of the colored population in the United States would be many times greater than the number that could possibly be transported to Africa. Such migration would also be tantamount to banning them from their own country.

Windom stated his conviction that there were several states where Negroes would be warmly welcomed and their rights protected. While he did not identify those states, he did mention specifically portions of the territories of Arizona, New Mexico, and especially the Indian Territory where they would be similarly received. He did not mention, however, Idaho, Montana, North Dakota, South Dakota, Utah or Wyoming, territories much closer to Minnesota. Even if it became necessary to organize a new territory for the Negroes, he continued, no constitutional difficulty would ensue, since it was not proposed to exclude any persons from the newly organized territory. Windom was not too precise on this point. He appears to have meant that if it were generally known that homesteads, of from forty to eighty acres, were for Negroes and that territorial officers would be mainly colored, then white settlers would voluntarily stay away. His proposal did not involve compulsory migration or federal support of the migrants. But his resolution did provide that the committee might report, by bill or otherwise, on the most effective way of encouraging the migration. It was in this speech that Windom made the perspicacious observation that "the black man does not excite antagonism because he is black, but because he is a *citizen*, and as such may control an election." He estimated that the migration of only a quarter of a million from the overcrowded districts of the South would accomplish the aims he had in view. No senator continued the discussion.

When Windom, on February 24, moved that the Senate consider his resolution, he was immediately challenged by the Democrat, Saulsbury of Delaware. Saulsbury had objected in 1862 to the recognition of Haiti, because it would lead to the eventual presence of a Haitian minister in the gallery reserved for diplomats. He declared, in 1879, that Windom's resolution would incur expense and would do no good. Later, Saulsbury probably revealed his real objection when he charged: "It contains an implied accusation against certain States and certain congressional districts in this country that colored people are not allowed to vote." He wanted specific proof that the charge was accurate. Windom was willing to strike out the words that seemed to reflect this accusation. Since the morning hour had expired, the Vice-President ruled that the Senate would proceed to unfinished business. Windom gave notice that he would press his resolution in the morning hour the next day. He was present on that day but he did not press his resolution.

He did not press it until December 15, 1879, when Voorhees, Democratic Senator from Indiana, alarmed by the migration of Negroes from North Carolina to Indiana, introduced a resolution for the appointment of a committee to investigate the causes of the migration. Windom on the next day offered an amendment that was substantially similar to his resolution of January 16, with the exception that it envisaged only territories as a refuge for the colored citizens of the South. Voorhees replied on December 18, that his purpose was to ascertain whether Negroes were leaving the South because of the injustice inflicted upon them, or because of "a conspiracy on the part of disreputable people, both white and black, to disturb the condition of the black race at the South and make them discontented and unhappy and point to them greater advantages elsewhere which do not exist, thus spreading a delusion and a snare before them, and getting them to move about." He was certain that the good people of Indiana had no objections to "legitimate" settlers. But, in what must have been an appeal especially to West Coast Senators, he said that Indiana no more wanted Negroes brought in by "regiments, divisions and corps" than the people of California wanted Chinese landed upon them by organized societies. Indiana, moreover, had no wastelands for the freedmen to take up cheaply. It would be fruitful of evil if the "well-behaved and decent colored population" of Indiana had thrust upon them the migrants from North Carolina. If he were motivated by party considerations, he would urge that Negroes be encouraged to enter Indiana, for there would be five new Democratic voters to every new Negro settler. But Voorhees objected to Windom's amendment as being "premature." Let the Committee ascertain the facts without being instructed what to do after it had ascertained them.

Windom defended his amendment briefly and then chided Voorhees for saying that Democrats in Indiana would violently object to the immigration of Negroes. The senator from Minnesota found this argument difficult to believe, since Southern Democrats had been giving the assurance that the reason why the votes in the South were almost solidly Democratic was the fact that Negroes there were supporting Democratic candidates.

Senator Benjamin H. Hill of Georgia, who announced that he would neither approve nor oppose the resolution, flatly denied that the colored people suffered cruel and unjust treatment in the South. On the contrary, he asserted: "The colored people of the Southern States are perfectly contented with their situation exactly in proportion to the length of time they have been under the government of what are known as the white people of that country, or the democratic party, if you choose that term." In evidence thereof, he cited the great increase in the number of colored children in school since the overthrow of the carpetbag governments. He also boasted that Negroes in Georgia had accumulated more than $5,000,000 worth of property, including 500,000 acres of land. Conkling, a Republican senator from New York, twitted Hill by asking how Negroes, in view of their well-known "inferiority" and "laziness" could possibly have accumulated so much capital. Although most Northerners probably no more accepted the rosy picture of the South painted by Hill than did Conkling, the prevailing mood was for peace at any price. Voorhees, for example, declared: "I believe the colored people, if left alone, and not operated upon by improper influences, would everywhere be as they are in Georgia."

Windom's amendment was rejected, 18 yeas to 25 nays. Sixteen Republicans and two Democrats, both from the South, voted for the amendment. Hill's vote for it was perhaps a kind of defiant justification of his own position. Since Kellogg of Louisiana—the other Southern yea—did not participate in the debate, it would be difficult to conjecture as to his reasons. Of the twenty-five negative votes, twelve were cast by senators from states that had seceded. Five were cast by Democratic senators from the border states of Kentucky, Delaware and Missouri that had been slaveholding states; two were from West Virginia, carved out of the former slaveholding state of Virginia. But six were from the Northern states of Illinois, Connecticut, Ohio, New Jersey, Oregon, and Indiana. These six votes could have swung the decision in favor of Windom's resolution, 24 to 19.

The debate was continued when Windom moved to add to the preamble of the resolution introduced by Voorhees the words "and by the denial or abridgment of personal and political rights and privileges." Voorhees declared that if the investigation revealed that Negroes were the subject of unjust and cruel treatment in the South, he would then be prepared to vote for Windom's motion. Garland, of Arkansas, gave the assurance that the Negroes of Arkansas were perfectly happy there. Vest, of Missouri, reminded the Senate that he had offered, at the previous session of Congress, a resolution inquiring of the Department of the Interior what land had been occupied in the Indian Territory by the Indians and by the freedmen from the South. A document was on file in the Senate, in response to that resolution, showing that no freedmen had ever been taken by the government from the Southern states and carried into the Indian Territory. Ransom of North Carolina intoned the Hill-Garland thesis. The real reason for the migration of Negroes to Indiana, he added, was the fact that the Negro vote was needed there to make the state Republican. Dawes, of Massachusetts, ridiculed the assertions of Hill and Ransom. The migration, Dawes insisted, was motivated by the universal desire of men to better their condition. Ingalls, Republican of Kansas, proclaimed his opposition to any exodus en masse, but asserted that the migration had no political significance. Most of the Negroes, he pointed out, had gone to Kansas, a solidly Republican state, and the few hundreds en route to Indiana would not alter the political complexion of that state. Every Negro with whom Ingalls had talked had given as his reason for moving to Kansas, "the purpose of obtaining protection of his political and civil rights and a fair day's wage for an honest day's work." The resolution introduced by Voorhees providing for an investigation of the causes of the Exodus was carried, 27 to 12.[19]

The report of the senatorial committee divided on party rather than sectional lines. Voorhees, Vance of North Carolina, and Pendleton of Ohio, all Democrats, concluded that the rights of Negroes in the South had not been curtailed. They also found that rents, wages, and sharecropping were about the same in all Southern States and that wages there were as good as those in the North. Conditions, on the whole, were better than they had expected to find them, but they did recognize that there was room for improvement. Educational facilities were not adequate for either whites or blacks. In conclusion, the majority felt that the Negro should be left to work out his own problems. The minority report of the two Republicans, Windom and Blair, on the other hand, found that the migration was confined more or less to the poor working class. It specified, as reasons for the migration, the abridgment of the rights of self-government, disadvantages in education, and discrimination in the courts. Referring specifically to Mississippi and Louisiana, the states from which most of the migrants had left, the minority added the system of labor, renting, and credit as reasons for the migration.[20]

While Congress was debating, investigating, reporting, and doing nothing to aid migration, the movement from the South had assumed such proportions in the spring of 1879 that it has been labeled the "Exodus." Led by Henry Adams of Louisiana and Moses ("Pap") Singleton of Tennessee, some 40,000 Negroes virtually stampeded from Mississippi, Louisiana, Alabama and Georgia for the Midwest. The largest number fled to Kansas where, at first, they received a friendly welcome. The Topeka *Commonwealth* on April 7, 1879, pointed out that it was only fitting that Kansas, which had fought to be a free state, should become the home of ex-slaves. The governor welcomed one group to "the State made immortal by Old John Brown." But, as the number increased, the attitude changed, especially since many of the migrants presented a woebegone spectacle. One author described them as follows:

> Hopeless, penniless and in rags, these poor people were thronging the wharves of St. Louis, crowding the steamers on the Mississippi River, hailing the passing steamers and imploring them for a passage to the land of freedom, where the rights of citizens are respected and honest toil rewarded by compensations.

As a consequence, messengers were sent from Kansas to advise the Negroes not to migrate and, if they insisted on doing so, to provide themselves with the necessary equipment. Some hotels and restaurants in Kansas refused the migrants accommodations. Singleton was so disappointed that he tried, unsuccessfully, to encourage Negroes to migrate to Liberia or Canada.[21]

The destitution of the migrants was only partly offset by the efforts of the Freedmen's Relief Association. Reviving something of the fervor that had given much needed support to the "Free Soilers" in the days of "Bleeding Kansas," the Association raised some $25,000 in cash and $100,000 in clothing, bedding, household goods and other necessities. About one-sixth of the cash and one-fourth of the furnishings came from England. Thus assisted, and further aided by the Homestead Act, the migrants bought about 20,000 acres of land. Lack of funds, however, made it impossible for many of the farmers to buy equipment. Many of them found employment on railroads, in coal mines, and in public works, while the women took in washing, worked as house servants, and kept apple stalls. There is no evidence available that the state contributed direct aid to the migrants, but it did build schools for children and maintained night classes for adults.

In addition to those who migrated to Kansas, some 4,000 moved to Iowa and Nebraska. Little is known about the fate of these migrants, but it is probable that it was similar to that of those who fled to Kansas. Until the Oklahoma Territory was thrown open to white settlement in 1889, a few

Negroes were warmly received by the Indians. A traveler in Indian Territory in 1880 gave a very favorable account of their homes, farms, churches and schoolhouses.[22]

It was thus clear that migration would not afford an effective avenue of escape for any considerable number of Negroes. The loss of Negro labor did, however, induce a re-examination of the treatment of black workers, especially in Mississippi. As early as May 6, 1879, a convention of leading white and colored citizens met in Vicksburg. It affirmed that the Constitution and laws of the United States had placed Negroes on a plane of absolute equality with the whites. The convention pledged its power and influence to protect the Negroes at the polls, and recommended the abolition of the mischievous credit system. But the convention rejected a proposal of ex-Governor Foote to establish in every county a committee, composed of men who had the confidence of both whites and Negroes, to hear their complaints.[23]

Ten years later, however, some Southerners favored the migration of Negroes from Southern states. This change of attitude was perhaps prompted by fear that Congress might pass a law providing for federal supervision of federal elections. President Harrison made such a proposal in his annual message of 1889. Senator M. C. Butler, of South Carolina—who had been one of the leaders in the Hamburg riot—almost immediately introduced a bill, December 12, "to provide for the migration of persons of color from the Southern States." Morgan, an influential senator from Alabama, who enjoyed friendly relations with many prominent Northerners, argued sarcastically that only a few statesmen wanted Negroes to remain massed in certain states, with a view to taking control of the state governments. In support of the thesis that Negroes were incapable of absorbing the white man's culture, Morgan contended that the Portuguese experience in Africa after four hundred years was conclusive. The failure of the Negroes of the Congo to organize a vast empire was further evidence of their incapacity for self-government, as was also the example of Haiti. Ingalls, of Kansas, opposed the bill because there was no reason to believe that the African could ever compete with the Anglo-Saxon in government, art, conquest, or practical affairs. Butler did not believe in the "total, hopeless depravity of the Negro race," but he reasoned that, since the United States realized the necessity of separating Indians from whites, the necessity of removing Negroes from the United States should be equally obvious. Wade Hampton contended that every race, save the Caucasian, "is and ought to be regarded as alien in the United States." Vance, of North Carolina, pointed out that the Negro, though outnumbering the whites in many parts of the South, permitted himself to be intimidated and defrauded in the matter of suffrage. Hoar, of Massachusetts, retorted that no senator had ever conducted himself with more propriety, dignity and intelligence than had Bruce, and that the colored members of the House were the equal of others in ability. He scoffed at the idea that Northerners should be silent on the problem of Negroes in the South, only to have to listen to a proposal for even voluntary emigration to Africa. Blair suggested that, if ten thousand carefully selected white men were sent to Africa, the whole problem would be settled. Apparently not even the Southern senators took Butler's bill seriously, for it did not come to a vote.[24]

Less well known than the Exodus of 1879 is the attempt of a colored man, Edwin P. McCabe, to create a Negro state out of the Oklahoma Territory. The Cherokee Strip was also considered as a possible new home for Negro migrants. McCabe, who had been state auditor of Kansas, is reported to have sent 300 colored families from North Carolina and 500 from South Carolina. Arrangements were said to have been made for 5,000 families to migrate to Oklahoma. But the federal government provided no aid to this project. Senators Ingalls and Plumb, of Kansas, supported the idea, as did several members of the House, and General E. H. Funston. President Harrison granted McCabe an interview but took no steps to support his enterprise.[25]

This movement failed, not only because of the lack of federal support and private financial assistance, but also because of the hostility of both Indians and whites. Professor Mozell Hill of Atlanta University has collected more than 200 newspaper articles, some of them extending over into the twentieth century, which reveal this hostility. Three of them during the period under study are as follows:

The Choctaws are driving the Negroes out of that Nation. Anyone employing a colored servant is subjected to a $50.00 fine.

In the Southern portion of the Oklahoma Territory, White Cappers are running the Negroes out of the country. At Norman, not one Negro remains.

Major H. C. Miller has issued a proclamation to the citizens of Sapulpa stating that if they are determined to rid the town of the Negro population, let them do so in a peaceable law-abiding manner.[26]

It may be presumed that the Indians, who had welcomed a few Negroes in the 1870's, took alarm at the influx of a large number. The New York *Times* reported, in 1891, that there were 22,000 Negroes in the Northeast Black Jack section.[27] Perhaps the Indians were also aroused by white settlers who were determined to keep the territory for themselves. In any case, the Oklahoma Territory was no more prepared than Kansas, Iowa or Nebraska to absorb enough Negroes to relieve appreciably their miserable condition in the Southern states.

Plans for Southern Negroes to migrate to other parts of the United States or to emigrate continued to be formulated until the end of the century. The fact that many of these were projected in the 1890's suggests that the general deterioration of the Negro's status prompted them, as it did earlier and later proposals. In 1894, the Knights of Labor proposed to send an organizer into the South to lecture on the advantages of colonization in the Congo Basin, Liberia and other parts of Africa. The Knights planned to petition Congress to make an appropriation to aid the project.[28] There is no evidence that the petition was presented, probably because the Knights had almost disappeared from the ranks of organized labor. It is clear, however, that the Knights had abandoned the hope, which had existed even until the late 1880's, of organizing black workers in the South.

One of the few undertakings in the 1890's that resulted in actual migration was that organized by a colored man, variously known as H. Ellis and W. H. Ellis. Early in 1895, some eight hundred Negroes, largely recruited from Alabama towns by Ellis, attempted to settle near the village of Mapimi in the Mexican state of Durango. A severe winter, inadequate housing facilities, and an outbreak of smallpox soon drove most of the settlers back to the United States. On the recommendation of President Cleveland, the railroads that had transported the migrants from the Texas border back to their homes were reimbursed,[29] but there is no evidence that the government assisted the distressed settlers.

One of the most interesting proposals was that in 1897, made by the Americans who had executed a revolution in Hawaii, that Negroes be imported from Louisiana, Texas and Mississippi. This plan would result in the displacement of Japanese laborers at the expiration of their contracts. The Hawaiian government also planned to issue no more six month residence permits to Chinese.[30] Evidence is lacking that the plan materialized.

Brief mention of a few other proposals and actual migrations completes the picture, as it is known to date, of the evident yearnings of some Negroes to escape from the South. In 1877, 1894, and 1895, three small ships chartered by private Negro enterprise, sailed for Liberia. A proposal for a Negro state within the United States, advanced in 1883, received scant attention. Lillian K. Ray, a wealthy English philanthropist, founded the town of Cedarlake, near Decatur, Alabama, as an experiment to make Negroes an industrial population distinct in themselves.[31] Other all-Negro towns, especially in Mississippi, attracted Negroes from rural areas.

The Spanish American War required no such expansion of Northern industries as that which, during World War I and World War II, finally led to the migration of hundreds of thousands of Negroes from the South. Foreign immigrants, moreover, more than supplied the need of Northern industries. Neither the North nor the sparsely settled West afforded an escape for the approximately nine million Negroes of the South, about one-half of whom were engaged in agriculture.

Nor did the Populist Revolt provide an escape from thralldom. The economic roots of the various organizations which since the 1870's had sought to improve the lot of farmers are well known. They included primarily a decline in the price of farm products without a corresponding decline in the cost of manufactured articles and of transportation. The South suffered perhaps even more than did the West, for the price of cotton fell more rapidly than did that of either corn or wheat. In the period after the Civil War, "Cotton was King" even more than it had been prior to the war. Production rose from five and a half million bales in 1880, to nine and a half at the end of the century. Overproduction led to a drop in price from twenty-nine cents in 1870, to seven cents in 1894. As in other farming areas, farmers were compelled to borrow from banks at usurious rates of interest; unable to repay loans, they were forced in many instances to mortgage and frequently to lose their farms. Throughout the South, nearly half the farms were tilled by renters whose exploitation by merchants through the mark-up or "pluck me" system has been already described. In brief, conditions in the South were surely no better, and probably worse, in the 1890's than they had been at the time of the Exodus of 1879. The political failure of the Populist Revolt has already been discussed. It is sufficient to point out here that the success of the Revolt would not necessarily have meant an improvement in agriculture in the South. After 1897, when the price of cotton began to rise, Negroes still were denied an equitable share in the rise. Free enterprise had not hurdled the "color line."

EIGHT

The Economic Roots of Second-Class Citizenship: Organized Labor

DURING the second half of the nineteenth century, the United States changed from a rural and agricultural nation to an urban and industrial nation. If Negroes could have participated equally with white workers in this transformation, many would have escaped the thralldom that engulfed agricultural workers in general, but black workers more than white. White industrial workers, however, failed to share equitably with Big Business in the tremendous profits reaped from the industrial expansion that transformed the face of America. Black workers obtained an even smaller share than did the white.

This difference was due in part to the fact that few Negroes lived in the former non-slaveholding states in which the greatest industrial growth developed. From 1870 to 1900 the percentage of Negroes in the North out of the total Negro population rose slowly from 9.3 to 10.00. In the West the percentage was infinitesimal—0.1 in 1870 and 0.3 in 1900. Both in the North and the West, large numbers of immigrants were given jobs that Negroes might have filled. It is true, of course, that a small number of immigrants brought with them skills that few Negroes—or whites—had been able to acquire. But the number of artisans before the Civil War leaves no doubt that black skilled workers could have been employed more widely in the expanding and newly opened industries than they were. When management or capital wanted to break strikes, however, it did not hesitate to give jobs to Negroes.

In the South, where nine out of ten Negroes lived, capital and management gave native white workers the same preference that was accorded immigrants in the North and West. The vast expansion of the cotton textile and tobacco factories was, indeed, looked upon with great fervor, as a crusade for the habilitation of the "poor white." It is difficult to determine the extent to which this denial of equal job opportunities to Negroes in both sections stemmed from interlocking control or management. In the years immediately after the war, Northern capital found investments in the North and West more profitable than those in the South. But Northern capital invested heavily in Southern railroads and frequently left their management in the hands of Southerners. By the end of the century, a fairly intelligent system of railroads in the South and between the South and the North had been established. The role of railroad lobbyists in the Compromise of 1877 has already been noted. Big Business continued to constitute the principal force for peace at almost any price, for "leaving the South alone." Further investigation may reveal close links between Northern capital and management and the supposedly predominantly Southern enterprises of cotton and tobacco factories. In any case, neither Northern nor Southern management and capital were disposed to give black workers equal job opportunities. This policy should not cause surprise in the Gilded Age and the Era of the Golden Calf. But organized labor might have been expected to manifest a more friendly attitude toward black workers. The failure of the one organization which made a serious effort to integrate all workers, male and female, native and foreign-born, skilled and unskilled, black and white into one body is another principal reason for the plight of the Negro at the end of the century.

In agriculture the greatest blunder of Reconstruction was the failure of the government to assist large numbers of Negroes to become landowners. In industry, as Du Bois has rightly contended, the greatest tragedy was the failure of organized labor to strengthen its forces by the wholehearted incorporation of the new contingent of free, black workers.[1] It is probable, however, that he minimized the difficulty of establishing a powerful labor organization, and that he overestimated its potentialities in the struggle with Big Business. Prior to the Civil War, only a relatively small number of workers, nearly all white males, had been unionized, and no nation-wide federation of unions had been achieved before the war. Organized labor after the war, therefore, had to grope its way and learn the intricacies of large-scale federated unionism in the face of bitter opposition by Big Business, before it could become a real force in American economy, politics and thought.

The pre-Civil War bitterness of white artisans, increased by the war, did not predispose them to an enthusiastic welcome for the new contingent of workers. They were generally considered as competitors for jobs rather than as allies in winning better conditions for all working men. Organized labor had to face the two dilemmas which it has not yet fully answered: (1) should Negro workers be organized or should they be left to swell the ranks of those who were willing (or forced) to work for lower wages; (2) if Negroes were organized, should the unions be mixed or separate? The National Labor Union, at its first meeting in 1866, decided to organize black workers. A way out of the second dilemma was sought at the Philadelphia Convention in 1869, where it was voted that the Union would recognize neither color nor sex, and the colored delegates were urged to form their own organization. Accepting the inevitable, a national Negro labor convention in the same year formed a separate body.[2] It is not without interest that the first large-scale exclusion of Negroes by private organizations in the post-bellum period was the handiwork of organized labor.

The exclusion policy of the National Labor Union drove Negro workers away from unionism and toward political action. At the same time, the National Labor Union abandoned political action but made little effort to organize Southern white workers. Weakened by auxiliary undertakings, such as cooperatives and educational enterprises, the Union virtually disappeared after the panic of 1873.

More radical labor movements met with even less success than had the National Labor Union. The "First International," founded by Karl Marx in London, 1864, never gained a solid foothold in the United States. In 1876, the International Workingman's Association was officially declared dead in the United States as well as abroad. The Socialist Labor Party, organized at Philadelphia in the same year, likewise won few adherents. Five years later, the anarchist-syndicalist element in the party split off and formed the Revolutionary Socialist Party which soon changed its name to the International Working People's Association. Dubbed the "Black International" by its opponents, it was completely discredited by the Haymarket Square Riot, Chicago, 1886. The Socialist Labor Party, even under the able leadership of Daniel De Leon, never acquired an important place in American unionism or party politics. The Social Democratic Party, founded in 1898, likewise failed appreciably to influence unionism or party politics.

In brief, organized labor in the United States could hope

to achieve its aims only if it were rooted in accepted American ideas and divorced from party politics. This hope rested, especially after the demise of the National Labor Union, with the Noble Order of the Knights of Labor, organized in 1869. This organization was just beginning to gather strength when pacification became the national policy, in 1877. Even without the benefit of the recent revelations of Woodward as to the role that the railroad lobbyists played in the Compromise of 1877, Du Bois called the "Revolution of 1876" a victory of Big Business over organized labor.[3] The victory of Big Business is not disputed. But one should not conclude that organized labor was prepared to launch an uprising in 1876. On the other hand, the Knights of Labor achieved its greatest growth in the decade after 1876.

It did so despite the fact that it sought more vigorously than had the National Labor Union to make "solidarity" something more than a by-word. The Knights pursued a dual system, in both the North and the South, of all-colored and of mixed locals. It used both white and colored organizers in both the North and the South. The success of the courageous organizers is well attested by the determined efforts made in many Southern communities to break up the assemblies of the Order. Vigilantes and lynch mobs joined officers of the law in intimidating and murdering organizers and Knights, breaking up meetings, and forcing the discharge of union workers. Nearly every Southern state, according to the colored newspaper, the New York *Freeman*, enacted laws making it a conspiracy for any persons to band together to interfere with any contract between any employer and employee, whether such contract were in writing or oral. Although such a law died in the South Carolina House Judiciary Committee after passing the state senate, 1886, a considerable number of Negroes left the state. The threats, intimidations, the increase of militia, and the wild rumors that Negroes were bent on murder, rape and the destruction of property prompted Henry George to berate the well-understood "pretense." The pretense, George continued:

> is as absurd as it is stale. . . . It is the manufactured excuse for murdering black men. . . . The fact is, evidently, that the black Knights of Labor are learning, like their white brothers at the North, that the land belongs to

all the people—to the workers as well as to the idler, to the black as well as to the white. . . . They must be accused of contemplated violence as an excuse for using violence against them.

In the North, the Knights had to confront the blacklist, the lockout, Pinkerton detectives, the "iron-clad oath," and other familiar devices for circumventing organized labor.

The Knights also had to face the issue of the employment of Negroes as strikebreakers. In some instances, scabbing was due to the failure of the Knights to accept colored workers. In other instances, Negroes did not know that they were being used to break strikes. The refusal of some Negroes to be used as scabs should be kept in mind when one considers the later attack upon Negroes as "cheap men" by Samuel Gompers. As one writer inquired in 1886:

> I would like to ask as a fair-minded man, if it is right for the strikers or their advocates to blame the Negroes for accepting the offer made by the capitalists to fill the places made vacant by the striking quarrymen, or any other trade unionist, when they are not recognized or respected enough by them for admittance into their great organizations as co-laborers and brothers in this great cause.

Despite these difficulties North and South—in the South, of course, greater racial prejudice on the part of workers themselves had made organization more difficult than in the North—the Knights had made notable gains by 1886. In that year, membership exceeded 700,000, of which some 60,000 were Negroes. In the following year, when the membership had dropped to 500,000, the most recent student of the subject accepts 90,000 as the total number of Negroes in the order.[4]

In the spring of 1886, the Order appeared to have gained a dominant place in the labor movement. It loomed in the minds of many capitalists, politicians and newspaper editors as a dire threat to business and to the government itself. They feared, not only the growing power of a centralized unit based upon an early concept of industrial unionism that included men and women, skilled and unskilled, white and black workers, but also the Order's ultimate aim of some sort of industrial commonwealth. But the spring of 1886 also witnessed the beginning of the decline of the Knights of Labor. On May 4 a strike and demonstration by the "Black International" resulted in the bloody riot of Haymarket Square, Chicago. The Knights of Labor joined in the general denunciation of the riot. But the enemies of organized labor contrived to discredit the Knights by charging that its unions were also anarchistic and communistic. The moment was propitious for the emergence of a new and "safe" labor movement.

The philosophy of this new labor movement was expressed by Adolph Strasser, president of the International Cigar Makers' Union, before the Senate Committee on Education and Labor, in 1885. When asked the ultimate ends of his union, Strasser replied: "We have no ultimate ends. . . . We are all practical men. . . . We are going on from day to day. We fight only for immediate objects—objects that can be realized from day to day." Samuel Gompers, president of the American Federation of Labor from 1886, except for the year 1895, to his death in 1924, was also a member of the International Cigar Makers' Union. He had the same narrow vision as did his co-worker, Strasser, and his early adviser, Ferdinand Laurrell, who had urged Gompers to use his union card as the guide for all his thinking. Gompers' almost entire program was higher wages and shorter hours for skilled workers of craft unions. He probably saved the labor movement from a complete breakdown,[5] just as Hayes had perhaps saved the Union from another Civil War in 1877.

The American Federation of Labor grew out of the Federation of Organized Trades and Labor Unions, organized in 1881. The composition of the convention at which the A. F. of L. emerged from this Federation, at Columbus, Ohio, December, 1886, presaged its later membership. The national unions represented were: iron molders, typographers, German-American typographers, granite cutters, stereotypers, miners and mine laborers, journeymen tailors, journeymen bakers, furniture workers, metal workers, carpenters and joiners, and cigar makers. Except for the miners and mine laborers, all these unions were almost entirely white in their membership. Evidence is lacking as to the number of colored workers among the local unions of barbers, waiters and bricklayers and among the city centrals in Baltimore, Chicago, St. Louis, Philadelphia and New York.[6]

The structure of the A. F. of L. was also radically different from that of the Knights of Labor. The constitution of the latter made the General Assembly the supreme authority with control over both the district and local assemblies. Membership was on an individual basis and not through affiliated trade unions. The structure of the A. F. of L., on the other hand, was implicit in its name—it was a federation. Each union was autonomous. Membership was through the union and not on an individual basis.

Personal rivalry, in addition to basic differences in structure, composition of membership, and ultimate aims, heightened the conflict between the two organizations. The struggle between Terence V. Powderly of the Knights and Gompers came to a head at the General Assembly of the Knights, at Richmond, Virginia, in October, 1886. The Knights had attempted to organize a dissident body of the Cigar Makers' International Union which belonged to the Federation of Organized Trades and Labor Unions. A "treaty" failed to resolve the differences between the parent organizations, and the dissident Progressive Cigar Makers were admitted to the Knights of Labor at the Richmond Assembly. The organization of the A. F. of L. two months later made clear that no compromise was possible. The two rivals continued their struggle until 1894, when the Knights of Labor virtually disappeared from the scene. The practical Gompers had eliminated the more idealistic Powderly. Opportunism, local autonomy, limited goals for the "aristocracy" of labor had won the day against more democratic ideals and membership, and central control. The victory of the A. F. of L. over the Knights of Labor was the economic counterpart of the political victory of pacification, local control and white supremacy.

It is debatable whether the tactics, structure and objectives of the A. F. of L. were consciously motivated by a desire to exclude Negroes. The hard-headed, practical men who directed the A. F. of L., however, realized that the heterogeneous membership of the Knights was one of the reasons for its declining power. Moreover, a federation of unions of craftsmen would not include many Negroes. There was, nevertheless, a sufficient number of them to embarrass the A. F. of L. at the turn of the century.

Gompers in his opening remarks at the Tenth Annual Convention, Detroit, 1890, referred vaguely to "deep-seated ignorance and prejudices." He eloquently recalled "the great struggle to free the black man and to sunder the shackles from his wrists." In his annual report, however, he again called attention, as he had done at previous conventions, "to the necessity of avoiding as far as possible all controversial questions."

But the controversial question of the admission of Negroes had already arisen through the exclusion clause in the constitution of the National Machinists' Union. The issue was decided in what might be called a hard-headed, practical manner. A motion was introduced by a delegate named Lennon as follows:

> Resolved, That it is the sense of this Convention, and it looks with disfavor upon trade unions having provisions which exclude from membership persons on account of race or color, and that we most respectfully request that the National Machinists' Union remove from their constitution such conditions, so that all machinists shall be eligible to membership.

A slightly milder substitute motion prevailed by a vote of 51 to 3. It declared: "Moved, as a substitute, that the matter be referred to the Executive Council, and the recommendation contained in the resolution of Mr. Lennon be carried out."[7]

The structure of the A. F. of L.—a federation of autonomous affiliates—made it impossible for the convention to order the Machinists to strike out the exclusion clause. The convention could only "most respectfully request" that they do so. The policy question of disapproving trade unions whose provisions excluded workers because of race or color was apparently not acted upon until 1895. Meanwhile, both the Thirteenth and Fourteenth Annual Conventions, 1893 and 1894, unanimously adopted a resolution which categorically proclaimed: "We here and now reaffirm as one of the cardinal principles of the labor movement that the working people must unite and organize, irrespective of creed, color, sex, nationality or politics."[8] Some delegates undoubtedly hoped that the resolution would have the moral effect of preventing unions from excluding persons for the reasons stated. Other delegates probably voted for the resolution precisely because it had no binding effect upon unions that violated the pious hope.

When the Machinists' Union refused to comply with the request to strike out the exclusion clause, the Executive Council organized a new union, the International Machinists Association, which was admitted to the A. F. of L. in 1895. But the Union found an easy way to evade the non-discrimination recommendation of the Annual Convention. The Machinists adopted a ritual in which the members pledged themselves to propose only white men for membership. The Boilermakers' and Shipbuilders' Union, which used the same device for excluding Negroes, was admitted to the A. F. of L. in the following year. Similarly, the Plumbers' and Steamfitters' Union disqualified large numbers of Negroes by their control over local license laws. Since the Brotherhood of Locomotive Engineers, the Order of Railway Conductors, and the Brotherhood of Locomotive Firemen and Engineers had been founded as fraternal and beneficial societies, these social features prevented the admission of Negroes. In 1899 the Trainmen called for the exclusion of Negroes. The following year the Tobacco Workers' International Union gave up the attempt to forbid discrimination on account of race and color and began to organize separate Negro locals. The Annual Convention of the A. F. of L. capitulated in 1900, when it adopted the explicit policy of organizing Negroes into separate locals or affiliated "central" unions when they were refused admission to existing locals because of their color.[9]

The attitude of the Executive Council was strikingly revealed in a statement on April 20, 1901, released by Gompers, in response to numerous inquiries. For years, the statement declared, the A. F. of L. had favored the organization of all workers without regard to creed, color, sex, nationality or politics. However, the A. F. of L.

does not necessarily proclaim that the social barriers which exist between the whites and blacks could or should be obliterated; but it realizes that when white and black workers are compelled to work side by side, under the same equally unfair and adverse conditions, it would be an anomaly to refuse to accord the right of organization to workers because of the difference in color.

Evidence of the interest of the Federation in the welfare of colored workers was seen in the fact that several organizers were devoting their time exclusively to organizing them. These colored workers, despite inquiries from "self-constituted 'superiors,'" should not be entitled to any "privileges" other than their chance to ply their trades as did white workers. Some of these white workers, especially those in New Orleans, had jeopardized their own interests a few years previously by going on strike. The statement specifically urged colored workers to organize, and in all cases to become affiliated with the organizations of white workers or form colored workers' unions "in full sympathy and co-operation of the white workers union." These separate unions generally worked together without any friction. To be sure, in an organization as large as the Federation some mistakes were bound to be made. When the mistake involved a colored worker, it was magnified into an attempt to convey the notions that it was the rule and not the exception and that the labor movement did not grant the right of the Negro to organize.

The real difficulty, the statement continued, stemmed from the fact that "the colored workers have allowed themselves to be used with too frequent telling effect by their employers as to injure the cause and interests of themselves, as well as of white workers." They had allowed themselves to be regarded as "'cheap men.'" Further placing upon Negro workers the responsibility for the failure to receive their due, the statement closed with the admonition:

If the colored workmen desire to accept the honest invitation of our movement to organize; if those who have influence over the minds of the colored workmen will encourage the earnest, honest effort put forth by our fellow unionists, we will find larger success attending their efforts, economic bitterness and antagonism between the races reduced, minimized and obliterated; but if the colored workers are taught to depend entirely upon the good will and control of their employers; that they can be brought from place to place at any time to thwart the struggle of the white workers for material, moral and social improvement; then hostilities will increase and thus counteract the very best efforts of those who are earnestly engaged in the endeavor for the unification of labor, the attainment of social improvement of all the people and their entire disenthrallment from every vestige of tyranny, wrong and injustice.[10]

This carefully prepared statement leaves no doubt: (1) that the Executive Council of the A. F. of L. fully approved separate locals as a matter of expediency; (2) that it took a dim view of the aspirations of Negroes for "social equality"; (3) that it denounced Negroes or scabbing despite the efforts of white unionizers to organize them. It is relevant to note that in 1900 the General Federation of Women's Clubs refused to admit a Negro club, although it recognized the credentials of the representative of the Negro club as a member of other state clubs.[11] The "Road to Reunion" was gaining increased momentum, expanding from the arena of politics to labor and cultural and civic organizations.

The answer to the question whether Negroes scabbed because they were cheap mean, or because they were frequently compelled to do so since they were not unionized, is seen in part at least in an analysis of the number of skilled Negro workers and the number who were unionized. Skilled Negro workers were engaged in every class of occupation listed in the 1890 and 1900 census schedules.[12] But, in 1890 they belonged, apparently, to only five unions, and in 1900 to only nine unions out of sixty. The following table shows the number of colored workers in those unions:[13]

	1890	1900
Barbers	200	800
Brick and clay workers	50	200
Carpenters and joiners		1,000
Coopers		200
Firemen and oilers		2,700
Longshoremen	1,500	6,000
Mine workers		20,000
Painters, decorators and paper hangers	33	169
Tobacco workers	1,500	1,000
Totals	3,283	32,069

In 1900, then, almost two-thirds of colored unionized workers were members of the United Mine Workers of America. One-fifth belonged to the International Longshoremen's Association, which likewise could hardly be called a union of skilled workers. One thousand, a decrease of one-third from

1890, were tobacco workers, few of whom were skilled workers.

Particularly in the building trades were Negroes not organized. In 1900 there were 22,435 colored carpenters and only 1,000 of them were unionized; 5,934 painters and only 169 unionized; 14,457 bricklayers and only 200 unionized. Perhaps one major reason for this small number of organized colored workers is the fact that most of them lived in the South: more than one-half of the colored bricklayers, more than two-thirds of the colored painters, and three-fourths of the colored carpenters. Evidence is lacking that colored workers belonged to the Operative Plasterers' and Cement Finishers' International Association or to the United Association of Journeymen Plumbers and Steamfitters. In 1900, there were 3,754 colored plasterers and cement finishers of whom 1,841 lived in the South; and 1,197 colored plumbers of whom 781 lived there. The colored carpenters in the South were organized into separate locals. The colored painters were placed in separate locals in both the North and the South. But the bricklayers and longshoremen had mixed locals, even in the South, as did the mine workers.[14]

The place of Negro workers in the building trades was, however, materially better than that in the vastly expanding Southern tobacco and textile factories. Although slaves had been skilled workers, especially in Southern textile mills, as free men they were relegated to the menial and other least desirable jobs. Probably the fact that Negroes had worked in tobacco factories after the war as leafers, stemmers, draymen and blenders accounts for their continuation in these jobs after large-scale mechanization was instituted. But the introduction of the huge textile mills was particularly looked upon as a kind of crusade to provide work for poverty-stricken whites. In order to rationalize the exclusion of Negroes from machine jobs, the argument was soon popularized that Negroes were clumsy and would be lulled to sleep by the whirring of the wheels. The distinguished Southern historian, Walter L. Fleming, for example, contended, in 1949, that "the negroes because of lack of quickness and sensitiveness of youth proved to be unfit for factory work. Besides, the noise of the machinery made them sleep and it was beyond their power to report for work at a regular hour each morning."[15] The denial of equal job opportunities in the tobacco and textile factories accounts, more than any other single factor perhaps, for the general economic decline of non-agricultural Southern Negro workers in the post-Reconstruction period.

Negroes in the North also encountered many difficulties in getting jobs in new and expanding enterprises. To be sure, the Negro population was relatively small in many of the regions. Consequently, cattle raising in the West, meat packing in Chicago and Kansas City, wheat growing and flour milling in Minnesota, oil wells in western Pennsylvania, oil refineries in Cleveland, steel mills in Pennsylvania, Ohio, and elsewhere found few Negroes seeking employment in them. But even where there were fairly sizable Negro populations, neither management nor labor unions welcomed colored workers with open arms. Northern cotton textile mills provided hardly more jobs, proportionately, for Negroes than did Southern. Woolen textile mills, shoe factories, iron and steel mills likewise gave few Negroes an escape from domestic and personal service. The opposition of the Amalgamated Association of Iron, Steel and Tin Workers, an affiliate of the A. F. of L., was dominated by the former members of the Sons of Vulcan which had barred Negroes by constitutional amendment. The attitude of the machinists has already been noted. It is not surprising that in 1900 there were only 1,263 colored machinists, 335 steam boiler makers, and 13,293 other iron and steel workers. These figures represent an increase from 1890, of 406, 178 and 5,836 respectively.[16]

It was especially in some of the big Northern industries that the employment of Negroes as strikebreakers had aroused the condemnation of the Executive Council of the A. F. of L. When management began to use Negroes as strikebreakers in the steel mills, the Amalgamated Association formed separate Negro locals. Small numbers of Negroes were first employed in the meat-packing industry during the 1894 Pullman strike. Stockyard workers struck in sympathy with the American Railway Union. Negroes formed the Anti-Strikers' Railroad Union in retaliation against its anti-Negro clause, and then joined strikebreakers at the stockyards. Some Negroes retained their jobs after the strike, because the packers saw in Negroes an almost inexhaustible supply of non-unionized and cheaper labor. They expected that Negroes would oppose unionization because of the antagonism of white workers.[17]

It is not strange that Negroes did not sympathize with the

railroad strikers, for the "Big Four" of Railroad Transportation had notoriously opposed not only the unionization but also the promotability of colored workers. While colored men, especially in the South, were employed as firemen, brakemen, switchmen, and flagmen, black firemen were not promoted to engineers nor black brakeman to conductors as were white workers.

Thus, management in large industries either relegated Negroes to unskilled jobs, or used them only occasionally as strikebreakers in better jobs; and the dominant labor organization, despite its protest to the contrary, had organized only a small number of colored workers. With due allowance for the shortcomings of the colored workers—shortcomings that may generally be explained by lack of incentive, encouragement, training and experience—it remains none the less true that they were widely discriminated against. It is understandable, then, that by comparison with other elements in the population, Negroes occupied the lowest rung of the economic ladder. The following tables present a graphic picture of their economic plight:[18]

1890

Occupation	Negroes	%	Native Whites	%	Foreign Whites	%
Agriculture, fishing and mining	1,757,403	57	5,122,613	47	1,305,901	26
Domestic and personal service	963,080	31	1,342,028	12	1,375,067	27
Manufacturing and mechanical industries	172,970	6	2,067,135	19	1,597,118	31
Trade and transportation	145,717	5	1,722,426	16	712,558	14
Professional service	33,994	1	640,785	6	114,113	2

1900

Occupation	Negroes	%	Native Whites	%	Foreign Whites	%
Agriculture, fishing and mining	2,143,176	53.7	6,004,039	43.3	1,074,211	18.7
Domestic and personal service	1,324,160	33	1,841,853	13.3	1,435,407	25
Manufacturing and mechanical industries	275,149	6.9	2,823,131	20.3	2,168,153	37.8
Trade and transportation	209,154	5.2	2,400,018	17.3	915,151	16
Professional service	41,524	1.2	806,288	5.8	143,896	2.5

The economic plight of the Negro can be even more clearly seen in the following table which shows the percentage of the Negro population of the total population in the five main occupational groups listed above.

	1890	1900
Agriculture, etc.	21.7	20.6
Domestic and personal service	22.6	23.6
Manufacturing, etc.	3.6	3.9
Trade and transportation	4.3	4.4
Professional service	3.6	3.7

Thus, the percentage of Negroes in agricultural pursuits, domestic and personal service was twice their percentage in the nation's population. On the other hand, the percentage in manufacturing and professional service was only a little more than a third of their percentage of the total population, and considerably less than half in trade and transportation. Most of those employed in manufacturing, trade and transportation were unskilled, unorganized and underpaid. The failure of the tremendous expansion of American industry to change materially the essentially peasant and domestic service status of most Negroes is evident from the fact that in 1890, 88 per cent and in 1900, 86.7 per cent of all Negroes were still employed in these least remunerative and least dignified occupations. Like most persons engaged in agriculture, Negroes had been caught between the hammer of lower prices for their products and proportionately higher prices for goods, loans and transportation. But Negroes had been more ruthlessly exploited than had white farm workers. Too little is known about domestic workers to permit the kind of statistical picture given for workers in industry. There is no reason, however, to believe that they were, relatively, better off than they are today, when most of them are the lowest paid, least appreciated, and least organized of all American workers. Many of them were women who sought to supplement the meager salaries of their menfolk. In 1900, 40.7 per cent of Negro women were gainfully employed, by contrast to 16 per cent of white women.

Because of the small income of most Negroes, Negro professionals and businessmen rose only slowly in numbers and in the accumulation of wealth. Their clientele was almost exclusively Negro. While this segregated market assured most of them an income that enabled them to become the "leaders" in their communities, their economic base was not broad enough to produce the capital that would enable Negro business to provide a sufficiently large number of jobs to offset the discriminations that black workers suffered at the hands of white capital and of organized labor. These professionals and businessmen did, however, constitute one of the roots for recovery from the nadir, a topic to be developed in Chapter Fifteen.

Part II

NINE

Introduction:
The Mind of the North, 1877–1901

THE reciprocal effect of events on the development of attitudes, and of attitudes in changing the course of events, constitutes an integral, though elusive, thread in the history of mankind. Part I of this book has traced the Negro's descent toward the nadir, from 1877 to the turn of the century. Part II will portray the attitudes toward this descent, as expressed especially in Northern newspapers and magazines. No attempt will be made to determine the extent to which these attitudes helped to mold events, but it will be clear that, on the whole, attitudes endorsed the policies and approved the events that steadily reduced the Negro to a subordinate place in American life. On this point, American thought generally conformed to American life.

While the analysis is focused upon the Negro, other minorities, especially Irishmen, Italians and Catholics in general, Swedes, Germans, Scotsmen, Indians, Chinese and Jews, were also attacked, caricatured and stereotyped. Negroes, however, suffered more than did other minorities. The stereotypes of these latter, except to some degree in the case of Indians, Chinese and Jews, were generally less derogatory and less comprehensive in scope than those lampooning Negroes. The "belligerent" Irishman, the "tight-fisted" Scotsman, the "dumb" Swede were inherently less objectionable than the "lazy, improvident, child-like, irresponsible, chicken-stealing, crap-shooting, policy-playing, razor-toting, immoral and criminal" Negro. Specifically, the Irishman was "belligerent," but the Negro was "uppity." The "tight-fisted" Scotsman was thrifty, while the Negro was a spendthrift. Although "tall tales" have constituted an amusing element in American folklore, they became deceitful lies in the mouths of Negroes. Moreover, the improved status of many peoples of European descent left them less vulnerable to gibes than did the deteriorating status of Negroes. The "fighting" Irishman was already gaining power in municipal politics; and the "dumb" Swede had acquired some of the best farm land in the Midwest.

Stereotypes of Indians and Chinese hurt more than did those of peoples of European descent. "The only good Indian is a dead Indian" was widely accepted, especially when Indians stood in the way of the filling up of the West. Their alleged fondness for "firewater," stories about their "viciousness" and "stupidity" were further invoked to rationalize the dictum. "Chink, Chink, Chinaman, eat dead rats" was a common saying among boys even in Washington, D. C., at the turn of the century. One of the famous stories in American folklore was based upon a report in the El Paso *Daily Times* for June 2, 1884, about Justice of the Peace Roy Bean. According to the report, "Somebody killed a Chinaman and was brought up standing before the irrepressible Roy, who looked through two or three dilapidated law books from stem to stern, and finally turned the culprit loose remarking that he'd be d————d if he could find any law against killing a Chinaman." Chinatown in many cities, especially on the West Coast, was portrayed as a sinister hot-bed of vice, gambling, opium-smoking and disease. The pigtail, bound feet, and even the exotic costumes made easy the caricaturing of "The Heathen Chinee" whose cheap labor provided abundant ammunition for attacks by workers and politicians. But, in the 1880's, the acuteness of the Chinese and Indian problems was somewhat assuaged by the Chinese Exclusion Act and by the Dawes Severalty Act—which latter permitted the government to reclaim and open up to settlement more than fifty million acres of land previously allotted to Indian reservations.

Jews, next to Negroes, were the target of the most harmful stereotypes. Because of their religion, the dress of some "Old" Jews, and the physical characteristics commonly attributed to all Jews, they were almost as easily identifiable as were Chinese, Indians and Negroes. They were caricatured and denounced because of their religion, their race, and their "parasitism" which led many of them into commerce, banking and the professions. Frequent "fire sales" and other sharp practices became fixed in the public mind as peculiarly Jewish. "Whoever heard of a Jewish farmer?" was a favorite loaded question. The very fact that some Jews did gain financial power and success in the professions added an element of fear to an anti-Semitism that was by no means confined to native-born Americans.

The cruel lampooning of minorities can be understood as,

in part, at least, a reaction of the Genteel Tradition against the uninhibited exuberance and even crudities of the riffraff. But not all of the riffraff were recent immigrants. Vernon Parrington has penned unforgettable portraits of the bucca-neer capitalists who feasted at the Great Barbecue: Jay Cooke, Drew, Fisk, Gould and Vanderbilt. Paced by these parvenu *nouveaux riches*—for the most part brawling, boisterous, os-tentatious "blackguards . . . , railway wreckers, cheaters and swindlers"—politicians, cranks, revivalists reveled in the de-struction of the "old ideals along with the old restraints." Alien peoples intruded their discordant manners, languages, customs and religions—Roman Catholic in increasing num-bers—upon an intellectual and social minority, predominantly Protestant, that was shocked and somewhat frightened by the passing of the old order. Thomas Bailey Aldrich, editor of the *Atlantic Monthly* from 1881 to 1890—whom Parrington selected as the personification of the Genteel Tradition—was revolted by the "wild motley throng" that was passing through our "Unguarded Gates." In 1892 he urged that "jailbirds, professional murderers, amateur lepers . . . and human goril-las should be closely questioned at our Gates." Two years later, he predicted that "we shall have bloody work in this country some of these days, when the lazy *canaille* get or-ganized."[1] In brief, the reaction of fastidious devotees of the Genteel Tradition against crudity not infrequently found ex-pression in crudity. The writings of Jacob Riis, Henry George, Edward Bellamy and others, exposing the ruthless exploitation of the downtrodden "Other Half," affected but little the in-tellectual conservatives.

Most of the books and volumes of poetry about the Negro that Northerners read were by Southerners: Mark Twain, George Washington Cable, Thomas Nelson Page, Joel Chand-ler Harris, Harry Stillwell Edwards, F. Hopkinson Smith, Grace King and Kate Chapin. With the exception of Cable, they developed—according to Professor Sterling Brown, the authoritative literary and historical critic—seven stereotypes: The Contented Slave, The Wretched Freedman, The Comic Negro, The Brute Negro, The Tragic Mulatto, The Local Color Negro and The Exotic Primitive. As he has observed, "All of these stereotypes are marked either by exaggeration or omission; they all agree in stressing the Negro's divergence from an Anglo-Saxon norm to the flattery of the latter." He pointed out that he should not "be accused of calling everything a stereotype that does not flatter Negro character, or of insisting that the stereotypes have no basis in reality. Few of the most apologistic of 'race' orators could deny the presence" of these seven stereotypes. But he rebelled against "the obvious unfairness of hardening racial character into fixed molds." Poems, except those by Walt Whitman, and most of the plays written during this period were cast in the same molds.[2]

I recognize that the stereotypes revealed in this first comprehensive analysis of Northern magazines and newspapers did exist, but I also believe that they gave an unbalanced picture of Negro life. Since they differ but little from the stereotypes found in books and plays, detailed analysis is reserved for Chapters Twelve and Thirteen. It will suffice here to indicate briefly the tone of two of the most popular writers. Thomas Nelson Page, the personification of the Plantation Tradition, as Aldrich was of the Genteel Tradition, called Moses in *Red Rock* (1898) "a hyena in a cage," "a reptile," "a species of worm," "a wild beast." Joel Chandler Harris, the famed exponent of friendship for the Negro, put these words into the mouth of Uncle Remus:

Hit's [education is] de ruinashun er dis country. . . . Put a spellin'-book in a nigger's han's, en right den en dar' you loozes a plow-hand. . . . What's a nigger gwineter 'larn outen books? I kin take a bar'l stave an' fling mo' sense inter a nigger in one minnit dan all de schoolhouses betwixt dis en de State er Midgigin. . . . Wid one bar'l stave I kin fa'rly lif' de vail er ignunce.

Non-conformists were almost completely overwhelmed. George Washington Cable, who deviated most from the stereotypes in *The Silent South* (1885), moved in the same year from Louisiana to Masachusetts, and thereby became almost as much of a "Dam-yankee" as was Albion W. Tourgee, whose *A Fool's Errand* (1879) has been called, with some exaggeration, "The Uncle Tom's Cabin of Reconstruction." Mark Twain was both a traditionalist and a non-conformist. *Huckleberry Finn* (1884), contains the classic devastating conversation between Huck and Aunt Sally after a steamboat blew out a cylinder head:

"Good gracious! anybody hurt?"

"No'm. Killed a nigger."

"Well, it's lucky because sometimes people do get hurt."

Sterling Brown believes that Jim in the same book "is the best example in nineteenth century fiction of the average Negro slave (not the tragic mulatto or the noble savage), illiterate, superstitious, yet clinging to his hope for freedom, to his love for his own." But in *Pudd'nhead Wilson* (1894) Twain reverted somewhat to the Page Plantation Tradition.[3] Charles Waddell Chesnutt, the first colored novelist of real merit and the first to have his books published by a prominent firm, had only short stories in magazines until 1899.[4]

On the stage also, Northerners saw, heard and laughed at familiar stereotypes, in such plays as *The White Slave*—which ran from 1882 to 1918—*Out of Bondage, Eph or the Slave's Devotion, Uncle Tom's Freedom*, and *Down on the Suwanee River*. Evidence is lacking that *My Old Southern Home*, 1900, which introduced a lynching scene, was produced. An extremely popular type of play developed the theme of reconciliation between the North and the South, cemented by a romance usually between a beautiful Southern girl and a dashing Union officer. The first important play employing this theme, *Held by the Enemy* by William Gillette, a Northerner, was produced in 1886—the year that Grady delivered his "New South" speech.

Minstrels, which were first introduced by black-faced white entertainers and later adopted by colored, became so popular that "Society" young women in Philadelphia put on such a show.[5] Consisting of dialogues between a "Center" and an "End Man," minstrels included also jokes, dances—especially the Cake-Walk—playing on the banjo, fiddle and guitar, and songs, among the most popular of which were "Old Black Joe" and "Carry Me Back to Ole Virginny." (It was not then known that the latter, Virginia's state song, was written and composed by a colored man, James P. Bland.) Occasionally a minstrel scene was included in a play as, for example, *Uncle Tom's Freedom*. A typical joke:

"Center: 'What did Uncle Abe mean by the sheep and the goats?'

"End: 'Dat paht of de document I intahpet dat he meant de goats for de mastahs, an' de sheep for de cullid man.'

"Center: 'I don't understand; explain.'

"End: 'Doan de cullid man wa'e de wool? He am, den, of de sheep fol', suah.'"

Edward Harrigan, author of the well-known Mulligan Cycle of plays, introduced what might be called The Bumptious Negro. The initiation song of the Society of the Full Moon urged:

> *In de by-laws of dis lodge*
> *You'll find dis rule right dere*
> *Don't you stand on de platform*
> *Of de one-horse bob-tailed car.*
> *Get in and grab a seat;*
> *Make white folks give you room*
> *Or—excommunication*
> *From de Third Degree Full Moon.*[6]

Negroes in the famous Currier and Ives prints of the period were also frequently in the minstrel tradition. Thomas Worth's "Darktown Comics" portrayed Negroes disporting themselves ludicrously in "Lawn Tennis at Darktown," "Wild West in Darktown," "The Darktown Fire Brigade," "The Darktown Yacht Club," and "The Darktown Hunt." They stood out in sharp contrast to the romantic joys of courtship, marriage and family life of genteel people, bucolic pleasures and frontier life.[7]

If the writings of three of the most eminent of the preachers of the Social Gospel—Washington Gladden and Lyman Abbott, Congregationalists, and Walter Rauschenbusch, a Baptist—are valid criteria, the Protestant church did little to alter prevailing attitudes toward the Negro. Originating in a group of Unitarian ministers in the 1820's, the Social Gospel has been defined as "the application of the teaching of Jesus and the total message of the Christian salvation to society, the economic life, and social institutions . . . as well as to individuals." In the period before the Civil War, the Social Gospel had embraced such reforms as prohibition, women's rights, prison reform, peace and the anti-slavery crusade. But after the war, the social impulse of Protestant Christianity concerned itself with the evils of the new industrial civilization that the war had helped to create. By 1900, according to the most authoritative interpreter of the Protestant Social Gospel, it had become "orthodox."[8] Although he did not examine the extent to which it was orthodox on the place of the Negro in American life, Protestant Christianity seems on this point to have conformed also to public opinion.

The foremost exponents of the Social Gospel manifested their orthodoxy both by their silence and by their statements. Gladden's astigmatism on a question vital to American democracy and Christianity is most evident in the essays which he brought together, in 1895, under the title *Ruling Ideas of the Present Age*. Although he discoursed at length upon practically every problem of American life, nowhere did he directly discuss the problem of the Negro after the Civil War. He insisted, for example, that the doctrine of the equality of rights, which sprang from the Christian doctrine of the Fatherhood of God, was well established. He recognized, vaguely, that the truth of the doctrine was not fully achieved in "our political and social life; vast injustices and inequalities are arrayed against it." In an essay on "Religion and Politics" in this volume he quoted the last two lines of a poem which read:

> My palace is the people's hall
> The ballot box my throne.

He also declared that the subordination of the citizen to laws should be as spontaneous as the franchise was free. His analysis of public opinion led him to point out that he had seen the mob spirit take possession of an ecclesiastical assembly, but he did not mention lynch mobs. Whether he intended to do so or not, he appeared to sanction white supremacy in the South when he asserted that it was absolutely essential that "the principle of local self-government be carefully cherished." The views of Gladden, Rauschenbusch and Abbott as voiced in magazine articles will be analyzed in Chapter Thirteen.

Social Darwinism contributed a more positive force than did the Social Gospel to the concept of the inferiority of the Negro. Applying Darwin's theories about the animal kingdom to man, the Social Darwinists compounded Gobineau's theories about the inferiority of races and Spencer's assertion of the "survival of the fittest" to prove the superiority of the white, especially the Teutonic and pre-eminently the Anglo-

Saxon, races. Richard Hofstadter's *Social Darwinism in American Thought, 1860–1915* reveals clearly the development of Spencer's social theories by their "most vigorous and influential American disciple," William Graham Sumner, professor of political and social science at Yale, 1872–1909. Hofstadter also shows the links between racism and imperialism, especially in the writings of Senator Albert T. Beveridge, Senator Henry Cabot Lodge, Secretary of State John Hay, Admiral Alfred T. Mahan, President Theodore Roosevelt and other advocates of the "Anglo-Saxon mystique," which for a brief period at the close of the century "became the rage among the upper classes." Among the laymen the most important were John Fiske, the famous historian, and Josiah Strong, whose book, *Our Country: Its Possible Future and Its Present Crisis,* was a great popular success.

Fiske's lecture on "Manifest Destiny," which was published in *Harper's* in 1885, was repeated more than twenty times in the United States, including the capital where he was presented to the Cabinet. Strong, who was resurrected by Hofstadter, might be termed a racist neo-Malthusian. Arguing that the unoccupied lands of the world were becoming crowded, and that population would soon be pressing upon subsistence in the United States as in Europe and Asia, Strong predicted:

> Then this race [the Anglo-Saxon] of unequaled energy, with all the majesty of numbers and the might of wealth behind it—will spread itself over the earth. If I read not amiss, this powerful race will move down upon Mexico, down upon Central and South America, out upon the islands of the seas, over upon Africa and beyond. And can anyone doubt that the result of this competition of races will be the "survival of the fittest"?[9]

But Strong, a Protestant clergyman, may also be classed among the Social Gospelers. Like them he was blind to the condition of Negroes in the United States, for he wrote in 1893:

> The meeting of many races here as nowhere else in the world, with equal rights before the law, with the educational, social, political and industrial opportunities open to

them, is peculiarly favorable to the eradication of race prejudice and the cultivation of a broad sympathy which must precede the coming of the brotherhood of man.

Sumner's racial views, like Strong's, were also ignored by Hofstadter. An examination of Sumner's writings prior to 1900 throws additional light on the effect of the new "science of sociology" in convincing American thought of the inherent inferiority of the Negro. As early as 1876 he advocated the restoration of home rule in the South. Whether or not a black man was the equal of a white man was not an essential question. Since the South considered the Negro to be inferior, the only practical question was how to deal with that opinion. Vigorously protesting the attempts on the part of Northerners to change it, he argued: "The Southern States have on their hands a race problem of the first magnitude; they will have all they can do to manage it, if they are left free under the natural social and economic laws." The Reconstruction laws proved the failure of what had happened "everywhere in history from coercive legislation enacted by one community against another." Repeatedly asserting that the doctrine of evolution, "instead of supporting the natural equality of man, would give a demonstration of their inequality," Sumner insisted in 1896 or 1897:

> Nothing is more certain . . . than that inequality is a law of life. . . . No two persons were ever born equal. They differ in physical characteristics and in mental capacity. . . . In fact no man ever yet asserted that "all men are equal," meaning what he said. Thus if you asked Thomas Jefferson, when he was writing the first paragraph of the Declaration of Independence, whether in "all men" he meant to include negroes, he would have said that he was not talking about negroes. Ask anyone who says it now whether he means to include foreigners—Russian Jews, Hungarians, Italians—he would draw his line somewhere. The laws of the United States draw it at the Chinamen.

In 1898, Sumner opposed the acquisition of territories from Spain because

> we must either hold them as inferior possessions to be ruled and exploited by us after the old colonial system, or

we must take them in on an equality with ourselves, where they will help to govern us and to corrupt a political system which they do not understand and in which they cannot participate. . . . Hayti has been independent for a century and has been a theater of revolution, tyranny, and bloodshed all the time.[10]

Thus, the simultaneous "failure" of the Reconstruction experiment to make ex-slaves and poor freedmen the equals of other American citizens, the emergence of Social Darwinism, and the scramble for Africa facilitated the acceptance, by the Northern mind, of the concept of the Negro's inherent inferiority. The conquest, at the end of the century, of territories inhabited by dark races placed the capstone upon that concept at the time when Northerners were content with the apparent solution of the race problem in the South. The "Lost Cause" had gained a notable victory in "the market place of free ideas" in the North.

Three excellent studies have included penetrating analyses of the American mind and thought during the last quarter of the nineteenth century. Professor Merle Curti devoted a considerable portion of *The Growth of American Thought* to this period. Professor Henry Steele Commager's *The American Mind* has for its subtitle: *An Interpretation of American Thought and Character Since the 1880's. The Road to Reunion*, by Paul Buck, won the Pulitzer Prize for his brilliant analysis of the social, economic and cultural forces that led to the reconciliation between the mind of the North and the mind of the South. But none of these scholars made, or could be expected to make, a detailed portrayal of the Negro in American mind and thought. One of them, Commager, arrived at a conclusion which is not borne out by the available evidence. He asserted that, "if popular practice failed to live up to the principles of the American Creed, it never repudiated them—not even where the Negro was involved."[11] The extent to which the American Creed was repudiated is revealed in the next four chapters.

TEN

National Issues in the Northern Press, 1877–1890

IT IS not surprising that Northern newspapers frequently repudiated the application to the Negro of the American Creed which stemmed from such libertarian antecedents as the Declaration of Independence, the Constitution of the United States and the Christian doctrine of the brotherhood of man. For the newspapers generally mirrored the views of Big Business, the principal engineer of the Compromise of 1877 and of the subsequent determination to leave the South alone. In the opinion of one historian of the period, "never before had newspaper owners been such creatures of the corporation financiers and the politicians who were being fed from the rich man's hand."[1]

Despite the dangers inherent in the sampling process, it is the only feasible method, since it would be well-nigh impossible to analyze all newspapers. Twelve papers were therefore selected for extensive analysis: the Boston *Evening Transcript*, the New Haven *Evening Register*, the New York *Times*, the Philadelphia *North American*, the Washington *Star*, the Cincinnati *Enquirer*, the Pittsburgh *Dispatch*, the Indianapolis *Journal*, the Detroit *Tribune* (*Post and Tribune*, October, 1877–July, 1884), the Chicago *Tribune*, the St. Louis *Globe-Democrat* and the San Francisco *Examiner*. Occasional excerpts from other papers expand this extensive geographical distribution. Southern papers were not investigated because they were assumed to support almost invariably the doctrine of white supremacy. This assumption is validated, at least in part, by the comprehensive examination of the Southern press at the time of Booker T. Washington's Atlanta address.

The *Evening Register, Enquirer, Dispatch* (until the mid-1890's) and the *Examiner* were staunchly Democratic, while the *Transcript, North American, Journal*, Detroit *Tribune* and Chicago *Tribune* were equally partisan in their support of Republicans. The *Times* was in turn Republican, Democratic from 1884 to 1896, and then again Republican. The *Star* and the *Globe-Democrat* tended to be independent with Republican leanings, but the latter had become definitely Republican by the campaign of 1896. Only two, the *Enquirer* and the *Examiner*, may be considered prototypes of "Yellow Journalism." Even George Hearst's *Examiner* began to be somewhat less sensational as San Francisco grew into a sophisticated city in the 1890's. About 1895 the *Enquirer* also toned down its lurid headlines and articles, perhaps as a result of the fact that John R. McLean had moved to Washington although he retained ownership.[2]

General approval by the press of Hayes's withdrawal of the troops from South Carolina and Louisiana has already been noted. Two years later, although evidence had begun to accrue that the president's "let-alone" policy was not a complete success, the Northern press, on the whole, wanted Negroes to remain in the South. With one exception, the twelve papers ignored, ridiculed or opposed the Exodus of 1878–1879 and Windom's proposal, February 7, 1879, to investigate the reasons therefor.

The *Transcript*, *Times*, *Star*, *Journal* and *Post and Tribune* did not during the month of February deem Windom's proposal worthy of comment. Three papers poked fun at it. For the *Evening Register* it was a "backyard" scheme, in the same category as reservations for Indians. The usually urbane *Globe-Democrat* jocularly asserted that the "hegira" of Negroes from the "naughty" Southern states would serve the Northwestern Territories right, "for they deserve a return for the swarm of locusts they have sent our way." Reviving one of the "jokes" of the Reconstruction era, the *Examiner* ridiculed the idea of "forty acres and a mule" for the migrants to Kansas. The San Francisco paper also reprinted the suggestion of the Baltimore *Gazette* that Windom induce Hayes to write a proclamation and distribute it throughout the South, "announcing that coons and possums are as plentiful as blackbirds in Minnesota and that sweet potatoes grow on sumac bushes. That will start the hegira."[3]

Only two papers, the *Times* and the Chicago *Tribune*, recognized that there might be valid reasons for the Exodus. But the former opposed wholesale and "indiscriminate" migration to the West since homes and labor might not be so plentiful as the migrants thought. Liberia would also be unsuitable because the Negroes, poor and unwanted, would be stranded in a strange land. On the other hand, when the Mobile *Register* condemned the " 'foolish hegira' " and warned that the Westerners would stamp out Negroes as they had Indians and Chinese, the *Times* observed that there was no comparison between Negroes and Indians, and that the migrants were not moving into sections where Chinese had lived. Needless to say, the *Times* did not suggest that some Negroes might migrate to New York.[4]

Nor did the Chicago *Tribune* suggest that Illinois would welcome them. Rarely missing an opportunity to remind its readers of the misdeeds of Southern Democrats, it pointed out that many persons believed that migration from the South was the true remedy for the "intimidation and violence" inflicted upon Negroes there. It condemned Douglass for urging them to stay in the South, buttressing its arguments by recalling that he had run away from slave territory, and by asserting that he had lived in the North for so long that he had lost touch with Negroes in the South. Migration would not only show the independence and enterprise of Negroes but would also teach Southerners the value of Negro labor. While Africa was not a suitable place, because of the climate there, a new look should be taken at ex-President Grant's proposal to annex the Dominican Republic as a place of refuge for the migrants.[5]

Three Democratic papers used the proposal and the migration to emphasize the generally accepted shortcomings of Negroes. Editorial comment in the *Enquirer*, although not entirely consistent, was subtly or openly anti-Negro. It generally opposed the Exodus on the grounds that it was unfair to the Negro who would encounter prejudice in the North, unfair to the productive interests of the South and to laborers in the North. It also labeled the migration a "damnable scheme," since, it alleged, one of its purposes was to create a Republican majority in Ohio and Indiana in 1880. On the other hand, the Cincinnati paper could not forego the opportunity of asserting that the Negro in the South would for a long time be a hewer of wood and a drawer of water, and suffer disabilities that were calculated to suppress his ambition, if he had any. It might be well, therefore, to see whether Negroes would show more ambition in states inhabited solely by Negroes. But the *Examiner* expressed the conviction that, if Negroes settled in a separate territory, they would soon lapse into a condition little better than barbarism. It was consequently better for them to remain in contact with whites so that they could be educated and protected and put on the path of progressive development. In those states where Negroes had escaped from the "debasing" influence of the carpetbagger, they were doing as well as one might reasonably expect. In similar vein the *Dispatch* contended that Negroes needed the guiding hand of whites in order to progress. Only the *North American*, published in the City of Brotherly Love, extended the hospitality of the state in which the paper was published to all comers, Europeans, Confederates, freedmen or Chinese without molestation.[6]

With the exceptions of the withdrawal of the troops from South Carolina and Louisiana, and the defeat of the Blair bill for federal aid to public education, the papers surveyed and two other New York papers revealed a closer approach to unanimity on the Civil Rights decision than on any other issue. Foremost among their reasons for opposing the Civil Rights law was the assertion of the principle which William Graham Sumner was already advocating and which he was later to popularize in the dictum, "Stateways cannot change folkways." The *Evening Register*—published in the city where Sumner taught—believed, for example, that there was a "grave doubt if the question of social principles can be settled satisfactorily by legislation." The same opinion was expressed in similar language by the *Times, Enquirer*, Chicago *Tribune, Dispatch* and New York *World*. Hence, in the opinion of the *Enquirer*, public opinion and the force of circumstances would accomplish more than legislation. The *Dispatch* and the *World* advised Negroes to exercise patience, forbearance, and the proper use of their citizenship. The Chicago *Tribune* and the *Enquirer* further insisted that the Civil Rights law had not resulted in any real benefits for the colored people, and the *Enquirer* gave the assurance that the issue was not a grave one anyway. The most extreme assertion of the Sumner thesis was expressed, rather surprisingly, by the *North American*; it declared that it had come to be understood that the difference which nature had made between the two races could not be nullified by any intervention of the law-making power. Only the *Star* cast doubt upon the validity of the thesis by quoting the satisfaction of the district attorney of Washington that, during his four years of office, there had been practically no cases of denial of public accommodations to colored people.[7]

Four papers raised the question of state rights. The *Enquirer* asserted that much had been said in the decision that would serve to limit the powers of states to pass such a "silly and wicked [civil rights] law." On the other hand, the *Transcript* and *Evening Register* declared that the Court had rightly left the problem to the states. The *Journal* concluded that the only way for Negroes to secure relief was through a constitutional amendment empowering Congress and the states to pass civil rights laws.[8] In reality, without benefit of an amendment to the federal Constitution, fifteen states passed new civil rights laws, and three strengthened already existing provisions.

The political implications of the decision were naturally not overlooked. The *Transcript* pointed out that, although the Supreme Court had been frequently criticized as a "Republican Court," it had not hesitated to give an "impartial" decision on a law passed by a Republican Congress. While the *Enquirer* also approved the decision, it perversely gibed at the "Republican Court." The *Examiner*, which considered the decision largely in political terms, warned that the decision had caused consternation among Negroes in San Francisco and elsewhere on the Pacific Coast. Bishop Alexander Walters of the African Methodist Episcopal Zion Church and P. A. Bell, the veteran colored editor of the *Elevator*, were quoted as saying that the decision would be disastrous to the Republican party. Two of the most prominent colored Republicans, Douglass and ex-Senator Bruce, also roundly denounced the decision. But John F. Cook, another well-known colored resident of the capital, believed that public sentiment would not be any more antagonistic to Negroes than before.[9]

Although the daily press almost unanimously approved the decision, opinion was divided as to its effect on future agitation. The *Journal* felt that the question had nearly adjusted itself and regretted that it had been reopened. The New York *Truth* was happy that the decision would put the quietus on the " 'fanatical' " legislation by which Congress sought to give colored people equal rights in public places. New York had a civil rights law, but it could be easily circumvented. Both the Democratic *Enquirer* and the Republican Chicago *Tribune* rejoiced that Negroes no longer enjoyed "superior rights." On the other hand, the *North American* feared that the territories and the District of Columbia "must still bow the knee to the supremacy of the negro" in public places, even when a white man could be refused. Although the *Globe-Democrat* stated that most people had grown tired of the race question, the St. Louis paper suggested that the denial of accommodations by hotels and theaters would probably result in renewed agitation "on the color line" both within states and as a national question.[10]

Of the papers surveyed, the Detroit *Post and Tribune* was the only one that supported Justice Harlan's dissenting opinion. The editor believed, as Harlan did, that the Civil Rights law "does express what the people of the United States desired and attempted to establish and thought they had established."[11] It might be noted that Detroit's Negro population was relatively small at that time.

The Civil Rights decision, and the attitude of most of the Northern press toward it, probably encouraged Southern leaders to believe that they had accomplished their mission of convincing the North that the South should be allowed to work out its own race problem. But the bitter criticism of the decision by many prominent Negroes, their support of Cleveland in 1884, and his election led many Republican politicians to the conclusion that their future control of the government could not be assured without the electoral votes of some of the Southern states. When, however, these Republican politicians urged a revival of "bloody shirt" tactics and federal supervision of federal elections to protect the Negro vote, Northern businessmen, especially those who had investments in the South, became uneasy, lest the economic rehabilitation of the South be retarded if the Negro question were reopened. Some of these businessmen, therefore, obtained an invitation for Henry W. Grady, one of the editors of the Atlanta *Constitution*, to deliver an oration on "The New South" at the annual dinner of the New England Society, in New York on December 22, 1886.

Neither the title nor the theme of this address was new. It had captioned a series of articles in *Harper's* beginning January, 1874, and an article that Grady had written in the Atlanta *Daily Herald* on March 14 of the same year. When Hayes ordered the withdrawal of the troops, the Atlanta *Constitution*—for which Grady had become an editorial writer—used the title to applaud the president's policy as one that would "invite and promote reconciliation." Moreover, practically every idea that Grady expounded in 1886 had been expressed by Benjamin H. Hill (later senator from Georgia) in his address before the Young Men's Democratic Union of New York, in 1868. Many other prominent Southerners, notably Representative L. Q. C. Lamar in 1874, Wade Hampton at Auburn, New York in 1877, and Senator John B. Gordon of Georgia before the Commercial Club of Boston in 1878, had reiterated the basic ideas.[12]

But Grady spoke his piece with an eloquence that his predecessors had not possessed, and at a time that was more propitious for his plea. He rang the changes on Abraham Lincoln, on the "chivalric grace and strength" of the South, and the return of the "footsore Confederate soldier." He reiterated the South's desire to let the issues of the war be looked upon as permanently settled and to begin a new era of peace and prosperity. He gave a fulsome description of the New South that

> challenged your spinners in Massachusetts and your iron-makers in Pennsylvania. . . . We have learned that one northern immigrant is worth fifty foreigners, and have smoothed the path to southward, wiped out the place where Mason and Dixon's line used to be and hung out our latch-string to you and yours. . . . Never was nobler duty confined to human hands than the uplifting and up-building of the prostrate and bleeding South, misguided, perhaps, but beautiful in her suffering, brave and generous always.

Grady then asked whether the South had progressed "in honor and equity" toward the solution of the Negro problem. The record would speak for itself, for no section showed a more prosperous laboring population than the Negroes of the South; no laboring class revealed more sympathy with the employing and landowning class. The Negro shared in the school fund, he had the "fullest protection" of laws and the friendship of the Southern people. The orator made a joke about the North's selling slaves, repeated the time-worn story of the faithful slave in the South while his masters were fighting the Civil War, and then made his plea that the South be allowed to handle its own race problem. But he first warned that legislation could carry the Negro only as far as liberty and enfranchisement. The rest must be left to conscience and common sense.

> It should be left to those among whom his lot is cast, with whom he is indissolubly connected and whose prosperity depends upon their possessing his intelligent sympathy and confidence. Faith has been kept with him in spite of calumnious assertions to the contrary by those who assume to speak for us or by frank opponents. Faith will be kept with him in the future, if the South holds her reason and integrity. [Applause]

In addition to these warnings, pleas and cajolery, Grady gilded the lily: "The new South presents a perfect Democracy, the oligarchs leading in the popular movement." He painted a glorious picture of the New South, declared that the "late struggle between the States was war and not rebellion," and waxed eloquent on "the indissoluble union of American states and the imperishable brotherhood of the American people." Would New England "permit the prejudice of war to remain in the hearts of the conquered? [Cries of 'No! No!']" If not, then the prophecy of Webster forty years ago before that same Society would be fulfilled when he had proclaimed: "'Standing hand to hand and clasping hands, we should remain united as we have been for sixty years, citizens of the same country, members of the same government, united, all united now and united forever.'"

To be sure, the speech in print cannot possibly reveal the fire and eloquence and, in the opinion of many contemporaries, the sincerity of the orator. Grady was frequently interrupted by applause. When he sat down, he was given a rising ovation, and the band played "'Way Down South in Dixie."[13] Most readers of the speech today, since we are far removed from the bitterness of that period, are likely to agree with Paul Buck's conclusion that "the content of his speech was a bundle of platitudes made trite by endless repetition."

Grady's speech ranks none the less—along with that of Booker T. Washington at Atlanta, which borrowed freely from it—as one of the most effective political speeches of this period. Its appeal was due not only to his eloquence but, in a large measure as was Washington's, to the simple fact that Grady said what a large and influential audience wanted to hear. In 1886, most Northerners were infernally tired of hearing about the Negro question, and business with the South was booming. Among the powerful businessmen whose names appear in the list of guests were J. Pierpont Morgan, H. M. Flagler, Cornelius N. Bliss, H. H. Rogers, Russell Sage, John H. Inman, Hugh D. Auchincloss, Edgar S. Auchincloss and Charles L. Tiffany. Others among the 240 listed guests who exercised great influence on American thought were Elihu Root, Generals Sherman and Schofield, Myles Standish, Lyman Abbott, F. Hopkinson Smith, Richard Watson Gilder, editor of *Century Magazine*, and Charles R. Miller, editor of the New York *Times*.[14] With one or two exceptions, perhaps, these distinguished and influential Northerners represented the attitudes and power that had effected the Compromise of 1877, and that were to help pave the way for the steady deterioration of the Negro's status.

Grady's speech received more attention in the press than did practically any other address at that time by a man not holding high public office, but it was not greeted with the thunderous acclaim that one would imagine in the light of its later fame. All or most of it was published in the *Times*, the *World* and New York *Daily Tribune* on December 23, the day after it was delivered; in the *Transcript* on the next day and in the *Enquirer* on Christmas day. By the end of the year the *Globe-Democrat*, *Journal*, *Evening Register* and Chicago *Tribune* had also published the text as it had appeared in the New York papers. Brief excerpts were included in a *Star* editorial on December 24. The other four papers did not publish even excerpts, and one of them, the far-distant *Examiner*, carried no editorial comment. The *Journal's* only editorial notice was the gibe, on December 28: "Southern people know how to treat their editors when the latter have returned home safely after long and perilous journeys." In the *Dispatch* the only editorial comment stated that the boom to make Grady Vice-President came from the fact that he had made a "fine speech" in New York. By the end of the year, however, all the other papers expressed editorial opinions, some of them quite lengthy. It is probable that the death, on December 26, of Senator John A. Logan, Union Civil War hero and past Commander-in-Chief of the Grand

Army of the Republic, delayed and limited the amount of space devoted to "the speech of the year." Until the end of the year, pages in the larger papers and columns in the smaller contained long obituaries, eulogies from prominent citizens, the state of Mrs. Logan's health, her precarious financial situation and arrangements for the funeral.[15]

Of the nine papers that commented editorially on Grady's speech, three endorsed its substance enthusiastically and two somewhat equivocally; one reproduced both favorable and unfavorable comment from other papers; three severely criticized it.

No paper "raved" about the speech as much as did the *Times* whose editor, Charles R. Miller, attended the banquet. On the day after the speech, when Miller was still under the spell of Grady's eloquence and the great ovation he had received, both the news article and an editorial heaped fulsome praise upon the editor of the *Constitution*. A long news article assured that "no postprandial oration of any recent occasion has aroused such enthusiasm in this city. . . . It was the matter, however, more than the manner of his speech that told with his audience." The editorial added that "it was an 'American' speech in the sense that those magnetic statesmen who boast of being American to their finger tips can never equal though they have the days of METHUSALEH." But the *Times*, until the end of the year, did not offer a sober evaluation of the speech. In fact, the only other references to Grady were two brief items about the enthusiastic reception given him on his return to Atlanta and the short-lived boom to nominate him as Vice-President.[16]

Since the *Enquirer* rarely had long editorials, the brevity of its comment on "New North—New South" was not unusual. It is significant, however, that comment on Grady appeared below a paragraph about William D. ("Pig-Iron") Kelley of Pennsylsvania who was also extolling the glories of the New South. Grady's speech gave evidence that "a new generation have arisen who have turned their faces to the future, and are yearning and struggling and working for all that lifts up and elevates American manhood and tends to perpetuate American institutions."[17]

The *Transcript* went further than any other paper in emphasizing the theme of Northern friendship for the South. The Boston paper was particularly concerned lest many

Southerners labor under the same misapprehension as Grady apparently did, namely, that the "best political classes" in New England were hostile to the South. Its editor, on December 24, assured the South that the "beating of war-drums and making threatening faces at the South is only campaigning buncombe, and that the best and most intelligent sentiment in New England wants no more of it." He reiterated this assurance in an editorial three days later. In order to buttress Grady's rosy picture, the *Transcript* added below the first editorial a paragraph calling attention to the fact that the Judiciary Committee of the South Carolina House of Representatives had adversely reported a bill passed by their senate which was "intended to manacle colored labor." In further support of its editorial position, the *Transcript*, on December 24, quoted a sentence from the influential Springfield *Republican*: " 'New England rejoices in the New South most heartily.' "[18]

But the *North American* and the *Star* were doubtful as to the extent of the support that Grady had in the South. The Philadelphia paper declared that he represented only a fraction. Conditions which had prevailed there after the Civil War and which still dominated would not "be tolerated by men who build up nations." But so soon as the South found "pluck and common sense enough to send its old traditions to the limbo . . . , so soon will the new south appear clad in all the panoply which has made the north an irresistible force, and weld the nation into a solid phalanx." While the *Star* was somewhat more optimistic than the *North American*, it also may have been unconvinced. Recognizing that there were doubtless many "unprogressive" men in the South who would not echo Grady's warm assurances of fraternity at a Northern gathering, its editorial on December 24 was sure that they were "like poor imbeciles who would try to stop a railway train by pulling at the rear car." Although these "imbeciles" might never be converted, Grady had the consolation that their posterity would be, a point that was much more important. Still looking to the future, the *Star* declared, deadpan, that Grady "drew with brilliant phrases a picture of a rich oligarchy, with negro slavery as a foundation, merging into a democracy with free labor, universal education and political equality as bases."[19]

Less enthusiastic than its two New England neighbors, the

Transcript and the Springfield *Republican*, the New Haven *Evening Register* on December 27 criticized the *Palladium* of the same city for ridiculing "the eloquent speech that has been the talk of the country." On the next day the *Evening Register* carried an excerpt from the Richmond (Virginia) *State* which praised Grady. But a week after the address an editorial paragraph reprinted from the Boston *Herald* the rather oblique compliment that Grady was equally at home "'in the editorial chair, making a commencement oration, pronouncing a funeral panegyric, rousing a political convention to enthusiasm, or making a witty postprandial speech.'"[20]

The three Midwestern papers—two of them robustly Republican and one independent with Republican leanings—joined in the chorus of praise for the eloquence and sincerity of the speaker. They rejected, however, the validity of Grady's "honor and equity" thesis. The Detroit *Tribune* pointed out that "bragging" about the New South showed that there had been "a flaw or two" in the Old South. When the New South would have proved by its deeds that the prejudice of war had died in its hearts, the North would applaud the New South as joyfully as the members of the New England Society had applauded Grady's speech. The North had been praying for the "abolition of the shotgun at the polls, the suppression of election frauds, the bulldozer and intimidator of the colored vote." Accepting in good faith what Grady had said, the editors insisted that, so long as fraudulent elections like that of Elliott over Smalls in South Carolina continued, they would have to believe that the prejudice of war remained in the hearts of some Southerners. Likewise, the editors of the Chicago *Tribune* felt constrained to doubt Grady, since they remembered "the bulldozing of Negroes in Louisiana, their horrible and murderous treatment in Mississippi and Virginia, their disfranchisement in the Gulf States and their industrial oppression in the Carolinas that is driving them out of those States by the thousands."[21]

The most comprehensive rebuttal of Grady appeared in the *Globe-Democrat* which waited until December 31 before devoting an editorial to his speech. However gratifying it would be if what Grady had said were true, there was overwhelming evidence to the contrary. The South had virtually suppressed the entire colored vote in order to insure and perpetuate Democratic rule. By a systematic course of "fraud and violence," the South had so thoroughly destroyed the idea of free speech that as a rule only Democratic candidates ran for office. There was a New South in the sense that, whereas there used to be two parties and fair contests between them, there was now only one party. The free Negro counted for more than he had as a slave, largely because he had increased Southern representation in the House of Representatives and in the electoral college. Statistics showed that the average yearly wage paid to colored laborers did not exceed $100,

> and in every Southern state there are statutes under which persons may be easily deprived of all their rights and condemned to a form of service which lacks only the lash of the overseer to make it as bad as their situation was when they were merely pieces of property in the hands of the whites. Facts like these go far toward spoiling pretty speeches like that of Mr. Grady; and so long as they exist it will be hard to convince the North that the miracle of a new South has truly come to pass.[22]

A number of incidents, reported in various papers immediately before and after Grady's speech, supported the criticisms voiced by the three Midwestern papers. Even though the Judiciary Committee of the South Carolina House of Representatives had adversely reported a bill making it a penal offense for Negroes to join labor organizations, several hundred Negroes had left the state for Arkansas, Texas and California. An even larger number would probably leave in the spring because, they said, "landlords under the law absorbed the proceeds of black labor," and colored voters were virtually disfranchised. Negro sharecroppers in Lincoln County, Georgia, were reported as being in armed revolt. Because of ill-treatment on farms in the Black Belt of Alabama, many were leaving for the mines in the northern part of the state. Others were leaving the state in such large numbers that planters were accused of using force to drive away emigration agents. Colored passengers had proclaimed a boycott of railroads in Florida because they had to pay first-class fare for worse than second-class accommodations. The protests charged "that young white men passed through the colored cars cursing and drinking, regardless of the presence of females; that no matter how well dressed or behaved a colored woman might be, she was recipient of treatment which the offenders would not dare to offer to a white woman." Frequent references were made to the defeat by "fraud and violence" of Robert Smalls, colored candidate for re-election in the Seventh Congressional district of South Carolina. A whole family of Negroes had been assassinated in Attala County, Mississippi; two colored men had been lynched near Vicksburg by a mob of white and colored men; a man and his wife at Kosciusko, Louisiana. An attempted lynching had been averted at Cynthis, Kentucky by a courageous jailer. During the same period, it is true, a white man was lynched in Eaton, Ohio, and two young white men poured turpentine over a colored porter employed in a saloon in Cairo, Illinois, struck a match and burned him to death.[23] Neither the "New North" nor the "New South" was free from violence inflicted upon Negroes. Since nine-tenths of the entire colored population lived in the Southern states, it is understandable that there were more acts of violence there. Whatever the reasons may be, and however guilty the North may have been of also violating the principles of American democracy, the New South of 1886 did not offer the bright prospects for Negroes portrayed by Grady. But only three of these newspapers questioned the validity of his thesis.

The fame of Grady's speech has obscured other evidence of the North's interest in strengthening business ties with the South—an interest that would have been jeopardized by the intrusion of extraneous issues. There was no danger of civil war in 1886, as there had been a decade earlier. But there was threat of the revival of "bloody shirt" tactics. The Northern press revealed clearly its interest in promoting a renewal of efforts by forces similar to those that had effected the Compromise of 1876–1877. Foremost among them was William D. Kelley. In some respects, his testimony was more important than Grady's, for Kelley had spent ten years after a Southern visit in 1867 waving the "bloody shirt." In 1886, however, he extolled the industrial resources of the South and the progress of colored workers, especially those in Chattanooga who lived in "neat, commodious and well-painted homes," and who had proved their skills in mining, smelting and mechanical pursuits. These views, which appeared in an article in the influential Baltimore *Manufacturer's Record* for December 25, 1886, won approval in editorials and long excerpts beginning with December 23.[24]

Even more significant perhaps was the presence in New York, at the time of Grady's speech, of several prominent Southern and Northern businessmen engaged in developing the coal and iron industries of the South. A long article, "The Southern Iron Trade," which appeared originally in the New York *Daily Tribune* on December 20, and which was reprinted three days later in the *Globe-Democrat* under the caption, "The New South," adds to C. Vann Woodward's array of evidence demonstrating that in the 1880's, business ties were being further strengthened between the North and the South.[25] The article began:

> The leading coal and iron men of the South, who have been in this city during the last ten days, will go home to spend the Christmas holidays, thoroughly satisfied with the business of the year, and more than hopeful for the future. And they have good reason to be. The time for which they have been waiting for nearly twenty years, when Northern capitalists would be convinced not only of the safety but of the immense profits to be gained from the investment of their money in developing the fabulously rich coal and iron resources of Alabama, Tennessee and Georgia, has come at last.

Among those who had been present in New York were General Willard Warner, president of the Tecumseh, Alabama, Iron Company; A. M. Shook of Tracy City, Tennessee, manager of the Tennessee Coal, Iron and Railroad Company; Professor J. B. Killebrew, secretary of the Alabama and Tennessee Coal and Iron Company and formerly state geologist of Tennessee; a "Mr. Parish" of Philadelphia, who was also largely interested in the development of coal and iron properties in the old Southwest. They all verified the glowing accounts that had been given by Kelley—there was no reference to Grady. More than a column was devoted to portraying the wealth of Southern resources. John H. Inman of New York, who had attended the New England dinner, had been interested in the region since 1882. "He had this year invested more than $1,000,000 in iron and coal properties there." Samuel Thomas, the "great iron-master" of Pennsylvania and president of the Thomas Iron Company, "has large iron and coal properties near Birmingham, and he is now preparing to build one, and probably two, large furnaces there."

General Warner was originally from Ohio, but, by virtue of twenty-five years' residence in Alabama and identification with Southern interests, was really a Southerner. All these men "agree in testifying to the pleasant relations existing between all classes of men, without regard to nativity, war or politics." A candidly revealing statement added: "These gentlemen are all pronounced protectionists, and agree practically on political questions, though called by different party names, and their union of opinion foreshadows the fast-coming union of all patriotic and progressive men in the South against the Bourbons and scoundrels of both political parties."[26]

An editorial in the *Globe-Democrat*, December 29, under the headline, "Industries Moving Southward," reported that John S. Perry, "the great stove manufacturer," was going to remove part if not all of his works from Albany, New York, to Alabama. The intolerance that had once stood in the way of Northern investments—especially in the "inexhaustible" coal and iron deposits of the South—was diminishing, as was

> evinced by the increase in the Republican vote and the decrease in the number of outrages on Republicans in certain sections of the South. It is true that a great deal of the proscriptive spirit still exists and probably will exist until the generation which were adults at the beginning of the war die. But a beginning has been made in uprooting it, and the good work will be actively prosecuted.[27]

This editorial, let it be noted, appeared two days before the most incisive attack of any of the papers on Grady's "honor and equity" thesis.

Further evidence of business opportunities in the South appeared in the Northern press during the last ten days of 1886. A headline of the *Globe-Democrat* boasted: "The Southern Giant—Alabama Defies the World of Manufactures." Steel manufacturers in Pittsburgh were undoubtedly excited by the news in the *Dispatch*: "Iron in Tennessee—Magnetic Ore Discovered that Will Make Fine Bessemer Steel"; "Iron in the South—Furnaces with Tremendous Capacity in Alabama, Tennessee and Georgia." The latter article was based upon one that had just appeared in *Bradstreet's*. For the speculative-minded there was attraction in a special dispatch from Pittsburgh to the Chicago *Tribune*, announcing that a Pittsburgh oil expert, just returned from Tennessee, spoke in glowing terms of the discovery of oil wells there. "Northern capital was flowing into Tennessee at a rate that astonishes the natives." Of course, the *Journal*, in an article reprinted from the Philadelphia *Press*, took pleasure in assuring the South that its progress would be even greater if it adopted the principles of tariff protection of the Republican party. Most revealing is an editorial in the *Examiner* (which made no reference to Grady until the end of the year) on December 23: "The forces that have been silently working for the rehabilitation of the Southern States are now manifest. . . . Just now the 'late rebel states' are attracting their full share of attention from capitalists, politicians and men of letters. . . . The days of sectional lines are past and can never be revived again."[28]

Grady won great popular success and enduring fame. It is probable, however, that it was less his eloquence than the "inexhaustible resources" of the South and the increasing investments of Northern capital in them that interested the hard-headed businessmen who controlled the Northern press. Grady's promises of fair treatment of the Negro was just about all they needed to leave the South alone, in 1887 as in 1877. Harrison's inaugural address becomes understandable in the light of this analysis. It was, so to speak, the response of the "New North" to the "New South."

During this second honeymoon period, the attempts of a few colored passengers to use the Interstate Commerce Law as a means of securing equal, though separate, railroad accommodations received little encouragement from the Northern press. The *Times* and *Enquirer* did not report any of the three rulings of the Interstate Commerce Commission, 1887, 1888 and 1889, that upheld the doctrine. The Chicago *Tribune* reported only the first and the Detroit *Tribune*, the first and third. The other papers carried items, usually brief, as a part of the general summaries of the ICC rulings. They all stressed the fact that Negroes were to be separated but that the accommodations should be equal. In the climate of Northern opinion at that time, occupancy of the same coaches by white and colored passengers was not likely to be approved. But only the *Transcript*, after the third ruling, began to express skepticism as to the effectiveness of the rulings in obtaining equal though separate accommodations.[29]

Harrison's disillusionment did not last as long as had

Hayes's. In his first annual message he referred to the violation in the South of the Negroes' right to vote. Almost immediately several Southern senators introduced resolutions for the migration, emigration or expulsion of Negroes. The senators probably saw in the proposed departure of a considerable number one answer to their participation in politics.

Senator Call of Florida wanted the United States to annex Cuba and set up a Negro republic there. Gibson of Louisiana urged that territory in the United States be set aside, and Morgan of Alabama favored the emigration of the "better class" of colored people to Africa. Still another proposal called for a protectorate over Haiti. Participants in the debates on these proposals repeated substantially the same arguments as those advanced at the time of Senator Butler's resolution. The discussion in the Northern press reveals little inclination to ease the burden of the Southern states by encouraging Negro migration to their states and little cooling off of the warmth of the honeymoon on the eve of the crisis of 1890–1891.

The *Transcript, Star, Enquirer* and *Examiner* merely ridiculed one or more of the proposals. There was a mild note of criticism in the headline of the Detroit *Tribune's* news article, "Want to Exile the Negro," but no editorial comment. The opposition of the *Journal* implicitly approved the thesis of the New South, for it insisted that Negro labor was needed there to build up its resources and to permit Negroes to establish "there what they had never had, a true civilization." The *North American* insisted that "the negro citizen is just as much an American as any Southern Senator and has just as much right to live wherever he pleases." The Chicago *Tribune*, as usual, denounced the treatment of Negroes in the South which desired their labor but not their suffrage. Negroes would, therefore, not object to migration since they realized that their situation in the South was hopeless. The paper consequently warmly supported the suggestion for the establishment of a United States protectorate over Haiti where whites could direct enterprises that would require American Negro labor. The *Tribune* was even more enthusiastic about the construction of a railroad in the Congo, where the climate was "well adapted" to the Negro's constitution. But there was little inducement for Negroes to come to the "Windy City" or the neighboring plains in the admonition:

A great migration of negroes from the Sunny South to the Northern land of ice, snow and blizzards would surely lead to sore distress. The instinct which has kept the Afro-Americans in the South has been kinder to them than mistaken philanthropists would be if they could carry out their plans for an exodus to the North.[30]

Thus, despite habitual criticism of the South's treatment of the Negro, the *Tribune* preferred for him to remain there rather than to come to the North. To this extent even the *Tribune* endorsed the thesis of the "New South."

The fullest endorsement was given by the *Times*. It insisted that Northerners did not understand the Negro question in the South, and that decent and sensible men in any community should not be called upon to submit to the kind of government that had been imposed upon South Carolina during Reconstruction. Loss of representation in Congress would be a smaller "calamity" than permitting Negroes to elect officials of their own race in districts where they outnumbered whites. It was idle to discuss whether the inferiority of the Negro was ineradicable and a matter of race, or whether it could be eradicated in one generation. To the people of that generation it was clear that the desire of Europeans and even Asiatics (the term did not have the derogatory connotation that it has had in recent years) to better their condition could be counted upon; but this betterment in the case of the mass of Negroes was not to be counted upon, "as educated and exceptional representatives of that race are free to admit." Haiti was cited as an example of the inability of the Negro to progress when left to himself. The *Times* revealed perhaps its basic fear when it stated bluntly that the Northern and Western states did not desire Negro migrants. Colonization abroad was, therefore, more "promising."[31]

Only two papers attributed the proposals of the Southern senators to fear that the new administration was about to reopen the question of the violation of the suffrage rights of Southern Negroes. The *Globe-Democrat* pointed out that Southern Negroes would not consent to be colonized, and that Southern whites were not so desirous of getting rid of their cheap labor as the Southern senators seemed to believe. Even South Carolina had expelled agents seeking to recruit Negro labor for other states. The St. Louis paper went so far as to assert that Negroes constituted the only reliable and adequate labor element in the South. Speeches by Southern senators in favor of colonization were merely for political effect; they sought to divert attention from "the shameful wrongs which are being perpetrated upon negro citizens and laborers." It was to the South's political advantage to make it appear that it was carrying a burden which it would gladly dispense with. "They think to create sympathy and avert unpleasant Federal legislation by pretending that the negro is a curse and a sorrow," the *Globe-Democrat* concluded.[32]

The *Dispatch* was equally severe in its condemnation of the treatment of Negroes in the South, and even more pointed in its interpretation of the motives of the Southern senators. In what was perhaps the most perspicacious comment of all the papers examined, the *Dispatch* warned:

> The South should rather be on its good behavior, seeing that the majority party in Congress is contemplating a reopening of the "race problem," and possibly a readjustment of the election laws. There is no telling how serious the situation may become if the relations of the white and black population in the South are further strained.[33]

National Issues in the Northern
Press, 1890–1901

THE decade that began with 1890 marked the greatest victories that the South won since the Compromise of 1877. The Blair bill for federal aid to public education and the Lodge bill for the federal supervision of federal elections were defeated, 1890–1891. Mississippi, South Carolina, Louisiana and North Carolina, in flagrant violation of the law which had "readmitted" them to the Union, amended their constitutions so as to disfranchise most Negroes and permit even unqualified whites to vote. The United States Supreme Court made it more difficult than it previously had been for Negroes to prove that failure to call them for jury service violated the equal protection clause in the Fourteenth Amendment. With only one dissenting vote, the highest tribunal, in 1896, invoked the principle of police powers to give sanction to the doctrine of "separate but equal accommodations"—although it was generally known that rarely if ever were the accommodations, especially in the South, equal. Cleveland virtually ignored the Negro question; the Republican party and McKinley revealed their lack of concern for Negroes by planks and official utterances that were at variance with the truth. The Populist Revolt and Fusion caused a revival of Southern demagoguery that in some instances won for "poor whites" the political power previously exercised by the more urbane "Bourbons." One hundred Americans, most of them Negroes living in the South, were lynched annually, but it was left to the last Negro in Congress to introduce the first resolution for a federal anti-lynching law. His retirement from Congress, in 1901, was hailed with public thanksgiving in his own state. Many others probably interpreted it as the end à tout jamais of Reconstruction. A new Negro "leader" had received national acclaim and international fame for his Atlanta Compromise which renounced "social equality," accepted at least temporarily a subordinate role in politics and promised by clear implication that Negroes would not engage in "strikes and labor wars." In return he counted upon a great expansion in industrial education to prepare Negroes for the jobs which their Southern friends would give them.

The expansion of educational facilities, however, had to be left to private philanthropy—largely Northern—and to the still relatively impoverished Southern states. For in 1890, the Senate rejected the Blair bill to provide federal aid to public education. During the debates several Southern senators admitted the inability of the Southern states to provide an adequate public school system for the children of either race. Despite venomous attacks upon the bill by other Southern senators, eight voted for the bill. But enough Northern senators joined Western silverites and a majority of the Southerners to defeat it. With one exception, the Northern press, regardless of party, opposed the bill strenuously, and most of them openly rejoiced over its defeat.

The newspapers manifested but little interest in the benefits that would accrue to colored children or even to white children. Most of the discussion repeated the objections made during the debate in the Senate. The measure would be a drain on the surplus in the Treasury; it was impracticable, novel. It was opposed by many "good men" of both the North and the South; it delayed consideration of matters that were much more urgent. Only the *Transcript* gave the bill strong support as an enlightened method of lifting all the Southern people to a higher level of education, and there is some indication that the Boston paper's attitude was determined in part at least by the opposition to the bill by advocates of parochial schools. Almost as an afterthought the Chicago *Tribune* pointed out that there was no provision in the bill which obligated Southern state governments to devote any of the money to the education of colored children.[1]

What is most striking is not the arguments advanced by practically all the papers but the abuse hurled at Blair and his bill. The senator was a "crank"; his bill was "quixotic," "preposterous," a "nuisance." But Blair would be forgiven for everything if, in the language of the *Dispatch*, he would take out his dead bill and give it a decent burial. While opposing cloture in principle, the *Enquirer* contended that a few "more doses" like the Blair bill might make a rule necessary. Most vituperative was the Republican warhorse, the Chicago *Tribune*, which characterized the bill as Blair's "Humbug Bill" to "demoralize self-reliance and self-help in the South." The "anti-self-help" bill was one of the "most mischievous measures ever presented to Congress."[2]

Herein lies perhaps one explanation for the well-nigh unanimous rejoicing over the defeat of the bill, and the harsh tone —especially on the part of papers that occasionally defended the interests of the colored people. Even if the editors had considered the bill unconstitutional—a point that was only broached; or even a novel experiment—which it was to only a limited degree; or an undue strain on the Treasury—which it clearly was not, these objections could hardly have provoked such great rejoicing and such strong abuse. Indeed, even the delaying of other important measures could have been criticized in more temperate terms. A deep-seated, though not always openly expressed, opposition to a nebulous concept of what is now called the "welfare state" was perhaps as much an underlying cause as it had been, openly, during the short-lived Freedmen's Bureau.

It is even more likely that an adamant determination to prevent the reopening of the Negro question in the South accounted in considerable measure for the fury of the opposition. This conjecture is all the more plausible in view of even harsher condemnation of the Lodge bill, which was passed by the House on July 2, 1890. The three Republican papers that supported the bill were motivated, probably, at least as much by party interest as by concern for the Negro.

The *Journal* declared, for example, that the Republican party had never appeared to better advantage than it had in presenting a "solid front" (!) for the passage of Lodge's measure. The Northern Democratic press, it charged, had opposed the bill for drafting recruits into the Union army in order to defeat the Union cause; in 1890, in order to sustain crimes at the ballot box, it opposed federal supervision of federal elections. Typical of this Northern Democratic opposition was an editorial in the New York *Sun* reprinted in the Indianapolis *Journal*. The *Sun* had charged that the proposed law would open the door of every householder to the domiciliary visits of a federal police, and would summon to the polls the drums and muskets of the federal army. "'It amounts,'" continued the organ of Tammany Hall, "'to a revolution in our form of government, wipes out home rule and tears away the main safeguard of our free institutions.'" Such ranting, asserted the *Journal*, was the worst kind of "idiocy"; it might excite ignorant Democrats but it would not frighten them as had similar ranting during the Civil War. Likewise accusing the Northern Democratic press of seeking to confuse the issue, of arousing race prejudice and stirring up sectional strife, the Detroit *Tribune* insisted that the bill would go a long way toward securing honest elections and government. The Chicago *Tribune* took the position that Congress had the constitutional right to pass the bill, and called attention to the laws in some Southern states, especially South Carolina, which contained objectionable provisions for electing members of the national House of Representatives.[3]

Another Republican paper, the *Transcript*—the only paper that had strongly supported the Blair bill—clearly approved the anticipated filibuster in the Senate by Democrats and some leading Republicans. The *North American* carried no editorial between July 1 and 8. Hope was expressed by the *Star* that the Senate would kill the bill, while the *Globe-Democrat* doubted that the upper house would have time to discuss it. The *Enquirer* merely reported the passage of the bill by the House.[4]

The accusations leveled at the Northern Democratic press by the *Journal* and the Detroit *Tribune* are supported by the views of the other four Democratic papers. Under the shadows of Yale University, the *Evening Register* obviously considered the Lodge bill worse than the Blair bill. It had termed the latter "preposterous," but the federal elections bill was the "worst" measure that had passed the House during that session. The Senate should refuse to enact such a "dangerous, unjust and odious measure." "The bill ought not to become a law," the *Dispatch* stated bluntly. If the Republican consciences had not been eased by a "tolerably clear assurance" that the Senate would have none of it, it would not have received even a small majority in the House. The trouble about such "ill-advised" attempts at legislation was that they delayed and endangered measures of the greatest value— such as the tariff particularly. Probably with regret, the Pittsburgh journal pointed out that the Louisiana "Klu Klux" had got in its work just in time to furnish the best ammunition that supporters of the bill could hope for. In even more violent language the *Examiner* asserted that the bill was "the most thoroughly sectional measure introduced since the war." The Republicans did not really wish a strong party in the South, but a "sickly exotic" that would have to be propped up by bayonets, so that they could fire Northerners with tales of Southern outrages and thus avoid the necessity of discussing the tariff and silver.[5]

Most surprising to readers of the New York *Times* today was its almost unbelievably intemperate denunciation of Lodge's bill. It had been "driven" through the House by a slender majority of six. Only a few Republicans had had the courage and firmness to "brave the tyranny of the caucus, the wrath of the Dictator Reed, and the resentment of the pigmy of the White House." The proposed law was "infamously wrong . . . , a stupid blunder as a matter of party politics." But it could be doubted that there was enough "partisan drunkenness" to carry it through the Senate and give Harrison the "ghoulish" joy of approving it.[6]

This editorial probably marks one of the low points in the history of the *Times*. Along with the editorials in the other Northern Democratic papers, it may be characterized as a kind of hoisting of the "Bourbon" flag, a generally overlooked counterpart of the waving of the "bloody shirt." On the other hand, three Democratic papers—the *Evening Register, Examiner* and *Enquirer*—remained silent on the Mississippi amendment, while two eminent Republican papers, the *Transcript* and the Chicago *Tribune*, succeeded in swallowing it.

Discussion of the amendment included, on the one hand, basic constitutional and legal questions and, on the other hand, the specific question of disfranchising Negroes while leaving many whites in possession of the suffrage. These constitutional and legal questions transcended the disfranchisement, since flagrant violation of the Constitution and laws breeds disrespect that might conceivably affect adversely all the American people. Five important questions were considered by one or more papers.

First, did the amendment violate the Act of Congress, approved February 23, 1870, by which Mississippi had been "readmitted" to the Union? One of the fundamental conditions of readmission was the pledge that the constitution of the state should never be "so amended or changed as to deprive any citizen, or class of citizens of the United States of the right to vote, who are entitled to vote by the constitution [of 1868] herein recognized, except as punishment for such crimes as are now felonies at common law." The *Transcript* contended that, while it was late in the day to raise the question, Mississippi had no recourse but to accept the law. But the editor was ready to let the question rest. Nor did the Chicago *Tribune* press the issue, merely pointing out that the act of readmission was a "snag" to disfranchisement of colored voters. Since the state Judiciary Committee had reported that the act of readmission was not binding, the *Journal* argued that Mississippi was no longer in the Union, and should therefore recall all its senators and representatives and become a territory. But the *Globe-Democrat* accepted the interpretation of the Judiciary Committee; indeed, if the Act were brought before the United States Supreme Court, it would decide that the federal government had had no power to pass the law.[7]

Second, was it necessary or customary to submit constitutional amendments to the people for ratification? On this point the *Transcript* was silent and the *Times* doubtful. Modern practice required submission, the *Star* pointed out, but non-submission had been considered good practice at one time, notably in the case of the Constitution of the United States. But this was the first time since then, contended the *Journal*, that a constitution had been "imposed" upon the people of a state without their ratification. While recognizing the preponderance of precedents in favor of submission, the *Globe-Democrat* was willing that it should not be submitted.[8]

Third, would not the adoption of the amendment require the application of the second section of the Fourteenth Amendment, which stipulates that disfranchisement should carry a proportionate reduction of the representation of the state in the House of Representatives and in the electoral college? By implication the *Transcript, Times* and *Dispatch* answered in the negative. The first two argued that Mississippi had as much right to enact an educational requirement as had Massachusetts—where apparently reduction had not become an issue. The *Dispatch* insisted that every state had the right to establish educational requirements. On the other hand, the Chicago *Tribune*, the Detroit *Tribune*, the *Journal* and the *Globe-Democrat*, asserted that the adoption of the amendment would necessarily require application of the second section of the Fourteenth Amendment.[9] At no time, however, was a serious effort made by these Republican stalwarts, or the *Globe-Democrat*, to launch a crusade in behalf of enforcement.

In the fourth place, did the amendment violate the Fifteenth Amendment? Instead of facing this issue squarely, the

Transcript warned that, if a petition from Mississippi for the repeal of the Fifteenth Amendment ever reached Congress, the petitioners would find that "there is considerable opinion in the United States outside Mississippi." By contrast, the *Journal* repeatedly insisted that disfranchisement would be an "outrageous conspiracy" to nullify the Fifteenth Amendment. In fact, the attempt to frame a state constitution without violating the federal constitution was the "Democratic puzzle of the times." Although the proposal to repeal the Fifteenth Amendment had excited little or no comment in the country, it was pretty well understood, even in the South, that "they might as well cry for the moon." The Detroit *Tribune* accused the convention of "conspiring" to nullify the Amendment. When Judge S. S. Calhoon, chairman of the convention, defied the federal government to enforce the Amendment, the Detroit *Tribune* inquired: "How much short of treason is it when the president of the . . . Convention talks like that?" After the Fifteenth Amendment should have been nullified, it would not be necessary to kill any Negroes. "How do Northern Democrats who fought for the preservation of the Union like the Mississippi Plan?" the editor queried on September 13.[10]

Although the fifth question has been largely ignored, two papers considered it pertinent. Did such disfranchisement violate Section four of Article four of the Constitution of the United States, which stipulates that "the United States shall guaranty to every state in this union a republican form of government?" The Chicago *Tribune* was unequivocal: "No form of government which disfranchises those who have the right to vote is republican." Although the *North American* devoted little space to what it called "The 'Massysip' Idea," it condemned the "reactionary" determination to shut out a whole class of the population. The glorious traditions of "the Democracy" were "streaked with blood and disfigured by inborn tyranny." Unless the moral senses of the Southern masses were awakened, there would not be a state in the old black belt with a republican form of government in ten years.[11]

A sixth question, the equal enforcement of the laws—which the Supreme Court has invoked in the twentieth century to declare unconstitutional various provisions for disfranchisement—was not raised at this time.

Although there was no specific reference to Grady's thesis

of "honor and equity," most of the papers looked closely at the fairness of the Mississippi amendment. It will be recalled that three Democratic papers, the *Evening Register, Examiner* and *Enquirer* did not discuss the amendment. The others, except the *North American, Journal* and Detroit *Tribune,* eventually accepted it.

Since three of the other Democratic papers were silent, the tergiversations of the *Dispatch* are particularly interesting. Early in August one editorial was headed "A Commendable Proposition." It made no difference that the great majority of voters excluded would be colored. No injustice would be done if the educational qualification was equally applied to black and white, and if the Negroes were permitted to exercise the suffrage when they had prepared themselves to meet the qualification. But on August 19, the *Dispatch,* even though in jocular vein, laid bare the intent and methods of the convention. Under the caption, "A Wonderful Constitution," the editor gibed:

> They are making a fearful and wonderful constitution down in Mississippi. Things from the heavens above and the earth beneath and the waters under the earth are being dragged into the constitutions [*sic*] as qualifications for the franchise. In the endeavor to fence the negroes out from political power the Mississippians have concocted some of the queerest legal dishes ever seen. . . . They have not yet decided to disfranchise the man who wears number twelve boots, or the unfortunate who has corns, or the villain who plays the banjo, or the enthusiast who loves "watermillions." But they would travel to their destination by a short cut if they disfranchised every man whose face is not white.

In more serious manner, an editorial on August 25 accused the Mississippians of being affected by a "color-blindness" that made them eager to shut out "black ignorance and viciousness, and leave white ignorance and vice in possession of the ballot."

The *Dispatch* was rescued from the logic of its position by Montgomery's advocacy of reduced voting power for Negroes. His acceptance of the educational qualification enabled the Pittsburgh paper to return to its original stand, namely, that such a qualification was the solution of Mississippi's difficulty. But the *Dispatch* was disturbed, late in September, by the clause requiring ability to understand the constitution, which left a loophole by which the educational provision could be nullified by the party in power. Like some other papers, the Steel City journal fell back upon the hope that "the spirit of civilization will have force enough in Mississippi to require an impartial educational qualification."[12]

Miller's *Times* was hardly more enthusiastic than the *Dispatch* in its acceptance of the amendment. It also recognized that the discretion given to the election officials would probably be abused for partisan purposes, but it softened this criticism also by reference to Montgomery's acceptance of the amendment. In almost the same spirit of resignation, the *Times* closed a long editorial on November 13 with the mild admonition: "It is claimed for the new Constitution . . . that it furnishes a solution of the race problem in that State, but that remains to be seen."[13]

In many respects these reactions of the Northern Democratic papers may be quite revealing. They had opposed the Blair and Lodge bills because, among other things, they constituted federal interference in the Southern question. But they were evidently somewhat embarrassed by the new evidence of how the New South intended to use its freedom in the solution of the Negro problem. Equally revealing is the fact that the position of the *Dispatch* and *Times* differed but little in substance from that of the *Transcript* and the Chicago *Tribune*.

The erudite organ of the "Proper Bostonians" at first disapproved the amendment. On August 8, it reported the advice of a Mississippi editor who favored disfranchisement: "'Disfranchise for petit larceny and build the henroost low.'" Nine days later the *Transcript* asked how the two races could advance equally while one was the legal inferior of the other. That, however, was a problem that Mississippi would have to solve after the convention was over. On August 25, the paper apparently failed to grasp clearly the fact, emphasized in other papers, that in the administration of the new constitution it would be easy to disfranchise literate Negroes while illiterate whites would be permitted to vote. On the other hand, the *Transcript* laughed at Governor Alcorn for indicting the Negro as being incapable of exercising self-government since, as everyone knew, all white men were capable of doing so.

It further ridiculed his assertion that designing white men controlled the Negro votes, for, of course, no white men had ever succeeded in voting large numbers of whites. But the editor seemed to be in dead earnest in supporting a proposal that white women in Mississippi be given the vote in order to

> temper the power of colored illiteracy. Crochet needles at the polls will have to do the work proposed for bayonets in the federal election bill; and by a fair vote for all who are qualified by property and education under the law, Mississippi will have an opportunity of wiping out the stains of former election frauds and getting nearer to equality than some of her less illiterate sister States.

In brief, so long as the Fifteenth Amendment remained a part of the Constitution, the *Transcript* seemed able to rationalize its violation.

The Chicago *Tribune* also emphasized at the beginning that the purpose of the amendment was to disfranchise colored voters and eliminate colored officeholders, and stressed the fact that it would assure Democratic domination in the state. But after several reiterations of these themes, the *Tribune*, like the *Times* and the *Dispatch*, fell back upon the great panaceas, time and education of the Negroes. The *Star* hopefully believed that the amendment would not go into effect until "all illiterates" had time to meet its qualifications.[14]

After taking a strong stand at first, which repeatedly denounced the amendment as aiming at the disfranchisement of intelligent Negroes, the *Journal* in midstream also observed that in view of the declining illiteracy of the Negroes the amendment might not prove effective in the future. But, on September 17, it bitterly denounced Montgomery as a "Traitor to His Race." On October 2, it asserted that Mississippi was too "modest" in asking for repeal of the Fifteenth Amendment. The state should seek the re-establishment of slavery since, in the honest opinion of Southern Democrats, that was the only solution of the race question. And finally, on November 8, the *Journal* condemned the New York *Times* for attempting to draw a parallel between the Massachusetts and Mississippi educational provisions, and concluded: "To decitizenize a man is an unparalleled outrage upon him and a disgrace upon free government."[15]

Only the Detroit *Tribune* consistently thundered in tones

that were reminiscent of some of the Abolitionists. As early
as August 17, the editor predicted that Mississippi was going
to disfranchise most of its colored voters, and that in three
years the other Southern states would complete the process,
and still claim full representation in Congress. On the next
day, he pointed out that, while an ignorant suffrage was a
dangerous one, it was not determined by race or color. Mississippi, instead of striving to educate the former slaves who
had been kept illiterate by their masters, had run Northern
teachers out of the state. An educational qualification im-
partially applied might work, but it was doubtful that Mississippi had men wise and influential enough to devise and secure
the adoption of such a provision. Constituting itself the watch-
dog of the convention, the paper warned, on September 13,
that the "Southern outrage mill" was grinding out great grists
in Mississippi. The next day appeared the admonition to keep
track of the convention since the federal government was
"pretty 'small potatoes' down that way." On the following
day, the *Tribune* credited the New York *World* with being
the only Northern Democratic paper that had even mildly
protested against the "treasonable" proposition of Judge Calhoon to nullify the Fifteenth Amendment. That same day, the
Tribune charged that the convention was being "run by a
pack of rebels and political cutthroats, some of whom ought
to have been hung 25 years ago." Two weeks later the Detroit
paper contended:

> It is as hard for the Southern Bourbon to abandon his love
> of injustice as for the leopard to change his spots. During
> slavery the defenders of the "peculiar institution" were
> wont to roll their eyes heavenward and declare that the
> bondage of the colored man was for his benefit and for
> the interest of civilization. The Democratic party now de-
> clares that nullification of the war amendments of the
> constitution and depriving the colored man of his vote is
> really for his own good![16]

The impassioned appeals of the *Tribune* clearly struck a discordant note in 1890. The editor was probably accused of
waving the "bloody shirt." Not only had these appeals long
since lost most of their effectiveness, but the Detroit *Tribune*
was one of the least important of the papers analyzed.

The more influential *Globe-Democrat* resorted to a sardonic cynicism tinged with fatalism. It interpreted a petition of the Mississippi Farmers' Alliance not to adopt an educational qualification as a desire to disfranchise Negroes in some way that would not affect the illiterate and shiftless white voters. As a matter of fact, "the Mississippi section of the Caucasian race stands near the foot of the list in the scale of illiteracy." Probably with his tongue in his cheek, the editor suggested a way by which Negroes might be disfranchised without the state's suffering a reduction in its representation. His proposal amounted in substance to wide-spread gerrymandering which would make the vote cast by a Negro in Mississippi as meaningless as one cast in Africa. But, while Mississippi Democrats were seeking to solve the riddle, they could console themselves with the fact that "the familiar and long-tried shotgun policy is equal to all the necessities of the party." Another solution would be the adoption of a liberal and progressive policy that would attract enough settlers to overcome the preponderance of Negroes in the state. But that sort of policy the "Bourbons" did not want. Nor did they favor an educational qualification that would disfranchise 12,000 whites along with 123,000 Negroes. The problem was quite simple: make ignorance a disqualification regardless of color, and "the political power of the State will be permanently confided to its intelligent and responsible citizens." (This solution, it will be remembered, had been advocated by President Hayes.) A property qualification would not work, because the wealth of the colored people of the South was estimated at $263,000,-000. (The source of this estimate was not indicated.) Since the people of the North were not so concerned about the Negro as they used to be, they would endorse any action that was "honestly and justly" directed to the end of elevating the standard of voting of both races. Anticipating the thesis advanced six years later by F. L. Hoffman that Negroes were not holding their own numerically with the whites and that therefore the problem would soon solve itself, the *Globe-Democrat* predicted that the Negro "will soon cease to be a disturbing factor, either politically or socially, anywhere in the United States."

When the constitution adopted the amendment, however, the *Globe-Democrat* concluded that the race problem could not be disposed of by waiting for the Negro to die out. The amendment was "in every sense discreditable" to the convention, but it would not permanently eliminate the colored vote. In support of its contention that the purpose was to prevent Negroes from voting, not on account of their ignorance but of their color, the *Globe-Democrat* reprinted an excerpt from the Charleston *News and Courier* which candidly stated: "'If every colored man in Mississippi were a graduate of Yale College, the two races would remain as widely separated in all political and social matters.'" It was a simple, practical truth, the *Globe-Democrat* added, that Negroes were hated because they were black. In fact, the "anti-negro prejudice is inbred and ineradicable. It is not possible for the proscribed race to overcome this fixed hostility by any improvement in its mental and moral condition, since it can not change the color of its skin." But after this expression of hopelessness, the editorial immediately called for action to solve the problem. The sheer inability of the Negro to get rid of the prejudice against him was

> the grave and controlling fact that our statesmen and philosophers have to grapple with. How it can be safely and satisfactorily disposed of is a question that can not be decided in a day; and yet it needs to be decided at the earliest possible moment. The present situation is at once both a reproach and a peril. We may postpone the matter in one way and another from year to year; but in the end a final settlement will have to be made—and the end may come suddenly at any time.[17]

Thus, no issue in the period under study had caused so much confusion in editorial offices. The confusion is all the more evident in the fact that two of the papers that at one time accepted the amendment urged the adoption of a federal elections law. More bluntly than any other paper, the Chicago *Tribune* declared on August 21: "If there can be a stronger argument for the 'force' bill than this present situation would present, what is it?" The *Journal*, which wavered in midstream, was less explicit. A member of the Mississippi convention had declared that, if the attempt were made to enforce a federal elections law in Mississippi, the colored voter would be forced to flee from the state in order to save his life. "This," commented the *Journal*, "is the first time a threat to commit wholesale murder has been made by a Democrat, but the Southern Democrat is speaking his mind with reckless fluency these days." The other two papers, the *North American* and the Detroit *Tribune*, which at the end still condemned the amendment, also favored the adoption of a federal elections law. The latter warned that "the reign of terror" would be continued without interruption until the control of federal elections passed out of the hands of the "bulldozers and regulators into federal hands."[18]

As may be expected, the defeat of the Lodge bill by the Senate, January 26, 1891, was hailed generally with a sigh of relief. Only two papers, the *Journal* and the Detroit *Tribune*, expressed definite disappointment. The former insisted that the bill was pre-eminently right in its purpose and constitutional in its methods. It was not a " 'force bill' " as Democrats and Mugwumps called it. It did not in any manner interfere with home rule; it interfered, in short, with nothing except fraud. The Detroit *Tribune* charged that Republicans who had voted against the bill had abandoned the party and its platform, and allied themselves with Democrats.[19]

The Chicago *Tribune*, which had not manifested much enthusiasm when the House had passed the bill, shed no tears over its defeat by the Senate. Most of its comment was devoted to an attack on New Jersey, the "head-center of Democratic rascality," which had feared the effects of the bill on the party there. The *North American*, which had insisted that the proposed Mississippi amendment showed the need for a federal elections law, confined itself to a condemnation of Senator Cameron for voting against the Lodge bill.[20]

The *Transcript, Evening Register*—which quoted also the Philadelphia *Inquirer*—*Star, Enquirer, Dispatch* and *Globe-Democrat* were restrained in expressing their satisfaction. In general, they emphasized the points that not many Republicans and only a few businessmen had really desired its passage and that, further, it was well for Congress to be able to move on to more important business.[21]

But the *Examiner* and the *Times* spoke out in stronger language. A few days before the defeat, the San Francisco paper condemned the bill as an "iridescent or putrescent dream," and a scheme of the Republicans once more to indulge in corruption and fraud with federal money. After the defeat, George Hearst's journal was content to observe: "Those Republican Senators who have saved the country the shame and danger that threatened in the Force bill deserve the unstinted thanks of every patriotic citizen." But the *Times* could not forego the opportunity once more to give its strong support to allowing the South to work out its own destiny. On the day after the defeat, it condemned the advocates of the bill for their faith in "mechanical as opposed to moral force in politics. That is to say, it was expected by them that the unscrupulous use of the Federal power in behalf of the Republican party would gain more seats in Congress than would be lost by the revolt of intelligent voters." Two days later, the *Times* attached even greater significance to the defeat of the bill. The "Force bill," which might be termed the last of the "war measures" was itself "so unintelligent, so uncalled for, so opposed to the sentiment of the country, so dangerous in its crude violation of the spirit of the Constitution; and the motive of some of its authors was so plainly corrupt, that in thinking of it we may easily mistake the character of the series of which it was the final one." That series of laws had had as its objective the restoration of civil order in the South at the close of the war, the protection of the freedom and civil rights of the emancipated slaves, and the resumption of the normal operation of the federal government. But during the preceding ten years the country had greatly suffered from the "lingering abuses" that grew out of the achievement of those objectives. During that time, however, the "Southern question" had become less and less engrossing. With the defeat of the "Force bill" it was hoped that the Southern question would disappear. "No such measure," the editorial concluded, "will again be brought forward to embody a sentiment no longer existing or to revive slumbering fires. Whatever may be the issues of the future, they will not be of this sort." The long editorial was appropriately captioned "The Close of an Era."[22] It would seem that Grady's "footsore Confederate soldier" had come to stand guard in the editorial rooms of the *Times*.

For reasons that can not be too precisely defined, the Northern press took a somewhat stronger stand against South Carolina's revision of its constitution than it had against Mississippi's. Perhaps Booker T. Washington's compromise had seemed so persuasive, that editors regretted to see so soon an untoward manifestation of "Southern friendship." Equally plausible is the conjecture that "Pitchfork" Ben Tillman's extremism created alarm, especially at a time when Populism, Free Silver and other "radical" demands still constituted a threat to the recovery that was beginning to emerge from the panic of 1893.

A detailed analysis of the press comments on South Carolina's revision deserves a separate monograph, especially since they were comprehensive and, in many instances, entertaining. Since, however, most of these comments repeated points of view expressed in 1890, a succinct comparison is more valuable.

One of the three papers that had remained silent in 1890, the *Evening Register*, again deemed it wise to refrain from discussing the South Carolina amendment. The *Examiner* began to show concern at Tillman's demagoguery which saw blood and fire in the future. Perhaps Tillman should consult an oculist—he had only one eye and that one had probably been overstrained. Until the end of October, the point at which this investigation ended, these constituted the *Examiner's* only remarks. On the other hand, the *Enquirer* strongly supported the revision and enthusiastically praised Tillman.[23]

The conscience of the *Transcript* was more disturbed than it had been in 1890; it concluded that the "dodge" would be more difficult than was generally supposed. Especially interesting is the shifting attitude of the *Times*. At first, it declared that the amendment would have to be accepted in good faith, although it was clearly designed to establish "white supremacy." Then the *Times* strongly criticized the ignorance and illiteracy upon which Tillman planned to erect his "white supremacy." But when the London *Spectator* vouchsafed that the amendment had for its sole purpose the exclusion of black voters, the *Times* asserted that it was better for this exclusion to be accomplished by constitutional means than by force or fraud. As in 1890, the *Times* envisioned the possibility that Negroes would eventually vote as freely as the whites.[24]

Naïve acquiescence by the *Star* in 1890, gave way, in 1895, to a blunt denunciation of the South Carolina revision as "an unmitigated flim-flam." But that was its only comment. Having in the earlier case expressed the view that Negroes would wait "patiently," the *Dispatch* reversed its 1890 position and unequivocally condemned Tillman's determination to keep Negroes illiterate while proclaiming to the world that South Carolina, like Mississippi, feared the ignorant Negro. The fact that the *Dispatch*, alarmed by the growing demands for Free Silver, was beginning to veer toward the Republican party may account in part for this change. Likewise, the steadfast Chicago *Tribune*, which in 1890 had left the solution of the problem to time and education, in 1895 strongly condemned revision, and introduced the argument that it would violate the Fourteenth Amendment.[25]

The *Globe-Democrat, Journal, North American* and Detroit *Tribune*, which had openly denounced Mississippi's amendment, stuck by their guns in 1895. The *Journal* buttressed its position by quoting the Democratic New York *Sun* which had observed that many Negroes would be forced to leave South Carolina. The *North American* gave much more coverage, of a highly sarcastic nature, to the South Carolina amendment than it had given in 1890. Sounding a new note, the Detroit *Tribune* referred to a resolution adopted by the South Carolina convention expressing sympathy for the Cubans, in order to mock: "How much more 'precious' liberty and independence are for the negroes of Cuba."[26]

Concern in 1895, about this new victory over the Reconstruction attempt to give Negroes political equality was not manifest early in 1896, when the Supreme Court denied them social equality. Plessy *v.* Ferguson, in which the Court first sanctioned the fiction of "separate but equal" accommodations, was argued on April 13. In sharp contrast to the nationwide interest when the public school cases—that frontally challenge this doctrine—were argued in 1952, none of the twelve papers mentioned the oral argument in 1896. The Washington *Post* (which was investigated because of its forthright opposition today to the doctrine) noted in its "Capitol Chat" that the counsel for Plessy was Albion W. Tourgee, author of *A Fool's Errand* (1879), which had severely criticized the South during Reconstruction. The writer of the *Post's* column added: "One of the visitors to the court expressed the opinion that it was another fool's errand," since the lower court had already decided the practical questions. After the decision was rendered, May 18, many papers carried brief summaries of it and of Harlan's dissent. But the *Times*, for example, reported in separate items on page one decisions in favor of the eccentric millionaire Hetty H. R. Green and of the famous playwright-producer Augustin Daly. The Plessy ruling—spelled Plassy—was included under railroad news on page three. The *Transcript*, which devoted forty lines to the Hetty Green decision, did not mention Plessy. The *Journal, Star, Globe-Democrat* and Chicago *Tribune* listed it along with other decisions handed down on the same day—more than thirty in the *Tribune's* list, plus a large number of Court orders. The only editorial comment found was, strangely enough, a short paragraph in the *Evening Register*: "Mr. Justice Harlan is sound in dissenting from the opinion," since it might be used to separate Protestants and Catholics, for instance. Perhaps a basic reason for the scant interest in a decision which was one of more than thirty is revealed in an editorial in the *Globe-Democrat* three days later: "For the first time in a Presidential year since the Republican party was founded there is an utter absence in Republican gatherings" of any allusion to the Southern question.[27]

Nor was the somewhat more forceful position taken by the press in respect of the South Carolina revision maintained when Louisiana became the third state effectively to disfranchise the Negro. Its constitutional convention convened on February 8, 1898, and lasted through the greater part of the year. The suffrage provision, which was the first important item considered, was approved in March. It introduced what is known as the "Grandfather clause," that is, it set up educational and property qualifications for voting, but provided that those whose ancestors could vote in 1867 did not have to meet those requirements. Since only a few thousand Negroes voted at that time, this provision virtually eliminated Negroes from suffrage and government in Louisiana.

While the convention was considering the amendment, Booker T. Washington sent a letter of protest on February 19. This letter—which was drafted with the utmost care after consultation with Emmett J. Scott, his confidential secretary, and T. Thomas Fortune, editor of the New York *Age*—pointed out that he had advised his race to give attention to the acquisition of property, intelligence and character as the necessary bases of good citizenship, rather than to "mere political agitation." He declared that the Negro agreed that it was necessary to the salvation of the South that restriction be placed upon the ballot. The Negroes, he continued, did not object to an educational and property test, but he urged that the law be so clear that no one clothed with state authority be tempted to perjure and degrade himself by putting one interpretation upon it for white men and another for the black man. The consideration for this agreement was stated in words that were to be frequently repeated—and ignored: "In the degree that you close the ballot box against the ignorant, . . . you open the school house."[28]

The Grandfather clause made it unnecessary for white men to perjure and degrade themselves, but it was such a crude device for disfranchising Negroes that a similar provision in the Oklahoma constitution resulted, in 1915, in the first decision of the United States Supreme Court which declared unconstitutional one of the various efforts to disfranchise Negroes. In passing, it should be noted that Washington had definitely assumed the role of "leader" in speaking for all Negroes.

Despite this letter, which was given wide circulation by the Associated Press, the papers gave less consideration to the Louisiana convention than they had to those in Mississippi and South Carolina. During February and March, six papers did not analyze the amendment. It is not at all surprising that the *Examiner* and *Enquirer* ignored it, and not very surprising that the *Star* did. But the *North American*, which had devoted a great deal of space to penetrating, sarcastic criticisms in 1895, was also silent. Perhaps as a result of the newly acquired control by Adolph S. Ochs, the *Times* also preferred to omit discussion of a measure that could not be justified by any reasonable interpretation of the United States Constitution or of the principles of democracy. Most surprising is the silence of the Detroit *Tribune*, which had been the most forceful of the papers in 1890, and which in 1895 had been one of the first papers to gibe about the greater sympathy for the independence and liberty of Cuban than of South Carolina Negroes.

The *Dispatch* and the *Evening Register* limited their comments to strong endorsement of Washington's letter. The former, revealing perhaps a doubt that his plea would be heeded, pointed to Mississippi as an illustration of the bad effects resulting from inadequate educational facilities. The *Evening Register* awakened sufficiently from its torpor in 1890 and 1895 to observe that Louisiana would be the principal loser if Washington's appeal were ignored. Perhaps the *Globe-Democrat* had Washington's letter in mind when it strongly condemned any "double standard"; but agreed that, if Louisiana were to apply an educational qualification equally, and at the same time expand facilities for black and white alike to gain a rudimentary education, the nation would hold it in higher esteem.[29]

The Chicago *Tribune* on three occasions strongly endorsed Washington's letter, but then cited statistics to show that Louisiana was discriminating against Negroes in public schools. Between 1891 and 1895 white male teachers had increased by 19 per cent and colored male teachers by one per cent; white female teachers by 21 per cent and colored by 8 per cent. Average salaries for white teachers had increased while those for colored had decreased. School terms for colored children were shorter than those for white. The Chicago *Tribune*—which had scoffed at the Blair bill—at least saw the need, for the strongest reasons of "public policy," for securing to all alike the needed education. It finally condemned the proposed amendment, not only for its discriminatory provisions, but also because of the possibility that they might be used to bar whites suspected of being Republicans.[30]

Taking direct issue with Washington, the *Journal* asserted that the Louisiana convention did not want to make the Negro intelligent so that he could become a voter, but rather it wanted to keep him "generation after generation, . . . a drudge, a slave, without incurring the responsibility which the slave system involved." Quite naturally, it blamed Democrats for this determination to deprive Negroes of the ballot and of "all equality before the law." It suggested that William Jennings Bryan himself favored the amendment, since he had addressed the convention without criticizing it. This paper was one of the few that gave a detailed analysis and interpretation of the Grandfather clause.[31]

The one paper that showed consistent advance, and understanding of the constitutional amendments was the *Transcript*. Its conscience had been troubled in 1890, but it had succeeded in swallowing Mississippi's amendment. It had concluded that South Carolina's "dodge," in 1895, would be more difficult than was generally supposed. In 1898, it bluntly declared that Louisiana was formulating a plan "that excludes from the right to vote all the ignorance and poverty of the State that is covered by a black skin, and admits to it all under a white skin, provided it is native." Louisiana's act made all the more timely Washington's warning, for "in this act of reckless discrimination the seeds of trouble have been sown, even more for the white man than for the black."[32] The most probable explanation for this growing awareness of the dangers ahead is the fact that the *Transcript* had "adopted" Booker T. Washington and Tuskegee Institute as one of the causes that it most consistently presented to the favorable consideration of its readers.

It is understandable that the imminence of war with Spain— the *Maine* was blown up on February 15, a week after the opening of the convention—reduced interest in Louisiana's new device for circumventing the Constitution of the United States. On the other hand, the imminence of war might have brought forth other expressions similar to the Detroit *Tribune's* contrast in 1895 between sympathy for Cuban Negroes and lack of concern for American Negroes. The absence of such comparisons, and the general failure to explain precisely the operation of the Grandfather clause, further strengthen the conclusion that the slight revival of concern for the Constitution and for the constitutional rights of Negroes had already waned. But the hunt for Aguinaldo, the Boxer War, and the Boer War at the very end of the century did not prevent at least a dim awareness that a line had to be drawn somewhere.

It is conceivable that the presence of even a slight majority of Negroes, practically all ex-slaves, in Mississippi, South Carolina and Louisiana, justified, in the minds of Northern editors—who were not informed about the ignorance and poverty of large numbers of "poor whites" in those states—the conclusion that good government was being furthered by the almost total elimination of colored men from the suffrage. In North Carolina, however, Negroes constituted only 34.7 per cent of the population in 1900. Moreover, by the use of force and of lurid appeals to race prejudice, white supremacy had regained control by 1898. A constitutional amendment would give an aura of legality to a *fait accompli*. Unless a halt was called to the disfranchising process, it was going to be increasingly difficult for Northern editors to explain and justify it.

The editor of the New Haven *Evening Register*, however, still had no doubts or qualms. People in the North, he contended, simply could not understand the political situation in the South which grew out of racial differences. It had always been the paper's belief that a great mistake had been made in conferring the suffrage upon a people only recently emancipated from slavery. The South should be left to handle this problem in its own way. But the *Evening Register's* support of American acquisitions overseas led it to comment that Democrats who were concerned over the "consent of the governed" in those possessions were hardly consistent in disfranchising American citizens.[33] The *Enquirer, Dispatch* and *Examiner* manifested no interest in the North Carolina amendment.

Charles R. Miller began to display some embarrassment and fear of the consequences. In order to justify its adoption, the *Times* declared that Negroes had shown little interest in the North Carolina campaign and that some had voted for the amendment. It could not be denied, moreover, "that the evils of what is described as black domination might be very great, since the mass of the colored vote was ignorant and blindly prejudiced." But the whites in the South were proceeding in a mistaken way to "protect themselves from such evils," since it perpetuated the ignorant and prejudiced white vote. A wiser and more manly method would have been to have legislated for the exclusion, temporarily, of the illiterate of both races. If a small property qualification had been added to the educational, "the effect must have been to offer the suffrage as a prize to education and thrift, while the affairs of the States in the meantime would have been in the hands of those best fitted to care for them." The white citizens would have only themselves to blame if the second section of the Fourteenth Amendment should be enforced.

The *Star* also manifested a growing concern. A penetrating editorial called attention to a catechism issued to reassure the illiterate white voters that their suffrage would not be affected by the amendment. This catechism was "deliciously explicit as to the process of juggling whereby a sharp line of distinction is to be drawn between the illiterate white and the illiterate black." Although the editor expected the Supreme Court to declare the North Carolina amendment a violation of the Fifteenth Amendment, if a case came before it; he also anticipated additional amendments that might disfranchise even larger numbers of colored voters.

The *North American* and the Detroit *Tribune*, which had remained silent when Louisiana introduced the Grandfather clause, condemned the action in North Carolina. The latter, after observing that the colored voters who had approved the amendment had found discretion the better part of valor, declared that the disfranchisement violated the spirit of the Constitution of the United States even if it did not clearly violate the Fifteenth Amendment. The *North American* bluntly charged that the race problem in the South would not be solved by flying in the face of the federal Constitution and by organized intimidation.[34]

The other stalwart Republican papers—the *Journal*, *Globe-Democrat*, Chicago *Tribune* and *Transcript*—repeated their former criticisms, with the *Journal* adding a new note: "The Czar of Russia never took from native-born citizens the privilege of voting in local affairs." *The Transcript's* editorials and news articles provide a fitting epitaph for the demise of Negro suffrage at the beginning of the twentieth century. On June 4, a strong editorial condemned the "White Supremacy" campaign of 1898, and the "bloody massacre" of Wilmington. On the next day, an editorial discussed the resolution introduced by Representative Edgar D. Crumpacker of Indiana to initiate an inquiry into the justice and expediency of reducing Southern representation. The matter had slumbered for some time, having been "put aside for questions of apparently greater urgency, but the developments now making in some of the more northerly States of the South in harmony with the 'Mississippi Plan' will make the reasons which activated Mr. Crumpacker stronger than ever." A reduction of about forty per cent in the South's representation in Congress and in the electoral college would be "just and logical." A news article from Washington—signed by its regular correspondent, "Lincoln"—concluded that McKinley had done nothing about the Crumpacker resolution because action would have been bad politics. But if McKinley were re-elected, and if the Republicans won a majority in both houses of Congress, "the time will seem ripe for this great action."[35]

TWELVE

The "Color Line" in the "New North," 1877–1901

THE expression, the "color line," was used as early as 1883 by the *Globe-Democrat* in its discussion of the agitation likely to ensue from the Civil Rights decision. Several other papers frequently employed the term long before Ray Stannard Baker gave it wide currency in an article, "Following the Color Line," in the *American Magazine*, April, 1907, and in a book by the same title the following year. It dealt with most phases of Negro life in the United States. The term, the "New North," a headline in an *Enquirer* editorial at the time of Grady's speech, did not catch on. Common usage would have suggested that the North had problems comparable to those in the South. There was, of course, no comparison between the South's need for developing its resources, and the great expansion of industry in the North during the last half of the nineteenth century. Immigrants rather than Negroes constituted the most serious local problems in the North. Only ten per cent of all Negroes lived there; they were less than two per cent of the total Northern population. They constituted a considerable proportion, one-fourth, of the population in only one of the cities whose papers have been analyzed, Washington, D. C.—which is included in the South in census statistics. Indianapolis stood second, with a little over nine per cent. In Philadelphia, Pittsburgh, Cincinnati and St. Louis Negroes constituted about five per cent. Even so, the colored people of Philadelphia encountered so many difficulties that they inspired what is generally considered the first intensive, scholarly, sociological study of Negroes in an urban community, *The Philadelphia Negro* (1899) by W. E. B. Du Bois. Their number was about two per cent in New York, Chicago and New Haven; and less than one per cent in Boston, Detroit and San Francisco. Numerically, then, Negroes in the North did not impinge upon the white population as much as they did in the South.

The two preceding chapters, which analyzed national issues, have made manifest that the Northern press was not reluctant to sacrifice the Negro on the altar of reconciliation, peace and prosperity. The discussion of the color line in this chapter is based, with a few additions, upon (1) an intensive study made by the author of all twelve papers at the time of Grady's and Washington's speeches and the meeting of the General Federation of Women's Clubs in June, 1900; (2) the theses of graduate students who searched the *Transcript*, *Times*, *Star*, *Enquirer* and *Examiner* from 1877 to 1900, and the Chicago *Tribune* from 1890 to 1900. Their intensive spot-check supplements but does not alter the larger picture. The synthesis from all these necessarily presents a more sharply focused picture than did any one paper. But if there were such a thing as an American Mind of the North, this synthesis delineates the composite portrait that it was drawing of the Negro.

Then, as now, most Americans made up their minds about local affairs and their relations with their fellow man on the basis of news articles, many of them slanted, and the other less weighty ingredients of the paper, such as anecdotes, jokes and cartoons, rather than from reading ponderous editorials. Letters to the editor were infrequent. Only one advertisement of a caricatured Negro, eating a watermelon, was noted. It appeared at irregular intervals in the *Evening Register* in the latter part of the century, to extol the virtues of a laxative, Sanford's Ginger. But in the 1890's editorial and comic cartoons were splashed upon the pages of the Chicago *Tribune*, the *Enquirer*, and the *Globe-Democrat*. Half-tone photographs replaced drawings at the end of the century. The first photographs noted of colored men—Robert Smalls of South Carolina and James Hill of Mississippi, delegates to the Republican National Convention—appeared in the *Globe-Democrat* on June 19, 1900.

Intensive checks made of the papers of December, 1886, September, 1895, and June, 1900, disclosed that, with the exception of the *Transcript, Evening Register, Times*, Detroit *Tribune* and *Examiner*—which emphasized rather the misdeeds of Chinese, Mexicans and Indians—there was a tendency to play up crimes in which Negroes were involved. This tendency does not necessarily indicate prejudice on the part of the men who controlled, owned, managed and edited the journals. Only a relatively small number of local Negroes had achieved sufficient fame for their names to "make the news."

Crimes committed by other minorities also occupied considerable space. The papers that seemed most preoccupied with crimes involving Negroes were, to some extent, those published in the cities that had a relatively high Negro ratio in the population, St. Louis, Philadelphia, Cincinnati and Washington. Exhaustive research would be necessary to permit a conclusion as to whether a disproportionate amount of space was allocated to crimes in which one or more of the principals was colored. (It is generally agreed that Negroes were more likely to be arrested, tried and convicted than other racial groups, except Chinese, Mexicans, Indians and other problem minorities.) More important than the number of articles, however, was the almost invariable racial identification of the Negroes and of the other "colored" minorities. On the other hand, except in the case of Italians in cities like Boston and Pittsburgh, and very rarely of Germans, Poles, and a few others, either the word "white" was used or no descriptive term was employed.

Such words as "colored" and "negro"—the latter was not capitalized by any paper until the *Transcript* did so in 1900—were not inherently harmful. But their constant repetition helped to build up the stereotype of the Criminal Negro, a stereotype that was hardened by the use of pejorative adjectives. While no one paper used all of them—and the *Transcript*, *Evening Register*, *Times* and Detroit *Tribune* rarely if at all—the following terms were used by one or more papers: "burly negro," "negro ruffian," "African Annie," "a Wild Western Negro," and "colored cannibal"—he had bitten off the lip of an opponent in a fight. "Mulatto," which has virtually disappeared today from news articles, was frequently employed, and a very precise reporter for the *Times* designated a colored woman as a "mulatta." Negress, which occasionally appears even today in Northern papers insensitive to the objections of colored readers, was also sometimes used.[1] "Coon," "darky," "pickaninny," "uncle," "nigger," or "niggah" were not employed in news articles, but they did appear in anecdotes, jokes, cartoons and narrative stories.

Whereas the editorial policies of the *Globe-Democrat* not infrequently showed more discernment on national issues than did more Northern papers, at one time it developed the stereotype of the Criminal Negro more than did any other journal. Between September 18 and 30, 1895, its three col-

umns regularly devoted to short articles about crime contained such headlines as these:

NEGROES SENTENCED FOR TWENTY-ONE YEARS
HELD UP BY MASKED NEGROES
SIX NEGROES DIE OF POISON
SHE KILLED HER LOVER—MINNIE HALL, A NEGRESS
KILLED AT A NEGRO FAIR
DRUNKEN FARMER KILLED BY A NEGRO
ST. LOUIS NEGRO SENTENCED
KILLED A NEGRO
NEGRO MINER MURDERED
COLORED DYNAMITER CONVICTED
STABBED A NEGRO
DEATH OF A MAN SHOT BY A DISSOLUTE NEGRESS
NEGRO'S HORSE STEALING METHODS

During that time the only other specific racial identifications
in its headlines were "Chinese Murderers Executed" and
"Indian Murderer Lynched."

The news articles were usually short and less inflammatory
than the headlines. One, however, reported the trial of four
Indians and a Negro charged with murder in Arkansas as
follows: "The jury was out three minutes. . . . The case will
not be appealed and the five demons will swing on the day
fixed by Judge Parker." The article about the "Dissolute
Negress" stated that she lived in a "neighborhood inhabited
only by negroes, and which has become notorious by reason
of the large number of robberies and murders which have
occurred there."[2] By the beginning of the century, however,
the *Globe-Democrat* had reduced the number of articles
about crime in general and those involving Negroes in particular.

The *North American, Enquirer* and *Star* rarely identified
Negroes in headlines, but their articles almost invariably did.
Thus, the headline in the *North American*, "Used His Razor
Fatally," was about the murder of a colored woman in Stam-
ford, Connecticut—a story that practically all the papers
carried. Under the headline, "Razzers Were A-Flying," the
Enquirer identified the persons involved in a fight at Elyria,
Ohio, as colored, although the *Dispatch* did not do so in that
particular case. On one occasion the *Star* specified: "A Hor-
rible Murder . . . By a Colored Man." The partisanship of the

Journal led it to portray Indianapolis Negro Democrats as selling their votes for small sums of money or for "Free Beer and Women." On the other hand, the Democratic *Times* headlined an article:

COLORED MAN AFTER SPOILS: CLAIMS OF RIVAL BODIES
MAY EMBARRASS NEW-JERSEY REPUBLICANS

In Indiana two colored men and their white wives were arrested, "Charged with Miscegenation," according to the *Globe-Democrat* in 1895. Two years earlier the Chicago *Tribune* headlined an article: "Miscegenation Causes Trouble." When a colored man in Fort Dodge, Iowa, took out a license to marry a white widow with four grown children, she was ordered to be examined by the Commissioners for the Insane.[3]

As in the *Globe-Democrat*, there were fewer articles, headlines and adjectives in the other papers in 1900. But the *Star* headlined a story: "Attacked by Footpad—Mrs. Mary Seaton Robbed by a Colored Ruffian." An article, a half-column long in the *Enquirer* reported: "Colored Fanatic Causes Death and Starvation in North Carolina." Two days later there was an account of a "Solemn Vigil Over the Body of a Colored Man in a 'Coke' [cocaine] Room." The article related that " 'Crippled Jumbo' was in charge, and among those who helped with the incantations were Cinthy Mason, Bettie Anne, 'Cocaine Lil,' 'Little Black Ginny' and many others." In a story about a fight between two colored women it was stated that "both are irascible and both will fight at the drop of a hat." The *Evening Register* called attention to the "Cocaine Habit in the South: How the Negroes Plan to Get the Drug Without Cost." The *Times* told the story of an apparently deranged colored man: "Camped on Miss Gould's Stoop: Negro with Sling Shot Insisted in Court that he was her Half-Brother." Two headlines in the Chicago *Tribune* used the word Negress: "Thief Deceives a Bishop. Atlanta Negress Steals Diamonds and Induces a Philadelphia Colored Churchman to Sell Them for Her"; "Two Killed in Street Fight. Attempt to Stop Kansas City Fracus Results in the Death of Negro and Negress." One of the most sensational stories in the *North American* was headlined: "Masked Lynchers Drag Brutal Wife Beater to the Jersey Woods" where they tarred and feathered him. All the parties were white, but it was finally revealed that the town of South Bridgeton was "populated largely by whites and negroes intermixed, and vice is commonly known to be present. It is the presence of negro women that has been the chief cause of complaint against the men toward whom the God-fearing people have turned their attention, and the general opinion is that tarring and feathering is not sufficient punishment for them."[4]

A similar emphasis on the race of Negroes, and to a less degree of Chinese and Mexicans and Indians, appeared in stories about lynchings. Lynchings were by no means limited to one section, one race of victims, or the "usual crime" of rape. In 1886 a white man was lynched in Eaton, Ohio. A white tramp was nearly lynched in Pennsylvania. There were threats to lynch white men in Arkansas, San Francisco, near Decatur, Illinois, and even of a sixteen-year-old white girl accused of murder in the first degree. Negroes in Huntingburg, Indiana, threatened to lynch two white boys who had poured oil over a respectable colored citizen and burned him to death; and whites in Iowa threatened to lynch a colored couple accused of murdering a little white boy. Nine years later there were threats or attempts to lynch white men in Ohio, Montana, South Dakota and Missouri; a railroad detective in Bristol, Tennessee; the president of a bank that had failed in Pawnee, Oklahoma Territory; a Catholic priest in St. Joseph, Missouri. Chinese in Hope, Idaho, threatened to avenge the murder of a Chinese "highbinder" (opium-smoker). An Indian was lynched near Bakersfield, California. Negroes in the South sometimes participated, alone or in company with whites, in lynching or attempting to lynch Negroes. The threat of a lynching in South Bridgeton, New Jersey, in 1900, has just been mentioned. The *North American*, in 1900, also pictured "Women Anxious to Catch Fiend and Lynch Him: Virginians Thirst for Blood of Man Who Attacked Southern Belles." Since no reference was made to his color, it may be fairly assumed that he was white. The *Enquirer* reported two attempts to lynch white men in Ohio.[5]

Although the *Enquirer* had become much less sensational by 1900 in reporting lynchings, it had previously been the most inflammatory of all the papers. A headline in 1883 reported:

RETRIBUTION

JACOB NELLING LYNCHED BY A MOB

RED-HANDED MURDERER OF ADA ATKINSON

PAYS THE PENALTY FOR HIS HORRIBLE CRIME

A suspicion that the *Enquirer* deliberately played up lynchings in order to build circulation was confirmed by its announcement on page one, in 1886, that "the Enquirer is highly praised here [in Eaton, Ohio] for the energy and persistency with which it pursued the murderer and finally brought about his capture. As evidence of the paper's popularity five hundred copies were sold this morning. . . . Country people offered as high as $1 for a single copy." But in the case of a Negro who had been jailed for robbing a store and clubbing the proprietor, a white woman, the *Enquirer* urged:

OUGHT TO BE LYNCHED

In 1892, a Negro accused of rape was burned to death in Texarkana, Arkansas. The victim declared his innocence to an *Enquirer* reporter twenty minutes before he was led to the stake, but the denial was given in such a manner as to carry a conviction of guilt with it. The lynching was justified by the people of the section "on the ground that a desperate disease requires a heroic remedy, and that hanging has not as great horror for the average colored man as death by fire." The next year, a Negro in Paris, Texas, accused of ravishing and murdering a four-year-old girl, was burned alive after his eyes had been gouged out with a red-hot poker. In the opinion of the *Enquirer* "unparalleled punishment had been meted out to the perpetrator of an unparalleled crime."[6]

Whereas the *Enquirer* had toned down its articles by the end of the century, the Washington *Star* became almost as inflammatory as the *Enquirer* had been when lynching mobs formed across the Potomac from the capital. A headline on April 19, 1897 announced:

NEGRO RAVISHER CAUGHT

The following paragraph would probably shock most readers of the *Star* today:

> The Fairfax County people are very much worked up, and it is feared that trouble will be had in landing Lewis in jail as in any event he will have to be carried along a country road for a distance of three miles and farmers will have a chance to get him from the officers, and there is a rumor afloat that if he is caught he will be summarily dealt with and a strange face will appear on the other shore a few minutes thereafter.

While Lewis was being tried at Fairfax County Courthouse, a mob overpowered police officers at the jail in Alexandria, Virginia, and lynched another Negro from an old iron gas lamp at the corner of Cameron and Lee Streets. The *Star's* reporter repeatedly referred to the victim as the "self-confessed ravisher" who had "raped" a little white girl. A piece of rope used by the mob and stained with the "fiend's" blood was put on exhibition at the *Star's* Alexandria Bureau. The *Star* also sat in judgment on Lewis during whose trial a crowd stood outside the court ready to lynch him if he were found innocent.[7]

But the *Star* and the *Enquirer* were not the only Northern papers that accepted accusation, "confession," and lynching as evidence of guilt. Even the *Transcript*, in a first-page article on July 21, 1886, headed an article, "A Negro Desperado Lynched." The article was not inflammatory, but it raised no question about the charge that he had killed a white woman in an argument over money. Two articles in the *Times* of the same year reported the lynching of three colored "murderers" by a mob of white and colored men near Vicksburg, and of another colored "murderer" in Louisiana. On the next day it was discovered that the three colored men had not been lynched. In 1900 the *Times* still sat in judgment:

NEGRO MURDERS A CITIZEN
POSSES ARE LOOKING FOR HIM AND HE WILL BE LYNCHED

The article, from Louisiana, explained that the Negro had committed the murder in a "particularly fiendish manner." The *North American*, which had become almost as sensational as the *Enquirer* had been, announced in 1900:

ARMED MEN HUNTING NEGRO IN MARYLAND
MAN WHO BRUTALLY ATTACKED PRETTY WHITE GIRL
WILL BE LYNCHED IF CAPTURED[8]

Only occasionally was doubt raised as to the guilt of the accused or of the victim. The *Enquirer*, on December 26, 1886, reported that a Negro who had "attempted rape" was saved from a mob by a courageous jailer who deserved credit "because the case is not clear against the negro although public sentiment is running against him." In the Detroit *Tribune*, the white man lynched to the satisfaction of the *Enquirer* in Eaton, Ohio, was called "The Supposed Murderer." One of the rare occasions when the word "alleged" was used was in the headline of an article in the Chicago *Tribune*, September 26, 1895: "Attempt to Lynch Alleged Fire Bug" in South Dakota. Toward the end of the century the *Transcript* began to report news in language used by most papers today as, for example in September, 1895, that "a negro boy, charged with assault, was taken forcibly from the train [near Shreveport] by a crowd of armed citizens and lynched." An editorialized headline in the same paper a few days later queried:

HOW MANY NEGROES WILL BE LYNCHED?

as the result of a fight between whites and Negroes near Jacksonville. The trend had become even more pronounced in 1900. The *North American* reported:

MOB THREATENED HIM
COLORED MAN CHARGED WITH ASSAULT SENT TO CHESTER JAIL

The *Enquirer* informed its readers:

WHIPPED, HANGED AND BLISTERED
BUT THE MAN PERSISTED IN DECLARING HIS INNOCENCE—
HORRIBLE TORTURES INFLICTED ON AN ALABAMA NEGRO
SUSPECTED OF MURDERING A CHILD

On June 3, 1900, the *Examiner* used three-fourths of a column to develop the headlines:

TERRIBLE FATE OF MISSISSIPPI SCHOOLGIRL:
UNKNOWN MURDERER LIES IN WAIT AND SLAYS THE CHILD
VICTIM IS 13 YEARS OLD—
ASSAILANT BELIEVED TO BE A NEGRO
AND IF CAUGHT WILL BE LYNCHED

Two were, in fact, caught and lynched. In the face of evidence that one of them was innocent the *Examiner* admitted that they had been "Suspected." The *Times* and the *Evening Register* reported flatly:

LYNCHED AN INNOCENT MAN[9]

Only a few editorials appeared in these Northern papers in condemnation of lynching, except in rebutting criticisms of the North by Southern papers, or in raising doubt as to the extent to which the New South had ceased its maltreatment of the Negro. In 1895, the *Enquirer* proclaimed that the hanging of a colored man was "Better Than 'Lynching.'" The *Dis-*

patch sarcastically commented, on June 7, 1900: "The report from Mississippi that a mob of negroes lynched one of their own color indicates that the black race there must be rising— or falling—to the white standard." While both the *Transcript* and the *Times* strongly denounced lynching, they offered as remedies time, patience and education. After the Mississippi lynching in which one of the victims was later declared to be innocent, the *Transcript* admonished: "As long as such brutality is possible and that on mere suspicion, and as long as men and women of standing publicly defend it, the South is a good section to stay away from. It is still a barbarous country." In somewhat the same vein, the Chicago *Tribune*, which gave at the beginning of each year the number of lynchings in the previous year, warned: "Each lynching in the South does more to discourage immigration than could be counteracted by spending thousands of dollars in advertising."[10]

In contrast to the tendentious straight reporting with racial identification and pejorative adjectives, the following story in the *Transcript* deserves a small niche in journalistic Americana:

> A colored man who gives his name as Henry W. Turner was arrested last night on suspicion of being a highway robber. He was taken this morning to Black's studio, where he had his picture taken for the "Rogue's Gallery." That angered him, and he made himself as disagreeable as he possibly could. Several times along the way to the photographer's he resisted the police with all his might, and had to be clubbed.[11]

One may be sure that the reporter in the staid *Transcript* was not trying to be amusing. Occasionally, however, Northern papers used for the small tragedies of Negro life the jocular tone that was standard in Southern papers. A reporter for the *Dispatch* had not quite mastered the technique in his account of an incident: "He Created A Scene: Lively One Act Comedy Rehearsed in an Alderman's Office." A young colored man who had beat his sweetheart "because he loved her" begged her to withdraw the charges and help him pay the costs in the case. "When last heard of they were trying to get the amount necessary, but the odds were against" him. Whether from practice or not, a *Times* reporter was more successful with his story, "They Fell Into the Pit":

Mrs. Emil Ezec Thompson, of Jamaica, gave a birthday reception, and a number of colored guests who attended are laid up with severe contusions and bruises. There was no fight or razors displayed, but the floor in Mrs. Thompson's house gave way and all the guests were precipitated into the cellar. A piano and three musicians went down with the guests. In the darkness and confusion, Miss Clara Bell Brown received a tight squeezing, but not at the hands of any of the male guests. She was caught under a beam and it had to be sawed in two before she could be released. The accident occurred while the guests were dancing.

An article in the *Star* in 1897, about a fight at a colored "parlor social" reported the judge in the police court as saying: " 'I suppose there were razors enough in the party to free Cuba.' " Stories about difficulties that Negro and other preachers encountered with their congregations were also presented in jocular style.[12]

Anecdotes, jokes and historical articles helped to build up the stereotype of the Comic Negro. The *Evening Register* in 1886, reprinted the following explanation from the Chicago *Herald* by a "dignified-looking darky":

" 'Coon's meat am a heap richer'n 'pos'ums, but cher got ter take de kernals out'n de coon's fo' legs if yo' spect ter enjoy him, 'cause dar's gall in dese yer kernals, an' they spile de meat when it am a cookin'. Coon's clim' de trees when de nights am da'k, while de 'pos'um wrestles with de wil' grapevine when de moon am a shinin' bright. Dar's de difference in de beasts.' "[13]

In 1886 also, the *Transcript* selected from the Detroit *Free Press*, which seemed to delight in such episodes, this story of a colored wedding in Mississippi attended by some white Northerners. When the happy couple stood before the minister, he said:

" 'Samuel, you an' Lucinda are shortly to be jined together. Does you desire to back out?' 'No, sah,' 'How am it wid you Lucinda? Does you want to flunk afore dese yere white folks?' 'No, sah.' 'Den you two hitch hands.' They hitched. 'Samuel, does you take her fur better or wuss? Am you gwine to do de fa'r thing by dis yere gurl, whose fadder was killed on de railroad up nigh Jackson?' 'Yas, sah.' 'Lucinda, does you realize de seriousness of dis opportunity? Am you gwine to stick to Samuel clean frew to de judgment day, or am you gwine to trifle around arter odder men?' 'Ize gwine to stick.' 'Den, chill'en, in de presence of dese yere white men from the Norf, one of whom subscribed two bits yesterday to help build de meetin' house dat was blowed down by de sighclone, I denounce you as hitched, jined an' mar'd 'cordin' to de law an' gospel. Now you go 'long an' behave yerselves.' "[14]

The Negro's hypersensitiveness about his "civil rights" is illustrated by the following story in the *Star* in 1897:

MORE DISCRIMINATION
THE DISCOVERY MADE BY A MAN WHO WAS ON THE ALERT FOR AN AFFRONT

"There was that about his attire and manner which showed that, although of African descent, he was fully alive to the respect due him as a citizen of the United States and an equal voter at the polls. The salesman in the men's furnishing store hastened to learn his wishes and ventured to wish him 'good morning.'

" 'What can we do for you today?'

" 'You can't do nuffin' much foh me,' was the reply. 'I come yuh ter do somefin' foh you.'

" 'We—er—we don't need any help.'

" 'I ain't lookin' foh wukh! I come yuh to give you all some money. I wants to trade an' ef somebody gits de bes' er de bahgain, I don't reckon its gwineter be me. Only I don' want no bowin' and scrapin' like yoh 'magined I was de Prince o' Wales, an' at de same time I don' want no sassiness. All I desiahs is ter put money on de counter an' kyah off de goods, ef dey suits me.'

" 'What do you wish to purchase?'

" 'Er shirt.'

" 'Ah yes, I'm sure we can give you a satisfactory article. Do you want a white shirt or a colored shirt?'

" 'What's dat?' and his hand reached ominously for his pocket [for the razor, probably, that Negroes were supposed to carry and to use on the slightest provocation].

" 'I merely asked you whether you wanted a white shirt or a colored shirt,' the salesman replied as he edged behind a pile of hat boxes.

" 'I s'pected it in de fus place; an' now I knows it. I'm in de wrong sto'. What's de good er civil rights? I goes ter de theayter an' dey has white seats an' colored seats. I goes ter de restaurant and dey has white vittles an' colored vittles. But when I come yuh ter get some cotton foh my back an' yoh stan's me up an' tells me dat yoh has white shirts foh white folks an' colored shirts foh colored folks, you's done got pas' de limit, an' dar ain' nuffin lef foh me ter do, 'ceppin' ter hire a lawyer.' "15

Four excerpts from narratives and one from a book review further sharpen the picture that was being drawn for Northern readers. General Sherman in his speech at the New England dinner told of an incident during his March to the Sea. He showed a Georgia planter the futility of the Civil War by pointing out that the planter had lost his "niggers." A long article in the *Dispatch*, 1886, narrated the visit of its author with a "genuine Virginia gentleman of the old regime." As the narrator was about to leave, he met a "decrepit old negro," and the following conversation ensued:

" 'Was your master a good master, uncle?'

" 'Wa-wa-wat you say sah? He-he good mawstah? Yo-yo-yo nebber head tell o' Maws—afore, has yo'? Goo-goo-good mawstah? Well, I sh'd—well, well, well! So! Dis ole niggah do' no what to say. He! He! he! whew! He was one ob de bes'! 'de berry bes'! I tell you [*sic*], sah! He! He! he! Whew!' "16

The *Enquirer* in 1895 reprinted an article from a Kentucky paper about " 'Mammy' " Carroll of that state. She was known to be 120 years of age, "and the old darky's former owner, Mrs. Carroll, thinks the good old woman must be at least five years older than that." Two years later the *Star* also ran a "darky" story. It began: "The African race in America, from the respectable 'colored person' all the way down the scale to 'niggers' (and please mark right here that all negroes are not 'niggers,' and all darkeys are not respectable persons) is strangely attracted by music, musk and the military." That the word darkey was unmistakably considered to be in good taste is further evident from the following paragraph in the same article: "An army darkey, with all his glee over free-dom, bragged of having belonged to rich people, and to some extent boasted of his state. Virginia darkeys certainly looked down on those of other states. Even a Kentucky darkey would observe in a quarrel: 'I never yit did see an Allerbarmer nigger wuff anything.' " The article continued in the same vein for almost two columns. A review in the *North American* in 1900, of *The Black Homer of Jimtown* described him as a "picturesque negro of the Uncle Rufus type, with all the ex-travagant fancy and boundless imagination of his race. His stories overflow with drollery and unctuous humor. Ed Mott, the author of the series of tales, has caught the spirit of the real old-time Southern darkey."[17]

The scramble for Africa led to numerous articles about the backwardness of the natives and the standard jokes about "cannibals," typified in a story told by Stanley during his visit to this country in 1886. Missionaries, he declared, did little good because "the natives all incline to the idea that they are only fit for roasts." On the other hand, articles in the Detroit *Tribune* and the *Globe-Democrat* in 1900 gave dramatic ac-counts, respectively, of "Atrocities" in the Belgian Congo and the "Belgian Monsters" there. Stories about superstitions in Africa and New Orleans appeared from time to time, and one death in Pittsburgh, 1895, was attributed to "Voodoo" or "Hoodoo." A colored woman whose color had slowly changed to white was termed a "freak" in nearly all the papers. In Sep-tember, 1895, the *Times* headlined a story about the arrival of Negroes from the South to take part in a play: "New Darkies for 'Black America.' " The same issue carried a story a column long about a Brooklyn woman's visit to the Eastern Shore of Virginia in which she stated: " 'It was on my first drive that I first saw the native darkies.' "[18]

While jokes in atrocious Irish, Jewish and German dialects must have rankled members of those minorities, Negro jokes appeared more frequently than those about any other minority. They were not particularly funny nor vicious, as the following selections indicate. The *Times* culled, in 1886, from *Texas Siftings* a slight exaggeration:

"Col. Yerger—Well, Uncle Mose, I expect you have seen many Christmases?

"Uncle Mose—Yas, Sah, tousands and tousands ob 'em."

One of the better chicken-stealing jokes appeared in the *Star* in 1895:

" 'I done tole de folks on Tuhkey Level dat dey orter git yoh ter settle in dah neighborhood,' said Elizabeth Crow.

" 'Whuffoh?' asked Erastus Pinkley.

" Dey was complainin' dat chickens got so common dat dey couldn't get no price for 'em, an' I tole em dat ef dey'd only get you in de place dey'd be purty sho' ter git skyace ergin."

The *Enquirer* liked this one about the Trifling Negro, also in 1895:

"Ferry—Rastus, you ought to be ashamed of yourself. The idea of a great, able-bodied man like you letting his wife support the family by taking in washing.

"Rastus—You don't understand de exemplary exigencies ob de situation, sah. I'se de promoter in dis partnership, sah. I goes around and gits her de jobs."

Uncle Ebem, the genial philosopher whose witticisms were an irregular small feature in the *Star*, admonished in 1897:

" 'Folks is nebber saterfied. Er white young lady is allus tryin' ter git frizzes in her hair an' culled young lady is allus tryin' to git 'em out.' "

The advent of automobiles led to a fairly good one, also in the *Star*, in 1900:

" 'Dese hoss'less kerriges ain't so much,' said Mr. Erastus Pinkley.

" 'Dey's all de talk,' replied Miss Miami Brown.

" 'Co'se dey is. But it's a back number scheme. What were de fust steamship but a mule-less canal boat?' "

A rare example of a joke against discrimination appeared in the *Dispatch* in 1895. A traveler asked:

" 'What's the reason I can't get a meal here, I'd like to know.'

"Dignified Proprietor (of a first-class restaurant in Central Africa)—'You'll have to go to that little chop-house down the street, sah. We don't entertain white people here, sah.' "[19]

Cartoons, both editorial and comic, made more vivid several stereotypes. On the front page of the *Enquirer* in 1895, appeared a drawing, three columns wide, of "Interested Spectators of the Passing Procession to the Chickamauga Park." They were a rather cute, though raggedy and barefooted, colored boy and girl—and a mule. A sequence of four incidents showed how an explorer saved his life from African "savages" by doing some magician's tricks. A third one in the *Enquirer*, taken from *Life*, pictured a short-haired colored boy yelling his head off to illustrate "An Old Adage: 'Much cry and little wool.' " "Stray Leaves from Comic Sketch Books" in the Chicago *Tribune* in July of the same year captioned a cartoon "An Impediment." A Negro, obviously ill at ease in white tie and tails, said to an equally uncomfortable big-footed colored "belle" in evening clothes: " 'Skuze me Miss Whitely, but woan yo' mobe two feet closer to de wall. We wants to dance.' " Some of the cartoons were evidently syndicated, for one appeared in the Chicago *Tribune*, *Globe-Democrat* and *Enquirer* in September, 1895. Somewhat in the style of Worth's Darktown Comics in the Currier and Ives Prints, it was entitled "The Reigning Craze." The hard-working colored woman was holding a broom in her hands; her husband, without coat or collar, was adorned with the standard big feet, hands, nose and mouth. "Br'er Johnsing" asked: " 'Whah am dem kyarpet beatin' sticks of mine?' " His wife replied: " 'I ain' quite shuah, but I t'ink Mary Jane done took 'em to play golf wid.' " Similar cartoons about mules, chickens, and cannibals appeared in 1900. A variation was syndicated: a little colored boy, made up to look like a scarecrow, was moaning: "Mammy! Mammy! Dese heah w'ite boys is callin' me 'niggah' wifout provocation."[20]

But news along the color line revealed to the discerning reader tragedy and "human interest" as well as crime and humor. If the reporter for the *Star* had possessed the insight and literary craftsmanship of a Charles W. Chesnutt, he might have been inspired to dig deeper into a story which appeared in 1895:

> Julia Pursall, a colored woman who for years conducted a small hairdressing establishment on M Street, under the name of "Mme" Pursall died suddenly last night. . . . For many years "Mme" Pursall lived exclusively to herself. She had education and a haughty bearing. For the past two or three years, though, she was compelled to waive her prejudice and live among her people.

What had been the relations between Charles H. McCallister, a colored physician practicing in Chicago, and his father, a former slave-owner in Kentucky, prior to the time that his father left him a substantial bequest on his death in 1886?

History would probably have been enriched by the reminiscences of Elias Polk, President Polk's body servant, if some one had deemed them worthy of being recorded prior to his death in 1886. Only students at Yale were eligible for membership in the Skull and Bones Society, but the colored janitor, Robert M. Park, had to be made a member so that he could perform his duties during the meetings. Lewis Bates, a former slave in North Carolina, lived alone in a dingy room at 400 Dearborn Street, Chicago. Although unlettered, he had amassed a fortune of some $500,000 through shrewd real-estate dealings. One of his holdings was "an elegant, new seven-story pressed-brick and terra cotta apartment house worth $80,000 on State Street which he rented to white tenants."[21]

Numerous articles related various incidents in the life of prominent colored men such as Bruce, Pinchback and Langston. The comments that were printed after the death of Frederick Douglass in 1895, must serve as a capsule of the appreciation for these "exceptional" Negroes.

In accordance with established custom, most of the dailies adhered to the tradition of *de mortuis, nil nisi bonum*. The *Enquirer* and the *Examiner* extolled him as a great colored statesman, and the *Evening Register* confined itself to the innocuous comment that few men had spoken more often or more effectively or to a larger number of people. Projecting its discussion against a broader background, the *Globe-Democrat* linked his death with the recent deaths of Theodore D. Weld, Judge E. R. Hoar and General John L. Swift as a reminder of the passing of the few survivors of the old anti-slavery champions. While the Chicago *Tribune* called him the most illustrious representative of his race, it added that no man, white or black, had been better known in the United States for almost half a century. "One of the most valuable characters in American public life" was the rather restrained appreciation in the Detroit *Tribune*.

When a tempest was created in North Carolina over reports in the North Carolina press that the Fusion-dominated legislature had adjourned out of respect for Douglass but not for Washington and Lee,[22] the *North American* retorted that "Frederick Douglass did more for man, for the South, for the country, a hundred times over than did Robert E. Lee." The *Transcript* not only saluted Douglass as "one of the best known men in this country," but added: "His mission on this planet was evidently to demolish color prejudice, because he did it with wonderful success by his example, unflinching attachment to principle, and never-failing cheerfulness." Going further than most of the papers, the *Journal* emphasized his demands for equal rights and predicted that remote history would accord him a much higher place among the world's great men than did that generation. The *Star*, which was most lavish in its praise, considered him one of the most remarkable men that the nation had produced, and warmly endorsed a proposal sent to it that a memorial be erected to his honor in Washington that would "fitly" honor him. (Nothing came of the proposal. Rochester, New York, is the only city that has a monument erected in his honor.)

Only two papers appeared hostile to Douglass. The *Dispatch* commented sarcastically that the North Carolina legislature had honored him above Washington and Lee. The *Times* was most unseemly in its attacks. In a rather vicious comment on the action of the North Carolina legislature and of Douglass's marriage to a white woman, one editorial asserted: "Fusion is a marriage of two parties having no principles in common. The indorsement of the miscegenation leader is the legitimate heir of the union." Another editorial recalled Douglass's resentment at being called "Fred" Douglass, and recognized that this diminutive was in truth a sign of patronage by the white race for a man of color "who had done remarkably well, 'considering.'" It was equally futile to argue against or to pass statutes against such prejudice. Douglass had qualities which no full-blooded African in American history had displayed. This long editorial concluded:

It is significant that the blacks should generally have regarded his espousal of a white woman for his second wife as an act of "treason" though indeed it was the natural consequence of his own development. He was a man of integrity, of intelligence, of dignity, of benevolence. But these qualities, instead of solving the "race question" in his case simply served to propound that question more sharply. They made it appear that a man who differed from his race for better was isolated and made unhappy by the difference, without being enabled to effect any thing for the benefit of his race.[23]

The great abolitionist had become the "tragic mulatto."

The Northern papers also revealed to their readers the successful careers of several Negroes who are not included in a kind of colored Who's Who, namely, *Men of Mark* published in 1887, and who have not been noted by historians. These stories will be summarized in Chapter Fifteen. They served perhaps to offset somewhat the generally derogatory material. But they could not hide the fact that colored people in general, even the "upper class" Negroes who were called Mr., Miss and Mrs., and even "Hon." and "esquire," were subjected to prejudice, discrimination and segregation in the North.

Evidences of these practices are not surprising since, despite considerable improvement, they have not yet been entirely eradicated. Well-to-do Negroes in New York encountered so much difficulty finding decent homes that they began moving to Brooklyn. Many prominent Negroes were denied hotel and restaurant accommodations in Washington, St. Louis, Cincinnati and Springfield, Ohio, and even in New York and Boston. Even the passage of new and strengthened civil rights provisions did not always prevent discrimination. In fact, when a stronger law was passed in New York, 1895, the *Times* felt that Negroes should not use it as a means to "rub shoulders with whites." During the Republican National Convention, at Philadelphia in 1900, Negro delegates were assigned to colored homes. One of these delegates, Dr. George W. Lee, pastor of the Vermont Avenue Baptist Church in Washington, was the subject of a cartoon by the *North American's* regular cartoonist, Walt McDougall, the nature of which may be judged by the accompanying article. In the election for the seat for which Lee was contesting, he had run "with weight in his favor but beauty against him. 'In one district,' said Doctor George, 'W. Calvin Brice [Chase], the editor of the Bee (he has 'em in his bonnet, he! he!) done polled 2900 votes. In dat district dere ain't no 2900 votes, countin' men, women, chillun, dawgs an' cats.' "[24]

Negroes, it was reported, were already being replaced in most of the first-class hotels because of their lack of dependability. Major Taylor, one of the best professional bicyclists, and the mixed Oakland, California, Club were denied membership in the League of American Wheelmen. Only after great agitation in the *Examiner* did the white Pacific Coast champion give Peter Jackson a chance to knock him "under the color line." A colored reporter for the Philadelphia *Times* was denied membership in the Philadelphia Journalists Club, solely because of his color, it was asserted. Negroes generally accepted exclusion from white churches, but in at least one instance, they tried unsuccessfully to be admitted to a church in Brazil, Indiana. Colored Protestant Episcopalians, in a meeting in Washington, 1895, protested that, while a few colored ministers were permitted to speak before white audiences, none was admitted to diocesan conventions.[25]

But there were many demands on the part of Negroes for improvement in colored schools, the abolition of separate schools, and the employment of colored teachers in mixed schools. It is probable that the cases cited are indicative of many others. In 1895, Negroes in New Haven unsuccessfully supported a colored candidate for the board of education in an effort to obtain better facilities for colored children. Colored citizens in Jamaica, Long Island, charged, in the same year, that not a single pupil had been graduated from the colored school built in 1874. Also in the same year, a young colored woman was denied an appointment in the public schools of East Providence on "no other grounds than color," according to the *Transcript*. One hundred and three delegates representing seventy-eight counties of Illinois organized the Illinois Afro-American Citizens' Protective Association, to "resist mob violence and lynch law; to demand fair and impartial trials for colored people, and to endeavor to secure for colored children equal school accommodations with the white children." That they were not entirely successful is seen in the fact that two years later colored pupils invaded the white school in Alton, struck the teacher, and sat in the school until police ejected them. After the repeal of the Ohio Black Laws in 1887, Cincinnati established a high school in a neighborhood inhabited almost exclusively by Negroes. When colored citizens of Oxford brought suit to gain admission to the white school, a merchant discharged all his colored employees. In the town of Felicity, a riot resulted, followed by the threat to close the school rather than open it to Negroes. A riot between white and colored pupils in Indianapolis, November, 1895, spread to the entire community. When colored teachers began to seek appointment in the Cincinnati schools in 1900, the *Enquirer* observed that it was not likely that any would be appointed because there was "said to be a strong sentiment, . . . against having colored teachers instruct white children." In the nation's capital, where segregation in the public schools was generally accepted, the overcrowding of colored schools and their location were frequently, heatedly and fruitlessly discussed. The Maryland Law School discontinued, in 1890, the admission of colored students when the white students threatened to leave.[26]

When the General Federation of Women's Clubs was faced with the question of the color line at the turn of the century, Southern clubs threatened to secede. One of the first expressions of the adamant opposition to the admission of colored clubs was disclosed by the Chicago *Tribune* and the *Examiner* during the great festivals of fraternization at the Atlanta Exposition, the Encampment of the GAR in Louisville, and the dedication of the Chickamauga Battlefield. The article, datelined Atlanta, September 19, 1895, the day after Washington spoke, began: " 'The color line' among women will not obtrude itself on the exposition, but there is no question that it will be fought out next May at Louisville," at the biennial meeting of the Federation. The Georgia Women's Press Club felt so strongly on the subject that members were in favor of withdrawing from the Federation if colored women were admitted there. Miss Corinne Stocker, a member of the Managing Board of the Georgia Women's Press Club and one of the editors of the Atlanta *Journal*, stated on September 19: " 'In this matter the Southern women are not narrow-minded or bigoted, but they simply cannot recognize the colored women socially. . . . At the same time we feel that the South is the colored woman's best friend.' "[27]

The issue came to a head neither at Louisville in 1896, nor at Denver in 1898, where Mrs. Rebecca Lowe of Georgia was elected president, but at Milwaukee in 1900. One problem was quickly disposed of. When the question was raised whether Mrs. Mary Church Terrell, president of the National Association of Colored Women, would be allowed to extend fraternal greetings, Mrs. Lowe ruled that it had been customary to limit the representation of so-called fraternal delegates to those societies which extended similar courtesies to the Federation, such as the National Council of Women, the Mother's Congress, the National Woman's Suffrage Association, and the Council of Jewish Women. Since the National

Association of Colored Women did not "extend similar courtesies" to the General Federation, Mrs. Terrell was not permitted to extend fraternal greetings at Milwaukee.[28]

The threat of secession arose from the fact that Mrs. Josephine St. Pierre Ruffin, the "octoroon" wife of a colored
graduate of the Harvard Law School and judge in the
Charlestown Court, represented not only the Massachusetts
State Federation and the New England Press Association but
also the New Era Club, a colored organization. If she were
permitted to represent the latter, then a Negro club would be
a member of the Federation. Mrs. Lowe skilfully evaded the
issue by rapidly calling the roll of delegates by clubs instead
of by individuals. Northern delegates who supported Mrs.
Ruffin were so surprised that the roll was approved before
they could discover a method of challenging the procedure.
On the other hand, the attempt to snatch Mrs. Ruffin's badge
from her was thwarted by her agility. She remained throughout the meeting, but the New Era Club was not admitted.
The re-election of Mrs. Lowe was rightly interpreted as a victory for the would-be "secessionists." The Southern clubs
held their lines, the powerful New York delegation was dis-
rupted by Mrs. Lowe's choice of Mrs. Charles Dennison,
president of Sorosis, as first vice-president. Mrs. William Tod
Wilmuth of New York withdrew her candidacy for president,
and Mrs. Lowe was re-elected by the overwhelming vote of
563 to 187.[29]

All the papers except the *Star* and the *Evening Register*
emphasized in bold headlines the issue of the "Color Line,"
and all except these two and the Detroit *Tribune* and the
Enquirer ran several long articles tracing the threats of secession of the Southern delegates and their final victory. The
Dispatch and the *Globe-Democrat* sent special feminine cor-
respondents. Inevitably, there was a good deal of editorializing in the news articles. Mrs. Cynthia Westover-Alden, the
special correspondent of the *Dispatch*, spoke very highly in
favor of Mrs. Ruffin whom she described as "a highly educated woman, very light in color and very lady-like in her
demeanor." On the other hand, Miss Jane Frances Winn, the
Globe-Democrat's special correspondent, soon was completely
in Mrs. Lowe's camp. "Mme" Ruffin was making very much
of a nuisance of herself, and the Massachusetts delegation was
tired of the whole question. But Mrs. Lowe was "a great

favorite with the colored race." A special dispatch to the *Globe-Democrat*, however, pointed out that the board of directors turned down the application of the New Era Club, "and at the same time took in half a dozen other clubs, so that it is plain that the only excuse for refusing the New Era Club is the colored [*sic*] line." All the other papers that reported the "color line" explicitly or implicitly underscored the discrimination.

But no paper deemed the treatment of Mrs. Ruffin worthy of extended editorial comment. In a short paragraph, the *Journal* chastised the Massachusetts delegation for not supporting a member in good standing even though such action would have "made trouble." The *Transcript*, rather facetiously, criticized clubwomen for taking matters so seriously. "Why cannot the clubwomen," it inquired, "do as the men do at their clubs, and tacitly agree to give soul-stirring, hair-raising questions the go-by?" In the most forthright condemnation of the Federation's action, the Chicago *Tribune* on June 7 admonished:

> Worst of all, the question on which the convention is so seriously divided is one which a large number of men thought was settled thirty years ago. If the women's clubs are to fight the war over again there would appear to be little hope for great progress in any of the reforms which the federation has set out to accomplish until peace has been finally declared.

Another editorial, four days later, quoted passages from Mrs. Lowe's address to show how meaningless they were:

> The one predominant thought which every member of the convention . . . , in this final year of the century, must carry away is that the federated white-faced women of the clubs have not had the courage to recognize their sisters of the colored race, and to this extent have stamped with insincerity their own protestations of sympathy "for all who have wrought with sorrow-laden hearts."[30]

In a letter to the editor, a man, W. A. Phelps, also condemned the Federation: "Here we have the spectacle of educated, refined, and Christian women, who have been protesting and laboring for years against the unjust discrimination practiced against them by men, now getting together and the first shot out of their reticules is fired at one of their own sex because she is black, no other reason or pretence of reason."[31]

This attempt to discover the Mind of the North may appropriately close with a statement by the woman whose election would not have been possible without the support of the "educated, refined, Christian women" of the North. In an interview reported by the Chicago *Tribune*, Mrs. Lowe declared: "Mrs. Ruffin belongs among her own people. Among them she would be a leader and could do much good, but among us she can create nothing but trouble." Mrs. Lowe had assisted in establishing kindergartens for colored children in the South, and the colored women in charge of them were all her good friends. She associated with them in a business way, but, of course, they would not think of sitting beside her at a reception or of standing with her on the platform of a convention. Negroes were "a race by themselves, and among themselves they can accomplish much, assisted by us and by the federation, which is ever ready to do all in its power to help them." If Mrs. Ruffin were the "cultured lady every one says she is, she should put her education and her talents to good uses as a colored woman among colored women." The interview closed with the assurance: "It is the 'high-caste' negroes who bring about all the ill-feeling. The ordinary colored woman understands her position thoroughly."[32]

THIRTEEN

The Negro as Portrayed in the Leading Literary Magazines

THREE of the leading literary magazines—*Harper's New Monthly Magazine, Scribner's (Century* after 1881) and the *Atlantic Monthly*—mirrored the refined tastes of the upper classes. Frederick Lewis Allen, editor of *Harper's* from 1941 to 1953, wrote in 1950 a penetrating evaluation of *Harper's* in 1891:

> To us today some of the *Harper's* fiction of 1891 seems naïve, some of its verse weakly sentimental, some of its pen-and-ink illustrations too daintily photographic; we wonder at its comparative neglect of the vital social and economic issues of the day, at its preoccupation with the safely remote, and the respectably classical, the second-hand literary; and its careful propriety. We have to remind ourselves that the public for which it was edited was the victim of an attractive but academic and timorous genteelism.

Harper's from 1877 to 1901 varied little from this sharply focused picture of 1891. Like *Harper's*, the *Atlantic* and *Century*, according to Commager, "made few concessions to the contemporary scene and none to vulgar taste."[1] Readers had to go to magazines like the *North American Review* and to *Forum*, established in 1886, for regular discussion of the vital issues of the day.

The editors of these five magazines were Northerners, except Walter Hines Page, editor of *Forum* from 1886 to 1895 and of the *Atlantic* after 1897. It would be difficult to ascertain a substantial difference between the portrayal of the Negro under Northern editorship and under Page's. In fact, the largest number of derogatory stereotypes appeared in *Harper's, Scribner's* and *Century*, partly because they contained drawings and cartoons that vividly depicted the antics of Negroes and more short stories in dialect than did the *Atlantic*. Most of the authors of fiction and poetry about

242

Negroes were Southerners whose lives were more closely associated, unavoidably, with Negroes than were those of Northerners. Most of the essays in all five magazines, however, were written by Northerners. It may be safely assumed that the majority of readers were Northerners. The composite picture of the Negro that emerges from this chapter is, therefore, that which appealed to editors who were overwhelmingly Northern, to writers who were largely Northern except in the case of fiction and poetry, and to readers who were predominantly Northern. A modern reader wonders why Northern devotees of the Genteel Tradition found such evident delight in the lampooning of Negroes. Perhaps these new-world aristocrats gloried all the more in their own faultless language, polished manners and physical attractiveness because of the outlandish speech, crude behavior and "ugliness" of those Americans who were most different from them.

Harper's, Scribner's, Century, and to a less degree the *Atlantic,* regularly employed derisive terms that are rarely used today, except in local color fiction, in private conversation, and by the most rabid of "wool-hat" politicians. Many stories, anecdotes, poems and cartoons referred to Negroes as "nigger," "niggah," "darkey," "coon," "pickaninny," "Mammy," "aunt," "uncle," "buck," "light-complected-yaller man," "yaller hussy." Pralines were "nigger candy." Thomas Nelson Page had an article in the Editor's Drawer of *Harper's* entitled, "All the Geography a Nigger Needs to Know." The *North American Review* rarely if ever permitted in its staid pages such uncomplimentary terms; when it published an article by General Sherman that referred to Negroes as "Darkies," the word was placed in quotation marks. The word Negro was practically never capitalized, and the dialect was generally strained, showing variations sometimes in the same story. But as the most eminent colored novelist, Chesnutt, himself explained:

> The fact is, of course, that there is no such thing as a Negro dialect; that what we call by that name is the attempt to express, with such a degree of phonetic correctness as to suggest the sound, English pronounced as an ignorant old southern Negro would be supposed to speak it, and at the same time to preserve a sufficient approximation to the correct spelling to make it easy reading.[2]

Negroes were described as being black, ebony, midnight black, black as a crow, or black as a total eclipse. A little white girl asked her mother whether God had made an "ebony" little boy. When her mother replied in the affirmative, the girl queried: "'Mama, do you suppose God thought he was *pretty?*'" Negroes were thick-lipped; they had flat noses, big ears and feet, kinky or woolly hair. An anonymous traveler in the "great black" regions of the South pictured "the uncouth, strangely shaped animal-looking Negro or mulatto, who seems mentally, even more than by his physical characteristics, to belong to a race entirely distinct from that of the white race around them." The writer of the article understood why white women were afraid of Negroes, since they were "a race alien, animal, half savage, easily made sullen or aroused to fury."[3]

Negroes were made ludicrous by the bestowal of titles, names of famous men or of folk expressions. Among the choice ones were Colonel, Senator, Sheriff, Apollo Belvedere, George Washington, Webster, Abraham Lincum, Napoleon Boneyfidey Waterloo, Venus Milo Clevins, Columbus, Pomp, Caesar, Lady Adeliza Chimpanzee, Prince Orang Outan, Hieronymous, Ananias, Solomon Crow, Piddlekins, Sosrus Dismal, Asmodeus, Bella Donna Mississippi Idaho, Violetta Marie Evalina Rose Christian, Nuttin 'Tal, Had-a-Plenty and Wan-na-Mo. The ultimate was achieved in Henri Ritter Demi Ritter Emmi Ritter Sweet-potato Cream Tarter Caroline Bostwick.

Virtually every derogatory stereotype was affixed upon the Negro. Sometimes several appeared in one passage of the same story. Thus, one colored woman was described as being a "typical Negro," since she was improvident, emotional, gossipy, kind-hearted, high-tempered, vain, dishonest, idle, working only two or three days a week and "'res'n'" up the rest of the week, with always a hearty appetite and "'miz'ry in de bres'.'" The Negro of Barbados was *sui generis*, for

There is nothing like him on earth, above it, or under it. He will lie, cheat, and steal beyond all comprehension. He is impudent to a degree hardly to be understood by an American. They are outwardly very devout, but it never enters their heads to practice what they preach. As an English clergyman living among them once said, "They will go to communion, and steal yams on the way home."[4]

In various articles, stories, anecdotes, poems and cartoons, the Negro was made to appear superstitious, dull, and stupid, imitative and hence not creative, ignorant, suspicious, happy-go-lucky, improvident, lazy, immoral, criminal; he was a liar, a thief and a drunkard. He used big words which he did not understand. He liked fine clothes and trinkets, chickens, " 'watermillions,' " " 'Sweet-'tators,' " and " ''possum.' " The inevitable razor-totin' Negro made his appearance. Preachers, and to a less degree lawyers, were the frequent butt of jokes. The Negro was portrayed in the plantation tradition as a faithful slave and servant. But he could not adapt to freedom. Occasionally he was revealed as the "tragic mulatto." While some articles and other contributions treated Chinese, Indians, Irish, Germans and other immigrants in general in an unfavorable light, these aliens and the oldest Americans fared better than did the Negro. Jews, partly because articles about them were written by Jews, received more kindly treatment than did other minorities.

Stealing was the characteristic most frequently attributed to Negroes. One prefaced his intention of stealing a turkey by vowing:

> Got to git out an' make hay
> Don't keer whut de preachah say.

The possible origin of one of the most famous jokes of Bert Williams, sometimes called the greatest comedian of the early twentieth century, is found in a story in which Webster resented being called a chicken thief. Mose, his accuser, sought to deny having made the charge. What he had really said was: " 'Dar was a dozen chicken thieves in Austin *not* includin' yerself.' " Thomas Nelson Page told a story about a Negro accused of stealing a steer. Despite all that Page could do for his client, he was found guilty. When Page informed him that an appeal would cost money, the Negro replied that he had none; if he had, he would have got himself a lawyer. Charlie had been haled into court on the charge of having stolen an opossum. Standing on his rights, he demanded the inclusion of six members of his race on the jury. Charlie confessed his guilt and described the tantalizing merits of a well-cooked opossum with " 'split sweet-'taters' " around it and " 'brown gravy leakin' down es sides.' " This evocation was more than certain members of the jury could endure. Joining

Charlie in visible manifestation of their delectation, they acquitted him. In similar vein, Lam (who was always lamentin') won the confidence of his congregation when he confessed that he was addicted to chicken stealing. When the wife of a Georgia " 'Cracker' " admonished her husband against stealing, she accused him of being like a " 'no 'count nigger.' " One writer attributed the Negro's alleged propensity for stealing to the fact that he knew that he had been wrongfully held in slavery and hence did not hesitate to feign sickness or to lay hands on any articles that he could appropriate without being detected. Judge Jeremiah S. Black, Southerner, contended that under the carpetbag government of Louisiana, Negroes stole everything possible that could not be kept under lock and key; pigs, poultry, the fruits of the garden and orchard, cotton and corn were carried away from the fields at night and traded for liquor and groceries at "stores" which had been established for this particular brand of commerce.[5]

Stealing frequently led to lying. A cartoon in *Century* showed a Negro mother wearing a polka-dot turban and holding a menacing switch in her hand as she asked her mammoth-eared son: " 'Abraham Lincum, whar's dat cooky?' " " 'I dunno,' " he replied. " 'Uncle Mose said dar was a cakewalk yest'day ebening, and maybe it hain't got back yet.' " Hebe, a small child, asked: " 'Unc' Isrul, mammy say, huccome de milk so watery on top in de mornin'?' " The "Patriarch" directed him to " 'tell you' mammy dat's de bes' sort o' milk; dats de *dew* on it—de cows been layin' in de dew.' " Ginger had prepared a splendid goose for a special dinner that his master had ordered, but the girl he "lubbed" had wheedled him into giving her one leg of the goose. When two guests asked to be served legs, Ginger called attention to the fact that all the geese in the yard were resting on one leg as proof of the general absence of a leg. But when the master made the geese run, Ginger had to call on all his ingenuity. As he told the story:

An' den I tu'n right roun' at Marse Ned, an' I say, solemn like, an' I say him loud, an' I say him strong, an' I look him straight in de whites ob his eyes—I say, "Marse Ned, when you see dat goose on de table in front ob you, wid just one leg afore de company, did you 'member to say 'shoo' to dat goose? I jist arsk you dat!"—and Marse Ned nebber had one word to say.

Although tall tales are a part of American folk humor, they became a racial penchant for lying when told by Negroes. Thomas Nelson Page emphasized this trait rather than exaggeration as a basis for humor when he told the story of a Negro who had assured him that he had held George Washington's horse while the general decapitated Cornwallis in personal combat. Several other stories summarized below also included this penchant, and one story was entitled "Lazarus Mart'n de Cullud Lieyer."[6]

While colored lawyers were held up to ridicule in that story, colored preachers were much more often the butt of jokes. Stealing and lying formed the basis for a sermon by "Bruddeh Isaac" who admonished:

> My breddren, somewhah in de 'Sa'ms, King David says, "All men am liahs." . . . I want to invite youh t'oughts dis mawnin' to de 'speyance [experience] ob one ob de liahs, showin' de trufe ob de secon' tex', "Reputations am ohfen got widout deservin'." [Here followed the story of Ananias.] An' you white folks in de back ob de church, if bruddeh Samule says he t'anks de Lawd he's hones'; if bruddeh 'Rastus tells you he hates de sight ob chicken pie, remembeh dat King David says, "All men am liahs," an' keep youh hen-house locked.

Another preacher informed his congregation: "'Now my breddern, . . . you all'll want to know de reason dat immussion is de only mode ob babtism. Well, now, my breddern, bless de Lawd, 'tain't none o' yoah business.'" More than twenty-five anecdotes in *Harper's* developed the theme that Negroes valued their preachers in proportion to their ability to excite emotion. Typical of these was one about a "darky" who was asked the relative merits of two Negro "'zorters" (exhorters). He replied: "'Dey's bofe of 'em mighty pow'ful 'zorters, but dat Rob Sheldon, he's de best, 'kase he's got de mos' tones.'"[7]

Parson Reub Taylor, who had gone through only the First Reader, liked to use big words. His congregation often remarked: "'Brer Taylor is got a black face, but his speech sholy is white.'" In order to expand his vocabulary the preacher sought the aid of "Marse John." His former master gave him the word "ratiocination," which pleased the preacher so mightily that he asked how it was spelled. When the first three letters were spelled out, Taylor became very angry and exclaimed:

> Well! Hits come ter dis is it? One o' ole marster's chillen settin' up, makin' spote o' me ter my face! I didn't spect it of yer, Marse John—I did not. It's bad enough when some o' dese heah low-down po'-white-trash town-boys hollers "rats" at me—let alone my own white chillen what I done toted in my arms! Lemme go home an' try ter forgit dis insult ole marster's chile insulted me wid!

After a good deal more conversation in this vein, Taylor finally left with the new word added to his vocabulary.[8]

Sometimes words were put into the mouths of preachers for the purpose of teaching Negroes "proper" behavior. "Brudder" Peter informed his congregation that every woman was possessed of seven devils. Although he quoted the Bible to prove his assertion, some members of his congregation attributed his diatribe to the fact that he had a shrewish wife. Others, however, believed that he had got his "fool notion" from some lawyers at the court house where he had served on the jury. Another old colored preacher warned his son, "P'laski," against attempting to be like white folks by entering a tournament that Negroes were planning to hold. The preacher attributed this strange aberration to "free issue" Negroes.[9]

One of the longest stories about a man of God emphasized differences in color among Negroes, and portrayed the "uppity" Negro as well as other stereotypes. Jerry's employer began the narrative by recalling that one morning his man-of-all work was not his usual happy self. Seeking to ascertain the nature of the sorrow that hung so heavily upon Jerry's heart, he learned that Jerry hated " 'little yaller niggers dat put on a gol' ring . . . an' stove-flute hats, an' p'inted-toe shoes' " and pretended to be humble in church. The special objects of Jerry's hatred were the pointed-toe shoes, for they had come between him and the shapely quadroon, Venus Milo Clevins. The revival going on at Mount Tabor had brought to the neighborhood an exhorter who was winning the favor of the women by his " 'patentized leather p'inted-toe shoes,' " rather than by the persuasion of the Gospel. Apparently Venus Milo had succumbed to the lure of the shoes, for

she had begun to act as if Jerry " 'done pass off de map.' "
As Jerry related his woes, there was on his features the expression which "among his race was only too often followed
by the shedding of somebody's blood." Later Jerry rejoiced
when pointed-toe shoe tracks made it clear that it was the
preacher who had been making nocturnal expeditions to his
employer's home for the purpose of stealing.[10]

Northern Negroes were occasionally made to appear as
ludicrous as those living in the South. The Editor's Drawer
of *Harper's*, in 1878, reproduced a debate by the Colored
Debating Society of Mount Vernon, Ohio, on the familiar
subject of the pen and the sword. The following three excerpts
probably provoked the greatest laughter from readers:

Dr. Crane: " 'Now, as de modern poet says, our swoards
rust in deir cubbards, an' peas, sweet peas, covers de lan'.
An' what has wrot all dis change? *De pen.* Do I take a swoard
now to git me a peck ob sweet-taters, a pair ob chickens, a
pair ob shoes? No, Saar. I jess take my pen an' write a order
for 'em. . . . ' "

Mr. Hunnicut: " 'If it hadden bin for de swoard ob ole
Bunker Hill, Saar, whaar'd we niggers be tonight, Saar? Where
Saar? Not hyar, Saar. In Georgia, Saar, or wuss, Saar. . . . ' "

The committee finally decided " 'dat de swoard has de most
pints an' de best backin', an dat de pen is de most beneficial,
an' dat de whole ting is about a stan'-off.' "[11]

The religious superstitions of Negroes were frequently portrayed. One story told of the nefarious influence of black devotees of voodooism upon a mulatto. In the Contributor's
Club of the *Atlantic*, it was pointed out that not all Negro
superstitions were "gently, mildly ridiculous and associated
with hooting owls and dogs," for Negroes had superstitions
of a higher order which they did not wish white folks to know
about. Negroes believed, for example, that sounds of spirits
of the underworld could be heard through holes in the ground
which provided entrance and exit for underworld folk. Negroes had special ghosts for special areas such as the path
ghost and the wood ghost. Another "Contributor" felt that
the weird tales told by Negroes were assisted by an "erratic
memory, a vivid imagination and a superstitious trend of
thought, translated into fantasies and invested with super-
natural accessories." He told a story about two Negro witches

who had the power to change themselves into Jay-birds, their satanic helpers. The Jay-bird theme was also the subject of a poem in *Century*. When a Negro feigned sleep in the presence of witches, he did so with the "cunning of his race." Another writer called these superstitions "savage African beliefs." Virginia Frazer Boyle of Louisiana contributed several stories to *Harper's* based on superstitions, among them "Dark er de Moon," "Asmodeus in the Quarters," "Old Cinder Cat" and "The Devil's Little Fly."[12]

Mrs. Ruth McEnery Stuart, a frequent contributor to *Harper's* took special delight in telling stories of domestic squabbles. The alleged unchastity of Negro women in general was analyzed in an article in the *Atlantic*. The practice was attributed to their lack of concern for sexual purity and to the free use that white men made of them. The author added that the sexual immorality of Negro women was a deterrent to loose morals between white men and white women.[13]

A number of poems also contained stereotypes, including the faithful slave and the freedman who could not adjust to free society. Praise for the former master was revealed in one poem:

> *I heahs a heap o' people talkin', ebrywhar I goes*
> *'Bout Washintun an' Franklum, an' sech genuses as dose:*
> *I s'pose dey's mighty fine, but heah's de p'int I 's bettin' on:*
> *Dere wuzn't nar a one ob 'em come up to Mahsr John.*

A yearning for the good old days, and dissatisfaction with the new prompted a Negro husband to complain:

> *She's got set-up dese las' few years,*
> *An' wheat bread's all de go;*
> *But somehow seems I'd like ter tas'e*
> *Some ash-cake pone onst mo'. . . .*
> *Dat broadclof coat she made me buy—*
> *It don't feel half so good*
> *As dat ole jeans I used ter w'ar*
> *A-cuttin' marseter's wood. . . .*
> *'Tis only one o' all her ways*
> *Dat troubles me for sho':*
> *I'd like ter eat some 'possum-fat*
> *An' ash-cake pone onst mo'.*[14]

The watermelon stealing theme was thus put to verse:

> *En next time you hook water-millions, you*
> *heered me, you ignant, you hunk,*
> *Ef you do' want a lickin' all over be sho*
> *dat day allers go "punk."*[15]

Fifteen verses were necessary to tell the story of fishing on Sunday:

> *Hiya! you nigger, dah, I like ter know*
> *Wut dat you up to e yere! Well, to be sho*
> *Ef you aint fishin' on de good Lawd's day,*
> *Des like you done done clah forgit de way*
> *Up to de meetin' house! Yere, come erlong*
> *Er me, en I'll show you de place you b'long.*
>
> *Fer members ud de church, dis yer gits me,*
> *Un all de owdacious doin's I ever see,*
> *Dis takin de Sabbaf-day in vain's de wuss*
> *Fer mortifyin' de morals us—You Gus!*
> *Look at dat bite you got Lord bless de Lan'*
> *He's a soedahter! Look out dah, doe jam*
> *Dat pole up dah! You trine peahs like to me,*
> *To knock de fish fumall dat 'simmon-tree;*
> *Now look! Doe jerk dat way! Law love my soul,*
> *You gwiner lose 'im! Yere, gimme dat pole;*
> *I'll sho you how to lan' him! Stiddy, now—*
> *Pulls like a cat-fish. Hit's de boss, I swow!*
> *Des wit a minute; one mo' pull is boun*
> *To git 'im. Dah he is, safe on de groun'.*

When the speaker realized that he had broken the Sabbath, he threw the fish back into the water. He told the rest of the men about a Sunday when he had tried to fish and the devil had caught his line and almost drowned him. He advised the men to put down their fishing tackle before they caught something for which they had not bargained.[16]

Other poems dealt with picking cotton and shucking corn. Opie P. Reade, a writer for the comic weekly, *Arkansas Traveler*, contributed four to *Harper's*, one of which had the following verse:

> *An' er roas' de ole 'possum, an' er po' on de greas',*
>   *Make er nigger's mouf go clik, clak, clop,*
> *Jes han' ter de ole man a mighty big piece*
>   *Make er nigger's mouf go flip, flap, flop.*

The first verse of a corn shucking song read:

> *Shuck erlong niggers, shuck dis co'n!*
>   *Dar's manny er bar'l in dis ya pile;*
>   *Dar's manny er rashin, sho's you bo'n*
> *Ter feed all de han's wid arter'wile.*
>   *Luk at Susing, dat fat gal,*
>   *Whar she git dat ballymeral? [balmoral]*
>   *Mus' er got hit fum ole Miss Sal,*
> *Shuck erlong niggers, shuck dis co'n.*

> Chorus
> *Shuck a ruck a shuck! shuck a ruck a shuck!*
>   *Pars dat tickler down dis way*
> *Shuck a ruck a shuck! shuck a ruck a shuck!*
>   *Ain' gwine home ez long ez I stay.*[17]

The "nigger" theme was continued in another song in
Harper's:

> *I'd rudder be er niggah*
>   *Dan ter be er whi' man*
> *Dough the whi' man considah*
>   *Hise'f biggah!*
> *But ef yo' mus' be white, w'y be hones' ef yo' can,*
> *An ac' es much es poss'ble like er niggah!*
>   *De colah ob yo' skin*
>   *Hit don't constertoot no sin,*
>   *An yo' fambly ain't er—*
>   *Cuttin' any figgah,*
> *Min' w'at yo's er—doin' and do de bes' yo' kin*
> *An ac' es much es poss'ble like er niggah.*[18]

Numerous drawings and cartoons in *Century* and *Harper's*,
in addition to those already mentioned, added perhaps to the
enjoyment of readers at the expense of the Negro. Four from
Century follow. One can not be sure of the extent of the

enjoyment since to modern readers most of them probably do not appear to be funny. But they reveal what the editors believed their readers wanted to see. Two shabbily dressed and badly frightened colored men and a terrified child saw their first bicycle. Exclaimed the eldest: " 'My king! ef dar ain't de berry ole Satan hisself, tail an' all, a-gwine about de kentry a-straddlin' of a buggy wheel.' " A Negro man servant was entreating his mistress not to enter a room which he had just entered to clean. An animal's head emerged from under a sofa. " 'Keep outen heah, missus, keep outen heah,' " he warned. " 'Dars a monst'us Hydraphobium under de sofa. So long ez I eyes him straight he doan dare move, but yer better call marster, quick!' " Two Negro men were grouped around a small boy who held a childish drawing. One inquired: " 'W'ere yo' son git dis mawkable talent from, mister Bradish?' " " 'Entirely it come from my side of de house, sah. My fadder before me was po'ter in a picture-gallery for six years befo' he died an' of co'se you know I done have de sole dustin' of Marse Crawford's picters while I was in his sarvice, sah.' " An old man with an ax across his shoulder addressed to his neighbor this question: " 'Whar's dat lazy rapscaleon Jeemes dat he ain' come to cut me dat load o' wood he promise me for dat pyah o' shoes I half-soled him?' " " 'Well, brer, you mus' 'scuse Jeemes dis mornin', he's daid.' " A full-page drawing of the Paris Exposition in 1900 included as its central figure a huge, bug-eyed type of "Mammy."[19]

The drawings and cartoons in *Harper's* followed the same general pattern. Under the caption, "Partiality," a ragged Negro boy was shielding a haughty, well-dressed girl from the rain with a worn umbrella while a bedraggled girl walked behind sheltered only by an oversized bonnet and shawl. "A Surprising Discovery" pictured a Negro girl and a white girl of the same size wearing identical clothes. The accompanying couplet recited:

> *"Now what's the matter, Susie Jones?"*
> *said Lucy Ovenshine.*
> *"Oh Look ee do!" cried dusky Sue.*
> *"Your shadow's black as mine."*

A sequence of four drawings, in 1900, narrated the following incident. De Faque, the manager of a small circus, told a colored man that " 'all you have to do is to stand still and look dangerous.' " The colored man was then dressed up to look like a "Filipino Giant Boy." De Faque instructed him: " 'Now, just as soon as you get that idiotic grin off your face we'll go into the museum and scare 'em silly.' " In the third scene, the "Filipino Giant Boy" was seated on the platform with a ferocious snarl, and de Faque was saying to a puzzled colored woman: " 'Don't git too near the Filipino, madam. He is very fierce and dangerous, especially when he is hungry. He is a cannibal.' " In the last scene "Aunt Mandy," ax in hand, was leading the crestfallen "Filipino" home, rope tied around his neck, while she scowled: " 'I reckon dey won't steal no mo' o' my chillun an' call 'em Philapenas while I has mah health.' " The introduction of slick paper, near the end of the century, made even more vivid the stereotyped behavior of Negroes in the drawings that accompanied, for example, Virginia Frazer Boyle's "Asmodeus in the Quarters" and "A Kingdom for Micajah."[20]

These magazines contributed not only to the fixing of stereotypes, but also to the interpretation of events in harmony with the trend of those events to the victory of the "Lost Cause." One foundation for this achievement was the portrayal of the beautiful plantation way of life. An article, published two months after the withdrawal of the troops from South Carolina and Louisiana, provides us with a nostalgic classic of the plantation tradition. " 'A South Carolinian" pulled out the stops:

The old plantation days are passed away, perhaps forever. My principles now lead me to abhor slavery and rejoice at its abolition. Yet sometimes, in the midst of the heat and toil of the struggle for existence, the thought involuntarily steals over me that we have seen better days. I think of the wild rides after the fox and the deer; of the lolling, the book, the delicious nap, on the balcony, in the summer house, or on the rustic seat on the lawn; of the long sittings at meals, and the after-dinner cigar; of the polished groups in easy but vivacious conversation in the parlor; of the chivalric devotion to the beautiful women; of the pleasant evening drives; of the visits to the plantation, with its long, broad expanse of waving green, dotted here and there with groups of industrious slaves; of the long rows of negro cabins with little pickaninnies playing about them; of the old well with its beam and pole for drawing, and of the women with pails of water on their heads; of the wild old field airs ringing out from the cabins at night; of the "Christmas gif', Massa," breaking your slumbers on the holiday morn; of the gay devices for fooling the dignified old darkies on the first of April; of the faithful old nurse who brought you through infancy, under whose humble roof you delighted to partake of an occasional meal; of the flattering, foot-scraping, clownish, knowing rascal to whom you tossed a silver piece when he brought up your boots; of the little darkies who scrambled for the rind after you had eaten your water-melon on the piazza in the afternoon—and, "as fond recollection presents them to view," I feel the intrusive swelling of the tear of regret.[21]

Thomas Nelson Page glorified the plantation tradition in *Harper's* more effusively than did any other writer. "Relius" was an old ex-Confederate who boasted of his severity but who refused to chastise Patsy, the Negro maid, who worked at the rooming house where he lived. Patsy neglected all the roomers except Relius, and attended to all his needs as though she were his personal slave. Her devotion prompted her to act almost like a mother to the old man—she would see that he wore his rubbers when it looked like rain, and she would wait up for him when he was out late. Another of Page's stories, about "Ole 'Stracted," limned an old Negro who had lost his mind and who constantly recalled the bygone days of the ante-bellum period. His sharecropping son and daughter-in-law hated the "po' white trash" who owned the land that they were working and who were suspected of wanting to make the old man leave the place since he could no longer work. One day the couple visited Ole 'Stracted's shack where they found that he had worked for forty years in order to save money to give to his old master. Ole 'Stracted died happy because he thought he had seen his old master come back just before he passed away. In still another story, Unc' Edinburg lamented that in slavery days: " 'Twuz Christmas den, sho' 'nough. . . . Des free issue niggers don' know what Christmas is. Hog meat an' pop crackers don't meck a sho' 'nough Christmas.' " But one Christmas had been really bad.

"Marse George" had ridden his horse across a swollen river and Edinburg had followed him. Edinburg said that he and his master had " 'drowned' " but in reality only the master had drowned in an attempt to save the life of his devoted slave. One other story by Page will have to suffice. Drinkwater Torm, the faithful servant, was a "drunken, trifling, good-for-nothing nigger." His master had given him this name because he contended that, if Torm ever drank water, he would surely die. The Colonel always threatened to get rid of Torm when he fell into a drunken stupor, but Torm was indispensable to the Colonel's needs.[22]

Virginia Frazer Boyle's "A Kingdom for Micajah" shows the persistence of the plantation tradition and the stereotype of The Wretched Freedman at the beginning of the twentieth century. One drawing showed Micajah during his days of freedom wearing a longtailed coat, a book under his arm, sporting a cane but barefooted, dressed " 'Perzackly Lack Ole Marse.' " He wanted a " 'little nigger' " just like his master, but the little boy was recalcitrant. Another drawing revealed Micajah as " 'He Collared His Astonished Little Nigger.' " His speech to his master when he returned, disillusioned, from his days of freedom should be ranked among the classics of The Wretched Freedman. Micajah moaned and pleaded:

> "I wants ter git shet er dis heah freedom! I hain't nuffin but des er po' fool nigger, Ole Marse. I hain't gwine ter as' fur nuffin ebber mo'—nuffin but sumpen ter eat, an' mighty little er dat! You knows what's de bestes' fur me, Ole Marse, an' you knows I hain't fitten ter breave de bref er life! Kill me, Ole Marse, kill me; but 'fore you does hit take de cuss er freedom offen my soul!"[23]

Joel Chandler Harris, whose interpretations and characterizations of the Southern Negro have been generally accepted as the kindliest and most authentic, reanimated the plantation tradition in both *Harper's* and *Century*. A review of his *Uncle Remus: His Songs and Sayings* in *Century* assured that his "gentle old darky—shrewd, yet simple-minded . . . will live forever in these pages." His book was considered the best and most elaborate study which literature possessed of the type "familiar to us all—the old plantation Negro." The conductor of the Editor's Drawer in *Harper's* observed that Harris's poems were "among the best if not the best" contributions the South had made to " 'cullud' " literature since the war, and that his hymns breathed the "genuine air of devotion which is characteristic of the Negro when he gives himself up to psalmody."[24]

Harris's story in *Harper's* was about Ananias, a devoted Negro with a "hang dog look." Although his master mistrusted him, Ananias stayed with him until the end of the Civil War. He worked diligently and stole to keep his master's larder full. After Ananias had been acquitted at a trial in recompense for this devotion, he meekly followed his master's command: " 'Come, boy, . . . let's go home.' " A story by Harris in *Century*, "Free Joe," revealed how unhappy he was after freedom while his wife, still a slave, retained the care-free happiness of slavery. Virginia Frazer Boyle, Frank R. Stockton, James Lane Allen and the less well known Maurice Thompson also glorified in the pages of *Century* the plantation tradition and the woes of the freedmen.[25]

The *Atlantic* also carried its quota. Constance Fenimore Woolson's "Rodman the Keeper" was not blind to deplorable conditions in the South after the war, but it revealed a special tenderness for the Negroes who were loyal to their white folks. Other stories followed the same pattern without laying as much emphasis as did this Northern writer on the unlovely scenes. "Uncle" Newton, who often recalled the days of "ease" that he had enjoyed with his master, died in an attempt to save the life of his former master's daughter. "Pomp" remained with his poverty-stricken former master. A Negro yard-boy expressed his joy because he had " 'done foun' some mo' aigs for ole Miss'!' " A colored body servant, who had stuck with his old master, was revealed going to the poor house with him. As in the days of slavery, Negroes were portrayed trooping from the fields, "happy at leaving their work and unconcerned by yesterday or tomorrow." Their virtues of obedience and loyalty seemed to be natural to Negroes, and it was easy to see that many of them sadly missed and needed the control of someone stronger than themselves. The reviewer of Edward E. Hale's novel, *Philip Nolan's Friends*, declared that the true hero was "the proud, positive, loyal, and ungrammatical old family servant, Ransom, with his furious patriotism, and his reckless contempt of all foreigners whom he included in a single class and indifferently as 'niggers' and 'eyedolaters.' "[26]

Even the erudite *North American Review* helped to perpetuate the stereotype of the faithful plantation Negro. James Parton, famous for his numerous biographies, especially those of Franklin, Jefferson and Jackson, described an "old mammy" as a "motherly negro nurse, black, corpulent, big-lipped and broad-nosed" whom refined little whites would welcome with kisses. A less well known author, J. W. Watson, narrated the story of the faithful servant who guarded Henry Clay "with a vigilance only a negro knows." Another author told the story of a Negro who was about twenty years old when Lee surrendered. The freedman learned at about the same time that his mistress, widowed by that war and reduced to poverty, did not know which way to turn. But this loyal black freedman consoled her: " 'Cheer up, missus, and doan't griebe. I knows how massa used ter make de nostrums. I'll make 'em, and I'll sell 'em, and 'fore long I'll hab you as well off as you eber was.' " And, according to the author, so he did. General Sherman strengthened the myth of the faithful slaves during the Civil War when he wrote that "best of all, in the crisis of their fate, they did not resort to the torch and dagger, as their race had done in San Domingo."[27]

Free Negroes who had escaped from the beneficient influences of the plantation, however, were generally portrayed in an unfriendly manner. Charles Gayarré, the famous Louisiana author, depicted them as follows whenever the Reconstruction legislature was in session: "Fixing their eyes steadfastly on the walls of the building with gaping mouths, in the vain hope that some celestial manna may fall into the aperture, there they stand the whole day, braving cold and rain, and returning on the next morning to gaze vacantly at the same imaginary object." Jefferson Davis revealed how utterly unfit the Negro was for jury service. When Robert E. Lee presented a case as clearly as he could, he saw before him a "big black negro" whose head had fallen back on the rail of the bench on which he sat, his mouth wide open and fast asleep. James Parton asserted in 1878: "We cannot yet name one negro of pure blood who has taken the first, the second, the third, or the tenth rank in business, politics, art, literature, scholarship, science, or philosophy. To the present hour the negro has contributed nothing to the intellectual resources of man." Another author consigned most Negroes to be house servants or farm laborers or unskilled mechanics. To the few who showed a capacity for intellectual activities opportunities should be provided, but he was convinced that not many would show that capacity, for

> two hundred years of ignorance and animalism have so beclouded his intellect that not one in a hundred can so much as understand purely intellectual studies. They learn the words as the parrot learns them, but of the ideas the words convey, they have no comprehension. This I have found to be true of every one of the "advanced scholars" I have met among Southern negroes.[28]

In addition to perpetuating the plantation tradition throughout most of the period, these magazines generally endorsed the trend in political, social and economic development. *Scribner's* and the *Atlantic* strongly approved Hayes's Southern policy. Editorials in the former supported the president both before and after the withdrawal of the troops. Even Thomas Wentworth Higginson of Massachusetts, who had commanded Negro troops during the Civil War, wrote in the *Atlantic* in 1878 that the only misfortune was that the troops had not been withdrawn sooner. On the other hand, "A South Carolinian" felt that the troops were needed because of the ill feeling between the two races. An unsigned article in the *Atlantic*, March, 1879, predicted that, since a reconciliation had been effected between the races, and since the South had been left to solve the Negro problem, the next Congress would leave it where Hayes had "wisely" left it. In June, 1880 (when there was abundant evidence that the South was not living up to its promises about fair treatment of the Negro), an anonymous author urged patience. The South, he argued, was made up predominantly of an "ignorant and brutal mass of whites and blacks." The intelligent people of the South were of "our own blood and lineage," and their faults grew naturally out of their experiences and inherited ideas and the many clogs that the past had laid upon them. In 1881 (when Hayes had himself recognized the virtual failure of his Southern policy), another article still urged Garfield to follow the "let-alone" policy.[29]

A symposium conducted by the *North American Review* resulted in almost unanimous approval of the withdrawal of the troops. Richard Dana, Jr., the "Duke of Cambridge"

(Massachusetts), one-time member of the Saturday Club along with the illuminati, Dr. Holmes, Emerson, Charles Francis Adams and others, insisted that the promise that Negroes should have freedom, civil and political equality was the most sacred promise ever made. The promise had to be kept even if military force had to be used. But he cautioned none the less against the use of force lest the South rise up in insurrection against the government. Two Southerners, Judge Jeremiah S. Black and Charles Gayarré, unreservedly approved the withdrawal. David Dudley Field, a prominent New York lawyer, argued, in 1881, that the troops should never have been stationed in the South; while Cassius M. Clay, who had been forced to leave the South because of his abolitionist views, warned, in 1886, that the experience of ten years should convince statesmen that they should not again attempt to use troops for dissolving the Solid South. These articles were capped by one in 1900, when M. E. Ingalls, president of the Chesapeake and Ohio Railroad, argued that the "true regeneration" of the South had begun with withdrawal, and that therefore the experiment should not be tried again.[30]

On the other hand, seven of eight contributors to the *North American's* symposium, "Ought the Negro to Be Disfranchised?; Ought He to Have Been Enfranchised?," March, 1879, favored enfranchisement, although two of them supported a partial disfranchisement. James G. Blaine contended that the South could not disfranchise Negroes without disfranchising a number of whites. Garfield was already thinking about the statement which he later made in his inaugural address, but which he on this occasion qualified, since he declared that there was no "safe middle ground between slavery and full citizenship." Wendell Phillips, an abolitionist who remained true to his faith until his death, staunchly declared that the Negro had proved his fitness for the suffrage. Thomas A. Hendricks of Indiana, who had been Tilden's running mate in 1876, and who was to be elected Vice-President in 1884, also argued against disfranchisement, but entered the plea that the possible evil of the Negro vote should be reduced as much as possible. Montgomery Blair, who had lived successively in Kentucky, Missouri and Maryland, served as counsel for Dred Scott, joined the Republicans on the issue of slavery and then forsaken the "Radicals," had founded the Washington *Union* in which he opposed

Tilden and the Compromise of 1877. He was the only contributor who argued that the Negro should be disfranchised because he was not, and could not be trained to be, self-governing. Three Southerners, Lamar, Hampton, and Alexander Stephens, supported the view that the Negro should not be deprived of the vote, but Hampton contended that the method of enfranchisement had been unconstitutional and that only partial suffrage should have been granted. Lamar and Stephens emphatically denied that the Negro vote had been suppressed. Subsequent articles, however, took a more dim view of Negro suffrage. Two little-known authors, H. H. Chalmers in 1881 and J. Harris Patton in 1886, argued in favor of educational and property qualifications.[31]

Meanwhile, disciples of the cult of the "New South" found a hearty welcome in these magazines, especially in *Century*. Indeed, it would seem that Grady's "New South" speech was immediately inspired, at least in part, by vigorous articles written by one of the few Southerners, George Washington Cable, who laid bare the rank inequalities in the former slave states. Cable's article, "The Freedman's Case in Equity," published in January, 1885, declared that the popular mind in the North had thrown the "Case" over to the South where 9,000,000 whites exercised tyranny over 6,000,000 blacks. He attacked the exclusion of Negroes from juries and asked why differentiation in public places was not based on conduct, manners, dress and the cost of the goods rather than on race. He spoofed the bugbear of social equality: "Our eyes are filled with absurd visions of all Shantytown pouring out its hordes of unmasked imps into the company and companionship of our own sunny-headed darlings." Cable especially condemned the system of leasing convicts to private persons, and the tendency to imprison Negroes on the slightest provocation in some states. His criticism of the Civil Rights decision was mild, but his analysis of the basic injustices in the South was forthright. The Southerner, Cable observed, forbade the Negro to go into the water until he had learned to swim and, then, for fear that he would learn, hung millstones about his neck.[32] In the judgment of the writer of this book, the failure of most Northerners to grasp or to accept the truth of this inequity constitutes convincing evidence that, as Cable stated, 30,000,000 other Americans had grown weary of trying to obtain equity for the freedmen.

Cable's article provoked so much discussion that the editor of *Century* announced that Henry W. Grady had been selected to speak for the Southern dissenters. Grady contended that Cable was sentimental rather than practical. The South would never allow intermingling of the races, for amalgamation of the races would result and amalgamation would debase the Anglo-Saxon race. As a matter of fact, the "racial instinct" of Negroes led them to want to remain apart. If the North had the same problem as the South, it would handle it in the same way. The Southerner, while not careless of the opinion of the outside world, was saying: "Leave this problem to my working out. I will solve it in calmness and deliberation, without passion or prejudice, and with full regard for the unspeakable equities it holds." He reminded his readers that the Civil Rights decision had placed the problem back in Southern hands.[33]

An editorial in "Topics of the Time," the next month, May, 1885, recognized the merits of both articles. Cable's next contribution, in September, was devoted in large part to the discussion of the Civil Rights decision, and evidences of inequities in the South. He contended that the decision had neither settled nor dismissed the question. The white man erred in thinking that the Negro's insistence on civil rights was a bid for social equality. The wishes of those Negroes who might not desire those rights should not be allowed to prevail over those who clearly showed that they wanted them. He complimented those Northern states that had enacted new civil rights measures. Anticipating the "separate but equal accommodations" fiction, he gave numerous examples to show that practically nowhere in the South were Negroes provided equal facilities. He agreed with those who demanded white dominance if it could be proved that character, intelligence and property were possessed only by white men. He lashed out again at the convict-lease system and contended that many Southerners, who wanted change to be through evolution rather than revolution, really were praying that the steps should be not logical but "geological."[34]

Century accepted Grady's point of view rather than Cable's. An editorial in October, 1886, affirmed:

Since the Civil Rights clause has been invalidated and Southern State judges have been thrown back upon their

professional honor and the Common Law, the lines of
Southern decisions are taking directions which are startling; and it begins to look as if the rights of the freedmen
were rather safer under the aegis of the Common Law
than even under a Ku Klux Act.[35]

Two months later Grady's speech also convinced a large number of prominent Northerners that the freedmen were safe in
the hands of the "New South." When an article, "The White
Man of the New South," by Wilbur F. Tillett of Vanderbilt
University in the March, 1887, issue of *Century*, revealed
striking similarities with Grady's speech, the editor deemed it
necessary to point out that the article had been accepted prior
to the speech. But the editor at the same time paid glowing
tribute to Grady's speech.[36]

Harper's, the *Atlantic* and even the *North American Review* strengthened the willingness of most Northerners to believe that a new day had dawned in the South. Following
Cleveland's election in 1884, a tour of the South was made
by Charles Dudley Warner, who wrote for a time for *Harper's*
Editor's Drawer, and contributed to its Editor's Chair before
becoming editor of the Hartford *Courant*. His article about
his tour probably provided both Grady and Washington with
views on "The New South." In the *Atlantic*, Rebecca Harding
Davis, who had some years earlier given a stark picture of
the plight of the industrial worker, reported after a trip to
the South that the Southern states were willingly "overtaxing
themselves in order to educate Negroes." As early as 1877,
Gayarré had urged in the *North American Review* that the
Southern states be allowed to solve their own problems. Two
years later Watterson, Lamar, Hampton and Hendricks advanced similar views; as did Senator Zebulon B. Vance of
North Carolina, in 1884. The Massachusetts-born Mary Abi-
gail Dodge—a charming and influential personality in the
salons of the nation's capital, who wrote under the pseudo-
nym of Gail Hamilton—in November, 1885, urged that problems in the South would be solved more quickly if outsiders
did not meddle. She insisted that it was the mixing and not
the separation of the races that had brought disaster. Murat
Halstead, proprietor of the Cincinnati *Commercial* whom
Watterson had accused of trying to buy Hayes's election,
sought to rebut the views presented in the *North American*

by Watterson. But his was a voice crying in the wilderness. A little more than five years after Grady's speech, Thomas Nelson Page not only insisted that the South be left alone but added: "We have educated him [the Negro]; we have aided him; we have sustained him in all right directions. We are ready to continue our aid; but we will not be dominated by him. When we shall be, it is our settled conviction that we shall deserve the degradation into which we shall have sunk."[37] The New South was almost as much glorified in the editorial rooms of Allen Thorndike Rice and Lloyd Bruce as it was in those of Charles R. Miller's New York *Times*.

During the last fifteen years of the century, the newly established *Forum* magazine presented in each of its monthly issues opposing points of view on controversial issues. The dominant figure from 1887 to 1895 was Walter Hines Page, whose personal and professional relations with Chesnutt reveal him as the superior type of "Southern gentleman." The Southern point of view was presented by such prominent men as Page himself, Wade Hampton, Senator Morgan of Alabama, John G. Carlisle (Secretary of the Treasury under Cleveland), Jabez L. M. Curry (a prominent educator), Henry Watterson, and less well-known writers. Among those who supported the cause of the Negro were Senator Hoar, Senator Chandler, Albion Tourgee, George Washington Cable and Murat Halstead. The *Forum* is notable for the fact that it had more Negro contributors than any other of the magazines of the period. In addition to Booker T. Washington, these contributors included Professor William S. Scarborough of Wilberforce University, who had published a widely used Greek text book; Edward T. Blyden, Minister from Liberia to England and a well known scholar; Professor Kelly Miller of Howard University; President J. C. Price of Livingstone College, and Professor William Hooper Councill who seemed destined to be the "leader" of the race until Washington delivered his Atlanta address. It is significant that Douglass was not a contributor. (Du Bois was still engaged in scholarly studies rather than in minor essays.) On the one hand, it was commendable that the *Forum* opened its pages to such a large number of colored contributors. On the other hand, some readers probably discounted the pleading of the Negroes' cause by members of that race. No extended analysis of the *Forum* is given here, as is the case of the other magazines, because the points of view expressed were similar to those already presented. Suffice it to say that the balance was, on the whole, firmly kept, even in articles dealing with lynching.[38]

It is probable that the *Forum* rather strengthened prevailing attitudes hostile to the Negro, for it is easier for readers to find confirmation of views strongly held than to accept evidence against them. What was needed to offset the hardening attitudes was a magazine whose editor would have proclaimed, as Garrison had done in the first issue of the *Liberator*: "I am in earnest—I will not equivocate—I will not excuse —I will not retreat a single inch—AND I WILL BE HEARD." No such magazine, or newspaper, is conceivable in the last years of the century. The nation was attuned to the soft strains of the "New South." Magazines and newspapers depended more and more on advertisers who held the baton for the new symphony. On a very restricted scale the *African Methodist Episcopal Review*, with a circulation of a little more than one thousand, most of whom were Negroes, pled their cause. While, as will be seen later, some of the articles were surprisingly well written, Negroes had to wait until the end of 1911 before W. E. B. Du Bois was as eloquently and as harshly unequivocal in the *Crisis* as Garrison had been in the *Liberator*.

In the last decade of the century, the most important relevant topics of discussion in the major magazines were Negro suffrage, education for Negroes, the emergence of Booker T. Washington, criminality among Negroes, emigration and immigration, the New South, and the extension of American control over colored peoples in foreign lands. This last topic revealed an almost complete endorsement of "Social Darwinism." A series of articles in the *North American Review*, between 1890 and 1892, on the Lodge bill, presented Speaker of the House Thomas B. Reed and Lodge in favor of the bill. Surprisingly, T. V. Powderly, Master Workman of the Knights of Labor, argued that the second section of the Fourteenth Amendment made additional legislation unnecessary. A. W. Shaffer, a "Southern Republican" of North Carolina, Representatives Benton A. McMillin of Tennessee and Richard P. Bland of Missouri opposed passage of the bill. Senator James McMillan of Michigan hoped that some type of legislation could be devised that the South would accept. James

Bryce, whose opinion of Negroes was scarcely higher than his better-known views on American municipal government, asserted that the grant of suffrage to the freedmen had been a great blunder. The majority of Negroes should be excluded from voting by an educational qualification; the only objection to that proposal was that illiterate whites would also be disfranchised. He expressed similar views in an article in *Century*, in 1898, while Professor Jerome Dowd, a Southerner, two years later, pointed out that, although the Louisiana "Grandfather Clause" seemed unjust, no state constitutional amendment would be approved if it immediately disfranchised illiterate whites. A writer in the *Atlantic* condemned the Mississippi amendment, and called for the enforcement of the second section of the Fourteenth Amendment. But, according to an article in the *Review*, the Mississippi amendment had created more harmonious relations between the races. Near the end of the century, a *Review* contributor proposed an amendment to the Constitution of the United States that would make the ability to read and write a requirement for voting and become the basis for the apportionment of members of the House of Representatives. If this amendment failed, he suggested vigorous enforcement of the second section of the Fourteenth Amendment. Hoar closed the discussion in the *Review*, in 1900, by pointing out that four of the Southern states had disfranchised Negroes, and two others were about to take similar steps. If they did, every other Southern state, with one or two exceptions, would eventually accomplish the disfranchisement of ten million Negroes.[39] The question, "Ought the Negro to Be Disfranchised?" which the *Review* had asked in 1879, had at last been answered.

Most of the articles, before and after Washington's Atlanta address, favored the industrial type of education. Washington made it clear that he believed that Negroes should not be confined to one type of education but that for the masses, industrial education was the supreme need. A large number of writers in *Harper's*, *Century*, *Atlantic* and *Forum* generally endorsed this view.[40]

Washington elaborated upon his general views in the *Atlantic* a year after his speech. Negroes should not be excited to arms by their Northern brothers. They should distinguish between the few lawless whites and the many law-abiding ones. One should remember that no race or people had ever succeeded without a struggle. Newspapers should not spread propaganda that the South was unsafe for Negroes because of outrages in certain sections. Negroes should guard against a reputation for crime due to increased idleness and lack of education. At the same time, others should not judge the Negro too harshly, since perfection could not be reached in one generation. White people should not feel that, in order to settle the race question, they had to repress the Negro by a discriminatory franchise. In order to settle the race question in the South, Washington advocated a fair and high standard of voting for both races, and the participation of Negroes in Southern affairs by becoming so efficient that it would be impossible to ignore them. Washington drove home his point by citing the example of the Jews. He proposed industrial education as a means of supplying an immediate need, and urged Negroes to stay in the South where "opportunities for them are best." If the Negro made progress, the South would be better for both races. The Southern white man recognized this fact and therefore wanted to help that progress.[41]

A number of articles in the 1890's developed the theme of the criminality of the Negro, with emphasis upon attacks on white women. As early as 1884, an article in the *North American Review* pointed out that an immense proportion of brutal crimes in the South were charged to Negroes. But it was in the 1890's that the most severe attacks upon Negroes were launched. They seem to have been inspired, in part at least, by an article by Douglass in the *Review*, July, 1892, which sought to show that the Negro was not a rapist. The charge was frequently made, he contended, because it was the most revolting of all crimes and Southerners felt that, in the eyes of the North, it was the best excuse for lynching. But it was not so much the nature of the crime as it was the color of the "rapist" that aroused wrath. He added, sarcastically, that it was strange that a docile race, to whom had been entrusted the care of Southern women and children during the Civil War, could suddenly change to a race of the most daring and repulsive criminals. W. Cabell Bruce, a Southerner in his early thirties—who in the twentieth century wrote well-received biographies of Franklin and John Randolph—retorted two months later that the Negro in the South had "violated the chastity of white women with appalling frequency, and under circumstances unutterably shocking to human nature." The Negro had become such a habitual offender because he was no longer subject to the authority of a master. Two other writers developed the same theme in the *Review*. Two months after the second of these, Washington, in August, 1900, conceded that the criminal rate among Negroes, North and South, was higher than that among whites. Like Douglass, earlier, he gave convincing reasons why larger numbers of Negroes than of whites were tried and sentenced. He answered the argument that Negroes committed fewer crimes when they were slaves by observing: "To say that the Negro was at his best, morally, during the period of slavery is about the same as to say that the two thousand prisoners in the State prison and the city penal institutions in the city of Boston are the most righteous two thousand people in Boston."[42] Thus, the two best-known Negroes had been called upon to answer the charges that were being increasingly advanced in the 1890's to justify the denial of constitutional rights to Negroes.

The emigration of Negroes, which had been frequently advocated during the 1880's, again became a favorite theme in the 1890's. Page saw no need, in 1892, for deportation since the Negro race in the United States would soon die out. Blyden opposed large-scale emigration until a new generation of both whites and blacks developed different ideas. At the turn of the century, John Roach Straton of Macon, Georgia, argued that conditions elsewhere should be made so inviting that Negroes would want to emigrate.[43]

Toward the latter part of the century, however, all other topics were submerged by the plethora of articles on American expansion. Social Darwinists[44] enjoyed the advantage of a generally accepted American belief in the inherent inferiority of the Negro when they justified that expansion on racial grounds. Reciprocally, the failure of Negroes and other dark peoples in distant lands to match strides with Europeans and Americans was invoked to justify the inability of the American Negro to exercise rights which the Constitution conferred upon him. As early as 1879, a writer in *Scribner's* concluded that the colored pupils in the Richmond, Virginia, public schools showed quite as good progress as the white pupils until the two groups reached the age of fourteen, at which time there appeared a marked difference in favor of the latter. (It would be interesting to discover whether this pontifical assertion that the Negro's brain "closed up" at this age had its roots, knowingly or not, in the Freudian association with the age of puberty and virility.) The personality of a colored man who had advanced from slavery to freedom, from freedom to a high position during Reconstruction, evoked this declaration: "There are aspects of evolution in the man which would astonish and possibly terrify Darwin himself." Still another article in *Century* endorsed the theory that the half-caste was lower mentally and morally than the parent stock. Brazil was also cited in 1879 as "proof" that "the mixed races are invariably bad; they seem to combine all the worst characteristics of the two parent stocks . . . A light mulatto or an almost black one may be a very decent sort of fellow; but the brown half-and-half is nearly always lazy, and stupid and vain." But shortly before this, another writer had offered Haiti as a "discouraging commentary on the theories of those humanitarians who believe in the ultimate elevation of the negro to the level of the Caucasian race. There is a backward tendency of which barbarism seems to be the inevitable goal unless a new people take possession of the soil."[45]

One of the most amazing examples of early Social Darwinism appeared in *Harper's* in 1877. Lady Adeliza Chimpanzee became alarmed when she noticed that she was turning white. Her mother reassured her by pointing out that this turning of color was evidence of the fact that she was of a superior race. Prince Orang Outan, who had been selected to marry her, was even whiter than she. The Prince realized his superior ancestry because he had no caudal appendage. But the child of Lady Adeliza and Prince Orang had no tail and no hair; on the other hand, he had flat feet and a white skin. Since no one knew what to call this strange creature, Lady Adeliza named him Man. An accompanying picture showed "the new species" as being quite similar to the caricatures of Negroes that frequently appeared in *Harper's*.[46]

Several articles in the *Atlantic*, during this early period, also revealed evidence of belief in the superiority of the Anglo-Saxon. But the *North American Review* surpassed all others in publishing articles which presented similar views. Typical of these was the prediction by Gayarré, in 1877, that, "if contrary to the teachings of history and science, the negro should rise to an equality of intelligence and energy with the Caucasian," there would be a final struggle between the two races from which the Caucasian would emerge victorious.[47]

The revived creed of racial superiority was nurtured in the

1880's by agitation for Chinese exclusion, the wiping out of the Indian frontier, and the growing momentum of the scramble for Africa. A review in the *Atlantic* of Francis Galton's *Inquiries into Human Faculty and Its Development*, 1883, agreed that Chinese, Indians and Negroes should be excluded from the earth, and the sooner the better. But Social Darwinism continued to find a sturdy rationale in the growing deterioriation of the Negro's status in the United States. A writer in the *Review*, 1881, asserted that "in no time or clime have the Caucasian race ever consented to live with inferior ones *save as rulers*." Numerous articles supporting the concept of the inherent inferiority of the American Negro appeared in the *Review* and *Century*. John Fiske's famous lecture, "Manifest Destiny," which glorified the progress made by the Teutonic and "Aryan" races, and praised English imperialism, was published in *Harper's* in 1885.[48]

The refrain continued in the 1890's, re-enforced undoubtedly by some of the speeches by Southerners who opposed the Lodge bill. Bryce argued that the Negro had not been able to protect himself in the exercise of the suffrage because he was naturally inferior to the white man. Thomas Nelson Page contended: "The Negro has not progressed, not because he was a slave, but because he does not possess the faculties to raise himself above slavery. He has not yet exhibited the qualities of any race which has advanced civilization or shown capacity to be greatly advanced." He also cited Liberia, Haiti and the Dominican Republic in order to establish the "fact" that the Negro did not possess the qualifications to conduct his own government. Theodore Roosevelt affirmed in 1895: "A perfectly stupid race can never rise to a very high plane; the negro, for instance, has been kept down as much by lack of intellectual development as anything else." Marion L. Dawson, former Judge Advocate-General of Virginia, explained, in 1897, that the South was influenced by the same ruling spirit which had characterized the Anglo-Saxon from the beginning of his history to that time. He believed that the whole problem of the South was "whether the negro or the white man should occupy the seat of power; whether the inferior should dominate the superior, and whether ignorance should rule intelligence." Straton, in 1900, declared that the Negro showed all the defects of a degenerate race—lessened fertility, prevalence of venereal and other diseases caused by immorality, and resulting in a large infant mortality. The Negro would not, therefore, be able to adapt to Anglo-Saxon civilization. Two articles by obscure authors, one in 1884, and another in 1889, probably did little to offset the barrage of articles by much better known authors. In 1900, Washington cited Jamaica as an example of the increase of Negro population in contact with white races. In the United States, he added, Negroes enjoyed advantages and incentives that were not possessed by the colored Jamaicans.[49]

A natural consequence of the acceptance of the concept of the inherent inferiority of the Negro was the advocacy of the "White Man's Burden." Bryce, however, wanted it clearly understood that assumption of the burden did not involve mixing of the races. On the contrary, he assured, white colonizers, especially in the Union of South Africa, repudiated the idea. (Bryce could hardly have been ignorant of the existence of the "Cape Coloured.") He also sought to dispel fear that the inferior race would predominate there any more than in the Southern states of the United States. *Harper's* ran in serial form "A White Man's Africa" by Poultney Bigelow, a well-known New York journalist and lawyer, which also gave the assurance that the English in South Africa were not mixing their blood with that of the natives. The "degeneracy" of the Portuguese in Africa stemmed from the fact that since the fifteenth century they had intermarried with Negroes. The *North American Review*, as usual, presented articles praising and condemning European imperialism in India, China and Africa, but the majority extolled the blessings of civilization that were being carried to the benighted heathen. The most effective answer may be summed up in the sarcastic conclusion of the Marquis of Lorne:

Truly it is a wonderful phenomenon—this pouncing of Northern eagles and lions upon the abodes and realms of the black man. And why is it? Oh, for their good, of course! We shall stop their mauling and enslaving each other, and they ought to be grateful, and would be so if they only knew what unselfish intentions we one and all of us have.

Most readers, however, probably agreed with the Reverend W. Garden Blaikie that European imperialism would "issue in great good to the Dark Continent." Even conditions in the Belgian Congo found favor in the eyes of a contributor to *Century* in 1896 and 1897. Stanley urged, in 1896, that European partitioning of Africa should be looked upon as "civilization" rather than as "colonization." Another writer endorsed Rudyard Kipling's well known views. There were, finally, undertones and overtones of racism in the "Anglo-Saxon mystique," which led Captain Alfred T. Mahan, Andrew Carnegie, Sir Charles Beresford and others to favor an alliance between the United States and Great Britain and their eventual unification.[50]

The way had thus been prepared for the acceptance of American imperialism on racial and moral grounds. One writer, reversing a position that he had taken in 1896, urged, in 1898, permanent American intervention in Cuba in order to prevent the domination of the whites by the blacks. While most of the writers in the *Review*, including General Leonard T. Wood, found the Cuban Negroes industrious, there was a tendency to emphasize that they constituted only about thirty per cent of the population (an estimate that is probably considerably too low). Several articles supported the annexation of Hawaii and the Philippines by the plea that it was the duty of the United States to assume the obligation of civilizing backward peoples. An article in the *Atlantic* described most Cuban Negroes as ignorant, boastful, untruthful, ungrateful, fond of trinkets; "docility, except under abuse, is their most marked trait." Several editorials in *Century* emphasized the "purity" of the motives of the United States and endorsed the assumption of responsibility toward backward races.[51]

But opposition to American expansion also stemmed from racial considerations. Senator Vest (Democrat) condemned the idea of conferring citizenship upon the "half-civilized piratical, muck-running inhabitants of two thousand islands seven thousand miles distant." A less well-known author added that American expansion would bring vexing problems similar to those in the South. "Pitchfork" Ben Tillman naturally expressed opposition to annexation on racial grounds in the most extreme language. There would always be racial antagonism, he contended, because the Anglo-Saxon walked on the necks of every race with which he came in contact and resistance to his will meant destruction to the weaker race. Since the United States had its own race problem, it would be foolhardy to incorporate nine million more brown men under the flag. How could the Republicans, he inquired, defend their abandonment of the Negroes at home, and at the same time defend McKinley's policy of subjugating the Filipinos with greater hardships than Southern Negroes had to endure? Probably more in triumph than in sorrow, Tillman concluded: "And no Republican leader . . . will now dare to wave the bloody shirt and preach a crusade against the South's treatment of the negro. The North has a bloody shirt of its own. Many thousands of them have been made into shrouds for murdered Filipinos, done to death because they were fighting for liberty." Even Carl Schurz, whom Du Bois has called "the finest type of immigrant American," and who had written a report shortly after the Civil War castigating the South, wrote in 1898:

We are vexed by a very troublesome race problem in the United States now. That race problem is still unsolved, and it would be very sanguine to say that there is a satisfactory solution in near prospect. Cool-headed men think that we have enough of that. What will be the consequence if we indefinitely add to it by bringing under this republican government big lots of other incompatible races—races far more intractable, too, than those with which we have so far had to deal?[52]

Two of the best-known advocates of the Social Gospel revealed their astigmatism on the plight of the American Negro. Walter Rauschenbusch—who was born of German parents in Rochester, New York, on April 15, 1861—was unconcerned, during the period under investigation, about the political condition of Negroes in the South. Purvis M. Carter, who made a detailed study of his writings, including *For the Right* in the Yale University Library, *Dawn* and *Independent*, found that the great Baptist leader devoted practically no attention prior to 1901 to this subject. In May, 1890, Rauschenbusch urged that a petition be circulated in behalf of the downtrodden people of Russia. But in September of the same year, when Mississippi was revising its constitution and the fate of the Lodge bill hung in the balance, he wrote in *For the Right*, the organ of the Brotherhood of the Kingdom: "Our institutions are the admiration and the inspirational beacon-light of noblemen from the Straits of Gibraltar to the bleak huts of Siberian exiles. Whenever a hand seeks to rear the banner of liberty, it is nerved by the thought of a great nation beyond the sea, in which men are free and equal." He recognized that social equality had not been achieved: "Political liberty is ours, now let us use it to secure social equality."[53]

Lyman Abbott went further than did Gladden or Rauschenbusch, for he explicitly endorsed some Southern viewpoints. This endorsement is all the more significant because of his previous views and activities. He had publicly favored emancipation before Lincoln issued his preliminary Emancipation Proclamation. He had opposed granting Negroes immediate political responsibility because he would confine the administration of government "always to the moral and the intelligent." Since the South possessed neither the free schools nor the free churches necessary to develop these qualities, he believed, as early as 1864, that the North should supply them. As corresponding secretary of the American Union Commission and as general secretary of the American Freedmen's Union Commission, from 1865 to July 1, 1869, he had "performed a useful service in co-ordinating the efforts of the non-denominational benevolent socieites, in acting as an intermediary between them and the Freedmen's Bureau, and in general stimulating interest in moral reconstruction." While he believed that children in the South might choose to attend school with companions of their own race, he insisted that no child should be barred from any Commission school because of his color. He was a gradualist as far as the abolition of segregation was concerned, but he was convinced that, once segregation was accepted, it would not be abolished. But in the 1880's Abbott began to be an apostle of the "New South." It is probable that his "conversion" was prompted by Henry W. Grady's speech which he heard in 1886. The *Christian Union*, which became the *Outlook* in 1891, and which frequently reflected Abbott's views, supported the Blair bill in 1884 and 1888, but it took a positive stand against the Lodge bill. By 1890, Abbott had come to believe that the wisest policy was to allow the South to administer her own future. "The negro problem," averred an editorial in the *Christian Union* on June 12, 1890, "must be worked out by the negroes and the white men of the South with the aid of the North, not by the North or the Federal government over the heads of the negroes and the white men."[54] His conversion is also apparent in an article in the *North American Review*, in 1898, in which he discussed the Indian problem in the United States. He advocated the abolition of reservations, and urged that the Indian be treated as a man. He then added:

> Treat them [the Indians] as we have treated the negro. As a race the African is less competent than the Indian, but we do not shut the negroes up in reservations and put them in charge of politically appointed parents called agents. The lazy grow hungry; the criminal are punished; the industrious get on. And though the sporadic cases of injustice are often tragic, they are the gradually disappearing relics of a slavery that is past, and the negro is finding his place in American life gradually, both as a race and as an individual.

Three years later, after touring South Atlantic schools and attending the conference of the Southern Educational Board at Winston-Salem, North Carolina, he again gave explicit endorsement of Southern points of view. He approved the Southern suffrage amendments. The Southerner, he found, had less prejudice against the Negro and more interest in his welfare than did the Northerner. The South desired education for the Negro but felt, realistically, that it should be industrial rather than literary. Attempts to force political or social equality would inflict "uncalculable" injury on the Negro and on the nation.[55] Professor William Warren Sweet, perhaps the most authoritative historian of the church in the United States, has concluded that "no religious leader in modern times has exercised a more abiding influence than has Lyman Abbott."[56] Professor Sweet was not, of course, endorsing the contributions, positive and negative—not one of some one hundred magazine articles by Abbott between 1890 and 1900 bore a title referring specifically to the Negro—that Abbott made to the development of the concept of the "New South" that religious and other intellectual molders of American thought were implanting in the mind of the American people.

FOURTEEN

The Atlanta Compromise

BOOKER T. WASHINGTON's speech in Atlanta, Georgia, on September 18, 1895 was one of the most effective pieces of political oratory in the history of the United States. It deserves a place alongside that in which Patrick Henry proclaimed "Give me liberty, or give me death," and that in which William Jennings Bryan portrayed the "Cross of Gold." It is, in this writer's judgment, superior to Henry W. Grady's oration on "The New South." Structurally it was a model of organization, unity, clarity and brevity. The language was simple; the word pictures, understandable by all; the gestures, unforgettable. More than a half century later the reader comprehends the drama of the occasion, and is moved by the speaker's eloquence and mastery of the art of public speaking.

The fact that there was practically nothing new in the address does not diminish its importance. On the contrary, its adherence to ideas that had been frequently asserted by others, notably by Grady, won for it wide approval. Its basic theme, compromise, was attuned to the climate of opinion that had increasingly prevailed since 1877. The pre-eminent significance of the speech stems from the acceptance of the doctrine of compromise by a Negro with close personal contacts with powerful men who had made compromise the national policy.

The national fame that Washington achieved overnight by his Atlanta speech constitutes an excellent yardstick for measuring the victory of "The New South," since he accepted a subordinate place for Negroes in American life. Inasmuch as his compromise was based upon the premise that the Negro enjoyed the friendship of the Southern whites, this book for the first time presents a comprehensive analysis of Southern newspapers, just before and after the speech, as an index to the quality of that friendship. A similar investigation of representative Northern newspapers permits an evaluation of the extent to which the North approved the compromise.

Washington was the slave son of a white father and colored mother. Born on April 5, 1856, in Franklin County, Virginia, he became, in 1872, a student and janitor-on-trial at Hampton Normal and Agricultural Institute, which General Samuel

Armstrong had started with the aim: "To train selected youth who shall go out and teach and lead their people, first by example, by getting land and homes; to give them not a dollar that they can earn for themselves; to teach respect for labor; to replace stupid drudgery with skilled hands; and to these ends to build up an industrial system for the sake of character." A Negro, Lewis Adams of Tuskegee, Alabama, a skilled craftsman in metals and leather had similar ideas. He bargained with a white candidate for the state legislature, to secure colored votes for him in return for his support for a school at Tuskegee. In 1881, the state legislature appropriated $2,000 to pay the salaries of the staff at a normal school for colored teachers in Tuskegee. Washington became principal of that school in the same year.

By the 1890's his travels to the North, to raise money for the school, brought him a widening circle of influential friends. In 1895, he was one of a group of white and colored businessmen from Atlanta who went to Washington to secure congressional aid for a Cotton States Exposition. Although Washington was the last speaker to appear before the relevant congressional committee, he contributed greatly to the success of the mission by emphasizing the need for assisting the intellectual and material growth of both races. The Negro should not be robbed of his vote by unfair means, he suggested, but political agitation alone would not advance his cause. The suffrage must rest upon property, industry, skill, economy, intelligence, and character. Within a few moments after Washington had concluded his remarks, the committee unanimously agreed to recommend the requested appropriation. As Washington's latest biographer, a professor of World Relations at Union College, British Columbia, has pointed out: "This short speech opened the eyes of Atlanta leaders to Washington's remarkable powers of persuasion."[1] It also undoubtedly convinced them that he would strike the right note if invited to speak at the Exposition. Neither Washington nor any of his biographers have discussed the fact that he did not at Atlanta include the remark that he had made to the congressional committee, that the Negro should not be robbed of his vote by unfair means.

The invitation to speak at the opening of the Cotton States and International Exposition in Atlanta on September 18, 1895, placed a responsibility upon Washington that few speakers have been called upon to accept. He realized that by one sentence he could have jeopardized, in a large degree, the success of the Exposition and made it impossible for a Negro to speak under similar circumstances for many years. He was "determined from the first not to say anything that would give undue offense to the South" and "equally determined to be true to the North and to the interests of my own people." His task was not made easy by the reception given him by the white persons in the audience when ex-Governor Bullock of Georgia introduced "Professor Booker T. Washington." The colored people in the audience cheered him wildly, but the white people gave him only scattered applause. Soon, however, the white people were cheering him wildly. At the close of the speech, Bullock, in violation of Southern etiquette, rushed across the platform to shake his hand as did other speakers on the platform. The volume of applause from the white people had hardly been witnessed before in the South. By the next morning, congratulatory telegrams began to pour in from practically all parts of the nation. Within a few days, one lecture bureau offered Washington $50,000, or $200 a night, for a specified period—an offer which Washington declined as he did many similar offers. President Cleveland, to whom Washington had sent a copy of his speech, thanked him "with much enthusiasm for making the address." Harvard University gave Washington the honorary degree of Master of Arts in 1896, the first time that a New England university had conferred an honorary degree upon a Negro.[2]

Washington's first sentence struck the keynote. He pointed out that, since one-third of the Southern population was colored, it could not be ignored if the section was to move forward. He praised the managers of the Exposition for the generous recognition given to the "value and manhood" of the colored people. This recognition would do more to cement the friendship of the two races than anything that had occurred since the dawn of freedom. Since Negroes had been "ignorant and inexperienced" at emancipation, it was not surprising that they had begun at the top in politics, rather than at the bottom in acquiring property and industrial skill.[3] To those Southern Negroes who depended upon migration to a foreign land in order to better their condition, or who underestimated the importance of cultivating friendly relations with their next-door neighbor, the Southern white man, he would say: "'Cast down your bucket where you are'—cast it down in making friends in every manly way of the people of all races by whom we are surrounded."

He urged the colored people of the South to cast down their bucket in agriculture, mechanics, commerce, domestic service and the professions. Whatever sins the South had to bear, it was in the South that the Negro was given a "man's chance" in the commercial world, as the Exposition clearly showed. The Negroes' greatest danger was that in the great leap from slavery to freedom they might overlook the facts that the masses were to live by the production of their hands, that they would prosper in proportion as they learned to dignify and glorify common labor, to put brains and skill into the common occupations of life, and to draw the line between the superficial and the substantial. "No race," he warned, "can prosper till it learns that there is as much dignity in tilling a field as in writing a poem." Negroes had to begin at the bottom and not at the top. They should not permit their grievances to overshadow their opportunities.

Turning to the white people, he urged them also to let down their bucket where they were, rather than to rely upon immigrants of "strange tongue and habits." Instead the Southern white people should cast down their bucket among the eight million Negroes whose habits they knew, whose fidelity and love they had tested during the Civil War.[4] He again urged the white people of the South to cast down their bucket among the people who had, "without strikes and labor wars," done so much to help make possible the progress of the South. The South could be sure that, in the future as in the past, it would be surrounded by the "most patient, faithful, law-abiding and unresentful people that the world has seen." After asserting that no foreigner could approach the Negro in this respect, Washington held his hand aloft and pronounced the statement that has been more frequently quoted than any other: "In all things that are purely social we can be as separate as the fingers, yet one as the hand in all things essential to mutual progress." This sentence aroused more frantic applause from the crowd than any other.

If there were efforts anywhere to curtail the fullest growth of the Negro, Washington continued, these efforts should be turned into stimulating, encouraging and making him the most useful and intelligent citizen. The fate of the white people of the South was inevitably bound up with that of the Negro. As the Negroes presented their "humble" effort at an exhibition of their progress, too much should not be expected of them. He reminded the audience of the little wealth that the freedmen had possessed after emancipation. While Negroes therefore took pride in what they exhibited, their participation would fall far short of expectations were it not for the constant aid to education given not only by the Southern states but also by Northern philanthropists.

He repeated his renunciation of social equality in these words: "The wisest among my race understand that the agitation of questions of social equality is the extremest folly and that progress in the enjoyment of all the privileges that will come to us must be the result of severe constant struggle rather than of artificial forcing." No race that had anything to contribute to the markets of the world would long find itself "ostracized." It was important and right that "all privileges of the law be ours," but it was vastly more important that Negroes be prepared to exercise those privileges. For "the opportunity to earn a dollar in a factory just now is worth infinitely more than the opportunity to spend a dollar in an opera house."

In his conclusion he spoke of the great encouragement and resulting friendship that the Exposition had revealed. In the future development of the South, the white people would find, at all times, the "patient, sympathetic help" of the colored people. While much material good would come from the economic growth of the South, one should pray to God that a higher good would come "in a blotting out of sectional differences and racial animosities and suspicions, in a determination to administer absolute justice, in a willing obedience among all classes to the mandates of law. This, coupled with our material prosperity, will bring into our beloved South a new heaven and a new earth."[5]

Washington unmistakably accepted a subordinate position for Southern Negroes. This position was far different from the unequivocal standard for equal citizenship advanced by Douglass in 1889. He definitely renounced social equality. His allusions to "citizenship," "all privileges of the law," and "obedience among all classes to the mandates of law" were so vague that one can find in them a demand for the suffrage only by reading back from what Washington said at a later date. In return he asked for a chance to gain a decent livelihood. Washington was convinced, and rightly so, that it would have been folly to ask in 1895 for equal rights for Negroes.

The Southern press naturally approved wholeheartedly Washington and his speech. The Atlanta *Constitution* and the Mobile *Daily Reigster* called it the "hit of the day." The *Constitution* added that it was "the most remarkable address delivered by a colored man in America" and referred to Washington as a "sensible and progressive negro educator." In the words of the New Orleans *Picayune*, "the Rev. Booker T. Washington, . . . a prominent" and "sensible" man had given a "most temperate address." As the Charleston *News and Courier* put it, Washington was "one of the great men of the South. His skin is colored, but his head is sound and his heart is in the right place." Another representative Southern paper, the Memphis *Commercial Appeal*, said that Washington's speech evoked much applause and pleased both whites and blacks.[6] On this latter point it may be noted that James Creelman, a well-known reporter of the New York *World*, observed that at the end of the speech "most of the Negroes in the audience were crying, perhaps without knowing just why."[7]

The editorial interpretations placed upon the speech by representative Southern journals, and the excerpts which they quoted from it, are even more significant. The *Constitution* quoted in full the figure of the finger and the hand, and referred to the other passage in which Washington renounced social equality. This paper, of which Henry W. Grady had been managing editor until his death in 1889, believed that Washington had solved the race problem in a few terse words and had illuminated the minds of those Northern philanthropists who imagined that the political advancement of the Negro meant social advancement. The Negro could advance only as he deserved to be advanced. He might have temporary success as a politician in an "abnormal" period, but he would surely have to find his proper level, and his proper level was that which he had won and would have to win by the work of his hands and brains. The Negro race would have to be judged by the same tests as the white race.[8] The *Constitution* did not point out how difficult it would be for the Negro to compete on equal terms with white men when he was disfranchised, segregated, discriminated against, treated with contempt and lynched.

Even more revealing was the editorial comment in the *Constitution* about a letter in which Washington had expressed his views on the question of suffrage, which he had not discussed in his Atlanta speech. This letter declared:

> Beginning from today let the negro register an oath in heaven that from henceforth he will cast his lot materially, civilly and morally with the best people of the South; that he will cultivate the closest friendship with the Southern white man; that when he can he will vote for and with the Southern white man.

The Hartford *Courant*, which called special attention to this letter, had declared that this view represented one school of thought. Atlanta University represented another school which was "uncompromising" and which felt that discrimination because of color was unreasonable and wicked. The Hartford paper had hoped that Washington's speech and letter would not lose for Tuskegee a single Northern friend or Northern dollar. The *Constitution* retorted that surely Northern philanthropists were not aiding Negroes solely for the purpose of organizing them against Southern whites. "Washington knows he's on the right line," the *Constitution* concluded, "and whites will stand at his back."[9]

In Washington's own state, the Mobile *Daily Register* and the Birmingham *Age-Herald* carried practically no editorial comment for at least a month after the speech. The *Daily Register* did, however, print the speech in full, and stated editorially that the Exposition would show that the South was not made up of lazy whites and shiftless Negroes. The *Age-Herald*, a much larger paper, carried only the last three paragraphs of the speech and no editorial comment. In New Orleans, the *Picayune* stressed the value of the speech for the considerable light it shed, for the benefit of Northern critics, on the relations between the two races in the South. Washington had grasped, more completely than most educated men of his race, the "great and salient truths" connected with the race problem in the South. If these views were placed before the people of his race, "instead of the misleading mouthings of selfish politicians," the race problem would be greatly simplified. The Memphis *Commercial Appeal* apparently did not deem the speech worthy of editorial comment.[10]

The reaction of the Charleston *News and Courier* is particularly interesting since the state convention called for the purpose of disfranchising colored voters was in session when Washington delivered his address. The paper therefore used it as a means of combatting Northern criticism and justifying Northern support of the proposed amendment.[11]

In the border state of Kentucky, Watterson's influential Louisville *Courier-Journal* interpreted Washington's speech to mean also a renunciation, temporary at least, of participation in government. Its editorial also quoted the passage about the "inexperienced and ignorant" Negro who had begun at the top. Like the *News and Courier*, the *Courier-Journal* placed the blame for this mistake on others and declared that the Negro's enfranchisement had been a political move for the benefit of Northern politicians. When these politicians could no longer use the Negro, they frankly confessed that his "premature" enfranchisement had been a mistake and they then lost all interest in him except at national party conventions. If the Negro had had disinterested friends in the beginning, they would have told him that no race ever raised itself to high position by politics. The first step would have to be in the realm of industry and economy, a fact which, the paper asserted, Washington clearly understood. A mistake had been made in the type of education given to the Negro, as well as in "seducing him prematurely into the field of politics." Repeating the theme, the *Courier-Journal* pointed out that the sooner the Negro ceased to look upon himself as a great political factor, the better it would be for him. To that end his education should be "constantly directed."[12]

While it is not surprising that the Southern press and "Marse" Watterson approved Washington's speech, the generally favorable reception accorded it by the Northern press is more revealing and significant. The *Transcript* felt that the speeches of men like Speer, one of the white orators, and Washington gave assurance that the South was passing into a stage of development which would prepare more of its people to support Southern editors in their "feuds" with Northern editors. In a rather confused fashion, the *Transcript* appeared to believe that the South was learning, in spite of itself, that crime did not pay. The erudite paper declared:

"The race question, which is only race prejudice, has been responsible for many of the crimes of violence that redden the annals of the South. White mobs that hunt down 'niggers' and are not greatly troubled if they catch and hang 'the wrong nigger,' soon, in the mere wantonness of bloodthirstiness, turn their weapons upon one another." The *Transcript* nevertheless accepted the assurances of Speer and Washington that the progress of the South was not alone industrial, but social as well, and that the two races were getting along much better than they had been a few years ago. "This," the *Transcript* added, "is enlightenment."[13] It is not easy to understand how the paper reconciled lynching " 'the wrong nigger' " with improved relations between the races and with "enlightenment."

The New Haven *Evening Register* was favorably impressed by the prominent place given to Negroes at the Exposition. It approved Washington's speech, and quoted his statement that no race that had anything to contribute to the markets of the world would be long ostracized. If the colored people could contrive to make progress in education and the industrial arts, the *Register* added, they would soon win recognition.[14] Strangely enough the New York *Times* did not comment editorially upon the speech, at least until the end of the month. Since the president of the Times Publishing Company was Charles R. Miller who had enthusiastically endorsed Grady's speech, this silence can be subject only to conjecture.

The Philadelphia *North American*, like the *Evening Register*, was favorably impressed by the generous space "set apart" for the exhibition of what the "African race" had accomplished. Washington's address attracted attention, not only because it marked a "new departure" in the South, was eloquent and able, but also because it indicated the course for the freedmen to follow in order to live down race prejudice. When Washington said that agitation for social equality was the veriest folly, he spoke words of truth and soberness. Placing its own interpretation upon Washington's words, the *North American* declared that Washington had told his colored fellow-citizens that, proceeding upon industrial lines, they would conquer prejudice and surely arrive at that political equality for which so many sighed as the *summum bonum* of life. Washington was wholly right when he had advised that Negroes would have to rise under the laws of progress rather than by favor of special statutes in the nature of "artificial forces [*sic*]." At the other end of Pennsylvania, the Pittsburgh *Dispatch* declared that, if the Exposition had no other feature than evidence of just and peaceable relations between the two races in the South, it would be a great success. The Indianapolis *Journal* pointed out that the remarkable exhibit of the colored people and the fact that Washington's speech was the best of the occasion ought to stop Southern people from saying that Negroes were " 'worthless.' "[15]

In the Midwest the reaction was hardly different from that elsewhere. The Chicago *Tribune* did not devote much attention to the speech, but it did agree with the Charleston *News and Courier* that Washington was " 'one of the great men of the South,' " and added its own comments that he delivered by all odds the best speech and that he was a credit to his race. The *Tribune* apparently could not go so far as to approve the views expressed by Washington, but did not take issue with them. Two other Chicago papers, however, expressed such favorable views that their editorials were reprinted in the Atlanta *Constitution*. The Chicago *Inter-Ocean* asserted:

> He [Washington] has done more for the improvement of the negro in the South than has been accomplished by all the political agitators. . . . The possession of a vote does not always insure respect, but the possession of a good character, a good home and a little money reserve always insures respect. . . . If every southern state had such an institution as that at Tuskegee, Alabama, presided over by such a man as Professor Washington, the race question would settle itself in ten years.[16]

One wonders whether the disfranchising constitutions adopted during the following ten years by Louisiana, North Carolina, Virginia, Alabama and Georgia fitted into the solution that the Chicago *Inter-Ocean* approved.

The other Chicago paper whose views pleased the *Constitution* was the *Times-Herald*, which rather naïvely asserted that the mere fact that Washington had spoken was proof of the statement made by Judge Speer that "there is no negro problem." Even the St. Louis *Globe-Democrat*, which occasionally made very penetrating observations, declared that Washington's speech, the best, was the kind calculated to put colored people in the way of making the best of their situation. "They have nothing to gain," the editorial continued, "by seeking political relief for the ills that limit and retard their prosperity. It is useless for them to ask special favors on account of their race or previous condition. They must work out their own salvation by means within their reach."[17]

Some important papers, such as the Cincinnati *Enquirer*, the Washington *Star* and the San Francisco *Examiner* did not, in the first few days at least, comment editorially. The *Examiner* did carry a long news article, with drawings of Washington and of the colored buildings, and the *Star* carried a reprint from an unnamed Atlanta paper headlined "The Colored Man Spoke Best."[18]

Fewer Northern papers pointed out the differences, between Washington's fancies and the facts, than had done so at the time of Grady's speech. The Detroit *Tribune*, finally on October 6, made the derisive gibe: "That latest Tennessee lynching should be exhibited at the Atlanta Exposition as a fine specimen of one of the staple products of the South."[19]

These contemporaneous interpretations are extremely valuable in view of the later controversy about Washington, because they reflect the reactions of editors at the time he spoke. Only one of the papers examined, the Detroit *Tribune*, openly criticized the compromise. The Chicago *Tribune* neither condemned nor approved. All the others were either silent, or believed that Washington renounced social equality, that he renounced Negro suffrage at least temporarily, that he emphasized industrial education and the opportunity to gain a livelihood, and that Negroes found many manifestations of friendship in the South. The editors strongly supported his program.

The South of September and October, 1895, was not so friendly as Washington and the press seemed to believe. The most glaring example of Southern "friendship" for the Negro was the evident determination of the South Carolina convention, then in session, to disfranchise the Negro and to maintain the suffrage for whites who were equally, and in many instances more, unqualified to vote.

In Washington's own state of Alabama, the law had been revised in such a way, in 1891, as to allow the distribution of funds for education at the discretion of the local authorities. The new distribution was so inequitable that no figures were published between 1890–1891 and 1907–1908, by which time the Negroes had been so completely disfranchised that their protests were ineffective. Some idea of what had been accomplished in the meanwhile is indicated by the salaries paid to white teachers and to colored teachers in Wilcox, one of the black belt counties, in these two bienniums. In 1890–1891 there were 2,482 white children of school age and total salaries for their teachers were $4,397. There were 9,931 colored children and salaries for their teachers were $6,545. In 1907–1908, there were 2,285 white children and salaries for their teachers $28,108; but only $3,940 was paid to the teachers of 10,745 colored children.[20] The generally deplorable state of education for colored youth in the South toward the end of the century has already been noted. Segregation by law and custom was becoming more and more general. The pages of representative urban papers reveal even more glaring indications of the lack of a friendly attitude toward the Negro, and the extent to which the Negro had been relegated, in fact and in the Southern mind, to an inferior status.

The Atlanta *Constitution* was not likely, during the period of the Exposition, to emphasize the more unlovely aspects of the Southern scene. But even during this honeymoon period its pages are illuminating. The *Constitution*, for example, did not wage a crusade in favor of the South Carolina disfranchising scheme, but it certainly did not oppose it. A news article from Columbia, a week before Washington's speech, pointed out that the plan would not attempt in any way to disfranchise the Negro but it would surely cause him to take little interest in state politics. There seemed to be no escape for the Negro, and the measure was said to be perfectly constitutional. The only editorial, during this time, on the subject declared that some people seemed surprised by Tillman's plain speech. In fact, he merely told "truths" in such a loud tone that they seemed to be new.[21]

Nor did the *Constitution* usually report lynchings in such a way as to inflame readers. These stories, moreover, did not occupy the conspicuous place assigned to them by the *Picayune* and the *Commercial Appeal*. An editorial on the day of Washington's speech even indicated that the *Constitution* was engaged in a campaign against lynching, and against sensationalism in news reporting in general. Only a few lines were used to tell the story of a white farmer who had killed a colored man after an argument about money. The colored man had become "abusive." No question was raised, however, as to the veracity of the farmer who was, of course, exonerated by a jury. The Atlanta paper, like most of the other Southern papers examined, assumed the guilt of a Negro who had been lynched or almost lynched. And, like most of them, the *Constitution* was singularly unimpressed by what is today called "legal" or, more accurately, "judicial" lynching. It reported, without comment, the fact that officials in Florida had promised a mob at the outset of the trial of a Negro that he would be hanged. Although, according to the paper, one Negro confessed to the crime, two others were also hanged. In still another instance, mobs made five ineffectual attempts to lynch the same Negroes.

Even the *Constitution* devoted more space to lynchings resulting from real or alleged attacks upon white women than in other cases. It was almost as rabid in its reporting of the most gruesome lynching of the period studied as was the most vicious of the papers, the Memphis *Commercial Appeal*. A colored trusty, Neal Smith, was accused of having assaulted a young white woman. A first story reported the lynching under bold headlines. A second story, captioned "An Eye for An Eye," described in detail the mutilation of the trusty before his body was riddled with bullets and his ears cut off. Strong feeling prevailed against Negroes in Chattanooga, not far from the lynching scene. Despite the previous editorial which had condemned lynching, the *Constitution*, two days after the lynching, pointed out that if the convict had not been a trusty he would not have had an opportunity to waylay and assault "his victim." What was needed, therefore, was a revision of the practice of making trusties. The editorial in no way condemned mob violence, and in no way raised any question as to the guilt of the colored man in this case or in the case of any other lynching. But when a colored preacher in Chicago urged that the torch be applied to towns where lynchings took place, the editorial comment was quite pungent. It asserted that "sensible" Negroes knew that their white friends were trying to prevent lynching, and that the best way to put an end to it was for Negroes to stop committing the "horrible crimes which provoke it. If a Negro wants to escape the danger of lynching, let him keep his hands off white women."[22]

Crimes and misdemeanors that did not "provoke" lynching were generally treated in jocular, derisive or otherwise derogatory fashion. Typical was the story of a colored man who "got himself into a deal of trouble" when "he armed himself with a big pistol and started out to see what he could steal." Another Negro had a "penchant" for stealing anything that he could lay his hands on. He would then flee with "race-horse speed." The *Constitution* frequently referred to Negroes as "darkies." Thus a "darky" got in a fight with a white election official who had accused him of fraudulent registration. Four "darkies" were caught in the act of raiding a watermelon patch. A "very black little darky," called a "pickaninny" in the headline, had stolen some bread from a baker's wagon. A "happy darky" had had his eyesight restored by a white doctor. Stereotypes frequently portrayed the Negro as ignorant, superstitious, indifferent to marital ties. Four Turks, who had lost their way in Atlanta, asked information of a colored woman who "had a big mouth and a long tongue, and evidently thought that the only difference between the Arabic and our choice Georgia dialect lay in the strength of the lungs and the lift of voice." Another colored woman attempted to burn her home because she thought there were snakes in it. A colored man left six "widows" to none of whom he had been married.[23]

The amount of space and the tone of articles that portrayed Negroes in a more favorable light hardly offset the derogatory, jocular, derisive stories and the stereotypes. A number of articles spoke of the Negroes' share in the Exposition. One very prominent article was written by I. Garland Penn, colored commissioner of the Exposition and author of *The Afro-American Press and Its Editors*. This article announced that there would be a number of special days showing the progress of the race in medicine, law, the ministry, education, business and journalism. Bishop Henry McNeal Turner of the A.M.E. Church was quoted as saying that the "New Negro" was the "Old Negro," for even slaves had been skilled artisans. The colored men who attended a "Race Convention" in Raleigh were described as "intelligent and conservative." Other articles referred to the excellent speeches at the Atlanta YMCA and the Baptist Convention in Atlanta; to the tile work of a Negro builder; to progress that Negroes were making in home building and education. Matthew Henson's[24] participation in Parry's early explorations of the Arctic drew forth the comments that it was perhaps a mistake to believe that Negroes could endure only the heat of the torrid zone, and that Henson had taken care of others in the party. The *Constitution* also took issue with the statement attributed to Professor Flinders Petrie in London, that it was useless to try to carry civilization to inferior races. The acceptance of his views, the *Constitution* declared, would leave savage lands in darkness for ages to come. The *Constitution* spoke approvingly of the appearance of the first issue of the *Daily Opinion*, "the only negro daily in the world."[25]

The Charleston *News and Courier*, like the *Constitution*, generally was not inflammatory, but its reporting of news did not justify Washington's glowing portrayal of Southern friendship for Negroes. The Charleston paper, in fact, repeatedly supported the idea of white supremacy. It approved the Mississippi disfranchisement device, and warned that "no trouble has been caused in Mississippi and there will be none in South Carolina if outsiders will let the Carolinians, white and black, settle the matter for themselves." The *News and Courier* also enthusiastically supported the proposal to limit suffrage to those who had not committed crimes, since "neglect or maltreatment of their wives and children are far too common offences among black and colored men." The suggestion to give women the right to vote was espoused in order to prevent Negroes from outnumbering whites at the ballot box, presumably on the ground that colored women would not bother to vote. By implication at least, the paper also favored a division of voters into three groups, white, colored and black, each to vote for its own candidates and thereby assure victory to the undivided white constituents. White immigration was also favorably considered as a means of increasing the white vote. The paper, on the other hand, denounced a suggestion that a poll tax of $3.00 be levied because, the paper feared, Northern philanthropists would pay the poll tax for Negroes who, in turn, would vote to use the revenue for the education of colored children. Ben Tillman's brother, George, argued that two-thirds of the Negroes would be ineligible to vote because of their "migratory habits," if a residence requirement were stipulated. The *News and Courier* also approved this device. To make assurance doubly sure, the paper opposed the suggestion that the constitution be submitted to the people for ratification. If the disfranchisement of the colored voters would result merely in a reduction of South Carolina's representation in Congress and in the Electoral College, the editors of the paper were willing to accept that penalty. The position of the journal was made clear in an editorial that declared: "The Republican theory of equal political rights and privileges for unlike and unequal races occupying the same territory has made no progress whatever towards popular acceptance in any of the states upon which it was forced nearly a third of a century ago."[26]

In order to buttress its own position, the journal frequently reprinted articles and editorials from other papers, Northern and Southern, using generally for these reprints the caption "The White Man Must Rule." On September 20, the *News and Courier* carried an editorial from the Brooklyn *Eagle* which declared that the most important task before the constitutional convention of South Carolina was the elimination of the Negro vote. "It was useless," asserted the *Eagle*, "to indulge in sentimental high falutinism on this subject. The whites ought to rule in the South and they will rule." The *Eagle* further asserted that the proposed amendment would provoke a "formal and perfunctory" protest from Northern Republicans, but at heart it would meet the approbation of the people of the North regardless of party. In fact, so long as the "colored brother" was content to keep out of politics, his treatment was "exceptionally considerate," more so by the former slaveholding element than by the forces which had combined to overthrow it. The *News and Courier* also carried an editorial from the Pittsburgh *Times* which pointed out that if the whole South was determined to disfranchise the Negro, a fact about which there could be no doubt, it was better to do it by law than by the shotgun. Still another editorial from the Cincinnati *Christian Standard*, quoted in the Charleston paper, approved an educational qualification for voting, not only in the South but in the nation as a whole, for the purpose of eliminating the voting of ignorant masses at the dictation of party bosses. Again resorting to the Northern press for approval of the proposed amendment, the *News and Courier*, two weeks later, quoted the Philadelphia *Record* as approving an educational and property qualification that would bear alike upon white and black voters. The Boston *Herald* was invoked to show the danger of the colored population outvoting the white minority in South Carolina. In Maryland, the Baltimore *Sun* pointed out that the influx of colored "idlers" into the cities of that state might lead to a special suffrage qualification to meet the situation. It was not likely that a restriction would be hazarded that would bring the state constitution into conflict with the federal Constitution.[27]

Lynchings occupied about the same amount of space in the *News and Courier* as in the *Constitution*. Although the news articles were generally not deliberately designed to arouse hatred, one was particularly vicious. It reported that a Negro in Tennessee was surrounded, "and before morning he will have met the fate usually meted out to black brutes who outrage white women in this section of the country." The paper also carried the gruesome details about the lynching of the Negro trusty, and denounced the colored pastor in Chicago for his "Misplaced Wrath in Regard to Lynchings for the Besetting Sin of His Race." In both news articles and an editorial the paper approved "judicial" lynching. The editorial specifically endorsed quicker trials when especially brutal crimes were committed, and when the "guilt of the accused was notorious or generally regarded as clearly established," and when a threat of violence was noticed.[28] It would be superfluous to point out that this view violated the Anglo-Saxon doctrine that a man is innocent until he is proved guilty.

As in the other papers, an element of supposed humor was injected into stories about lesser crimes. "Two Negroes Walking Bar Rooms" was the headline for a jocular story of their trial. When a colored man was robbed of $280, the paper expressed mild surprise that he had obtained it honestly, and added that "like all such darkies he carried it about with him and showed it around." An article about some colored boys arrested for throwing rocks at one another regretted that the boys had not "exterminated" one another and thereby rid the city of a nuisance. Parson Jenkins's "pickaninnies" could hardly play music that was worth hearing. Some Negroes stranded in Texas were "cantankerous"; they had been so "spoiled" by being furnished with supplies that they refused to work. A letter to the paper urged that Negroes above a certain shade of whiteness should be deported, preferably to Africa. After that wholesale deportation, the birth of a light-colored child would be *ipso-facto* evidence of miscegenation.[29]

Even in poetry the Negro was scoffed at. Private Miles

O'Reilly of the United States Army contributed this gem, entitled "Sambo as a Soldier":[30]

> Some tell us its a burning shame
>   To make the naygiers fight;
> And that the thrade of being kilt
>   Belongs but to the white;
> But as for me, upon my sowl,
>   So liberal are we here,
> I'll let Sambo be murdered in place of myself
>   On every day of the year.
> So hear me all, boys, darlings
>   Don't think I'm tipping you chaff,
> The right to be kilt, I'll divide wid him,
>   And give him the largest half.

Except for articles praising Washington's Atlanta speech and his work at Tuskegee, the *News and Courier* offered little that portrayed the Negro in a creditable light or revealed a friendly attitude on its part. It characterized the Raleigh Convention of Negroes as intelligent, and reported that its resolutions urged Negroes to decide on their best interests, socially, morally and politically. Reference was made to Matthew Henson without identifying him as a Negro. Like other Southern papers, the Charleston journal had words of praise for the meeting of colored Baptists in Atlanta. Separate education for white and colored students was naturally approved, but the paper opposed the proposal to make the colored people support their own public schools. The *News and Courier* also supported the resolution of one of the colored delegates to the South Carolina convention, Robert B. Anderson, for compulsory education for children between the ages of seven and twelve. While the journal, of course, opposed miscegenation, it favored a liberal interpretation of "Negro." Before the war, it pointed out, people of "tainted blood," that is of less than one-eighth Negro blood, were accepted as white. More severe provisions would have dire ramifications. The paper also printed a letter from John N. Gregg, a well-known colored Charlestonian, who queried how one-eighth of Negro blood could "vitiate" seven-eighths of white blood.[31]

Both the Mobile *Daily Register* and the Birmingham *Age-Herald* were relatively mild. The first carried so little news that the items mentioned below were more prominent than they would have been in a less provincial journal. During the period from September 12 to October 18, 1895, the Gulf paper reported briefly the lynching of a Negro in Florida and of another in South Carolina. In the latter case, three Negroes had been convicted of murder. Two had been sentenced to death and the third, on the recommendation of the jury, to life imprisonment. A mob took him from the constables and lynched him. An editorial and a news article reported the deplorable plight of Negroes returning from Mexico who had been dumped at the railway station in Birmingham. Some attention was given to the South Carolina convention. United States Senator Irby of South Carolina was quoted as fearing that the proposed suffrage plan would disfranchise poor whites and permit intelligent and property-owning colored people to vote. An editorial quoted the New York *Tribune* as saying that South Carolina's representation in Congress should be reduced; the Philadelphia *Press* as pointing out that the proposed suffrage amendment was for the purpose of disfranchising the colored illiterates and permitting the white illiterates to vote; the New York *Herald* as insisting that it violated the Fourteenth and Fifteenth Amendments. But the *Daily Register* contended that the only limitation allowable under the Constitution would have to apply to white and black alike. Two days later, however, another editorial asserted that since the whites in South Carolina frequently divided while Negroes never did, the whites were forced, in self-defense, either to hold together or invent some mechanical way of eliminating the Negro majority. The whites could not surrender the control of public affairs to the "ignorant and incompetent. That has been done once in the South. It will never be done again."[32] Since Alabama was already considering the revision of its constitution, this observation was rather ominous. It is not necessary to point out once more the implication that all whites were educated and competent and all Negroes ignorant and incompetent. The *Daily Register* reported in straight, friendly fashion a meeting of over twelve hundred delegates to the National Baptist Convention in Atlanta, and spoke favorably of plans to establish a school for girls at Anniston with the support of Northern philanthropy.[33]

The larger Alabama paper, the Birmingham *Age-Herald*, stood about midway between the mild *Daily Register* and the vicious *Commercial Appeal.* A week before Washington's speech it reported that fifty special policemen in Bristol, Tennessee, guarded a "negro rapist" from some three to four hundred men and boys. The judge ordered the policemen to shoot if an outbreak were made by the crowd. The colored man was tried for "attempted rape" and the jury returned with a verdict of guilty in a few minutes. On the same day, was a report of a lynching at Osceola, Arkansas. But while the *Age-Herald* was less vicious than the *Commercial Appeal,* it too treated stories of lesser crimes by Negroes in the standard jocular fashion. One story was headlined:

ASKED TO BE LOCKED UP
A Nervous Young Negro at Police Headquarters
STABBED HIS STEPFATHER
Who was Engaged in the Innocent Pastime of
Beating His Wife

This momentous news was evidently more important than the fact that cotton was coming in very fast, for this latter headline appeared after those relating the domestic squabble. Another story, headlined "Carved Her Husband," began: "Lou Pleasant is in the city prison for too free use of a knife." News items from Gadsden, on one day, reported that a Negro had died from hydrophobia; another was fined for stealing a ham; an unknown Negro corn-thief had made a murderous assault on a twelve-year-old white boy; colored preachers were making an effort to build a school at Attalla to train colored preachers. On September 17 and 18, the *Age-Herald* carried a story about an "unruly" Negro; about another who was taken to Kentucky, charged with theft; about a third who, though buried beneath a ton of doors, suffered no broken bones. A dispatch from Anniston stated that a Negro was accused of murdering a two-month-old baby. In that town also, about twenty able-bodied men, mostly Negroes, who had more time than money, reported at the city hall to work on the streets rather than pay the three dollar street tax. There was a story of the attempt to lynch two Negroes in Lexington, Tennessee, and finally, one about a Negro who was hit in the face with a beer glass by a "negress." Thomas E. Miller, a mulatto member of the South Carolina convention, was referred to as " 'Canary' Miller." One of the most revealing stories dealt with a meeting to form a local of carpenters and joiners who complained that they were out of work while unskilled Negro painters who did not have on "enough clothes to flag a train" were painting a bridge.[34]

Proportionately, the *Age-Herald* contained more news that portrayed the Negro in a respectable light than did the other papers. It headlined a speech by Smalls at the South Carolina convention: "TILLMAN CALLED DOWN—A Negro Tells Him of His Duty to His State." But this article was more than offset, two days later, by an editorial as follows: "The Secretary of State of Florida says that its ballot reform law 'is equivalent to an educational qualification and it virtually trumps the ignorant darky,' and the same may be said of the Mississippi law. South Carolina will enact a similar law." A brief dispatch reported a meeting of a Negro committee of fifty delegates from fifteen counties in North Carolina as "an intelligent body." There was a straight friendly article about a meeting of the Supreme Lodge of the Knights of Pythias in St. Louis, a segregated brotherhood.[35]

Since Louisiana in the 1890's revealed more of the frontier lawlessness than did South Carolina, it is not surprising that its leading paper, the New Orleans *Picayune*, was more violent than was the *News and Courier*. The former paper devoted few editorials, during the two months studied, to problems concerning the Negroes, but its many news articles contained much editorializing that left little doubt of the general contempt in which Negroes were held.

One editorial on the South Carolina convention, moreover, suggested that the Pelican state would not be far behind the Palmetto state in disfranchising the Negro. Two and two-thirds columns, a week before Washington spoke in Atlanta, were deemed necessary to substantiate the thesis that "men who are not fit to vote should not be allowed to vote, and that is all of it." South Carolina was merely doing what Mississippi had done and what was proposed in Louisiana. In justification of the proposed disfranchisement in Louisiana, the *Picayune* argued that the elimination of the colored vote would put an end to domination by the "ring" of politicians who controlled the colored vote. In further justification, the paper contended that Negroes were ignorant, shiftless and shifting, depraved and criminal-minded. Another editorial, two-thirds of a column long, declared, on October 3, that the

Negro population of South Carolina, like that of Mississippi, was "poor and illiterate, with a low state of morals." Although the census figures for 1890, quoted by the *Picayune*, showed a Negro majority of only 1,697 in Louisiana, by contrast with almost 200,000 in Mississippi, and more than 225,000 in South Carolina, the New Orleans paper insisted that Louisiana was "trifling" with the question of the Negro in politics.[36]

In addition to approving an educational qualification for voting, the *Picayune* was the only paper surveyed at this time that gave attention to a white primary. Some prominent Democrats opposed it, preferring a primary in which only accredited Democrats should have the right to vote. Others opposed it on the ground that Republicans and Populists would outvote Democrats, or set up a separate ticket after the primary and appeal to the colored vote. A "Pow Wow" of the central committee of the Negro Republican Party in Louisiana was held for the purpose of harmonizing the various elements of the "mongrel party." The *Picayune* charged that these Republicans planned to combine with the Populists. White members of the Republican Party would be willing to accept subordinate positions on the ticket, hoping that they would be able to "boss the negroes in all matters of interest." A plea by John R. Lynch in Mississippi that Negroes stand together, even though they had been forced out of politics there, prompted the *Picayune* to charge that, if Republicans got control of the national government, they would declare the constitution of Mississippi unconstitutional. In rather threatening tone, the *Picayune* asserted that their action would not work.[37]

Lynchings were reported at greater length and in a more inflammatory manner than in the *Constitution* or *News and Courier*. These murders by self-constituted guardians of the law had not been confined to Negroes, since eleven Italians had been lynched in New Orleans in 1891. In September, 1895, the *Picayune* treated almost as a joke the lynching of a Negro in Mississippi on a charge of stealing a goat. The presence of the carcass of the goat near the body of the dead man was obviously evidence that the victim had stolen the animal. The same issue reported that some Negroes were shot down in Florida by masked white men because the Negroes were employed at a saw mill from which some white men had been discharged. The lynching at Osceola, Arkansas, was reported the next day under the headline "Justice Was Swift." On the day of Washington's speech, the *Picayune* reported an "Unsuccessful Lynching Bee" in Memphis. Two days later, a Negro was lynched at Shreveport for attempted rape. Again two days later, a Negro described as a "big, burly negro" and "black wretch" was lynched at Hammond, Louisiana, for robberty. The town had hailed the news with delight when the victim was apprehended. The townspeople were satisfied after the lynching that justice had been done. A later article, about the same lynching, reported that the victim's "body is gayly hanging in the breeze from the tank, and no one has expressed any regret over the matter. A certain class of blacks along the line between here and New Orleans have committed such a series of outrages that this community, for one, seems to think that summary justice is necessary as a lesson and warning." Still another article, on the same lynching, was captioned: "Smith Was Hurried to his Fate with a Lie Upon his Lips." Although one letter to the Hammond *Graphic*, reprinted in the *Picayune*, regretted that the laws of the state had been transgressed, another letter from the Hammond *News* stated that a speedy lynching would prove more beneficial in the suppression of "this type of crime" than a legal execution a few months later. In this same month of September, 1895, a Negro was lynched at Plaquemine, Louisiana, for no specified reason. The rope-bound body of a Negro was found near Gretna, Louisiana. In October, the *Picayune* gave most of the gruesome details about the lynching of Neal Smith near Chattanooga. An editorial that commented on the threat of the colored preacher in Chicago warned that "the negroes, North and South, are not strong enough for a race war, which would inevitably follow. Negroes are not lynched in the South as negroes, but as rapists. White men, guilty of the same crime, suffer the same condign punishment."[38] Either white men did not commit rape or else the news of these lynchings was not published. More important is the fact that the *Picayune* reported many lynchings in which rape was not even charged.

A great deal of space was devoted to reporting crimes by Negroes that did not result in lynching. A "Dr. Brown" was found guilty in five minutes of manslaughter. The usual jocular tone described the plight of a "medicine divine" who was languishing in jail because his two colored bondsmen had given him up to the authorities. A colored witness in the trial of "Black Murderers" identified one of the accused as a "Moss Point nigger." Little importance was attached to the beating of a colored man by a white man whom the former had accused of being drunk. But another article showed a Negro "brutally beating a white man almost to death." A column, "Southern States Items," almost daily had articles about crimes committed by Negroes, including one by a "Desperate Negress." Some white people complained that Negroes working at night sang with "loud-mouthed . . . frightful noises."[39]

An editorial held Negroes almost entirely responsible for an outbreak of smallpox. It was next to impossible to isolate a case in the Negro quarters because "these people commonly herd together and do not seem to fear the disease. . . . If the disease be allowed to linger on until cold weather forces the negro population to crowd into their houses until they are packed like sardines in a box, the danger of a serious outbreak of the plague will be very great." Neither this editorial nor two others even hinted at the economic factor involved in the housing conditions, or the inadequate medical facilities available to the colored population. The Negroes stranded in Texas after their return from Mexico were called "Bad Negroes," a "shiftless gang." When they arrived in Georgia and Carolina, they expressed their great joy on getting back to the "home of the black man. . . . They swore with many manifestations of loyalty that the white man was the only friend the 'nigger' had in the world—a fact which, perhaps, is not so generally accepted by everybody." A poem in dialect, "Mammy's Baby Gal," praised the good, pretty white baby in the language of the colored "mammy." "Congo," a "sleepy darky" in the washroom of the Capitol in Washington, was the frequent butt of jokes by the head page. Since the Negro was "imitative," he could only attempt to retaliate in the same way against the page. But alas and alack, the man whom the "darky" kicked was Senator Hoar, who looked very much like the head page. "The darky did not faint, for the reason that darkies never faint. But he grew several shades lighter at the thought of what he had done." A story about a "razor-toting" Negro was reprinted from the Washington Star.[40]

Except for the comments about Washington's address, already noted, the Picayune carried only two items that differed in tone from those analyzed above. One was a letter from

the Colored Military Club of New Orleans asking: "Do we
as law-abiding colored citizens of the city of New Orleans,
some of whom are taxpayers, ask too much of our state to
have one 'Negro' military company therein?" In Chicago, Mrs.
Ellen M. Henrotin, President of the General Federation of
Women's Clubs, discussed with Miss Sophie B. Wright, Vice-
President of the New Orleans Women's Club, the admission
of Negroes to local Women's Clubs. Mrs. Henrotin felt that
the less said about the matter the better—"each locality
should choose for itself what is best for its own good." She
could understand why New Orleans could not have Negroes,
but other cities had the right to determine the matter for
themselves. In 470 clubs not more than three or four colored
women were members.[41] Even the reporting of the possibility
that a few colored women could be members of local clubs
in Northern cities is thus listed in this analysis as an example of favorable news about the Negro. Whether it belongs
in this category or not, the pages of the *Picayune* do not
seem to reveal a friendly feeling toward the Negro.

The Memphis *Commercial Appeal* was the most rabidly
vicious of the Southern papers examined. Tennessee revealed
then, as now, three points of view on the Negro. Eastern,
mountainous Tennessee had relatively few Negroes and consequently the least hateful attitude toward the freedmen.
Nashville and Chattanooga were the "border states" of Tennessee, and Memphis was the Deep South of the same state. It
is therefore understandable that although Tennessee had not
undergone "Radical Reconstruction," and although Memphis
was a fairly large and important commercial city, the paper
was the most violent of all those surveyed.

A week before Washington's speech, the paper reported that
two Negroes had been lynched in Osceola, Arkansas. On the
day of the speech, an unsuccessful attempt had been made to
lynch two colored men in Lexington, Tennessee. Four days
later, another attempt was made to lynch the same two men.
Ten days after Washington's speech, a Negro was being taken
back to Fayetteville County, Tennessee where he would probably be lynched. On September 30, headlines announced:

A LYNCHING BEE IS ON TAP
THE CIRCUMSTANCES, TOO, COME
MIGHTY NEAR WARRANTING IT

FIENDISH OUTRAGE OF A YOUNG GIRL IN THE
VICINITY OF ATOKA—HUNDREDS OF CITIZENS IN
PURSUIT—OCCASIONAL SHOTS AT THE FUGITIVE

Of course, in the article the victim of the lynching was a
"negro rapist." Five days later another headline proclaimed:
"Lynched a Murderous Beast." The next day, headlines told
practically the complete story to which almost an entire column in addition was devoted. On page 1 the *Commercial
Appeal* reported:

WHAT BECAME OF HIM?
HORROR REIGNS IN FAYETTE
A NEGRO RAVISHER RECEIVES THE
USUAL PUNISHMENT
BESTIALITY OF THE CRIME
ALMOST WITHOUT A PARALLEL
WHITE VICTIM OUTRAGED IN THE
PRESENCE OF HER SISTERS

The Fiend Chased All Day by Infuriated
Neighbors of the Afflicted Family, and Besieged
Last Night About Four Miles from Mason—
Support Accorded Him by a Gang of His Race
Whom the Whites Were Determined to Burn
To Death Unless the Monster Should Be Surrendered

Immediately below this article was another, giving the gruesome details of the lynching of the Negro trusty, Neal Smith.
This article reported:

After being mutilated in a fearful manner by the father
. . . who subsequently cut off the negro's ears, he was
seized and held while one of the crowd pounded his fingers, joint by joint, one finger at a time until the hand was
a shapeless mass of blood. This was because in the struggle
to subdue Miss Henderson he had bitten off one of her
fingers. Each man in the crowd then took a turn at shooting at him, until when he died he must have had four or
five pounds of lead in him. He was literally shot to pieces
and the bloody pulp, which only an hour before had been
Neal Smith, was thrown into a hastily prepared pile of
brushwood and burned until not a scrap of bone remained.

Below this article was another about the lynching of a Negro in Alabama who had "assaulted" a white woman. Below this, was still another article about the probable lynching of a Negro in Arkansas. Needless to say, the question of the guilt or the absence of a trial was not mentioned. The paper carried no editorials against lynching. It did, however, point out editorially that the massacre of Armenians "becomes very much a neighborhood matter." And when the colored preacher in Chicago urged that the torch be applied to cities where lynchings of Negroes occurred, the *Commercial Appeal* retorted that when a Negro assaulted a white woman, "whether from a spirit of lust or otherwise," he would be killed if seized. The editor also enjoined Negro preachers to urge morality upon members of their congregation.[42]

The Negro was rarely treated seriously in the *Commercial Appeal*, except in lynching stories and political matters. If a crime committed by a Negro—and it will be remembered that arrest meant guilt—did not result in lynching, the culprit was generally a " 'bad nigger,' " or a " 'fool nigger.' " For less grave crimes, especially when they were committed upon other Negroes, a jocular vein was standard. Thus, a colored man had committed assault and battery upon "one of his discarded women"; there was "a graveyard rookus" about some financial dealings in connection with a colored cemetery. The most important news next to lynching, if space allocation is an indication, was the difficulties at the colored Beale Street Baptist Church. Several articles, many of them a column long, were devoted to this highly important situation. A long article, headlined " 'Hoodoo' Plague Rampant," began as follows: "Darkest Africa is not in it when compared with the Senegambian descendants in Memphis. They are more superstitious than were the people in the days of witchcraft, and may be duped and gulled in the most surprising manner without resistance."[43]

Occasionally some signs of Negro progress or of a reasonably objective attitude on the part of the paper were evident. A long letter from Isaiah T. Montgomery denied that a merchant had been barred from the colored town of Mound Bayou because he was a Jew. The report about Negro Baptists in Mississippi contained nothing funny nor derogatory. In one respect at least, the *Commercial Appeal* was ahead of many Southern papers today—it called colored women Miss and Mrs. in the list of applications for licenses to wed. In crime stories, of course, they were, for example, Mary and Maud.

One article, from the Jackson, Mississippi, bureau of the paper, declared that Mississippi was doing more for Negro education than any other Southern state. But another article in the *Commercial Appeal*, from the Vicksburg *Herald*, pointed out that such a liberal policy was unduly burdensome and that it wholly lacked

rational design and practical purpose. Theoretically we are seeking to fit the negro for the same position in the State, for the same duties and vocations as the white man. Besides being repugnant to sentiment, this theory, if susceptible of practical test, would be found at variance with the welfare of the races. Practically considered, the recognition in law of such an absurdity is grotesque and gross.[44]

Another revealing indication of Southern attitudes is found in the well-nigh forgotten address of Judge Emory Speer, the orator of the day, who followed Washington. One reason why Washington's speech overshadowed his is the fact that Washington's was about twenty minutes while Speer's must have been more than an hour. One of its principal themes was that in the United States "the old Anglo-Saxon stock has ever predominated." Those persons who had feared, after the Civil War, that the Negro race would continue to control the Southern states should have remembered that, of all the American people, the Southern people had the largest percentage of old Anglo-Saxon stock. Those persons would have done well to consider the "imperious and commanding nature of the Anglo-Saxon race." This race, moreover, had never mingled its blood with a darker race. Not a drop of the Indian's blood flowed in the veins of the white men who had succeeded him. With respect to the Negro, he then asserted that the "so-called 'race question' does not exist. . . . Why shall any one forge a race issue?" Honest and decent men would accord the Negro that just measure of favor as a member of society that the laws afforded him, that his conduct deserved, and in due time it would be determined whether his presence was a benefit to himself and to the nation. No process of reasoning, no fertility of conjecture would afford any other solution to the so-called race question. Why agitate it, then? Agitation awakened prejudice, which caused the idle, the ignorant and lawless to become enemies of the Negro. "There is one thing," he continued, "since his emancipation the South has ever guaranteed to the negro, that is no matter what his trade or occupation, the privilege of earning a living." It was common to see whites and Negroes in the South working side by side. He regretted that this situation was not true in the North. In the South the Negro was taught a trade. "How incomparably superior is his condition to one of his race who is trained for a profession where he must depend upon the patronage and slender means of his own people," Speer contended. The people of Georgia respected and enforced laws; the people of the South were distinctively a religious people. He then added this fascinating statement of responsibility and firm prediction:

> We are the trustees for humanity, the trust is free government, and the beneficiaries of that trust are our fellowmen everywhere. . . . Our responsibilities are tremendous, but we must, in the future as in the past, see to it that the American stock which made the country shall dominate its institutions and direct its policy and work out its destiny on the lines our fathers marked.[45]

It is regrettable that Washington's speech, "the hit of the day," has led practically all writers to ignore Speer's oration. His views are as indispensable for an evaluation of The New South in 1895, as are those of Grady in 1886.

In addition to ignoring Speer's address, the interpretation given by the Southern press to Washington's speech, and revelations of actual contemporary conditions and attitudes in the South, most writers have failed to pay sufficient attention to Washington's clearly implied renunciation of Negro organized labor in the South. Horace Mann Bond and Abram Harris are two of the few writers who have emphasized the pro-capitalistic aspects of Washington's economics;[46] especially his reminder that Negroes had tilled the fields and worked "without strikes and labor wars." Even less attention has been given to the paragraph in which Washington denounced "the incoming of those of foreign birth and strange tongues and habits." In other words, not only would faithful Negroes not strike, but they would not succumb to the so-called radical and socialistic ideas usually attributed especially to alien workers.

While Washington's astute appeal to capitalists is thus clear, his views on politics—which have also been generally overlooked—are debatable. He probably concluded that it would have been inadvisable to tell his Atlanta audience, as he had the congressional committee, that the Negro should not be robbed of his vote by unfair means. He did not even repeat what he had said in his letter published by the Hartford *Courant*, namely, that when the Negro could vote he would vote for, and with, white men. Nor did Washington include this letter in either his *Up from Slavery* or *The Story of My Life and Work*, both published in 1900. But he did, with evident pride, include in the latter, though not in the former, an open letter to Ben Tillman written while the Atlanta Exposition and the South Carolina constitutional convention were in progress. The relevant passage, quoted in several papers, declared: "An appalling fact that may not be obvious at a first glance, is that the course proposed means the end of Negro education and Negro progress in South Carolina. This is openly admitted by Senator Tillman and his friends." Washington hoped that Tillman had been misunderstood on this question of education. There was not one word in this letter about the proposed disfranchisement of the Negro.[47] Reference has also been made to the letter which Washington sent to the Louisiana constitutional convention in 1898, urging that, as the ballot box was closed, the schools should be opened. In *Up from Slavery* he recognized that he had been often urged to express himself more freely upon the political condition and future of the race than he had done. Although he had never said so in so many words, his belief was that "the time will come when the Negro in the South will be accorded all the political rights which his ability, character, and material possessions entitle him to." He did not believe, however, that the opportunity freely to exercise such political rights would come in any large degree "through outside or artificial forcing, but will be accorded to the Negro by the Southern white people themselves, and that they will protect him in the exercise of those rights." The right to vote would be the result of "natural, slow growth, not an over-night, gourd-vine affair." The Negro should not cease voting, but in voting he should be more and more influenced by those of intelligence and character who were his next-door neighbors, namely, the Southern white man. He summarized his views in a closing paragraph:

As a rule, I believe in universal, free suffrage, but I believe that in the South we are confronted with peculiar conditions that justify the protection of the ballot in many of the states, for a while at least, either by an educational test, a property test, or by both combined; but whatever tests are required, they should be made to apply with equal justice to both races.[48]

The change from Washington's silence on Negro suffrage in his Atlanta speech and in his letter to Tillman in 1895, to his publicly expressed views on the subject in 1898 and 1900, can perhaps be attributed to disillusionment. During the intervening years, Louisiana had disfranchised the Negro; North Carolina, Virginia and his own state of Alabama had clearly indicated their intention also to disfranchise the Negro.

The fullest statement by Washington on the participation of Southern Negroes in politics was made before the Bethel Historical and Literary Society of Washington, D. C., on May 29, 1900. He realized that in the audience of the most important lyceum of colored people at the turn of the century were many opponents of his views. This speech, therefore, represents probably the limit to which he was prepared to go in order to retain his position as the spokesman acceptable to Negroes, without alienating his staunch white supporters in the North and the South. As reported, *in extenso*, in the *Transcript*, June 2, 1900, he urged that beyond all else Negroes should not lose hope or courage. No settlement would be permanent and satisfactory that did not command the "confidence and the respect" of Southern and Northern white men and of Negroes. He was emphatically in favor of encouraging Negroes "to secure all the mental strength, all the mental culture, whether gleaned from science, mathematics, history, language or literature, that his pocketbook and circumstances" would enable him to pay for. But the greatest proportion of the "masses" should be directed toward toil that would permit them to work in the community where they resided. He then attacked the delicate problem of participation in politics.

In national politics, he was a Republican, and he expected to remain one until he could discover something better. Yet he was "free to say that there is little reason why in the future we should pursue the policy of arraying ourselves in all our local matters solidly in politics against the men whose interests are naturally our own, and to whom we go naturally for assistance and advice." The Fifteenth Amendment, "the precious Magna Charta of our citizenship," despite demands for its repeal, "would remain while the Constitution itself still stands. . . . The minute you recognize a law which taxes a Negro for support of government and denies him the opportunity to make his wishes felt at the ballot box, that minute you begin to undermine our whole theory of government."

But after this resounding statement of no taxation without the right to vote for representation, he hedged. "I stand today where I have always stood," he continued, "advising my race that in their present condition it is a mistake for them to enter actively into general political agitation and activity; but when the foundation of our citizenship is attacked, I think I have the right to speak and I speak here in the same spirit that I have already spoken in the heart of the South." He then reasserted, in part, the principle that he had insisted upon in his letter to the Louisiana constitutional convention: "Any subterfuge, any makeshift in the form of a law that gives the white man a right to express his wants at the ballot box and withholds the same privilege from the ignorant Negro is an injustice to both races."[49]

Washington thus laid down the following principles:

1. In national politics Negroes should vote Republican, but in local Southern politics, Democratic.

2. The Fifteenth Amendment should remain a part of the Constitution, but it should not be generally enforced.

3. Ignorant whites and Negroes should be excluded from, or admitted to, the ballot on equal terms.

In the light of what Washington had written to the Louisiana convention, he probably meant that the few "intelligent" Negroes in the South should be permitted to vote for Republicans in presidential elections, in which their votes would hardly change the outcome, and for Democrats in state and local elections. This limited participation would have constituted fuller enjoyment of the suffrage than Mississippi, South Carolina, Louisiana and, in a few months, Virginia,

North Carolina and Alabama were willing to permit. Meanwhile, however, Washington did not call for a reduction in the representation of these states in the House of Representatives and in the electoral college.

There remains to be considered the reaction of the Northern press to Washington's address. All twelve papers bestowed high praise upon it, either in news articles or editorials. They commended his "wisdom," "common sense"—"Afro-American common sense" as the *North American* put it—or repeated the refrain of many Southern papers: "The Colored Man Spoke Best." All except the *Evening Register, North American, Enquirer, Dispatch* and Detroit *Tribune* carried long excerpts from the speech. (The issue of the *Globe-Democrat* for September 19, the date when it would most probably have carried the speech, is missing in the Library of Congress volume.) But these five, like the others, devoted considerable space to the Fair and the events of the opening day, and the Detroit *Tribune* reproduced drawings of several buildings, including the Negro Building. Drawings of Washington and of the Woman's Building appeared in the *Examiner*, and of Washington and I. Garland Penn in the Chicago *Tribune*.[50] But only four papers gave significant comment in their editorial columns. Two others editorialized in news articles. Their endorsement was almost as enthusiastic as that given by Southern papers.

The fulsome approval of the *Transcript* was almost inevitable, since it had for a long time made appeals for financial support of Washington's industrial program at Tuskegee. But the fervor of the editor led him to appear to endorse the disfranchisement of Negroes in the South at that time. "Intelligent and sympathetic observers," he asserted, had long since been aware that it was through "the silent and serious and steady work of the schools that the solution of the race problem was coming and not through the passions of politics, stirred and kept hot by tricky professional party managers for use in Presidential elections." On the issue of social equality, he was unclear. It was to be noted that "this wise leader of his race abates nothing of the *ultimate* claims of manhood and womanhood to social *respect* and *privilege*; he merely advises against pressing those claims until they can be backed up."

The other New England paper, the *Evening Register,*

lauded the progress that had been made from " 'the ownership here and there in a few quilts and pumpkins and chickens (gathered from various sources)' as he humorously put it." It then quoted the statement that was obviously drafted by Exhibition officials: "The [Negro] building was designed by a negro architect, was constructed by a negro contractor, and no white man has had any part in its making." If the colored people continued to make progress in education and the industrial arts, they would win recognition, the *Evening Register* added at the end.[51]

The *North American*, which at the time of the Civil Rights decision had given the most extreme expression of the folly of seeking to change by legislation the relationships between races, approved Washington's assertion of the same thesis, and agreed that he "spoke words of truth and soberness" when he said that "any agitation for social equality is the veriest folly." Equally categoric was the *Globe-Democrat*: "They [the Negroes] have nothing to gain by seeking political relief for the ills that limit and retard their prosperity. . . . They must work out their own salvation by means within their own reach."[52]

The *Times* limited its editorial comment to its news article in which it approved the claim of Southerners that the Negro had greater chances for practical advancement in the South "than he has ever had, or than he could have, in any other part of the country." The article also included the sentence about the construction of the Negro Building, and ended with praise for education along manual training and technical lines.[53]

But the news article in the *Enquirer* outdid all others, even those in Southern papers. Although McLean's paper had toned down its articles and headlines, its reporting of the Exposition and of the speeches is perhaps unsurpassed. In large black-faced type on page one, the poetic headlines proclaimed:

DREAMS,
Only Dreams, They Said,
But It Blazed in Glory and
Sparkled in Light
An Unseen Power Came
Down in Awful Might,

And Shed Its Brilliance in the
Darkness of the Night,
Swept Over the Maze of Grassy
Glades and Rolling Hills,
Bathed the Southland in Gor-
geous Hues of Love
That Lingers and Languishes as
the Coo of the Dove,
The Bird, God-Given, That Car-
ries the Olive Branch
To the Peoples of the Earth and
Restores Peace, Good Will
The Opening of the Atlanta Exposi-
tion, Blending North and South
Hearts and Hands

After describing the other events of the day, the article declared that "the greatest single event" at the auditorium was
the reception accorded Washington. The scene was

AN INSPIRING ONE

that marked an epoch in the history of the South. "As he dwelt
on the gospel of the brotherhood of man and rejected the
baneful doctrine of social equality, the bugbear of whites, he
was forced to cease speaking several times in order that his
auditors might cheer." The Negro Building spoke louder than
did the words of Washington,

GIFTED AND ELOQUENT

though he was, and told the grand story of true emancipation. . . . If peace hath her victories no less renowned than
war, then the battle of Atlanta of 1895 was as decisive a
victory over race prejudice as the world has ever seen.
Separate socially, but in all things else united, is the new
doctrine that is bound to lead the South back to glory and
supremacy once more.[54]

At the time of Grady's speech there was considerable evidence that many Northern papers were impressed more by
"the inexhaustible resources" of the South, especially in coal
and iron, than they were concerned about the treatment of
the Negro. Washington's speech had to compete with en-

couraging evidence of fraternization between the North and the South. Many papers devoted as much space in their news columns to the dedication of the Chickamauga Battlefield as they did to the Atlanta Exposition. Frequent mention was made also of the Encampment of the Grand Army of the Republic at Louisville. Typical of the comments about the significance of these three events was the assurance by the *Evening Register* that they would result in "an utter absence of the race issue and the waving of the bloody shirt" in the presidential campaign of 1896. The *Examiner* was even more enthusiastic: "The official announcement of this complete obliteration of sectional lines will come with the election of a Southern man to the Presidency."[55]

There was less criticism of the New South in 1895 than there had been in 1886. The *Evening Register* disagreed with the assertion in the Atlanta *Journal* that "'the idea that the negro is fit only for menial service previals not in the south, but in the north.'" After stressing, on September 20, the significance of the events in Louisville, Chickamauga and Atlanta, the *Globe-Democrat*, two days later, warned that, despite much rhetoric about reconciliation, the Northerner was much less tolerated in the South than the Southerner in the North. And it was "equally true that many who profess to be thoroughly reconstructed would much rather hear 'Dixie' than the 'Star-Spangled Banner.'" The *North American* condemned Senator Bate of Tennessee for saying during the Chickamauga exercises that the South had gone to war to vindicate its rights under the Constitution. The *Transcript* hit back at the Macon (Georgia) *Telegraph* which had accused the Boston paper of "sectional prejudice." The *Transcript* retorted that it would continue to condemn lynchings until speeches like those of Speer and Washington had brought the enlightenment which would put an end to crimes of violence. Then there would be fewer occasions for Northern papers to speak of Southern crimes, and "for Southern journals to fall back upon the charge that the critics are moved by sectional prejudice." But, from September 18 to the end of the month, no paper evaluated Washington's speech against the background of events in the making, not even the South Carolina constitutional convention.[56] The New South had gained greatly in favor during the nine years that had elapsed since Grady's speech. Washington's address was the most convincing reply to those who had doubted the validity of Grady's most vulnerable point, "honor and equity" in the treatment of the Negro. The author of this book hazards the guess that Washington's Atlanta Compromise address consoled the consciences of the judges of the Supreme Court who in Plessy v. Ferguson, the following year, wrote into American jurisprudence one of its least defensible doctrines, the constitutionality of equal but separate accommodations. The Supreme Court, in 1953, found this doctrine so difficult to resolve that it instructed the litigants in the public school cases, which for the first time clearly presented the question of the constitutionality of segregation under the Fourteenth Amendment, to ascertain whether the Congress which submitted the Fourteenth Amendment for ratification by the states intended for the Amendment to abolish segregation in public schools.

In 1900, T. Thomas Fortune, the fiery editor of the New York *Age*, urged "revolution" at a meeting in Brooklyn to celebrate the one hundredth anniversary of the birth of John Brown. Fortune was reported as proclaiming: "It took tons of blood to put the fifteenth amendment into the constitution and it will take tons to put it out. You want to organize and keep your powder dry, and be ready to demand an eye for an eye and a tooth for a tooth, for there is coming a great crisis for the negro in this country." Fortune was generally condemned in the daily press for his utterances. In the same year, a group of prominent Negroes met in Philadelphia to form a separate Negro party. Some of the Negroes, including Booker T. Washington who was mentioned as a possible candidate for Vice-President, immediately disavowed the proposal. W. E. B. Du Bois, who was later to become the most eloquent critic of compromise, was so little known that the papers which mentioned him also as one of the possible vice-presidential candidates on the separate Negro ticket spelled his name De Boise.[57]

FIFTEEN

The Roots of Recovery

THE Negro in the United States has achieved today the highest status in his history. More American people than ever before are participating in movements to encourage, consolidate and accelerate his progress. Of course, unconscionable inequalities still exist. But it is now conceivable that "American justice, American liberty, American civilization, American law, and American Christianity could be made to include and protect alike and forever all American citizens in the rights which have been guaranteed to them by the organic and fundamental laws of the land."

Looking backward, we who were boys at the beginning of the century, can see clearly that the cold war, World War II, the Great Depression and World War I have greatly altered the outlook for Negroes, and changed the attitude of many other Americans. It is less easy to identify and evaluate the foundation stones upon which these changes were erected, especially since they were hardly discernible in the latter part of the nineteenth century. By contrast, the superstructure of the Terminal at the end of the Road to Reunion was massive and apparently indestructible. It was also ugly. On the pediments of the separate wing reserved for Negroes were carved Exploitation, Disfranchisement, Segregation, Discrimination, Lynching, Contempt. Few of the architects and engineers who had designed and erected the Terminal would have believed that their handiwork would be replaced within half a century by a monument that more fittingly represents American ideals.

These ideals, which have been called the American Creed, are one of the basic reasons for the change. Peace and Prosperity had dictated the compromising of those ideals, and even their repudiation in practice, as far as the Negro was concerned. Lip service to those ideals did not, however, destroy them. Not all the Northern and Southern conciliators, Southern demagogues, Social Darwinists, Social Gospelers, social philosophers on the Supreme Court, in Big Business and organized labor could exorcise from the Declaration of Independence the assertion that "All men are created equal

313

and endowed by their creator with certain unalienable rights, among which are life, liberty and the pursuit of happiness." Party platforms, inaugural addresses and messages to Congress all too frequently were meaningless, and sometimes hypocritical. But they almost always proclaimed allegiance to the principles of American democracy and to the Constitution of the United States. Churches that denied membership to Negroes still preached the Fatherhood of God and the Brotherhood of Man.

These ideals were honored, then, more in the breach than in the observance. They constituted, none the less, a yardstick by which Gideon's band could measure the shortcomings of the multitude. A few must have been aware of their hypocrisy when they violated by word or deed the ideals to which they paid laud and reverence on July Fourth and on Sundays. The multitude could forget, ignore or rationalize its violations of the American Creed but it did not formally adopt a new set of ideals like that in the Transvaal Republic, for example, which proclaimed that the Boers "will suffer no equality of whites and blacks, either in state or in church." The American Creed was dormant at the end of the century but it was not dead and buried.

"Radical" movements had done little to halt the deterioration of the Negro's plight. The spirit of vehement protest nevertheless remained a healthy American tradition and muckrackers were soon to castigate some of the most cherished and honored American institutions. Perhaps these attacks, which preceded the most militant period of muckraking in the early part of the twentieth century, helped to make the American mind more receptive to criticisms of one of the most sacred of these institutions, the denial of equal rights. Du Bois' *The Souls of Black Folk*, first published in 1903, was surely taking shape in his mind by the end of the century.

Less well known is the fact that the Conservative Mind had begun to fear the effects of the possible extension of lawlessness and the virtual nullification of the Fifteenth Amendment. Senator Evarts of New York, Hayes's secretary of state, had expressed this fear in 1891, when he declared in support of the Lodge bill: "Unless we can keep the suffrage within the regulation of legal obligation and maintain it by authority and obedience to it on the part of the whole country as a working force in our affairs, wider and wider estrangements from these methods will extend themselves among the people."

Even the intemperate denunciations of the Negro constituted one of the roots of recovery from the nadir. The very extremism of the demagogues led them to shout such absurdities that they must have repelled some Americans who might have been won by more persuasive enticement. When others were silent, the demagogues kept the subject before the public. The value of discussion itself was impressed upon the author by a visit to Venezuela a few years ago. Although even a casual observer could see that most Negroes were employed in the least remunerative jobs and that few of them were customers in the best hotels, restaurants and theaters, the visitor was assured: "We have no Negro problem." In the latter part of the nineteenth century, the Negro in the United States was a constant subject of discussion, even though he was frequently the object of obloquy, contempt and patronizing humor. The widespread discussion today of the largest racial minority is no new development. It stems directly from the impossibility, in the latter part of the nineteenth century, of ignoring the outcome of the most delicate problem in American democracy. Demagoguery shocked some Americans into a realization of the fruits of their own tinkering with the principles in which they professed belief.

Freedom of the press assured continued attention to this problem. Since many papers were controlled by large corporations and politicians under their influence, the freedom enabled the controlling forces to use the papers to win popular support for the trend in politics, industry and labor which steadily pushed the Negro farther down. A few papers occasionally departed from this trend in their treatment of the basic issues concerning the Negro. Some of them gave evidence of the achievements of colored men and women who gained recognition in many aspects of American life. A few of them are almost unknown, since they were not included in William J. Simmons's *Men of Mark*, which in 1887 listed some 150 living "eminent" American Negroes.

Two of the papers most hostile to the Negro on basic issues were the San Francisco *Examiner* and the Cincinnati *Enquirer*. Yet both, not infrequently, allowed their readers to see that not all Negroes were clowns, petty thieves, lazy and improvident workers, or rapists. These items also reveal another of the sources of recovery, the steady advance of some Negroes. The *Examiner* lavished great praise upon Paul Laurence Dunbar, the most eminent Negro poet of the period, and commented that the Negro had proved himself in music, oratory and several other arts. It pointed out that Pushkin and the elder Dumas were mulattoes. Captain Joseph Bounty, an ex-slave, the oldest resident in Astoria in 1879 and one of the largest boat owners there, was "industrious and thrifty to an extraordinary degree for one of his race." George A. Butler, manager of the Chinese Merchants Navigation Company, had been educated in France and Germany. After his return to the United States, he had gone to China as private secretary to Anson Burlingame, the United States minister. Butler's career had demonstrated that "a colored manager can make a great success where Chinese brains are no good." In 1894, Ida Platt became the first Negro woman admitted to the Chicago bar. Sissieretta Jones, "as black as a chunk of anthracite coal," was an accomplished artist whose voice was, "like all the voices of the Negro race, extremely dramatic." When Clement Morgan was class-day orator at Harvard in 1890, the *Examiner* reported that his "manner was easy and graceful, his voice, while rather heavy, was smooth, agreeable and persuasive." A colored citizen of San Francisco, who had successfully brought suit against the San Francisco Omnibus Line for denying him the right to ride on its buses, was said in 1890 to be the first colored notary public in the United States. Hearst's paper carried also brief sketches of Negroes who held minor offices in the state government.[1]

John R. McLean's Cincinnati *Enquirer* similarly related the accomplishments of exceptional Negroes. While it flailed such prominent Negro Republicans as Douglass, Langston and Lynch, it commended Fortune. Even in its commendation, however, it struck a few blows. It advised Fortune to devote himself to the Negro in the North and not to fret about the "grafter" in the South. "Mr. Fortune," it added, "is amply justified in taking up the cudgel for them [Negroes] but let him champion only those who are deserving." It mentioned the little-known fact that Cleveland had appointed C. H. J. Taylor consul to Bolivia in 1893. (The Senate refused to confirm his appointment.) The *Enquirer* reported many activities by Taylor in behalf of Negroes. Bud Lindsay was "one of the shrewdest and most adroit politicians" in Lincoln, Nebraska. Lutie A. Little was the first colored woman admitted to the bar in Tennessee, and the only colored woman in 1897 licensed to practice law in the South.[2]

Readers of the New York *Times* also got occasional glimpses of Negroes who were not going to jail or being laughed at. An article called attention to the fact that colored people in Chattanooga, Roanoke, and Lynchburg were investing in real estate. Negroes in Washington were on different social levels: doctors, lawyers, hawkers, servants and laborers. One colored man was suing to perfect his title to a coal and iron business valued at $100,000. When the League of American Wheelmen barred Major Taylor, one of the champion bicyclists of that era, the *Times* observed that he was a great sportsman caught in the web of race prejudice. Although it considered Dunbar an exception, he was a "true singer of the people—white or black."[3]

The Chicago *Tribune*, in addition to its crusade against lynching, frequently deplored individual acts of segregation. In 1895, it commented favorably upon the admission of a colored woman, Mrs. Fannie Barries Williams, to the Chicago Woman's Club. The next year it condemned the Republicans for holding their national convention in St. Louis where the hotels were "still dominated by the old Negro-hating feeling. It is too soon to hold a Republican National Convention South of the Mason-Dixon Line because a decent and fair treatment of the delegates will depend upon their color." A former steward on a Liverpool liner had built a theater on Mercer Street in New York City. Charles P. Graves, president of the Gold Leaf Consolidated Company of Montana and president of the Montana and Illinois Mining Company, was reported to be a millionaire. A. J. Arneaux, a Negro actor of French extraction, had gained fame abroad as had the better known Ira Aldridge (who had become famous in England for his Shakespearean roles, but who could not play Othello in the United States). Also mentioned were the achievements of Edmonia Lewis, a sculptress, Henrietta Venton Davis, an actress on the legitimate stage, and Ida B. Wells, a prominent clubwoman.[4]

The *Transcript* added to the list of "unusual" Negroes during the latter part of the century. George L. Ruffin was appointed district judge in the Charlestown Court in 1883. General Dodds, a colored Frenchman who had fought in the

Franco-Prussian War, was a graduate of Saint Cyr. George
Melburn was the author of the song, "Listen to the Mocking
Bird," and Harry T. Burleigh was "the most finished Negro composer." When many papers doubted the ability of
Negroes to make good officers during the Spanish-American
War, the *Transcript* expressed its confidence that "the time
will come when the courage and devotion of the colored
soldier will open to him the same chances that his white
brother possesses." Americans would not forever be so blind
to their own interests as to bar the door to men of talent.[5]

Since the capital of the nation was the mecca of the largest
number of prominent Negroes at the turn of the century, their
activities were reported more widely in the Washington *Star*
than in any other daily. It frequently carried articles about
chapel services, vespers, speeches and athletic contests at
Howard University. The meetings of the then well-known
Bethel Literary and Historical Society at the Metropolitan
A. M. E. Church, where some of the most noted colored
men and women of the day spoke to large audiences, were
also regularly reported. The favorable attitude of the *Star*
toward Douglass has already been recorded. In 1897, the paper reported at length exercises in connection with Douglass
Day. A column and a half was devoted to the oration by
the Reverend F. J. Grimké, the polished pastor of the fashionable Fifteenth Street Presbyterian Church. A portrait of
Douglass was accepted at the M Street High School by Mrs.
Mary Church Terrell, a colored member of the Board of
Trustees of the public schools, already well-known and highly
esteemed by some of the most eminent American women of
her day. Grimké's speech, as well as those delivered at exercises on February 14, demonstrated that some Negroes possessed not only the eloquence that is supposed to be one of
the gifts of the race but also a clarity of expression and
felicity of style that must have amazed readers who know
only the "Yassuh" Negro. Miss Lucy Moten was principal of
the Miner Normal School, now Miner Teachers College
(On her death in 1933, she left a bequest to Howard University that yields annually some $2,100 which has been used
to help defray annually the study abroad of three of the University's best students.) Other Negroes, who later became
well-known for their activities in restoring the faith of Negroes in themselves, and in changing the prevailing attitude

toward Negroes, were Kelly Miller of Howard University, one of the most effective pamphleteers of the first half of this century, and Dwight O. W. Holmes, then a student athlete at Howard University who later became the first colored president of Morgan State College and the first colored member of the Maryland State Board of Education. Drawings of Negroes not infrequently appeared which showed that not all Negroes looked like savages or baboons.[6]

It is, of course, impossible to evaluate the impact of these articles and drawings on the minds of readers. They hardly changed the attitude of those who considered Negroes, *as a race*, to be inferior. These individuals were undoubtedly classed as exceptions that proved the rule. Some attributed the achievements of the exceptions to their white blood, while others held fast to the theory that Negroes of mixed blood inherited the vices of both parents and the virtues of neither. In either case, they were compelled to think about the Negro and his place in American life.

The leading Negro newspapers today, the Pittsburgh *Courier*, Chicago *Defender*, Baltimore *Afro-American* and Norfolk *Journal and Guide*, are read not only by millions of Negroes but by a considerable number of other persons in government, politics, business and labor. One incident will have to suffice to suggest the importance of these weeklies. The first newspaper reporter to obtain an exclusive interview with General of the Army Douglas MacArthur, after his return from Japan in 1951, was Stanley Roberts, Washington editor of the Pittsburgh *Courier*.[7]

Negro weeklies in the latter part of the nineteenth century were as far different from the Negro "Big Four" today as most metropolitan dailies then were from the New York *Times*, New York *Herald-Tribune*, Washington *Post* and Chicago *Tribune*, for example, today. The most widely read of the colored papers, named successively the New York *Globe*, *Freeman* and *Age*, had an average weekly circulation in 1887 of about 6,000. (When Ochs took over the New York *Times* in 1896, the actual paid circulation was 9,000.) The *Age*, containing four pages of six columns, two and a half inches wide, sold for five cents a copy; a year's subscription cost $1.50. Fortune maintained correspondents in many parts of the country who regularly sent in "News Letters." Much space was given to such social activities as weddings, banquets and parties—Negroes also had their "Four Hundred." Not much space was devoted to crimes committed by Negroes, but many articles reported "injustices" inflicted upon them, and numerous articles excoriated the perpetrators of these injustices. In 1884, it listed a number of wealthy Negroes in Washington: James Wormley, proprietor of the famous Wormley Hotel, was reputedly worth $150,000; John F. Cook, collector of taxes, $70,000; Langston, from $60,000 to $70,000; Richard Francis, owner of one of the oldest restaurants on Pennsylvania Avenue, about $80,000. Others were worth from $10,000 to $50,000. If this emphasis on the acquisition of wealth seems crude, it was typical of the period. The figures were probably somewhat inflated. Other articles reported well-to-do Negroes elsewhere in the country.[8]

Second in importance to the *Age* was the Washington *Bee*, edited by W. Calvin Chase. I. Garland Penn, historian of the Negro press in the nineteenth century, stated, probably on the authority of the editor: "The *Bee* is read by all, and can be found in nearly every house in Washington, from the Executive Mansion to the most humble hut." The Cleveland *Gazette*, edited by H. C. Smith, ranked after the *Bee*. J. B. Foraker, later senator, was said to have owed his first election as governor in 1885 more to the *Gazette* than to any other paper, weekly or daily. Colored members of the Ohio legislature were also reported as relying upon the *Gazette* for their factual material. Pinchback's *Lousianian* and Hendley's Huntsville (Alabama) *Gazette* are known to investigators since the Library of Congress has more complete files of them than of most other colored papers of the period, but they did not wield the influence of the *Age*, *Bee* and Cleveland *Gazette*.[9] Professor C. A. Bacote of Atlanta University, who has studied the Savannah *Tribune*, is convinced that it should be ranked with the New York *Age*.

Penn lists 31 colored papers in 1880, and 154 in 1890. Most of them were ephemeral and had small local circulation. But the Negro press as an institution clamoring for the rights of Negroes was a lusty infant at the turn of the century. Some of their cries have been reported, especially in criticism of the Civil Rights Decision, President Arthur's Southern policy, the election of Cleveland and the defeat of the Blair and Lodge bills. Today investigators at Johns Hopkins University, the University of Notre Dame, the universities in New York City and probably elsewhere are making intensive studies of the nineteenth-century Negro newspapers as one of the most valuable of the untapped sources for a study of the struggles of Negroes to keep from falling lower than they did. The Negro press today has continued to be one of the most effective critics of injustice and one of the most insistent advocates of equal rights.

Only two Negro magazines of importance have been found for the period under study. One was the *Woman's Era*, discussed later in this chapter. The other was the *A. M. E. Review*, the organ of the African Methodist Episcopal Church. First established in 1841, it reappeared in January, 1884. A quarterly, it resembled *Harper's Magazine* in size and color, but it had smaller print on more roughly finished paper. Its circulation rose from 1,000 in 1884, to 2,800 in 1889. At that time, according to the *Review*, white church publications also had small circulations: the *Methodist Review*, 4,400; the *Presbyterian Review*, 3,000; the *Baptist Review*, 2,000; the *Unitarian Review*, 1,300; and the *Bibliotheca Sacra Universalist Quarterly*, 500. In 1900, the editor of the *A. M. E. Review* declared that its sixteen volumes constituted an encyclopedia on all subjects affecting the race. This is an exaggeration, but the *Review's* articles were surprisingly well written, and covered not only subjects of direct importance to Negroes but broader topics such as the tariff and currency. Among its principal contributors were Douglass, Blyden, Mrs. Terrell, Bishop R. H. Cain (former member of Congress from South Carolina), Judge Ruffin, John R. Lynch, Francis Cardozo (state treasurer of South Carolina during Reconstruction), Reverend Grimké, H. C. C. Astwood and R. R. Wright, who later became a banker in Philadelphia and as a nonagenarian attended the San Francisco Conference on the Organization of the United Nations. The magazine was not denominational in its contents,[10] but it was probably widely read by ministers many of whom sorely needed the extra-curricular education provided in its columns.

All too many Negro ministers resembled the ignorant, humble, immoral, class-conscious buffoons caricatured in the leading literary magazines. They could hardly have been otherwise. Not only had most of them been only recently emancipated but the Negro preacher in the South had been especially selected for his humility and docility. Because Nat

Turner, leader of the bloodiest slave insurrection, had been a preacher, all Negro preachers were suspect. It was after Nat Turner's insurrection in Southampton County, Virginia, 1831, that it had become customary in the slave states for a "discreet" white man to be present at religious exercises for Negroes. The catechistical method of teaching the Bible was commonly used in order to obviate the necessity of teaching slaves to read and write. In brief, the Negro church in the South and its ministers were promoted to the role of instruments of social control for the security of the slave system.

After emancipation, some Negro preachers obtained education and training in the colleges, universities and seminaries established in the South. But these schools, of course, did not have the rigid requirements exacted by Northern universities or, indeed, by the few Northern institutions of higher learning for Negroes. One of the ablest of the Southern ministers, J. C. Price, president of the A. M. E. Zion Livingstone University, Salisbury, North Carolina, for example, was a graduate of Lincoln University in Pennsylvania.

In the North, Negroes had been driven literally by force to form their own churches. While this enforced segregation led to the first large-scale organization of Negroes across state boundaries, it also excluded them from the enlightenment of the Northern churches. Despite this exclusion, a few Negro ministers obtained an education in the pre-Civil War period and gave Negroes after the war the intelligent spiritual leadership that in no way resembled the popular caricatures. Alexander Crummell, denied education in Episcopal seminaries in the United States, received the degree of Bachelor of Arts from Cambridge University in 1853. After serving for some twenty years as a missionary in Liberia and Sierra Leone, he became rector of Saint Mary's in Washington, and was the founder of the American Negro Academy. Bishop Daniel A. Payne of the A. M. E. Church had been graduated from the Lutheran Seminary at Gettysburg. In addition to lifting the moral and intellectual tone of his denomination, he had helped to found Union Seminary in Ohio, which was merged with Wilberforce University, the first Negro institution of higher learning for Negroes. White Presbyterians had founded Ashmun Institute in 1854, near Philadelphia, for the purpose of training Negro ministers. Some of the best-trained ministers in the United States, not all of them Presbyterians, were educated at the successor to Ashmun Institute, Lincoln University. In addition to Price, one of the most eminent graduates was the Reverend Walter H. Brooks who pastored the Nineteenth Street Baptist Church in Washington from 1882 to 1945. Henry Highland Garnet, denied admission to Canaan Academy in New Hampshire, was educated at Oneida Institute in New York. In addition to serving as a Presbyterian minister, he lectured on abolition platforms in England, was an educator of note, and was appointed minister to Liberia. Francis Grimké, after studying law at Lincoln and Howard, was graduated, in 1878, from Princeton Theological Seminary.[11]

After the Civil War, most Southern Negro churches asserted their spiritual independence just as American churches severed their connection with England following the American Revolution. Thus freed from the controls established during slavery, the Negro church served the freedmen in many ways. It provided an escape from their earthly woes. It gave them an opportunity to develop qualities of leadership, and it is no mere coincidence that many of the Negro leaders in the latter part of the nineteenth century were ministers. Many of the preachers inculcated habits of thrift, good manners and conduct, neatness in dress. A few of them preached a social gospel for their particular congregations. The churches that were organized on a national basis, such as the A. M. E., the A. M. E. Z., the National Baptist Convention, and the Lott Carey (Baptist) Convention, served as a training ground for directing large organizations with considerable funds. The National Baptist Publishing Company of Nashville, for example, which began circulating Sunday school literature in the late 1880's, has today grown into a thriving enterprise whose head is also engaged in banking, the hotel business, and other commercial enterprises.

Just as segregation has promoted the growth of the Negro press and the Negro church, similarly it accounted for the development of Negro business and professional men. The accumulation of capital by Negroes had been considerably retarded by the failure of the Freedmen's Savings Bank and Trust Company in 1874. It had close to $3,000,000 in deposits and 61,131 depositors, almost all of whom were Negroes. Although dividends amounting to $1,882,752.62 were declared between 1875 and 1883, the depositors lost a part of their first savings after emancipation and many others lost their faith in banks. As Du Bois later concluded: "Not even ten additional years of slavery could have done so much to throttle the thrift of the freedmen as the mismanagement and bankruptcy of the series of savings banks chartered by the Nation for their especial aid."[12] In 1888, however, Negroes began to organize their own banks: the Capital Savings Bank of Washington, with a capital stock of $6,000 later increased to $50,000; and the Bank of the Grand United Order of True Reformers of Richmond, with a capital of $100,000. In 1900, there were still only four banks owned by Negroes, with a total capital amounting to $94,605.61.[13] In 1948, there were fourteen Negro-owned banks with total assets of $31,307,345.[14]

Negro insurance companies evolved from secret fraternal organizations like the Masons, Odd Fellows, St. Luke's, True Reformers and Knights of Pythias and others which did not have a secret ritual. Their development was made almost imperative by the refusal of most white companies to write policies for Negroes, or to charge them at the same rate as other policyholders. White companies were even less willing to write policies for them after Frederick L. Hoffman, in 1896, published his widely read *Race Traits and Tendencies of the American Negro* which sought to prove that Negroes were a poor insurance risk.[15] Two years later, S. W. Rutherford formed in Washington the first Negro insurance company on an actuarial basis, the National Benefit Insurance Company. C. C. Spaulding and others organized the North Carolina Mutual Benefit Insurance Company in the same year. In 1948, there were sixty-two member companies of the National Negro Insurance Association with total admitted assets of over $108,000,000, and with a little less than $1,000,000,000 worth of insurance in force. The annual income of these companies was more than $55,000,000.[16]

Negro undertakers began to flourish, largely because most white undertakers had a repugnance against serving Negroes. In 1899, it was estimated that more than $500,000 was invested in Negro undertaking establishments. Negro physicians and dentists developed prosperous clienteles for the same reason. The number of physicians and surgeons increased from 909 in 1890, to 1,734 in 1900, and dentists from 120 to 212. The success of Negro physicians encouraged the growth of Negro drug stores of which there were 64 at the end of the century, each with a capital of $1,000 or more. Negro clergymen increased from 12,159 in 1890, to 15,528 in 1900; teachers and professors from 15,100 to 21,267. Negro journalists, practically all of whom worked on Negro newspapers, rose from 134 to 310. Although colored lawyers had special difficulties in pleading cases, particularly in the South, they too benefited from the segregation imposed upon Negroes; they increased from 431 to 728. In 1900, there were also 2,020 actors and showmen; 52 architects, designers, draftsmen and inventors; 236 artists, sculptors and teachers of art; 3,915 musicians and teachers of music; and 247 photographers. While Negro professionals and businessmen thus constituted only a small percentage of the total number of Negroes gainfully employed—a much smaller percentage than that for native born and foreign born whites[17]—they were the forerunners of men and women who are recognized among the national leaders in their respective professions.

A few Negroes found employment in the federal government. An infinitesimal number held the top "Negro jobs," register of the treasury, recorder of deeds of the District of Columbia, minister to Haiti and minister to Liberia. Most were in the menial and custodial categories, but a few held clerical jobs.[18] The writer, who grew up in Washington in the early part of the century, recalls that these latter were solid, respectable, progressive citizens, leaders in church, civic and educational organizations. They ranked only below the professionals and businessmen and the school teachers.

The firmest foundation for Negro progress was more clearly seen than any other, namely, the remarkable increase in literacy. That very advance, from 18.6 per cent in 1870, to 55.5 per cent in 1890, may have been one reason for the introduction of the "understanding" clause in the new constitutional amendments designed to disfranchise Negroes. If ability to read and write had alone been sufficient to qualify, large numbers of Southern Negroes would have been eligible to vote. Available statistics to not permit a breakdown as to graduates of elementary and high schools. It may be assumed, however, that most of them went only to the elementary schools, since the vast majority of students at colored "universities" in the South were in the elementary grades.[19]

Most of the teachers of these colored youth had been graduated from colleges and universities founded by Northern philanthropy and Negro church groups. During, and immediately after, Reconstruction, Alabama, Arkansas, Mississippi, Kentucky, Missouri, Maryland, Texas, Louisiana, North Carolina and Virginia had created state-supported schools for Negroes, all of them of a sub-college standard. Although the First Morrill Act, 1862, had provided for the establishment of land-grant colleges, it was not until 1871 that Mississippi created the first one for Negroes. After the passage of the Second Morrill Act, 1890, seventeen land-grant colleges were operated for Negroes. Ten of them had been privately supported institutions. None of them provided curricula of collegiate grade prior to 1916, or courses of a standard comparable to those afforded by Negro colleges that were supported by private funds.[20] Today, partly in order to maintain the segregated pattern, Southern state legislatures have gladly appropriated funds which have greatly improved and expanded the offerings of these state-supported and land-grant colleges. But an undetermined number—some estimates, probably too high, place them at one hundred—of Negroes are enrolled in graduate and professional schools for white students in Texas, Louisiana, Arkansas, Oklahoma, North Carolina, Kentucky, Virginia, Maryland, West Virginia and Delaware. Not content with using Plessy v. Ferguson as a lever to compel Southern white state universities to provide facilities not afforded at the state schools for Negroes, they have instituted suits to test the constitutionality of segregation itself in public schools. The most optimistic of Negro lawyers believe that the United States Supreme Court will rule in their favor.*

The saga of the private schools for Negroes in the South is one of the most inspiring in the history of Negro education. While most of these "universities" had more students in the elementary and secondary classes than on the college level, they embodied the concept of a university that is beginning to be achieved today. New England schoolma'ms defied ostracism, snide accusations concerning their morals (sexual, that is), and even violence to bring to the freedmen the "glory that was Greece and the grandeur that was Rome"; the splendors of the Renaissance, the Enlightenment of the eight-

* See footnote on page 106.

eenth-century French philosophers and encyclopedists, the Great Awakening in New England, and even the transcendentalism of Emerson. Quixotic? Of course, it was. But a few students, as in ancient Greece, Rome, Renaissance Florence, eighteenth-century France and nineteenth-century New England, were inspired by the Divine Afflatus. It ignited a spark which burst into flame in the twentieth century.

When General O. O. Howard, Commissioner of the Freedmen's Bureau, came to Atlanta during Reconstruction and asked the students what message he should take back to the North, a young boy in a shrill voice piped up: "Tell them that we are rising." The boy was R. R. Wright, already mentioned as the head of a bank in Philadelphia who attended the San Francisco Conference in 1945 to add the weight of his ninety years to writing into the Charter of the United Nations the aspirations for all people that he, an ex-slave, had glimpsed in Georgia. Mary McLeod (Mrs. Mary McLeod Bethune) was graduated from Scotia Seminary, a normal school in North Carolina, in 1893. She founded Bethune (later Bethune-Cookman) College, became an honored and intimate adviser to President and Mrs. Franklin D. Roosevelt and to President Truman. She, too, was in San Francisco in 1945, to demonstrate by her person, her charm and her prestige that the time had come to "promote human rights and fundamental freedoms for all without distinction as to race, sex, language or religion." Channing H. Tobias was a student at Paine College, Augusta, Georgia, at the turn of the century. After heading the Colored Department of the YMCA for a number of years, he is the first colored director of a white bank in New York and former director of the Phelps-Stokes Fund. In 1951, President Truman named him an alternate delegate to the United Nations General Assembly meeting in Paris. James Weldon Johnson, a graduate of Atlanta University in 1894, was the author of several well-written and widely read books, author of the lyrics of the "Negro National Anthem," a poet who (as Sterling Brown has observed) gave to "material which is usually made ridiculous . . . dignity, power and beauty." National organizer and secretary of the National Association for the Advancement of Colored People from 1917 to 1930, United States consul to Venezuela and Nicaragua, 1906–1912, he was professor of creative literature at Fisk University and visiting professor of literature at New York University at the time of his tragic death in a train wreck in 1938. Others became leaders in their local communities and states.

But many of the Negro leaders were educated in the North. Retrospectively, it is clear to this author that one of the greatest blunders committed by those who sought to relegate the freedmen permanently to the position of a "disfranchised pesantry" was the failure to capture the citadels of learning in the North. John Hope finished Brown University in 1894, and became the president of Morehouse College (from which more Negro college presidents have been graduated than from any other) and, in 1929, president of Atlanta University, the first Negro institution to offer only graduate work. Almost as white as his Scotch ancestors, the Autocrat of the Breakfast Table and of his faculty, a stern Baptist who inspired fear rather than love, he kept alive in the home of the Ku-Klux Klan the torch of learning that he had seized in a New England university. William S. Scarborough was graduated from Oberlin in 1875, where Mrs. Terrell received her A.B. in 1883, and her A.M. in 1888. E. M. Brawley, graduated from Bucknell in 1875, was president of Selma University in Alabama and the father of Benjamin Brawley, a great teacher at Shaw, Morehouse and Howard, and a gifted writer. Thomas Edward Beysolow attended Williams College, 1891–1892, and became associate justice of the Liberian Supreme Court. Edward E. Wilson, of the class of 1893, was an assistant state's attorney in Chicago. George M. Lightfoot, 1891, was for many years professor of Latin at Howard University. They and others handed down to eager young Negroes the tradition of liberalism at Williams, which attracted in the twentieth century Sterling Brown; W. Allison Davis, an expert in childhood education on the faculty of the University of Chicago; his brother John A. Davis, associate professor at the City College of New York; and Rupert Lloyd, first secretary and consul at the United States Embassy in Paris and Budapest. Amherst has vied with Williams in opening its portals to brilliant Negro students. William H. Lewis, captain of the Amherst football team and class orator in 1892, won fame as a brilliant trial lawyer in Massachusetts, and as an Assistant United States Attorney-General under Taft. The Amherst tradition has been continued in the twentieth century by the late Dr. Charles R. Drew, chief surgeon and medical officer at Howard University, director of the plasma project in the dark days after Dunkirk, and director of the first American Red Cross plasma bank; by William H. Hastie, first Negro governor of the Virgin Islands, and the first Negro to be appointed a circuit court judge; the late Charles H. Houston, one of the most successful legal advocates of equal rights for Negroes. Others have gained eminence in education and the professions.

Fittingly, the largest number of noted Negro scholars in the nineteenth century attended Harvard. In 1889, the Boston *Globe* listed the colored "Roll of Honor" from America's oldest university. Drs. Charles Miller and Samuel Boyd were graduated in medicine, 1868, George L. Ruffin (later judge in Charlestown) in law, 1870, and Robert T. Freeman in dentisty, the following year. Richard T. Greener, the first to receive the A. B. degree, 1870, became United States consul to Vladivostok and Bombay. George F. Grant, who finished dentistry in 1870, was elected president of the Harvard Dental Alumni Association in 1882. From 1884 to 1889, he was instructor in the treatment of the cleft palate and cognate diseases at the Harvard Dental School. Dr. James F. Still received his medical degree in 1871, and Archibald H. Grimké his law degree in 1874. Parker N. Bailey, who finished college shortly thereafter, taught English to some of the most famous graduates of the M Street High School, Washington, in the early part of the century. Otis F. Smith was graduated in dentisty, 1881. Robert H. Terrell, who received his A. B. degree in 1884, later became a municipal judge in Washington. Henry L. Bailey, of the class of 1889, taught Greek at the M Street High School to students preparing to enter the best New England colleges and universities. William L. Lewis received his law degree in 1895, an eminent forerunner for Hastie, Houston, Raymond Pace Alexander and others. Some of the best known Negro scholars today, especially in history, received their doctorate from Harvard.

None of these, however, was the peer of William Edward Burghardt Du Bois, the first Negro, 1895, to receive the degree of doctor of philosophy from Harvard. Author of the first monograph in the Harvard Historical Series and of what was probably the first scientific study of a Negro community in the United States, he inaugurated, at the turn of the century, the Atlanta University Studies which still are an indispensable source for the study of Negroes in virtually all phases of life. His *The Souls of Black Folk* likewise remains the classic statement of the demands of Negroes for equal rights. Eloquent advocate of "The Talented Tenth," he not only challenged the Atlanta Compromise of Booker T. Washington but inspired practically all the most distinguished Negroes of the early decades of the twentieth century. As editor of the *Crisis*, the organ of the National Association for the Advancement of Colored People, he castigated in matchless style the injustices inflicted upon Negroes in the twentieth century. Founder of the Pan-African Congresses and of the Pan-African Association, he focused attention, especially in his later writings, on the inequities of colonialism. His *Black Reconstruction in America* not only emphasized the economic aspects of that crucial period, but as Howard K. Beale has said, "presented a mass of material, formerly ignored, that every future historian must reckon with."[21]

Du Bois was not, however, the first Negro historian of note in the latter part of the nineteenth century. George Washington Williams wrote, in 1882, a two-volume *History of the Negro Race in America* which has been used by all subsequent historians of the Negro. Not always scientific or restrained, it was well documented and filled with evidence that Negroes had not always been hewers of wood and drawers of water. Carter G. Woodson, who founded the Association for the Study of Negro Life and History in 1915 and began the publication, still continued, of the *Journal of Negro History*, relied heavily upon Williams and was undoubtedly inspired by him. Among the contributors to the *Journal of Negro History* are white historians who have refused to accept the uncritical judgments of the Burgess-Dunning school at the turn of the century which was attuned to the reconciliation between North and South.

In the fine arts also, Negroes were beginning to receive recognition. Of the Negro authors, Paul Laurence Dunbar followed the Page-Harris tradition in two of his books of short stories published prior to 1901, *Folks from Dixie* and *The Strength of Gideon*. His wife, Alice Dunbar, on the other hand, was inspired by Cable in her book, *The Goodness of St. Rocque and Other Stories*. A less well-known author, J. McHenry Jones used his *Hearts of Gold* as a vehicle for denouncing legal injustice, the convict peonage system, the exploitation of women, and lynching. His novel was one of the first written in the United States which had as a leading character the offspring of the lawful marriage of a white woman and a colored man. *Iola Leroy, or Shadows Uplifted* (1892) by Frances Ellen Watkins Harper, the best-known colored writer of abolitionist verse, was the first published novel after the Civil War by a colored author. Its principal theme portrayed the life of well-mannered, educated Negroes for the definite purpose of offsetting the Plantation Tradition. Pauline Hopkins continued this theme in *Contending Forces: A Romance Illustrative of Negro Life North and South.*[22] Except for Dunbar's collections of short stories, which were rather widely read both because of the author's fame as a poet and because of his adherence to the Plantation Tradition, these novels had a restricted public.

Charles Waddell Chesnutt, on the other hand, was widely read, not because he was colored but because he was a skilled craftsman who won the praise of Walter Hines Page and of William Dean Howells. He was also the first colored novelist exposing the sordid side of plantation life to have a book published by a prominent firm. This book, *The Conjure Woman* (1899), was published by Houghton Mifflin as were *The Wife of His Youth and Other Stories of the Color Line* (1899), *The House Behind the Cedars* (1900) and *The Marrow of Tradition* (1901). These treated primarily questions of the color line, both between whites and blacks and between different classes of Negroes.[23] How much they modified attitudes on these questions is, of course, debatable. But once more, an individual colored man had demonstrated that, afforded equal opportunity, he could give a performance on a level that few persons would have been willing to believe in advance.

Alberry Whitman set this task for himself when he composed a poem in "stately verse," *Rape of Florida, or Twasintas Seminoles*. But Sterling Brown has found it "diffuse, obscure, and pretentious." The Negro during the latter part of the nineteenth century revealed greater gifts in folk rhymes. The most famous to write in this form, Paul Laurence Dunbar, followed, however, closely in the path of Page and other glorifiers of the Plantation Tradition.[24]

In the year of the disputed Hayes-Tilden election, a painting, "Under the Oaks," won a medal of the first class at the Centennial Exhibition in Philadelphia and was bought for

$1,500. When the artist, Edward M. Bannister, presented himself for the award, he was insulted by the guards who had not known that he was a Negro. Edmonia Lewis, who had gained renown for her sculptures in Rome, scored a great success at the Centennial Exposition. The greatest of all the Negro artists was Henry O. Tanner, a painter who was acclaimed by his fellow Americans in Paris as the "dean of American painters." His "Resurrection of Lazarus" was a salon sensation in Paris in 1897. Awarded a medal of the third class, Tanner sold the painting to the French Ministry of Fine Arts. Tanner, however, was little-known in the United States until later, as was Meta Vaux Warrick, a sculptress who went to Paris to study in 1899.[25] In our own day, Roland Hayes and Marian Anderson were acclaimed in Europe before they received the recognition in the United States which their consummate art merits.

Like other Americans, Negroes had the habit of assembling in conventions for the purposes of discussing their problems, promoting their personal ambitions and drafting resolutions. From 1817 to the eve of the Civil War, the Convention Movement brought together many of the most prominent Negroes and their supporters to discuss such subjects as colonization, abolition, the establishment of a colored college, the admission of Negroes to white universities, and migration to Canada. The League of Colored Laborers met at New York in 1850. During Reconstruction, the National Labor Convention of Colored Men met in 1869, January, 1871, and October, 1871, at the time of the Southern Convention, a political gathering in Columbia, South Carolina. Despite the efforts of some colored labor leaders, the politicians headed by Douglass succeeded more and more in making the convention a forum for promoting the interests of the Republican party. By 1874, the colored National Labor Union, like its white counterpart, had ceased to be an effective organization.[26]

So many national, state and special interest conventions met from the end of Reconstruction to the turn of the century that it would be tedious to list them all. Since, however, this post-Reconstruction Convention Movement is not so well known as that of the pre-Civil War, a brief discussion is necessary to indicate the extent to which Negroes were vitally concerned with their own advancement. As early as 1877, a colored teachers' convention in Missouri adopted resolutions supporting the First Morrill Act and urging better educational facilities and opportunities for Negroes in the state. The Exodus of 1879, and less important migrations in the 1880's led to a number of meetings to demand federal support and assistance by Negroes to the migrants. Conventions in Richmond, Virginia, 1879, and in Washington the following year were devoted largely to political considerations. More and more, the national conventions were primarily for the purpose of endorsing one or the other of the two major parties. At one of the most important of these, that at Louisville, 1883, the convention refused to adopt a resolution endorsing the Republican party. But at that same convention, Douglass made a demand for federal aid to public education. A number of conventions during the 1890's denounced lynching. The Afro-American Convention in Columbus, Ohio, 1890, deprecated the attempt to modify the system of mixed schools established by law three years earlier. The Afro-American Press Convention, in 1891, opposed the expatriation of Negroes and favored migration from the South to the West and Southwest; it denounced Congress for its failure to pass the Blair and Lodge bills, and condemned Jim Crow cars and discrimination in public places. It urged the appointment of a capable Negro lawyer to a federal court. In the South, conventions were held, notably at Nashville, 1879; Goldsboro, North Carolina, 1882; Richmond, 1885, and Raleigh, 1895.[27] Church groups met frequently as did many others.

Toward the end of the century, colored women began to take a more active part in civic as well as social matters. Patterned after the program of the General Federation of Women's Clubs, the Colored Women's League was founded in Washington by Mrs. Helen Cook in 1892, and chartered under the laws of the District in 1894. One of the signers of the act of incorporation was Mrs. Terrell. In 1893, she wrote an article in which she urged:

A national organization of Colored Women would accomplish so much good in such a variety of ways that thoughtful, provident women are strenuously urging their sisters all over the country to cooperate with them in this important matter. . . . There is every reason for all who have the interests of the race at heart, to associate themselves with the League, so that there may be a vast chain of organizations extending the length and breadth of the land devising ways and means to advance our cause.

In 1895, the Woman's New Era Club of Boston called a convention out of which grew the National Federation of Afro-American Women. The meeting was attended by representatives from more than twenty clubs. Mrs. Josephine St. Pierre Ruffin, wife of Judge Ruffin, declared that colored women were not drawing the color line, but that they recognized the opposition of Southern women to the admission of colored women to the General Federation of Women's Clubs. Among the topics listed for discussion were: Woman and Higher Education; Need of Organization; Individual Work for Mental Education and Elevation; Value of Race Literature; Political Equality; Social Purity; Temperance; Industrial Training. In 1896, the National Federation of Afro-American Women and the Colored Women's League combined to form the National Association of Colored Women, with Mrs. Terrell as its first president. It continued publication of the *Woman's Era* which had been started by the Boston club. Like the *A. M. E. Review*, it contained not only articles of special concern to Negroes but general articles on such subjects as Bryan and Free Silver. The topics of discussion at the Nashville Convention, 1897, and Chicago, 1899, similarly dealt with both types of subjects. At the latter convention, there were 146 delegates representing 46 clubs and 16 states. More than 300 clubs were said to be in existence. One of the speakers was Mrs. Ellen M. Henrotin, former president of the General Federation of Women's Clubs. But the Boston New Era Club was denied membership in the General Federation at its Milwaukee Convention in 1900.[28]

Driven back into their own organizations, colored women continued to focus attention upon their special problems and to increase their membership. Today the National Association of Colored Women has a membership of some 40,000. The National Council of Negro Women, whose founder, 1935, and president until 1949, was Mrs. Mary McLeod Bethune, has a membership of close to a million, and is a potent force in the struggle for equal rights for those Americans whose equality is most violated, colored women. Mrs. Terrell was honored at a reception on her eighty-eighth birthday, in special recognition of her participation in a suit designed to test the constitutionality of anti-discrimination laws enacted by the territorial government of Washington in 1872 and 1873. The decision of the United States Supreme Court in 1953 opened restaurants generally to individual Negroes many of whom had already been served in them as members of mixed groups. Some eight hundred friends honored Mrs. Terrell on her ninetieth birthday, 1953, at the Statler Hotel in Washington and launched a Mary Church Terrell Fund to help eliminate segregation from the nation's capital.

Not only scarcely discernible then, but well-nigh forgotten now, was the effect on the minds of Americans, white and black, of the magnificent record of the four colored regular army regiments in the Spanish-American War. Negroes had little, at the turn of the century, to help sustain our faith in ourselves except the pride we took in the Ninth and Tenth Cavalry, the Twenty-fourth and Twenty-fifth Infantry. Many Negro homes had prints of the famous charge of the colored troops up San Juan Hill. They were our Ralph Bunche, Marian Anderson, Joe Louis and Jackie Robinson. In the then prevailing climate of opinion, they were the only regiments to which the handful of Negro West Point graduates could be regularly assigned. One of these graduates, of the class of 1889, Charles Young, rose, despite little encouragement, to the rank of colonel. His soldierly and manly qualities undoubtedly helped to re-open the doors of West Point in recent years to a steady flow of colored cadets, and to encourage President Franklin D. Roosevelt in 1940 to commission the only Negro brigadier-general in the regular army, Benjamin O. Davis, Sr. (now retired). The proved ability of Negroes to meet the rigid requirements of West Point in these recent years facilitated the admission of Negroes to the Naval Academy at Annapolis. The long, hard road from a fixed policy of segregation in the army, adopted immediately after the Civil War[29] to the real beginnings of integration in the armed forces could hardly have been covered without the aid of these landmarks along the way.

The Spanish-American War not only gave to Negroes a much needed feeling of pride, and to some other Americans a respect for Negroes that was rarely manifested; the United States emerged from the war a "world power," with commitments, especially in the Caribbean and the Far East. The effects of these commitments are evident to historians. But it is probable that no American could have foreseen the dire portent of a sketch of Pearl Harbor published in the Washington *Star* on March 27, 1897. While the forward march toward equality had begun long before December 7, 1941, the "arsenal of democracy" has since then been peculiarly and increasingly sensitive to foreign criticism, not all of it by Communists, of the lingering inequities practiced by the leader of the "free world."

The penumbra of compromise and reconciliation that prevailed at the turn of the century, obscured also the intangible effects of equal treatment accorded to Negroes studying in the Library of Congress and the Washington Public Library. The author of this book who began using these libraries early in the century realizes now that this mingling on equal terms with other Americans probably kept the minds of young Washington Negroes from being warped and seared. As boys and girls we must have learned, though not fully appreciated, the privileged position enjoyed by students and scholars using these libraries. Schools, hotels, many restaurants and theaters, even churches were segregated. But men and women, boys and girls of both races sat side by side at desks in these treasuries of the accumulated knowledge of the ages. The colored students who went to New England colleges had this joint experience to help relieve the strain of our first association with our white classmates. Native white Washingtonians who have contributed to the peaceful revolution of social change in the capital have been encouraged by their recollection that there was no friction in these two libraries.

Perhaps the most significant event, however, that was to transform America occurred when Henry Ford trundled his first two-seater automobile out into the alley back of Bagley Avenue in Detroit and ran it around the block. The Norman Rockwell painting, "The Street Was Never the Same Again," recently reproduced in many newspapers and popular magazines, graphically portrays the amazement that this revolution in transport produced. In the course of time, the "horseless buggy" was to penetrate the American hinterland, link remote villages with bustling cities and change attitudes as well as the landscape. One authentic folk story relates that when a Negro first bought an automobile in Atlanta, Georgia, he was asked, "Whose road are you going to drive it on?" Unless one had lived in the South at the beginning of the century, he can hardly understand what a revolution was involved in the servicing of a Negro's car at a white filling station. Nor in the yielding by a white driver to a colored driver who had the right of way. Nor the effect on the mind of the Jeeter Lesters of Tobacco Road of the mere sight of a Negro driving an automobile. Nor of indubitable proof that, given the opportunity, Negroes were good automobile mechanics, and skilled craftsmen in the automotive industry. A fascinating volume could be written on "The Effects of the Automobile on Race Relations, Especially in the South."

It can hardly be gainsaid that the greatest acceleration of progress toward first-class citizenship has developed since the outbreak of World War II and especially during the Cold War with the Soviet Union. One can hardly deny, however, that the descent toward the nadir, in the last quarter of the nineteenth century, had not extirpated the roots of recovery. They awaited the phenomenal surge of the United States as the greatest power in history to bear the fruit which encourages the belief today that the experiment in American democracy can "include forever and alike all American citizens."

Part III

SIXTEEN

"A Low, Rugged Plateau"

IN the early years of the twentieth century, the Roots of Recovery confronted deeply entrenched customs, prejudices and a hostile economic system fortified by federal, state, and local sanctions. A continuing tug-of-war between these opposing forces makes it difficult to determine which side was gaining ground at the end of a tug. Henry Arthur Callis, a physician who was an undergraduate at Cornell University, 1905–1909, and who in the early 1960's was still diagnosing the nation's ills, recently described the early years as "a low, rugged plateau."[1]

The élan of a new century probably encouraged Negroes in their quest for equal rights. Most historians date this concept from 1925 when Alain L. Locke published *The New Negro: An Interpretation*. This Rhodes scholar, 1907–1910, sounded the keynote in his foreword: "There is ample evidence of a New Negro in the latest phases of social change and progress, but still more in the internal world of the Negro mind and spirit." Actually, Booker T. Washington had adumbrated the concept in an article on "The New Negro Woman" in the magazine, *Lend a Hand*, 1895. Washington had also collaborated in writing a book, *A New Negro for a New Century* in 1900.[2]

This same élan was perhaps partly responsible for the calling of the Pan-African Conference in London in 1900. The conference naturally devoted most of its attention to Africa. But William Edward Burghardt Du Bois[3] there warned, probably for the first time:

The problem of the Twentieth Century is the problem of the color line, the question as to how far differences of race, which show themselves chiefly in the color of the skin and the texture of the hair, are going to be made, hereafter, the basis of denying to over half the world the right of sharing to their utmost ability the opportunities and privileges of modern civilization.[4]

Three years later, in his classic, *The Souls of Black Folk*, Du Bois launched a trenchant protest against Booker T.

Washington's policies of seeking an accommodation with "Southern white friends." Du Bois repeated in slightly different words the same theme he had expressed at the Pan-African Conference: "The problem of the twentieth century is the problem of the color line, the relation of the darker to the lighter races of men in Asia and Africa, in America and the islands of the sea." Negro leaders, he urged, must seek the right to vote, civic equality, and the education of youth according to ability. "By every civilized and peaceful method we must strive for the rights which the world accords to men, clinging unwaveringly to those great words [of the Declaration of Independence] which the sons of the Fathers would fain forget."

In July of that same year, 1903, in the Columbus Avenue A. M. E. Zion Church, Boston, Monroe Trotter and his sister, Bernard Charles, and Martin Granville heckled Booker T. Washington so vigorously that Granville had to pay a fine and Trotter had to serve a short sentence in jail. Many white Americans thus realized that not all Negroes followed the leadership of Booker T. Washington. In 1903, too, Alabama Negroes made the first frontal attack on the constitutionality of state disfranchising amendments, in the little known case of Giles v. Harris. Though even Oliver Wendell Holmes, Jr., joined in denying federal intervention, this case also shows that Negroes had begun their long, tortuous climb.

Du Bois, seeking further to assert his leadership of "The Talented Tenth" against Booker T. Washington, organized the Niagara Movement in 1905. At Harpers Ferry in the following year, he presented an eloquent, unequivocal resolution for equality: "We will not be satisfied to take one jot or tittle less than our full manhood rights. We claim for ourselves every single right that belongs to a freeborn American, political, civil and social; and until we get these rights we will never cease to protest and assail the ears of America."[5]

The Niagara Movement foundered because of the opposition of Booker T. Washington, because only a small number of "The Talented Tenth" had the courage to follow Du Bois (President John Hope of Morehouse College was the only college president who dared attend the Harpers Ferry Meeting), because of the acidulous criticism of the leading national weekly, the *Outlook*, and because of Du Bois's arrogance.[6]

But the Niagara Movement is generally considered the principal forerunner of the National Association for the Advancement of Colored People, which was organized in 1909. Some of the organizers, white and colored, hesitated in 1910 to select Du Bois as Director of Publications and Research lest he use this position for a stronger assault upon Booker T. Washington's program. Writing thirty years later, Du Bois asked how, "in 1910, could one discuss the Negro problem and not touch upon Booker T. Washington and Tuskegee?" Du Bois, perhaps because of the restraints imposed upon him by the directors of the NAACP, attacked Washington less vigorously than he had done in *Horizon*, the magazine he had published from 1907 to 1910. None the less, Du Bois, as editor of another magazine, *The Crisis*, on the whole fulfilled until 1918 the vow that he had made at Harpers Ferry in 1906.[7] My high school classmates and I do not recall this vow or the early issues of *The Crisis*. But practically all of us and, indeed, most Negro intellectuals until the 1950's—when Du Bois's pro-Soviet feelings became obvious—were the disciples of this authentic American radical. The end of the first decade of the twentieth century may, therefore, constitute an important milestone in the Negro's quest for equal rights, as well as an important milestone in the intellectual history of the United States.

Despite the clarion call of Du Bois at Harpers Ferry in 1906, few Negroes at that time sought any kind of equality. In retrospect, therefore, the doctrine of "separate but equal" first sanctioned by the United States Supreme Court in Plessy *v.* Ferguson, 1896, was a "radical" concept. But, perhaps unwittingly, Negroes continued to use segregation as a weapon to remove segregation.

In 1904 five Negro physicians and one dentist organized in Philadelphia the Sigma Pi Phi Fraternity, because they were generally denied the opportunity to associate professionally and socially with white men of similar interests. Ten Negro professional men organized the second chapter or subordinate Boulé at Chicago in 1907, and ten others, largely educators, formed the third subordinate Boulé at Baltimore in 1908.[8]

Negro college students in the North generally encountered the same kind of isolation as did Negro professional men. At Cornell University in 1906, colored students organized their first Greek-letter fraternity, Alpha Phi Alpha. Henry Arthur

Callis, one of the founders, recalls that in addition to this isolation, the Niagara Movement, and the increase in disfranchisement and segregation led them to serious discussions of these problems. The desire to exchange views with other Negro college students prompted the founding of the second chapter at Howard University in 1907. Since few young colored women at that time attended Northern colleges and universities, they founded their first sorority, 1908, Alpha Kappa Alpha, at Howard.[9]

The founding of the Sigma Pi Phi Fraternity, the Alpha Phi Alpha Fraternity and the Alpha Kappa Alpha Sorority conformed to the pattern of segregation in Negro churches, colleges and universities, business institutions, and the press. Negroes had little choice at that time. Younger generations which have benefited from the advantages which leaders—whose names in some instances they do not know—gained behind the walls of segregation, should try to recognize this fact. The general acceptance of segregation and the rejection of "our full manhood rights" constitute two of the most important landmarks on the "low, rugged, plateau."

Booker T. Washington's rule during this period, on the other hand, requires a new assessment of his views, techniques and goals. The author's research in the Washington Papers in the Library of Congress reveal shiftings that make increasingly difficult the attempt to determine when the Nadir ended.

In an address before the Women's New England Club, in Boston on January 27, 1889, Washington excoriated Henry W. Grady's image of "The New South." He condemned the share-cropping system more vehemently than Frederick Douglass had done ten years earlier in his address to the American Social Science Association. Washington pointed out that schools for Negroes were kept open only three and a half months in the rural areas of Alabama. He flatly contradicted Grady and stated that railway accommodations for Negroes in the South were inferior to those for whites. Washington went further and accused Grady of not telling the truth about the "New South." Here are Washington's exact words:

It would have been the simple truth if Mr. Grady had said that in the whole of Georgia and Alabama, and other Southern states not a Negro juror is allowed to sit in the jury box, and while on that subject Mr. Grady might have added, even at the risk of spoiling his rhetoric, the information that since freedom there have been at least ten thousand colored men in the South, murdered by white men, and yet with perhaps a single exception, the record of no court shows that a single white man had been hanged for these murders. If time would admit an analysis of Mr. Grady's speech, I would reveal other equally untrue statements.

Washington did take time later in this speech to state that Southern white men privately admitted that they kept the Negro vote from being counted whenever that vote might have a controlling influence in an election.

As late as September 26, 1894, Washington continued in his public addresses to attack the myth of Grady's "New South," especially with respect to the inequities of sharecropping and of the short school term for Negro children. But, less than a year later, Washington extolled the "New South" in even more rapturous terms than Grady had done. Washington concluded his famous Atlanta Address of September 18, 1895 with a prayer to God that "a determination to administer absolute justice," coupled with material prosperity, "will bring into our beloved South a new heaven and a new earth."[10]

Descendants of Negroes who had achieved prominence prior to Washington's Atlanta Address attribute his shift to his conviction that he had to adopt a conciliatory attitude toward the South in order to establish his personal leadership. This explanation is plausible, especially in the light of the new evidence.

This recent research led to an equally astounding discovery, namely, clear evidence of Washington's disillusionment with his 1895 portrayal of the New South.[11] He repeatedly stated that many Negroes left rural areas in the South because of four-month school terms and of lynchings; and especially after 1908 he gave convincing evidence of the disproportionate sums spent by Southern states for the education of white and colored children.[12]

Washington had abundant additional reasons for his disillusionment. The Southern states had not accepted his formula for a restricted suffrage provided that "whatever tests are required, they should be made to apply with equal justice to both races." Mississippi had begun this discriminatory disfranchisement in 1890, followed by South Carolina in 1895, Louisiana in 1898 and North Carolina in 1900. Washington's own state, Alabama, joined the procession in 1901. Carter Glass declared on the floor of the Virginia Constitutional Convention, 1901–1902, that it had been elected specifically for the purpose of disfranchising Negroes, and that he would not submit the proposed amendment to be voted upon by "146,000 ignorant Negro voters." By 1910, all eleven of the former Confederate states and the new state of Oklahoma had accomplished, by various devices, discriminatory disfranchisement.[13]

The Republican platform of 1900 stated that "it was the plain purpose of the Fifteenth Amendment to prevent discrimination on account of race or color in regulating the elective franchise. Devices of State governments, whether by statutory or constitutional enactment, to avoid the purpose of this amendment are revolutionary, and should be condemned." The "Negro" plank in the 1904 platform demanded congressional action to determine whether the second section of the Fourteenth Amendment was being violated and, if so, that it be enforced.[14]

Four years later the Republicans drafted one of their most rapturous statements about the Negro. The Republican party, this plank asserted, had been for more than fifty years "the consistent friend of the American Negro." The Party

gave him freedom and citizenship. It wrote into the organic law the declarations that proclaim his civil and political rights, and it believes to-day that his noteworthy progress in intelligence, industry and good citizenship has earned the respect and encouragement of the nation. We demand equal justice for all men, without regard to race or color; we declare once more, and without reservation, for the enforcement in letter and spirit of the Thirteenth, Fourteenth, and Fifteenth amendments to the Constitution which were designed for the protection and advancement of the negro, and we condemn all devices that have for their real aim his disfranchisement for reasons of color alone, as unfair, unAmerican and repugnant to the Supreme law of the land.[15]

The Republicans, who held the presidency, and controlled both Houses of Congress from 1900 until the 1910 elections, did nothing to fulfill their promises. Peonage and the convict-lease system[16] continued to violate the Thirteenth Amendment. Congress refused to enact legislation for the enforcement of the second section of the Fourteenth Amendment despite increased disfranchisement of Negroes; nor did it seek to enforce the Fifteenth Amendment.

The Democrats, in 1904, instead of demanding the enforcement of any of these amendments, deprecated and condemned "the Bourbon-like selfish, and narrow spirit of the recent Republican Convention at Chicago which sought to kindle anew the embers of racial and sectional strife, and we appeal from it to the sober common sense and patriotic spirit of the American people." Four years later a plank on the "Protection of American Citizens" concerned primarily the negotiation of treaties to protect Americans abroad.[17]

After 1904, the Democrats had little reason to be distressed about Republican concern for the Negroes. To be sure, Theodore Roosevelt had aroused the ire of the South by inviting Booker T. Washington to dinner at the White House in October, 1901.[18] But Roosevelt had at times supported the "Lily-white" Republicans in the South and even the White Supremacy Democrats. In 1905, Roosevelt made a tour through the South not unlike that of Hayes in 1877. Du Bois and most other Negroes condemned Roosevelt's silence on the disfranchisement of the Negro. Booker T. Washington was one of the few Negroes who approved the tour.[19] One must conjecture whether Roosevelt's abrupt order for the dishonorable discharge of three companies of the Twenty-fifth Infantry after the Brownsville Riot[20] stemmed from a further desire to propitiate the South. Taft, in 1909, was the first Republican candidate for the presidency who visited the South in the course of his campaign. Shortly after his election Taft revisited the South; one of his speeches he called "Winning the South." The themes of this and other speeches surpassed those of Hayes and Roosevelt in expressions of confidence in the South: the Southern white man was the best friend of the Negro; the South need have no fear of federal enforcement of "social equality." Despite the grandiose pronouncement of the Republican plank in 1908, Taft gave the assurance that there was no inconsistency between the Fifteenth Amendment and disfranchisement.[21] Thus, by 1910, Negroes felt even less secure in their political rights than in 1900.

Lynchings constituted, until recently, one of the greatest shames of the United States. Substantially accurate statistics reveal the following number of lynchings from 1901 through 1910: 130, 92, 99, 83, 62, 65, 60, 97, 82, 76; for a total of 846. Of these, 92 were white and 754, Negroes. From 1889 through 1899, approximately 82 per cent of all lynchings occurred in the Southern states—the eleven former Confederate states, plus, Missouri, Kentucky and what became Oklahoma in 1907. During the first decade of the new century, 91.1 per cent of lynchings were in these states. Between 1889 and 1899, 32.2 per cent of all persons lynched were white; in the first decade of the twentieth century, 11.4 per cent were white.[22]

These statistics mean little to most Americans in the 1960's, for lynchings have almost ceased. Even an unimpassioned account of one lynching will suggest one of the most disgraceful facets, until 1964, of American life. Two Negroes, Will Cato and Paul Reed, were sentenced to be hanged at Statesboro, Georgia, for the alleged murder of a white farmer, Henry Hodges, and his family. Before the execution could be carried out, a mob of five hundred persons stormed the jail and took the prisoners to the Hodges farm. They were bound hand and foot and tied to stakes where burning torches were applied to hay. Cato and Reed burned to death while the mob looked on with sadistic glee.[23]

Another lynching resulted in what was reported as the first time that the Supreme Court of the United States punished anyone for contempt of that court. In March, 1906, a Negro, Ed Johnson, was hanged in Chattanooga, Tennessee, on the charge of rape. The trial court denied him the aid of counsel and a petition for a writ of habeas corpus. The United States Supreme Court granted him the right of appeal and a stay of execution until the case could be reviewed. On March 19, 1906, the sheriff and his deputy in Chattanooga left the jail unguarded; a mob seized Johnson and hanged him. The Supreme Court of the United States, on November 1909, sentenced six members of the mob to short prison terms for contempt of the Court.[24]

Since the platform of neither of the two major parties made specific reference to lynching,[25] it is not surprising that neither

Congress nor the Presidents of the United States took action to prevent the lynching of Negroes. Representative Crumpacker introduced a bill on December 12, 1907, to punish the lynching of aliens. It did not survive the Committee on the Judiciary.[26] Meanwhile, "Pitchfork" Ben Tillman voiced the hatred of extreme white Southerners when he declared, "to hell with the Constitution," if it interfered with the lynching of rapists.[27] This appeal to the sex psychosis of the South disregarded the facts. During the first decade of the twentieth century and thereafter, only about one-sixth of the Negroes lynched were accused of rape; more than one-third were accused of homicide, and almost one-half of other crimes.[28] How many were guilty of the alleged crimes may never be known.

The number and scope of race riots indicate the difficulty of determining the winner at a particular tug in the tug-of-war. How important were these riots in the sum total of race relations? Within this framework, were they more important in the first decade than in the second decade? An answer is perhaps impossible; it is certainly not easy, especially since the North vied with the South in both the number and scope of race riots, and in evidence of deeply rooted hostility against Negroes.

Six major riots occurred between 1900 and 1910: two in Springfield, Ohio; one in Greensburg, Indiana; one each in Atlanta, Georgia, and Brownsville, Texas; one in Springfield, Illinois. The anatomy of these six riots, like the anatomy of revolutions, charts the underlying causes, the immediate occasions, the reasons for the subsidence and the aftermath during convalescence.

Both in the Northern and the Southern cities, racial hostility had increased. The immediate causes, which varied, are difficult to determine—as difficult as the immediate cause of the race riots in Harlem, Brooklyn, and Rochester, New York, and other Northern cities and Southern cities during 1964. (Even though the riots in Northern cities involved hoodlums rather than advocates of civil rights, the confinement of Negroes to ghettos, segregation and discrimination were underlying causes.) A Negro killed a white officer in Springfield, Ohio, 1904. Who was the aggressor? Did the Negro shoot in self-defense? The mob did not seek the answers to these basic questions. The latent hatred of Negroes led a white mob to hang the Negro, riddle his body with bullets, and destroy the Negro section of Springfield. Neither there nor in Greensburg, Indiana, 1906, did a judicial body determine the guilt of the accused prior to a similar attack on the Negro part of the town.

The riot in Brownsville, Texas, August, 1906, caused the most dismay to Negroes, because it involved the Negro Twenty-fifth Regiment, which had fought gallantly at El Caney, Cuba, during the Spanish American War. It also caused Negroes to reverse their judgment about President Theodore Roosevelt whom many Americans still considered their friend and ally. Accepting a report by an inspector whom he had sent to Brownsville, Roosevelt dismissed the entire battalion stationed there without honor and disqualified its members for service in either the military or the civil service of the United States. Senator Joseph B. Foraker of Ohio (whom I remember from my boyhood days as a kind of Sir Galahad, but whom William Randolph Hearst revealed in 1908 as the recipient of retainers from the Standard Oil Company) persuaded the Senate to authorize a full-scale investigation. A majority of the Senate Committee accepted the guilt of the accused soldiers. In 1909, Congress, yielding to the insistence of Foraker, enacted a bill establishing a court of inquiry under the Secretary of War to make a final report within one year from the date of its appointment.[29]

A month after the Brownsville riot, a more bloody riot occurred in Atlanta, Georgia. Du Bois and President John Hope of Morehouse College had returned there shortly after the Harpers Ferry meeting of the Niagara Movement. Du Bois itemized the basic grievances of Negroes: "They had fought disfranchisement; they had resented the Carnegie Library which admitted no Negroes; they had boycotted unfair stores, railroads and streetcars." He accused Tom Watson—who had sought Negro support in the early days of the Populist Crusade—and Hoke Smith, who had been elected Governor of Georgia in August, 1906, of deliberately provoking whites to attack Negroes. John Temple Graves, editor of the Atlanta *Georgian*, defended the attacks by whites as a spontaneous flare-up against black rapists. Much of the "spontaneity" of these race-baiters had its source in a play that had attracted large crowds in Atlanta—a play based upon Thomas Dixon's inflammatory *The Clansman*. ("The Birth of a Nation," the *classic* of the motion-picture world, 1915, which was also based upon the hate-mongering writings of Dixon, triggered race riots in many parts of the nation.)

The economic interpretation of the causes of the Atlanta riot was expressed also by J. Max Barber in an article in the New York *World.* Barber and his magazine, *The Voice of the Negro,* are known to few students of history today. This remarkable magazine, in some respects the precursor of *The Crisis,* ended publication soon after threats on the life of Barber forced him to leave Atlanta. This riot perhaps contributed also to Du Bois's decision to leave Atlanta in 1910. But, his detractors to the contrary notwithstanding, he did not flee from the riot. He was in Lowdnes County, Georgia, for research in connection with his Atlanta University Studies. When he received news of the Atlanta riot, he "took the next train for Atlanta." On the way he wrote "The Litany of Atlanta."[30]

In retrospect these riots seem insignificant because only a few persons were killed. They are indeed insignificant, numerically, as compared with the number of Frenchmen and Muslims killed in French and Algerian cities. To be sure, lethal weapons had less firepower then than now. But I wonder whether the hatred was greater then than now. I am almost tempted to say (and I know that I will incur seething denunciation) that, in view of the deep-seated hatred, these race riots killed a surprisingly small number of persons. They were insignificant, perhaps; but not inconsequential. Responsible Negro citizens told me, when I taught at Atlanta University, 1933–1938, that one reason the riots subsided was that Negroes fought back. Negroes at that time, fortunately, knew little, perhaps nothing, about nonviolent resistance.

The beneficial consequences of a riot find perhaps their most authentic validation in the Springfield, Illinois, riot, August, 1908. The pattern of the anatomy of American race riots had congealed: the alleged rape of a white woman by a Negro. The evidence did not matter; indeed, an admission by the woman before a special grand jury that the Negro who had been arrested had not attacked her infuriated a mob. The state militia could not prevent the lynching of two Negroes and the destruction of many homes and buildings in the Negro section. Four white men were killed and more than seventy persons injured. The alleged leaders of the mob suffered no punishment. However, this riot, in the year before the one hundredth anniversary of Lincoln's birthday and close to the place where he was buried, shocked both Negroes and whites. William English Walling and his wife, Anna Strunsky, visited Springfield, and his subsequent article, "Race War in the North," in the *Independent*, September 3, 1908, must be counted as one of the more important articles in the history of American magazines. For it triggered a meeting in New York City on the one hundredth anniversary of the birth of Abraham Lincoln that was to lead to the organization of the National Association for the Advancement of Colored People.

Most of the fifty-three men and women who signed the call had already established their right to membership in a truly great American Hall of Fame. Oswald Garrison Villard was the grandson of William Lloyd Garrison, founder of *The Liberator* in 1830 and militant abolitionist who had validated his warning "I will be heard." Jane Addams had founded Hull House in Chicago, one of the first settlement houses in the United States. John Dewey, already one of the movers and shakers in education, contributed his ideas of pragmatism and instrumentalism. William Dean Howells, editor of *Harper's Magazine* since 1900, and the sponsor of Charles Waddell Chesnutt, gave an impeccably distinguished literary aura to the meeting. John Haynes Holmes spoke for the undenominational Protestant clergy and for nonviolent resistance. Hamilton Holt was editor of the *Independent* which had published Walling's article. Henry Moscowitz, a Jew from New York, enriched this all-American gathering by his presence. Charles Henry Parkhurst, Congregationalist and Presbyterian minister, had spearheaded the campaign which led to the appointment of the Low Committee and the defeat of Tammany Hall in 1904. The title of his book—*A Little Lower than the Angels*—was probably the most appropriate description possible of the dream of American democracy in 1909. William H. Ward, editor of the *Independent*, had published many of Du Bois's writings, including his "The Litany of Atlanta."

Other eminent liberals signed the call. A leading "muck-raker," Lincoln Steffens, had written a series of articles, "The Shame of the Cities," in *McClure's*. Rabbi Stephen S. Wise, who had been born in Budapest, founded, in 1902, what is generally recognized as the first city school-nursing work in the world. A year before the call, Congress had established the Federal Children's Bureau, based upon an idea which Lillian D. Wald had originated. Mary E. Wooley had become, in 1900, president of Mount Holyoke College.

Five Negroes in addition to Du Bois signed the call. William L. Buckley, a New York high school principal, merited distinction for this act alone. Francis J. Grimké, nephew of the noted abolitionist Angelina Grimké who had married the even more eminent abolitionist, Theodore Dwight Weld, was pastor of the fashionable Fifteenth Street Presbyterian Church in Washington, D. C. Bishop Alexander Walters of the African Methodist Episcopal Zion Church had signed the call, in 1889, for the organization of the Afro-American League, 1890–1892, and resurrected it as the Afro-American Council in 1898. As president of the Council he repeatedly urged achievement of the Council's aims, notably the investigation of lynchings; legislation to enforce the Thirteenth, Fourteenth and Fifteenth Amendments; the appropriation of federal funds to provide education for "citizens who are denied school privileges by discriminating State laws." At the Baltimore meeting of the Council, June 27–31, 1907, he not only denounced lynching but also insisted: "The humiliating Jim-Crow law is still with us and must be fought to the death. Surely we are not going to cry peace, peace, as long as the coaches are in existence. It is a badge of inferiority, a stigma upon the race, a disgrace to our civilization." There was need for the Afro-American Council so long as Negro citizens were "deprived of the ballot by unjust enactments. The ballot is a badge of political equality . . . and obtaining it should be the ambition of every man, whether white or black."[31] Walters and the Afro-American Council, which had a wider following than did the Niagara Movement, have not received the credit which they deserve as precursors of the NAACP.[32] Mrs. Ida B. Wells-Barnett, chairman of the Anti-Lynching League, who had signed the call for the Afro-American Council, was one of the most prominent club women of the era. I remember Dr. J. Milton Waldron, treasurer of the Niagara Movement, as the militant pastor of two of the most influential Baptist churches in Washington, D. C., Berean and Shiloh.

The NAACP, formally organized in 1910, chose as its first president Moorfield Storey who had served as private secretary to Senator Charles Sumner, November, 1867 to

May, 1869. Mark A. DeWolfe Howe believed that Storey's presidency of the NAACP "may be counted his most constructive piece of work in the field of public service."[33]

Rarely have so many talents joined in what might be called a new Declaration of Independence.

The Negro in Literature, the Theater, Music and Sports

Thomas Dixon's *The Leopard's Spots* (1902) surpassed in bigotry and vituperation his *The Clansman* (1905) and Thomas Nelson Page's *Bred in the Bone* (1904). Perhaps the most scurrilous book—one of the most vicious in American literature—was Charles Carroll's *The Negro Is a Beast*, published in 1900. Two years later, the title of Carroll's second book further reveals his *idée fixe*: *The Tempter of Eve; or The Criminality of Man's Social, Political, and Religious Equality with the Negro, and The Amalgamation to Which These Crimes Inevitably Lead. Discussed in the Light of the Scriptures, the Sciences, Profane History, Tradition and the Testimony of the Scriptures.*

William P. Calhoun continued the attack in *The Caucasian and the Negro in the United States* (1902). William B. Smith's *The Color Line: A Brief in Behalf of the Unborn* (1905) predicted consequences almost as dire from miscegenation as those predicted from fallout today, though of course on a smaller scale. The title of Robert W. Shufeldt's *The Negro, A Menace to American Civilization* (1907) is almost equally ominous. Carroll's and Calhoun's books were published in St. Louis, and Columbia, South Carolina, respectively. But Smith's book was published in New York, by McClure, Phillips and Company, and Shufeldt's in Boston, by R. G. Badger.

It may be doubted that W. S. Armistead's *The Negro Is a Man; A Reply to Professor Charles Carroll's Book The Negro Is a Beast* (1903) changed the minds of many readers. Edgar Gardner Murphy's *Problems of the Present South* (1904) and his *The Basis of Ascendency* (1909) likewise had little effect upon the warped ideas of his contemporaries.

Negro poetry ranged from the dialect and standard English poems of Dunbar who died in 1906, to the "Non-Negro" poetry of William Stanley Braithwaite whose *Lyrics of Life and Love* appeared in 1904. My colleague at Howard University, Professor Sterling A. Brown, gifted poet (whose poems cannot, unfortunately, be appropriately discussed here, since they appeared after the period covered by this book) and eminent critic has written perceptive, pithy summaries of these and other poets. Of Dunbar's poems of the "propaganda of aspiration," Professor Brown wrote: "Like so much of Negro expression of the period, it praises the nobility of forgetting and forgiving." Braithwaite (my colleague at Atlanta University during the 1930's) "through his criticisms and anthologies, was to become one of the pioneers in the poetry revival in America." A friend of Edwin Arlington Robinson and Amy Lowell, "his poetry is derivative of the romantic tradition, the Pre-Raphaelites, and at the end of the century, such poets as Swinburne and Ernest Dowson."[34] Unfortunately few persons knew that Braithwaite was colored —most of them probably assumed, as I did for many years, that an eminent anthologist had to be white. His impact on his audiences and readers thereby did little to convince intellectuals that a Negro was capable of selecting, annually, some of the best poetry published in the United States.

Sterling Brown's capsule description of John Charles Mc-Neill is another gem about one of the "Strong Men"[35] who were in New England colleges during and after the period covered by this book. In 1937, Professor Brown wrote:

John Charles McNeill in *Lyrics From Cotton Land* (1907) is a local color realist. Conventionally jocular in poems like "The Coon From The College Town," "Ligion" and "A Soft Nap," he is at times a shrewd witness, as in "August Meeting," which is a Tarheel variant of Burn's "Holy Fair":

> *Dar wus razors, knives en wrenches;*
> *Planks fum offen busted benches. . . .*
> *En I seed one fool er-fightin' wid his han's.*

"Protest" and "The Red Shirts" are a folk Negro's grumbling at the chain gang and the night riders, but too humorous to be completely truthful. "Mr. Nigger" states how necessary the Negro is to America (to ragtime composers, planters, politicians whose stock-in-trade is Negro abuse, lynchers "who burn to excite the North);" it con-

cludes: "Don't you fear expatriation, Mr. Nigger." If Mc-
Neill had not been so hot on the trail of jokes, he might
have said something about his native South worth listening
to.[36]

The influence of Negroes in the theater was probably less
at the time than later, when movies, radio and television permitted large numbers of Americans to view and hear the
Negro stars of these media. But these early Negro composers
and performers paved the way for acceptance today of the
great names without the limiting derogation of Negro; and
they did win friends in Bohemia if not on Main Street.

James Weldon Johnson, national organizer and secretary
of the NAACP from 1917 to 1930, United States consul to
Nicaragua from 1906 to 1912, portrayed in *Black Manhattan*,
1940, the changing role of these early Negroes. He knew
many of them. John Ishman's *Oriental America*, 1896, had
continued the trend away from minstrelsy by adding solos and
choruses from the classic operas to the show's finale; and it
was the first colored show to play on Broadway proper—at
Palmer's, later the famous Wallack's Theatre. Two years
later, Bob Cole whom Johnson described as "the greatest
single force in the middle period of the development of the
Negro in the American theatre," broke away completely from
the minstrel tradition. His "A Trip to Coontown" was the first
Negro musical comedy, the first colored show organized,
produced and managed by Negroes.[37] Will Marion Cook,
father of the present United States Ambassador to the Republic of Senegal, was the brilliant composer of this middle
period. In his successful "Clorindy—The Origin of the Cake-
Walk," with lyrics by Dunbar, and in later playlets, he developed his style in composing the music which helped Williams
and Walker on their road to fame.

George Walker, the dandy of this remarkable team, suffered from an illness which prevented his stage appearance
after "Band and Land" in 1907. Bert Williams, who joined
the Ziegfeld Follies in 1910, is generally recognized as one
of the greatest comedians of the American stage. One of his
most famous jokes (which some of our contemporaries have
borrowed without attributions to him—he may also have borrowed it) was the classic "Include me out."

During this middle period also, the first Negro jazz band

to play on a New York stage made its debut early in 1905. Such present-day performers as Louis Armstrong have scored triumphs as "ambassadors of good-will" to Russia, Africa and other countries. In the latter part of May, 1962, an international jazz festival in Washington, D. C., highlighted the recognition of this genre to which many Negroes have made significant contributions.

Negroes were losing the pre-eminent place which they had once held as jockeys. Isaac Murphy had won the Kentucky Derby in 1884, 1890 and 1891, and the American Derby in 1884, 1885, 1886 and 1888. The less well known Jimmie Lee won all six of the races at Louisville in 1907. By that time, however, jockeys were earning such large salaries, $10,000 to $20,000 a year, that white jockeys soon replaced them.

Then as now Negroes almost dominated prize fighting. Joe Gans was at times (1901–1908) the lightweight champion; Sam Langford, Sam McVey and Joe Jeanette were perhaps the equal of Jack Johnson who knocked out Jim Jefferies in the epic fight at Reno, Nevada, on July 4, 1910.

Most historians of professional baseball consider Jackie Robinson as the first Negro to break the "Big League" color-line when he joined the Brooklyn Dodgers in 1947. He and many other Negroes had served their apprenticeship on all-colored teams, another illustration of the skills which Negroes acquired behind the walls of segregation.

Negroes lost the propaganda battle in literature. Chesnutt's second novel *The Marrow of Tradition* (1901), and his last novel, *The Colonel's Dream* (1905), reveal his pessimism. The former powerfully presented a view of the anatomy of race riots that was hardly borne out by actuality. The second's theme added discrimination in labor unions to peonage, the convict-lease system, disfranchisement, unequal public education, and the North's exploitation of its Southern "colony" as entrenched forces which defeated Colonel Henry French's dream of social engineering by establishing a cotton mill with a mixed labor force. Paul Laurence Dunbar's novel, *The Sport of the Gods* (1902), and most of his short stories in *In Old Plantation Days* (1903) and *The Heart of Happy Hollow* (1904) glorified the Plantation Tradition almost as fulsomely as did Thomas Nelson Page. Sutton E. Griggs, though scarcely known today except to historians of literature by Negroes, probably had more Negro readers than did

Chesnutt and Dunbar. His novels, however, had little literary merit and presaged the black chauvinism of Marcus Garvey.[38]

Thus, on balance, the historian today finds it almost impossible to determine how far Negroes had inched forward by 1910. Perhaps, to borrow a current expression about newly emerging nations, American Negroes were ready for the "take-off."

SEVENTEEN

"A Shore, Dimly Seen"

BALANCING the losses and gains from 1910 to 1918 constitutes less of a problem for earlier than for contemporary historians. The election of Woodrow Wilson in 1912 and his re-election in 1916 caused grave concern, but the assaults upon equal rights achieved less success than many Negro leaders feared. Congress did nothing to protect the civil rights of Negroes; surprisingly, however, it enacted no legislation to curtail those rights. The death of Booker T. Washington in 1915 did not create dismay among those who had looked upon him as "The Leader," for the election of a Democratic President had deprived him of most of his political power. In 1918 Marcus Garvey's "Black Chauvinism" was less of a divisive force among Negroes than it would be soon thereafter. Trade unions continued their policies of exclusion, segregation, and minimal inclusion; but the emergence of new trade unions offered hope. The National Association for the Advancement of Colored People gained strength and *The Crisis* increased its circulation. In 1911, the National Urban League began a persuasive campaign to convince management of the wisdom of employing and upgrading Negro workers.

Two events opened new vistas which contemporaries could not adequately evaluate. First in 1911, and more particularly in 1915, the United States Supreme Court began a series of decisions which was to make this branch of the government the most powerful force in changing the legal status and thereby—albeit to a lesser degree—the *actual* status of the Negro. Second, World War I started a chain of developments which, more than any event since the American Civil War, made it increasingly difficult for die-hard Southerners and their Northern allies to "keep the Negro in his place."

Woodrow Wilson's election in 1912 did less harm to Negroes than many anticipated. Contemporaries could not, of course, judge him from the perspective of Arthur S. Link's perceptive biography *Wilson, The Road to the White House,* published in 1947. But they knew that he was the first Democrat since Cleveland to be elected President; worse, he was the first Southerner to enter the White House since the Civil

War. During the 1912 election campaign, the Negro news-paper, the New York *Age*, warned that "both by inheritance and absorption, he has most of the prejudices of the narrow-est type of Southern white people against the Negro."[1] Some Negroes knew that Princeton University, of which Wilson was president from 1902 to 1910, was perhaps the only great Northern university that excluded Negro students. Moreover, as governor of New Jersey, 1911–1912, his "Progressivism" did not embrace the Negro.

Some Negro leaders, nevertheless, supported Wilson's can-didacy. Taft's appointment of William H. Lewis, a graduate of Amherst College and of Harvard Law School, as Assist-ant Attorney General of the United States[2] was not sufficient to offset Taft's obvious wooing of the South. The Republican platform of 1912 omitted the specific plank on "Rights of the Negro" which the 1908 platform had piously proclaimed. The 1912 platform did "call upon the people to quicken their interest in public affairs, to condemn and punish lynchings and other forms of lawlessness, and to strengthen in all pos-sible ways a respect for law and the observance of it." But the Republican platform made no specific mention of the Negro. Roosevelt's Progressive Party pledged itself to the "task of securing equal suffrage to men and women alike." Consequently, the failure of the Democratic platform in 1912 to mention the Negro made that platform no worse than those of the other two major parties or, indeed, those of the So-cialist or the Socialist Labor parties.[3]

In 1908, Bishop Alexander Walters had campaigned for the Democratic ticket. He took an even more active part in the 1912 campaign. As President of the Colored Democratic League, in 1912, Walters declared that "the dullest mind can see at a glance the difference between the [Republican] party as represented by Charles Sumner in 1870 and Theodore Roosevelt and William Howard Taft in 1912." In addition, Bishop Walters believed, as did many liberals, that on the questions of the tariff and the curbing of trusts Negroes should support the Democratic Party.[4]

Walters persuaded Du Bois to support Wilson and to throw the weight of *The Crisis* against Roosevelt and Taft, if Wilson would make a statement in behalf of Negroes. Wilson, in October, 1912, sent Walters a categorical statement over his signature "of earnest wish to see justice done the colored people in every matter; and not mere grudging justice, but justice executed with liberality and cordial good feeling . . . I want to assure them that should I become President of the United States they may count upon me for absolute fair dealing, for everything by which I could assist in advancing the interests of their race in the United States."[5]

This promise gave Du Bois such satisfaction that he resigned from New York Local No. 1 of the Socialist Party in order to escape discipline for not voting the Socialist ticket. Shortly before the election he wrote in *The Crisis*:

We sincerely believe that even in the face of promises disconcertingly vague, and in the face of the solid caste-ridden South, it is better to elect Woodrow Wilson President of the United States and to prove once for all if the Democratic Party dares to be democratic when it comes to black men. It has proven that it can be in many Northern states and cities. Can it be in the nation? We hope so, and we are willing to risk a trial.[6]

Walters—despite the fact that Wilson offered him the post of Minister to Liberia in 1915—voiced, in 1917, his keen disappointment in Wilson. The President's "New Freedom" had been "all for the white man and little for the Negro." Wilson had not visited "any colored school, church or gathering of colored people of any nature whatever."[7] According to Du Bois, moreover, Wilson said in the course of a visit by the bishop to the White House in 1915: "'By the way, what about that letter that I wrote to you during the campaign? I do not seem to remember it.'" When Walters handed the letter to Wilson, "the President forgot to return it."[8]

Wilson's promise to Walters in this letter was soon contradicted by the expansion of segregation in the federal department buildings in Washington, a policy which Taft had begun. In mid-August, 1913, Moorfield Storey, Du Bois and Villard wrote Wilson a strong letter of protest. On August 18, Villard wrote Archibald H. Grimké, head of the Washington chapter of the NAACP, that "soon we may expect to have 'nigger' sections in all the Washington departments."[9]

Although Archibald Grimké, in a letter to Wilson on October 29, 1913, protested against these "reactionary and undemocratic practices," a report of the NAACP's special agent of November 17 stated that the effect of segregation was "startling." It had been effected without official orders on the excuse that it increased efficiency. One of the worst examples was found in the Dead-Letter Office of the Post Office Department, where colored employees had been segregated back of a row of lockers in a corner of the room.

A few days later, Monroe Trotter, Executive Secretary of the National Equal Rights League, had such a rowdy conference with Wilson that the President declared he had never been addressed "in such insulting fashion before." Trotter, in an interview after the conference, placed most of the blame for segregation on Secretary of the Treasury William J. McAdoo and Postmaster General Albert S. Burleson.[10]

Segregation practices were not consistent; sometimes they were ridiculous. An employee in the State, War, and Navy Department Building sent Grimké an order—dated August 7, 1916 and signed by the superintendent of the Building— which assigned men but not women to separate rest rooms. The order did not forbid, however, the use before 9:00 A.M. by either white or Negro messengers or laborers of the nearest men's toilet "equipped with a slop sink for filling and washing water bottles, slop jars, etc." Assistant Secretary of the Navy Franklin D. Roosevelt sent the order to employees of his Department with the comment that it was "for the information and guidance of the Bureaus and offices concerned."

Another Wilson administration innovation that irked Negroes was the requirement that applicants for civil service jobs file their photographs with their application. The NAACP engaged the Assistant Secretary of the Civil Service Reform Association to conduct an investigation. Civil Service officials denied that race was a motivating factor. Charles M. Calloway, Acting President of the Commission, wrote Grimké on July 28, 1914 that the requirement was an "extension to certain other parts" of the classified service that had been followed in the Philippines, the Isthmian Canal, and employment of Indian and penitentiary guards. Both Calloway and the Commission's President, A. McHennys, who wrote Grimké on July 29, 1914, gave the naïve assurance that the only reason for this requirement was "the interests of the public service."

I was in my last year of high school in Washington when Wilson was elected. Negroes showed grave concern, especially when some newly elected Southerners publicly declared that they had come to Washington to "fight niggers and likker." For a time we wondered whether the colored high school cadets would march, as they had done for many years, in the inaugural procession. We did, and folklore to the contrary notwithstanding, Wilson did not turn his back on us. (I was captain of the front Negro cadet company.)

Congress, which had done nothing to protect civil rights during Republican administrations, also did nothing under Wilson. On the other hand, the Wilson administration Congresses did not pass any anti-Negro legislation either. In fact, the defeats of the racists were as decisive as those which occurred after the United States declared a state of war against Germany in April, 1917.

Congress had considered many anti-Negro bills before Wilson's election. On January 14, 1909, Senator William H. Milton of Florida introduced a bill to ban intermarriage. Milton listed the following as evidence that Negroes were members of an inferior race:

1. Abnormal length of arms, averaging two inches more than the Caucasian.
2. Projection of the jaw at a facial angle of 70 degrees, as against 82 for Caucasian.
3. Average weight of brain, being for gorilla 20 ounces, negro 35 ounces, European 45 ounces.
4. Full black eyes with black iris and yellowish sclerotic coat.
5. Short, flat snub nose, depressed at base, broad at the extremity, dilating nostrils, and concave ridge.
6. Thick protruding lips showing inner red surface.
7. Exceedingly thick cranium enabling him to butt with the head and resist blows that would break an ordinary European skull.
8. Correspondingly weak lower limbs, broad flat foot, divergent and sometimes prehensile big toe and projecting heel.
9. Complexion brown or blackish, due to abundance of coloring matter.
10. Short black hair and distinctly woolly.
11. Thick epidermis, emitting a peculiar rancid odor.
12. Frame of medium height and sometimes out of perpendicular.
13. The early ossification of the skull.

Senator Foraker presented the motion to table Milton's resolution. The vote was yeas, 43, nays, 21; not voting, 28.[11]

The marriage of the Negro heavyweight champion, Jack Johnson, to a white girl infuriated many white Americans. Representative Seaborn A. Roddenbery of Georgia introduced, on December 11, 1912, a constitutional amendment to ban intermarriages. In defense of his proposed amendment, he said that Johnson's marriage was "more revolting than white slavery." Carried away, perhaps by his own eloquence, he asserted: "No brutality, no infamy, no degradation in all the years of southern slavery possessed such villainous character and such atrocious qualities as the provisions of [State] laws . . . which allow the marriage of the negro Jack Johnson to a woman of the caucasian strain." The Roddenbery bill died in the Committee on the Judiciary.[12]

Absorbingly interesting is the fact that, when bills prohibiting intermarriage included white-Mongolian and even white-Malay marriages, they gained wider support. Such a bill received, on February 10, 1913, the overwhelming majority of 92 to 12. The Senate did not even discuss this bill.[13]

I offer the unorthodox interpretation that the defeat of these and other bills opposing intermarriage is more important than the introduction of such bills. Sidney S. Tobin, who has made the most comprehensive study of this proposed legislation, has stated that between 1907 and 1921 "at least twenty-one anti-intermarriage bills were introduced—two and a half times more than the anti-lynching bills. They were sponsored by Southern Democrats but were supported by many Northerners." Equally important is the fact that several such bills and one constitutional amendment had been introduced prior to March 4, 1913 when Wilson took office.

Of the score of bills to prohibit intermarriage, only one in addition to that passed on February 10, 1913, which was introduced by Representative Frank Clark of Florida, passed the House: 238 to 60; 126 not voting. This bill apparently was not voted upon in the Senate.[14]

Several bills for the segregation of the races also met defeat. Representative Martin B. Madden, Republican of Illinois, was one of the few who vigorously protested the Jim Crow bills. He gained support when on February 11, 1916, a notable group of Negroes protested to the House District Committee. Archibald Grimké emphasized the point that laws forbidding intermarriage would permit a white man to "do what he wants with impunity." Professor Kelly Miller of Howard University, a vigorous pamphleteer, gibed that Congress did not have "wisdom enough" to determine who was a Negro, and added an argument which some persons believe originated with the Cold War, namely, that such a law would have a bad effect on the United States in the eyes of the world. Two other Negroes contributed to the debt that the present generation owes to men almost unknown today, for its rise from the Nadir. Whitefield McKinley, the collector of the Port of Georgetown under Taft, cited his own family as evidence of the fact that laws enacted by Southern states against intermarriage accounted for the "passing" of several thousands of Negroes as whites. Assistant District Attorney James A. Cobb advanced an argument that the courts have evaded, namely, what penalty, if any, would be inflicted upon an interracial couple who married in a state permitting such marriages when they moved to a state whose laws prohibited such marriages.[15]

Congress also refused to adopt legislation to segregate Negroes in the federal departments. This refusal is doubly significant: (1) it did not sanction executive action; (2) it prevailed against bitter racist arguments. Representative James B. Aswell of Louisiana asserted, in 1914, for example, that the United States was "a white man's country" and that it was "unjust" for a Negro to be put in a position of authority over a Caucasian; in fact, the Negro was "by inheritance . . . a misfit when in authority even over his own race." One of the staunchest supporters of the bill was Representative Martin Dies of Texas who later made his name synonymous with "Un-American Activities." Madden again had little support in his opposition to the bill. Archibald Grimké's contention before the House Committee on Reform in the Civil Service that "you cannot separate the colored people in the government service without humiliating them" led to this spirited exchange:

Dies: The point I make is that one of the races must be the ruling race. Both cannot rule, and the Negro race as rulers is unthinkable.

Grimké: That cannot be in this country.

Dies: I am only giving you my views.

Grimké: I am telling you the truth in this matter. I am a

man sixty-four years old and I have the blood of both races. I was born in the South and I will tell you frankly you cannot do that. There will not be two ruling classes.

Dies: I said one.

Grimké: I say you cannot have one ruling class, . . .

Dies: We have solved the question in the South and white supremacy is a fixture.

Grimké: You cannot solve it that way. You think you have solved it, but you cannot do it. It is not going to be done that way, because in fifty years everything is going to be changed. . . . Separation always means inferiority, and these people are going to be your equal if God made them your equal. You are not going to deport them; they are valuable laborers.

Chairman Godwin: The white people are taxed to educate the colored people in my State. We have compulsory education in North Carolina.

Grimké: For example, does anyone imagine that if the Government collect from Mr. Rockefeller an income tax of $12,000,000 that he would not transfer it ultimately to the backs of the consumers of Standard Oil? Labor in the last analysis bears the whole burden of taxes. Therefore, the colored people of the South support their own schools and much more besides. It is the poor man who pays the taxes.

Dies: You go on the wrong supposition when you impute prejudice to these people who believe that the Negro ought not to be of the governing class.

Madden: It comes with bad grace to have a man put his arms around your neck and tell you how much he loves you and then sticks a knife under your fifth rib.

Scott: Have you been in Government service?

Grimké: Yes, sir. I was consul at San Domingo under Mr. Cleveland.

Scott: Are you familiar with the . . . desires of the colored people in the Government service in the District of Columbia in respect to this question?

Grimké: Yes, sir; they are objecting to it.

Scott: Do you know of any colored people in the District of Columbia in the Government service who has expressed a desire to have rules of segregation adopted?

Grimké: I have not heard of any.

The NAACP rightly hailed Grimké's testimony as a decisive factor in the defeat of bills providing for segregation in the Civil Service.[16] Other attempts to introduce similar legislation likewise died in the Committee on Reform in the Civil Service. On the other hand, Republican efforts, in 1913, to investigate and check such legislation also died in the same Committee.[17]

Many historians have emphasized the legislative attempts of the Wilson administration to curtail the civil rights of Negroes without, however, noting adequately the defeat either of such laws, or of laws designed to promote the advancement of Negroes. These historians have generally overlooked, on the one hand, for instance, the defeat of a proposal to ensure equitable distribution of federal funds to Negro land-grant colleges and, on the other hand, the defeat of a bill to prohibit the immigration to the United States of "all aliens not of the Caucasian race."

Congressman Justin Smith Morrill of Vermont had engineered, in 1862, the passage of the First Morrill Act, which provided for the

> endowment, support, and maintenance of at least one college in each State . . . where the leading object shall be, without excluding other scientific and classical studies, and including military tactics, to teach such branches of learning as are related to agriculture and the mechanic arts . . . in order to promote the liberal and practical education of the industrial classes in the several pursuits and professions in life.

The first Negro land-grant college, Lincoln University, was established at Jefferson City, Missouri, in 1866. By 1896, all the former Confederate states except Tennessee had established land-grant colleges for Negroes. In addition, Kentucky (1886), West Virginia (1891), Delaware (1895), and Oklahoma (1897) had institutions which were and came to be designated as land-grant colleges for Negroes. Tennessee Agricultural and Industrial State College was designated a Negro land-grant college in 1919, and Princess Anne College, Maryland, in 1935.

These seventeen land-grant institutions came into being as the result of the Second Morrill Act, passed by Congress in 1890. This Act provided:

No money shall be paid under this act to any state or territory for the support and maintenance of a college where a distinction of race or color is made in the admission of students, but the establishment and maintenance of such college separately for white and colored students shall be held to be a compliance with the provisions of this act if the funds received in such State or Territory be equitably divided.

Equitably divided was construed to mean that the legislature of a state in which there were separate land-grant colleges might propose and report to the Secretary of the Interior "a just and equitable division of the fund." No provision was made for action by the Secretary of the Interior if he deemed the division unjust or inequitable.

Meanwhile, the Hatch Act, 1887, supplementing the Morrill Act of 1862, provided for the establishment of agricultural experiment stations in connection with the land-grant colleges. Since neither this Act, nor another in 1906, contained the provision that funds should be "equitably divided" as in the Second Morrill Act, Republican Senator Wesley L. Jones of Washington introduced an amendment for this purpose, to the Smith-Lever Act for federal funds for agricultural extension work among Southern Negro and white land-grant colleges. Jones further declared that the aggregate value— buildings, farm lands and grounds, apparatus and machinery, libraries, livestock—of the white colleges was $21,516,000 while that of the colored schools was $3,841,769.

The debate on the Jones Amendment, February 5–8, 1914, evoked typical rationalizations by Southerners to justify the inequitable distribution. Hoke Smith, for example, asserted that Negroes went to school for a few months, to learn saddlery, shoemaking, bricklaying and carpentry; these courses did not cost as much as did the teaching of "higher chemistry" at the white land-grant college. He did not believe that such courses as civil engineering, mechanical engineering and chemical engineering were taught at the Negro land-grant college since Negroes were not ready for such courses. James K. Vardaman of Mississippi, one of the worst race-baiters of the era, found an opportunity to express his "love" for the Negro and for his "old black mammy." The Senator averred that the Negro "does not vote much in Mississippi but I really think he votes more than he ought to vote, if he votes at all. I do not think that it was ever intended by the creator that the two races should live together upon equal terms." The Jones Amendment was defeated 23 to 32; 40 not voting. Republicans cast most of the affirmative votes, and all but two Democrats opposed it.[18]

The fiftieth anniversary of Lincoln's Emancipation Proclamation led to lukewarm celebrations. Of the several bills introduced to have Congress sponsor a national celebration, only one passed the House and one, the Senate. Neither became law. Congress did, however, appropriate $55,000 for an exposition held in Richmond, Virginia, in 1915. The state legislatures of Illinois and New York voted small appropriations for well-organized observances. An Emancipation Commission, created by an act of the Assembly of New Jersey in 1912, and appointed by Governor Woodrow Wilson, arranged for an exposition in Philadelphia in conjunction with the State of Pennsylvania, October 6–11, 1913. The commemoration had little effect upon either whites or Negroes.[19]

Negroes soon learned that the war by which the world was to be "made safe for democracy" would not revolutionize their subordinate status in American society. One of the first questions involved the appointment of Negro noncommissioned and commissioned officers. Although Negroes had long served in both capacities, Representative Frank Park of Georgia introduced a bill to make it unlawful to appoint them to either rank. A liberal Southern Republican, Representative Richard W. Austin, sponsored three bills between February 14 and April 9, 1917 to establish a commission to secure a site for the training of Negro officers. All three bills died in committee.[20]

In the spring of 1917, the problem of separate camps for Negro officers aroused heated debate outside of Congress. The NAACP reluctantly approved a separate camp as better than no camp. Negro college students, especially those who had been officers in the Washington High School Cadet Corps, grudgingly accepted the alternative. Du Bois urged Negroes in one of his most famous editorials to "Close Ranks."[21]

Negro officer candidates had to spend four months in training instead of three as did white officer candidates. The belief that Negroes needed more time to learn—and even then learned less than whites—found expression in two ways that especially shocked Negroes. First, because Negroes could not learn enough mathematics to serve as artillery officers, those who, prior to the war, had been assigned to artillery regiments were transferred. Second, most Negroes were made to serve as noncombatants. Segregation was, of course, rigidly enforced. Negro troops from the North, stationed in such Southern cities as Newport News, Virginia, and Spartanburg, South Carolina, refused to accept segregation. They were promptly sent overseas. When Armistice sounded on November 11, 1918, few Negroes believed that their country appreciated their services on the battlefield, behind the lines, or on the home front.[22] Most Negro troops, disillusioned and embittered, returned from France to find race riots erupting in different parts of the nation, including the Capital, and a black chauvinism movement led by Marcus Garvey.

EIGHTEEN

The Negro as Portrayed in Representative Northern Magazines and Newspapers

REPRESENTATIVE Northern magazines and newspapers continued to mirror preponderantly hostile attitudes to the Negro.

Magazines

The magazines repeated derogatory epithets, inconsistent dialect, and stereotypes; they glorified the Plantation Tradition and condemned Reconstruction; they praised Booker T. Washington, rationalized lynchings and the failure to enforce the second section of the Fourteenth Amendment. Only occasionally did these magazines publish articles by Negro authors; rarely did white authors defend with any vigor the Negroes' quest for equal rights.[1] The magazines surveyed were *Atlantic Monthly*, *Century Monthly*, *Harper's* and *North American Review* from 1901 to 1918. Students made the surveys for these magazines through 1918 except *Atlantic Monthly*, for which the author completed the survey for the years 1913 to 1918.

Century Monthly, which published the largest number of short stories, had more kinds of "niggers," "niggahs" and "darkies" than did the other magazines. Outrageous names such as "Mr. Napoleon Jackson, Esq.," familiarly known as "Poleon," Epaphrodites Plumer, Neuralgia, and Homicide appeared less frequently. In *Harper's* Sir Arthur Sullivan "worked like a 'nigger'"; one group of Negroes was compared to a "swarm of blackbirds," and one Negro was called "snowball." "Nigger" and "darky" appeared frequently also in *Atlantic Monthly*.[2] Since *North American Review* did not publish fiction, such epithets rarely disgraced its pages.

A long poem in *Century Monthly*, 1916, portrayed the longing for the Old South:

> *Wish I was home agin*
> *Way down Souf once mo*
> *Roses blooming in de sun*

> Round de lil ole cabin do
> Cotton fiels a gleaming white
> All de niggah picking
> Smells o' suppah time long todes night
> Lou done kill a chicken.
> Ef I was home agin
> Way down Souf once mo'
> Reckon I'd be standing hyah
> Shet out side de kitchen do
> Y'ole black rascal, cunnel say
> Damn yo' wufless hide
> Git in dah to de good hot stove
> En fill you' fool inside.[3]

Owen Wister, best known for his novel *The Virginian*, also used a Western setting for this poem in *Harper's*:

> Dar is a big Carolina nigger,
> About de size of dis chile or p'raps a little bigger
> By de name of Jim Crow.
> Dat what de white folks call him.
> If ever I sees him I 'tends for to maul him,
> Just to let de white folks see
> Such an animos as he
> Can't walk around de streets and scandalize me.
> Great big fool, he hasn't any knowledge.
> Gosh! how could he, when he's never been to scollege?
> Neither has I.
> But I's come mighty nigh:
> I peaked through de do' as I went by.[4]

Century Monthly did publish, in 1908, James Weldon Johnson's "O Black and Unknown Bards," a poetic form and theme which later Negro poets also used effectively. Four lines suffice:

> O Slave Singers, gone, forgot, unfamed
> You—you alone, of all the long, long line
> Of those who've sung untaught, unknown, unnamed
> Have stretched out upward, seeking the divine.[5]

In 1902, *Century Monthly* awarded three prizes for cartoons. The first prize cartoon portrayed an Irishman and the third prize, a German-Jew. A full-page cartoon, which won the second prize, presented a Negro dressed in a black tattered outfit with a tall top hat. An ink black face, half-hidden by a lily-white beard, wore a silly grin. Another cartoon, five years later, caricatured an old Negro, unusually black and scrawny, with a white beard and large white eyes; his clothes, too, were tattered. His son was a small image of the father. Under the cartoon appeared this dialogue:

Uncle Rastus: "Now dat you daddy too ole to work, why don't yah get a job?"

Young Rastus: "No! indeed. Ain' going to have folks say everybody works but father 'bout mah family."

A story by Bret Harte in *Harper's* was illustrated by a cowering, bewildered Negro, in ill-fitting clothes, round-shouldered, long of arm, while Colonel Starbottle stood tall, stately, handsome and well dressed.[6]

Less frequently, drawings presented a more commendable picture of Negroes. One industrial worker was receiving his play in line with white workers.[7] Readers of *Moby Dick* will particularly appreciate the drawing which made a Negro an integral part of a crew battling a whale in mid-ocean. *Century Monthly* had one portrait of a Negro, a bust of Booker T. Washington, in 1903. *Harper's* reminded readers of the abominable conditions under which slaves traveled below decks during The Middle Passage; the magazine also reproduced the famous oil painting of Dred Scott which hung in the Missouri Historical Society Building. In one story, a courageous Negro saved the life of a Confederate soldier, a young white girl and her Negro maid by throwing a lighted bomb out of a cave. Albert Bigelow Paine's article on Mark Twain carried a picture of Mary Quarles, a colored slave-girl belonging to the uncle of Samuel Clemens.[8] *Atlantic Monthly* carried no drawings or photographs.

Short stories still portrayed Negroes in a most unfavorable light. Gilder, the editor of *Century Monthly* until 1909, justified the use of Negro dialect on the ground that it, like other dialects, was a not "unimportant part of the United States social history, and has distinct value as folklore."[9] True, but Chesnutt's criticism has as much validity for this period as it did for the quarter century, 1877–1901.[10] Moreover, it appears that neither *Century Monthly* nor the other magazines surveyed provided folklorists with an equal opportunity to evaluate the contribution of other dialects to the social history of the United States.

Familiar names from the last quarter of the nineteenth century reappear: Thomas Nelson Page, Henry Stillwell Edwards, Virginia Frazer Boyle and Ruth McEnery Stuart in *Century Monthly*.

Page remained without peer in glorifying the Plantation Tradition and in bemoaning the miseries of freedom. Old Jabe, according to his overseers, was "the laziest nigger on the place." After Jabe became free, his master had to support him. Jabe had no respect for marital ties; he wanted, for example, to marry the cook of his master's wife before his former wife had been buried. The master's wife asked Jabe how he managed to fool all the women. Jabe: "Well I declare mist'is, I hardly know, but dee [they] wants to be fooled." Scratching his "nappy" chin, Jabe added: "I think it is becus dee wants to see what de urrs [others] marry me fur, and what dee one lef' me." Jabe then propounded a profound remark, though Page did not intend it to be so: "Women is mighty currisome folk."[11]

Edwards stereotyped the feuding of Negro preachers; they still called in their white friends, for "nothing so much pleases the negro as a realization of the fact that he is attracting attention in the courts of the mighty." Edwards ridiculed both the Negro who spoke in dialect and the Negro who aped the language of a high-Church Episcopalian. But Isam, a character in several of Edwards' short stories, strayed from the stereotype. When told to pay his poll tax, Isam went fishing. His former master rebuked him: " 'Why you black rascal, are you not a citizen and a voter?' " The deviationist Isam answered: " 'Yas Suh. I sholy is when dere is a tight race twixt two dimmercrats for some'pin other. But in time of peace, I'm des er country nigger owing a poll tax.' " When Isam's former master tried to convince him that, if he paid his poll tax, he would have the right to vote by pointing out to him that " 'You have a voice in the management in this great nation and the development of your own race' " and asked him whether he could imagine anything better than that, Isam replied: " 'Yas suh, fried catfish.' "[12]

Another example of supposed humor which cut two ways recorded, in 1909, the wry comment of a Negro soldier who had fought in foreign lands. Upon his return to the United States, he wondered: " 'But ah cain't neber understand why it don't neber seem lak we had any kentry [country] no mo when we get back to it.' "[13] Many Negroes made the same wry comment in more elegant and forceful manner after World War I.

Mark Twain's and Bret Harte's stories in *Harper's* rankled less than did those in *Century Monthly*. Twain in 1902 described two Negro nurses as "good nurses both, white souls with black skins, watchful, loving, tender,—just perfect nurses!—and competent liars from the cradle." Twain's Negro characters generally played much less conspicuous roles than did Huck Finn's Jim. Bret Harte's faithful slave and freedom-spoiled Negro likewise played minor parts in his work.

Atlantic Monthly contended with *Century Monthly* for the number of unlovely Negro stereotypes speaking almost unintelligible dialect. A story in 1902 may be viewed as a continuation of the Plantation Tradition. An old snowy white-haired Negro told a young colored boy: "'Dey wez good times, . . . but mo' speshully wuz I studyin' 'bout Chris'mus, kaze dis 'yer Chris'mus night, when I study 'bout fofe July I recterlec' mo' 'bout young niggers an' barb' cue, an' when I study 'bout Chris'mus I recterlec mo' 'bout Marse George and Old Miss and de ole niggers what done daid; but de mo' I study, 'bout dem times, hit pears like de wus all good times.' "[14]

But one wonders why this type of story appeared intermittently until the outbreak of World War I. One example of a more easily understood dialect: "'Kitty Sharp! Why, she's one third Nigger, one third Injun, an't'other third devil. Ef ye want ter c'nsult a witch, why don't ye go ter Rehoboth an see Poll Jinkins? Polly's a white woman ef she does hev dealin's with the Ole Harry.' "[15]

One story ran during November and December, 1914, and January, 1915. More revealing than this or other stories was this introduction to the second installment:

> [In the first installment of this true chronicle, the author told of her adoption, under tragic and dramatic circumstances, of two pickaninnies, Jonadab and Rechab. They grew plump and prosperous under the care of Patience Pennington and her colored servants, but developed an appalling aptitude for chicken-stealing and general devilishness.—The Editors.][16]

Articles in a serious vein probably did more harm to the Negro than did the poems, drawings, and short stories. While some of these articles defended him, most of them argued against accepting him as an equal citizen. The stature of the authors gave great weight to their suggestions and conclusions. There follows a sampling of articles during the early (1901–1905), the middle (1906–1910), and the late (1912–1917) periods.

Woodrow Wilson's article in the *Atlantic Monthly*, "Reconstruction in the Southern States," (January, 1901) gives the tone of many articles on the subject. In a literary style superior to that of most other authors, and with more restraint than some, the future President wrote:

> An extraordinary and very perilous state of affairs had been created in the South by the sudden and absolute emancipation of the Negroes, and it was not strange that the Southern legislatures should deem it necessary to take extraordinary steps to guard against the manifest and pressing dangers which it entailed. Here was a vast laboring, landless, homeless class, once slaves; now free; unpracticed in liberty, unschooled in self-control; never sobered by the discipline of self-support; never established in any habit of prudence; excited by a freedom they did not understand, exalted by false hopes, bewildered and without leaders, and yet insolent and aggressive; sick of work, covetous of pleasure, a host of dusky children untimely put out of school.

But Wilson, unlike most other writers, applied to Reconstruction the basic principles which he had outlined in his *Congressional Government* (1885). Enamored of the British system of an executive responsible to a majority in the legislature, Wilson portrayed Congress as the most important of the three branches of government. And so, in 1901, Wilson accepted the "War Amendments." He pointed out that "additional prohibitions were put upon the states; the suffrage was in a measure made subject to national regulation."[17] Of course, when Wilson became President, he made the executive the most important of the three branches of government. But he did not attempt to have Congress enforce the amendments he had advocated in 1901.

William A. Dunning, one of the most influential pro-Southern revisionist historians, argued in the same year that the principal difficulty in the South before the Civil War had not been slavery, but the coexistence of two races with widely different characteristics. The new society after emancipation had to rest upon an acceptance of the racial inferiority of the Negro. In 1901 also, Thomas Nelson Page lamented the loss of the ideals and charms of the Old South, the destruction after emancipation of the former slaves' habits of industry. Reconstruction had introduced electoral frauds and lynchings. He found encouragement in the new era of good feelings between the North and the South. Even Daniel H. Chamberlain, Massachusetts-born Governor of South Carolina (1874–1877), condemned Reconstruction as a "frightful experiment."[18]

Only one article presented the views of Northern Republicans who upheld the Reconstruction measures as a political necessity. An editorial which summarized the articles referred specifically to this article in asserting that the war measures had been a necessity for the victorious party; they had also represented in part a sincere desire to render abstract justice to a race that had been deeply wronged. But the editorial agreed with the vast majority of the contributors—it was dangerous to give the ballot to those who were wholly unprepared to use it wisely and, since partisan motives were apparent, partisanship had paid the penalty. A gradual program of education, based upon a recognition of actual conditions in the South and the granting of suffrage to all citizens who proved themselves worthy of it, would bring victory to those who believed, as did *Atlantic Monthly*, in the long established doctrine of political equality, irrespective of race, color, or station. As for social equality, the editor agreed with Booker T. Washington that "In all things purely social we can be as separate as the fingers, yet one as the hand in all things essential to mutual progress."[19]

An Alabama lawyer in 1905 vigorously opposed enforcement of the second section of the Fourteenth Amendment: a liberal construction would prevent a state from denying the right to vote to idiots or insane persons and from requiring a residence qualification for voting. The author doubted the authority to enforce the section if a state violated it and he revived the argument that the Fifteenth Amendment made unnecessary the second section of the Fourteenth Amendment. An Ohioan argued for the repeal of the Fifteenth Amendment since it had been a "stupendous fraud" on the rights of local self-government. The Amendment should be repealed also because Cuba was seeking admission to the United States as a state. On the other hand, he pointed out, repeal of the Fifteenth Amendment would revive the constitutionality of the Fourteenth.[20]

Charles Francis Adams, Jr., president of the Massachusetts Historical Society (1895–1915), contributed a surprisingly unsympathetic article to *Century Monthly* in 1906. The Negro, he declared, had contributed nothing to civilization; Africa stood at its highest point of development because of the presence of the white man. Developing a theme used by a number of other writers, the brother of Henry Adams stated categorically: "The negro mind did not expand—it promises fruit but it does not ripen." Only chaos would result if the Negro were given equality. Robert Bean, M.D., in similar vein asserted that Negroes had "never risen to the eminence of a nation." This failure was due to the fact that the Negro's brain was smaller than that of the white man; the size of the Negro's brain varied directly in proportion to the amount of white blood in his veins.[21]

The editor of *Harper's*, in a review in 1906 of Moncure D. Conway's *Autobiography*, agreed that slavery could have been abolished without a war, and expressed the belief that Lincoln would have had the insight and ability to guide the nation toward a peaceful reconciliation.[22]

Ray Stannard Baker, one of the best-known muckrakers, argued four years later that the Fifteenth Amendment was natural and necessary, that if a Negro in the South "can meet the requirements of education, property or both he can cast his ballot on a basis of equality with the white man." (This was one of the greatest distortions of fact encountered during the period, 1901–1918.) Large numbers of Negroes and whites did not vote because they did not have sufficient interest to pay their poll tax; Negroes, moreover, suffered open or concealed intimidation when they tried to vote. The kind of joint meetings that leaders like Booker T. Washington promoted would lead to a better understanding between the races which might provide the basis for an expanded franchise.[23]

When Booker T. Washington, in 1912, gave a generally affirmative answer to his question, "Is the Negro Having a Fair Chance?," Robert Underwood Johnson, the new editor of

Century Monthly, strongly challenged Washington in the same issue. Johnson declared that many Negroes wanted to know why they were finding opportunities for advancement closed to them. Negroes were burned at the stake; they had only a "phantom ballot" and received inadequate education.[24] Daniel D. Simmons, who has made an exhaustive study of the magazine, could not discover why Johnson was replaced as editor six months later. Not until 1919, wrote Simmons, did *Century Monthly* again discuss the Negro problem.[25]

World War I had little effect on the patterns of portraying Negroes. William Dean Howells concluded that the poverty of Negroes in Charleston was just a reflection of world-wide poverty; but in the country sections around Charleston, Negroes seemed to be reverting to the "African jungle culture." Another contributor to *Harper's* concluded that "toiling blacks and turbaned negresses" made one realize that Washington, D.C., was like a Southern town. In restaurants were cheerful grinning black waiters and an even blacker cook whom you instinctively addressed " 'snowball.' " In April, 1917, the month when the United States entered the war, and in May, Howells compared Negroes in St. Augustine, Florida, to "a swarm of blackbirds." As a race they were evidently "content" with working in menial roles and seldom had any "hope or endeavor for higher things." Decrepit cabins gave proof of Negroes' racial spendthrift.[26] Lawrence M. Bott concluded that during the almost quarter century covered in his investigation, *Harper's* published only one serious article, in 1920, which had as its principal concern the so-called race problem in the United States.[27]

James C. Hemphill of South Carolina, onetime editor of the Charleston *News and Courier* and the Philadelphia *Ledger* and Bromley Lecturer on Journalism at Yale from 1909 to 1910, contended in 1915 that the Negro deserved disfranchisement as a result of the conditions which he had wrought upon the South during Reconstruction. Although the decision, Guinn *v.* the United States, 1915, which had invalidated the "Grandfather Clause" in Oklahoma, was one of the most important decisions in fifty years, it hardly precipitated "a ripple in the great sea of American public sentiment." The decision "will not add a cubit to the voting stature of the Negro, and it will not take away from the white man any of his rights."[28]

Another article by Hemphill reviewed *Negro Education, A*

Study of the Private and Higher Schools for Colored in the United States by Thomas Jesse Jones of the United States Bureau of Education, one of the most important studies of that period. The per capita public school expenditure for white children in the Southern states was four and five times that for Negroes, but no more than one-half the per capita expenditures for white children in the North. "It is becoming more and more obvious to thoughtful men of both races," Hemphill observed, "that the negro in the South is in no large sense a political factor but an economic unit whose full efficiency can be secured *only* by education." Booker T. Washington was the "wisest and best man of his race this country has ever known."[29]

Thomas Walker Page, a Virginian who had degrees from Oxford and the University of Paris, a former professor of economics at the University of California, the University of Texas and the University of Virginia, argued that Negroes were lynched not because of race prejudice, but because they were an element of the poorer population which was given to committing more crimes than the white race. Therefore, innocent Negroes were often accused and lynched for crimes which they had not committed. Southern white people had opposed state intervention to prevent lynching because they had inherited the Saxon tradition. But the expansion of state control, which substituted state-wide prohibition for local option and which regulated banks, public utilities and other corporations, gave evidence that the states might adopt effective legislation against lynching. It would be premature, however, to forecast the effect of a mood which William Penn had called " 'governmentish' " on race relations.[30]

Negroes contributed articles through most of the period. Washington, naturally, appeared most frequently. One article in *Atlantic Monthly*, 1903, repeated some of the themes of his Atlanta Address, particularly the undue emphasis placed upon the Negro's role in politics during Reconstruction and the bitterness of debates about Negroes in Congress and during electoral campaigns. His "Heroes in Black Skins" in *Century Monthly* at about the same time had tones of the Page Plantation Tradition. Uncle Zeke, an ex-slave still in the service of his master, received no tip from the Yankee guests at dinner. The impecunious former master gave Uncle Zeke a dollar. After the Yankees had gone, Uncle Zeke said: " 'Massa,

I was powerful glad to see you mak dat front dem Yanks, and teach dem a lesson; but Massa, I know dat is de las dollar you got, and I can't keep it. I want you to take it and get Miss Genie a new dress dis year.'" A hero honored by Negroes today was Sergeant William H. Carney of the Fifty-fourth Massachusetts Regiment of Infantry who was killed in the attack on Fort Wagner in South Carolina. Most historians report Carney as having said: "The old flag never touched the ground, boys." In Washington's version, Carney said: " 'Well, boys she never tetched the ground.' "[31]

Washington argued in 1912 that the Negro, on the whole, was having a fair chance in the United States—a better chance than in the Negro Republic of Haiti. The Negro skilled laborer fared better in the South than in the North. Segregation in the South had led to the establishment of Negro business firms. But the Negro voted more freely in the North than in the South. He made a plea for equal justice in the courtroom and for Negro jurors. He roundly condemned the convict-lease system and, more mildly, lynching. He reiterated his theme that Negroes should not make politics and the holding of office "an important thing in life"; and that the "intelligent Negro" in the South should be allowed to vote.[32]

The other Negro contributors wrote more forthrightly in defense of equal rights for Negroes. Du Bois insisted that industrial training was not sufficient to elevate the Negro; separate education precluded sympathetic and effective group training and leadership. The most important article by Du Bois, "The African Roots of War," listed imperialism in Africa as one of the most important roots of World War I. One should not forget that "the white workingman has been asked to share the spoil of exploiting 'chinks and niggers.' " In typical poetic prose he concluded: "What shall the end be? The world-old and fearful things, War and Wealth, Murder and Luxury? Or shall it be a new thing—a new peace and new democracy of all races: a great humanity of equal men? *Semper novi quid ex Africa!*"[33]

Six years earlier, Professor Kelly Miller of Howard University had expressed the belief that the adjustment of the races of mankind throughout the world was the most urgent problem facing the twentieth century. The white races were superior in fact to the darker races, not because of inherent differences but because of different environments. The darker races would catch up with the white races because the latter passed on to those whom they exploited knowledge, skill and the development of resources.[34]

North American Review, in 1904, provided Mrs. Mary Church Terrell, Honorary President of the National Association for the Advancement of Colored People, with an opportunity to reply to several articles which had given the usual rationalizations for lynching. These, of course, emphasized rape as a cause.[35] Mrs. Terrell contended that white men who lived in the South, where nine-tenths of lynchings occurred, did not dare tell the truth. It was not the nature of the crime that aroused wrath, but rather the race and color of those lynched. She pointed out that of every one hundred Negroes lynched, from seventy-five to eighty-five were not even accused of rape. A second basic reason for lynchings was the lawlessness of the South.[36]

Archibald H. Grimké wrote in the vein of Du Bois: "If the disfranchisement of the Negro by the South could settle permanently the Negro question, I think that the action of that section would find its justification that achievement, according to the jesuitical principle that the end justifies the means." Disfranchisement would not be a permanent solution of the Negro question if it proved injurious to Northern and national interests.[37] Negroes who knew that the Constitution guaranteed their political and civil rights would not accept the violation of those rights. The South would suffer from disfranchisement of the Negro because it would cause unrest among Negro workers; the South had already suffered because disfranchisement had contributed to the backwardness of the region. This backwardness, which affected the nation as a whole, was a handicap in the struggle for world markets.[38]

The outbreak of World War I shifted attention from domestic problems to world problems. One must conclude that the principal literary magazines in the United States had made slim contribution to a clear understanding of a problem that after the war became even more complicated and pressing—an increased determination to deny, and an increased insistence to gain, equal rights for Negroes.

Newspapers

The analysis of newspapers included for 1901–1918 the New York *Times*, the Boston *Evening Transcript*, the Indianapolis *Journal,* the Chicago *Tribune* and the Cincinnati *Enquirer.* The investigation included also the San Francisco *Examiner,* 1901–1912 and the Washington *Star,* 1901–1912.

In general, the papers tended to give a less unfavorable picture of the Negro toward the end of the period. They continued to use, but less frequently, such familiar terms as "nigger," "niggah" and "darky"; "coon" tended to disappear. But as late as World War I the Cincinnati *Enquirer,* which continued more than did other papers its late nineteenth-century treatment, carried a headline: "Yah Suh!—Black Boys are Happy." The headline referred to Negro troops in France.[39]

Dialect jokes also appeared less frequently. In 1902, the Chicago *Tribune* published "by request" an article widely circulated in the *Club Woman,* the official magazine of the Federation of Women's Clubs. The story, "The Rushing in of Fools," developed the theme of atavism: The daughter of a fine, old New Orleans family had married a man who was suspected of having "one or two drops" of Negro blood. Their child was a coal-black, wooley-haired baby. The mulatto maid wailed: "Oh, missy, it was the black blood that did it." The mother died of mortification.

A regular column by Dorothy Dix in the San Francisco *Examiner* featured "Mirandy" on questions of interest to women. On one occasion "Mirandy" said: " 'Dey sho is having a good time when dey got some sorrer dey can prognosticate about.' " As for the woman's place, "Mirandy" said: " 'If home is a woman's sphere, she might servigrous in hit.' " This column continued at least until 1907. As late as 1913 the New York *Times* published this prayer by a Negro preacher:

> Gibe dis pore brudder de eye of de eagle, dat he spy out sin afar off. Glue his hands to de gospel plow. Tie his tongue to de line of truf. Nail his years to de gospel pole. Bow his head way down between his knees, Oh Lord, and fix his knees way down in some lonely, dark, and narrow valley, where prayer is much wanted to be made. 'Noint him with de kerosine ile of salvation and set him afire.

The San Francisco *Examiner* continued to ridicule the Negro in comic strips. In one, 1910, a Negro remonstrated: " 'Don't be bumping into me, white man: Don't rile me. I'se tough, I'se. Remembah, da civil war is ovah. Yar heard me

white man. I'se tough. I'se little Johnson, dats who I is.'"
Many of the Negroes in the *Examiner's* strips were named
Johnson—the *Examiner* bitterly opposed Jack Johnson who
had won the title as heavyweight champion. The Chicago
Tribune ran a not particularly funny comic, "Danny Dreamer
Sr. and Sambo Remo Rastus Brown," in 1912.[40]

A few tidbits are revealing. "A race war" threatened to result from a Negro's moving into a white neighborhood in
Chicago, 1908. A news article in the Chicago *Tribune* said
that white house-owners had denounced the act as "'outrageous'" and as "'an insult to the community.'" They feared
that this marked the beginning of an invasion that would ruin
property values. It was rumored that the invader was "a
notorious negro gambler. This, while it has not been corrobo-
rated, has not served to allay the feeling of the people in any
degree." In 1911, a white girl refused to pose at the Chicago
Art Institute life class because there were Negroes in the
class. Under a headline, "Blacks Will Be Barred," a story revealed that there had been some opposition before. The
model's action solved the situation: "She did what every one
seemed to want to have done and what no one seemed willing to do." An editorial in the Chicago *Tribune* in 1912,
"Three Generations of Dumas," praised the erection of a
statue of General Dumas, father of Alexandre Dumas *père*
and grandfather of Alexandre Dumas *fils* in the Place Male-
sherbes, Paris. But the editorial made no mention of the fact
that the latter two were colored.[41]

In Ohio, where segregated schools were illegal, the problem
was solved by the fact that Negroes tended to live in segregated areas. In 1916, white students at Walnut High School
threatened to walk out unless the Negro students were expelled. The Superintendent of Schools threatened to close the
doors against any white deserters and pointed out that neither
he nor the Board of Education had the right to abrogate the
state law which permitted no discrimination in color or creed
in education. The newspaper had no comment.[42]

There is some evidence that the Supreme Court decision,
Bailey *v.* Alabama, 1911, which declared that peonage violated the Thirteenth Amendment, resulted, at least in part,
from the holding of white immigrants in "slavery." A grand
jury in Vicksburg, Mississippi, refused to indict a planter
accused of holding Italians in peonage. The Italian and Aus-

tro-Hungarian governments had warned their citizens not to go to Mississippi. The Chicago *Tribune* pointed out that foreigners in the United States would receive " 'the most constant protection and security for their persons and property.' " Treaties could not be enforced in Mississippi, for "It is the great misfortune of the cotton south—a misfortune due to its long dependence on the negro, especially for agricultural labor—that it has no concept of the 'dignity of labor and little respect for the rights of labor.' " It was common practice, declared an article in the *Tribune*, 1908, for a planter to read rapidly the terms of an understanding which "no ordinary negro mind could comprehend. . . . As a matter of course the alleged 'contract' was interpreted against the poor darky."[43] Debates in Congress in 1910 dealt with the peonage of white immigrants rather than that of Negroes.

Negroes received little support from newspapers as far as their right to vote was concerned. The New York *Times* praised the disfranchisement provisions of the Virginia constitution of 1902, provided that its provisions were administered fairly. But it stated that "whatever excuses we may admit for such [literacy] measures in Mississippi with more than half its population colored, or even of Virginia with a third of its population colored, do not hold at all with reference to Maryland, since only one-fifth of the population was colored." The *Times* assured Southerners and Northern business interests in 1904 that the Republicans would pass no legislation to enforce the second section of the Fourteenth Amendment. President Theodore Roosevelt gave further assurance in 1905 that he opposed "any legislation cutting down representation of the Southern states in the Congress and the electoral college."[44]

When Republican Senator Thomas C. Platt of New York introduced, in December, 1904, a bill for the congressional reduction of the former Confederate states by nineteen, the Washington *Evening Star* quoted the New York *Sun* as predicting that the bill would be pigeonholed in the Committee on the Census. And so it was. But the *Star* pointed out, correctly, that the Republican platform of 1904 had promised to investigate suffrage conditions in the South before considering reduction. Like the New York *Times*, the *Star* opposed, in 1905, and again in 1909, the attempt of the Maryland legislature to disfranchise Negroes.[45]

Despite Roosevelt's wooing of "Lily-whites" during his first administration, many Negroes supported Roosevelt in the 1904 campaign. "The largest political gathering" held in Washington during a political campaign, according to the Washington *Star*, heard representatives of the Roosevelt and Fairbanks Club, the United Order of the Elks, and the Blaine Invincibles praise the President's "Square Deal" Policy. In November, Booker T. Washington urged Negroes to live a life of increased usefulness, soberness and simplicity, and not to lose their heads as a result of Roosevelt's policy.[46]

Contemporary accounts of the Republican National Conventions in Chicago, 1908 and 1912, reveal that sober historians have not exaggerated the unfavorable image of the Negro that emerged from them. Although by 1908 Negroes had been largely disfranchised in the Southern states, they continued to hold conventions which sent Negroes to Republican national conventions. (In the early twentieth century, Democratic primaries had not been devised for the purpose of eliminating Negroes from state and national politics. Only a few Negroes at that time could be persuaded to vote for Democrats.) After Theodore Roosevelt began intermittently to woo "Lily-white Republicans," contests over the seating of these and of the "Black and Tan" delegates became a quadrennial quarrel of the Credentials Committee at the Republican National Convention. If a candidate controlled the "Black and Tans," the Credentials Committee seated them, especially if he needed their votes for nomination. This procedure led the "Lily-whites" to charge the Black and Tan Delegates with venality. (The Lily-white Republicans were, of course incorruptible!)

In 1908, the Chicago *Tribune*, which supported Taft, condemned the "Black Troops" of the "Allies" who opposed him. Many Negroes opposed Taft because he had been picked by Theodore Roosevelt whose handling of the Brownsville riot, 1906, had left a bitter feeling. Other Negro delegates—some of whom, like some white delegates, had been bought—supported Taft. The *Tribune* took delight in reporting what it considered typical antics of Negroes. A Negro church barred its doors to anti-Taftmen. Some Negro delegates almost got into a fight. One of the would-be fighters was allegedly a college professor who said: " 'I'll whup him—I'll whup him if it costs me $5.00.' " Some Negroes even threatened to form their own Ku-Klux Klan to defeat Taft. But when his election seemed assured, Negro politicians began to climb on the band wagon. The *Tribune* added this editorial comment: "Already the rodomontade of the anti-Roosevelt, anti-[Booker T.] Washington Ku-Klux negroes has discredited the influence of negroes in the convention. If it should be followed by any considerable bolt to the Democratic ticket, the negro will have achieved in one campaign his own political annihilation." One wonders whether the *Tribune* understood the implications of a news article a few days earlier which stated: "As usual, the platform will declare for the protection of the civil liberties of the negro race. A special effort will be made to have this plank comprehensive and emphatic."[47]

But, in 1912 the *Tribune* supported Roosevelt against Taft and contended that the latter should withdraw since, of eleven Republican states which had voted directly for candidates, only one was for Taft. After condemning Negroes who opposed the nomination of Roosevelt, the *Tribune* warned: "If the Republican party in the South is to remain a mere shell of an organization, just continue the methods which hand it over to placeholders and a few negro voters."[48]

The Boston *Evening Transcript*, which steadfastly opposed measures to enforce the second section of the Fourteenth Amendment, revealed almost unbelievable naïveté in its editorial comment on the United States Supreme Court decisions which declared the "Grandfather Clauses" in Oklahoma and Maryland unconstitutional. After praising the Court for the decision and pointing out that neither state was in danger of "Negro ascendancy," the editorial concluded:

The decision does not stand in the way of a literacy test honestly applied to both races and honestly enforced. If the South puts into operation compulsory school laws it will have educated electorates with which the Supreme Court will not interfere. It is up to the South to accept the teachings of the decision, and the quicker it leaves off every attempt to adjust itself politically to the conditions of 1866, the quicker it abandons the effort to turn time backward, the better it will be for the South and the Nation. The South has blinded itself to its own interests. Let it tear the disfranchisement bandage from its eyes and accustom them to the sunlight of human progress.[49]

James C. Hemphill's article in *North American Review*, August, 1915, gave a more perceptive evaluation, for it did not expect the decisions to increase the Negro vote and it stoutly defended suffrage laws in the South.

Booker T. Washington periodically received support for his views on the race question. The New York *Times* considered the White House dinner unfortunate, but defended Roosevelt's right to confer with Washington at the dinner table. But the *Times* reported the incident in a colored Boston church, 1903, when a few members heckled Washington and Monroe Trotter's sister stuck him with a hat pin. On that occasion, the *Times* commented editorially that "underlying the trouble is the belief of certain negroes, most of them residents of the North, that Mr. Washington is too much a counselor of peace; of making the best of bad conditions, and of moving slowly when rapid motion is dangerous or impossible." In 1906, the *Times* published a ringing indictment of Washington by the Reverend Adam Clayton Powell, Sr., the father of the present-day Congressman from New York City:

> For years he has counselled colored men to "meekly wait and murmur not," and a large number of us have obeyed him. He has also advised the North to let the South solve in its own way the negro problem, and in its greed for gold the North gladly accepted advice from such a distinguished source. What are the results? Lynchings are increasing and riots are more numerous, the race is humiliated by Jim Crow laws, and woefully handicapped in its intellectual and moral development by inferior schools. In a word, under Dr. Washington's policy the two races in the South are a thousand times further apart than they were fifteen years ago and the breach is widening every day."[50]

Newspapers generally gave a balanced account of an ugly situation involving the Principal of Tuskegee. The Chicago *Tribune*, in fat, banner headlines, began its article on March 20, 1911:

BOOKER T. WASHINGTON
BEATEN IN FIGHT WITH WHITE MAN

This account differed somewhat from those which appeared, for example, in the New York *Times*. A March 21 *Times* account stated that Washington had been taken to Flower Hospital where "several severe wounds on the head, caused by blows struck with a club, were dressed." It went on to report that Mrs. Albert Ulrich appeared at the neighborhood station house and charged that Washington had said to her in the hallway of an apartment house at 11½ West Sixty-third Street, New York City: "'Hello sweetheart'"; that she had, moreover, seen him walking up and down in front of the apartment house. According to accounts in the *Tribune*, *Times*, and other papers the next day, Washington was looking for D. C. Smith, the auditor (in some papers treasurer) of Tuskegee. But a caretaker at the Smith residence in Monclair, New Jersey, said that Smith had been at Tuskegee for the past month. Smith later said that he had had no appointment with Washington on March 19. Dr. Emmett J. Scott, Washington's confidential secretary, was reported as having written a letter to Washington making the appointment but had destroyed the letter.

Seth Low, President of the Board of Trustees, issued a statement that Washington had entered the vestibule, but got no answer to the bell which he had rung. He returned twice thereafter to the vestibule. On his third visit, while he was leaning over to look at the name plates, a man rushed in from the street and began to assault him. Ulrich, sometimes called Henry and at other times Albert, said that he had watched Washington for some time and had seen him looking through the keyhole of the apartment of a Mrs. Revett who lived on the first floor. Ulrich entered the apartment and asked Washington what he was doing. When "the negro" did not answer, Ulrich pursued him into the street where "they struggled, rolling around the street, until the negro got away from him and ran east on Sixty-third street." Washington was arrested and charged by Ulrich with illegal entry.

The mystery deepened when the real wife of Ulrich was found living in Orange, New Jersey; she was willing to prefer charges against Ulrich, whose real name was Henry Adams Ulrich, for desertion. The woman with whom he was "boarding" at the apartment house was not his legal wife.

Washington changed his charge on March 21 from felonious assault to simple assault. President Taft wrote Washington: "I am greatly distressed at your misfortune and I hasten to write you of my sympathy. . . . I want you to know your friends are standing by you in every trial and that I am proud to subscribe myself as one." Senator Vardaman of Mississippi, who was campaigning for re-election was reported as having said that Ulrich had "proved himself not a man by not killing Washington on the spot." The horrible fire in the Triangle Waist Company Factory on March 25, which killed scores of young women and children, temporarily removed the Ulrich-Washington incident from the papers.

On November 6, 1911, the Court of Special Sessions, by a vote of two to one, acquitted Ulrich of assault. One of the two commented: "Dr. Washington had no business in the house." Immediately following Ulrich's acquittal, he was arrested on the charge of deserting his wife in Orange, New Jersey.[51]

When Washington died, on November 14, 1915, the *Times* commented editorially that "it is doubtful if any American within the forty years of his active life has rendered to the nation greater service of greater or more lasting value than his." The *Times* pointed out in the same editorial, however, that many Negroes did not accept him as their leader.[52]

Newspapers contributed little to the decline in lynching. Negroes appeared more frequently in articles involving crime and lynching than in any other type of news. Northerners, accustomed to reading about crimes in their own communities, easily accepted the stereotype of the Negro "brute" who provided the principal basis for Southern justifications of lynchings.

The Cincinnati *Enquirer* continued to present lynchings in a most sensational and lurid fashion that generally upheld the mob. Lynching was "not necessarily a mark of a disorderly or non-law-abiding community. On the contrary it might be argued that where the unspeakable crime [rape] had been committed which leads to the greatest number of lynchings, that the work of the mob is the highest testimony to the civilization and enlightenment and moral character of the people." When Negroes lynched Negroes, this border newspaper apparently considered their act also the highest testimony to civilization. Not so, however, when Negroes tried to hang a white man. The *Enquirer* quoted with approval, in 1912, this promise by Governor Cole Blease of South Carolina: "Therefore let it be understood in South Carolina that when a negro attacks a white woman all that is needed is that they get the right man and they who get him will neither need nor receive a trial."[53]

The *Enquirer* generally approved whites who were involved in riots. But, after the East St. Louis riot and the Houston riot in 1917, the *Enquirer* changed its position. The paper did not accept the argument that the influx of Negroes into East St. Louis justified the "anarchical . . . conditions" there. "The defiance and desecration of law is never justified and certainly in this instance cannot be condemned too vigorously." In September of the same year a riot in Houston, Texas, was much more grave than that in Brownsville in 1906. Men of the Twenty-fifth Infantry, after a riot with white civilians, seized weapons and killed seventeen whites. With only the semblance of a trial, thirteen Negroes were hanged for murder and mutiny, forty-one were imprisoned for life, and forty others held for further investigation. The *Enquirer* at first accepted reports that the troops were responsible for the riot, but later presented evidence that they had been goaded into attacking white civilians. The paper also reported the slogan of the troops before the riot: " 'To hell with going to France, let's clean up this dirty town.' "[54]

The San Francisco *Examiner* also generally condoned lynchings while the Washington *Evening Star*, the Chicago *Tribune* and the Boston *Evening Transcript* criticized them.[55] The *Transcript*, however, did not support Boston Negroes who sought to have the movie, "Birth of a Nation," banned. The governor sought to have the state legislature prohibit the showing of all films and plays which aroused racial and religious prejudice, but the city government permitted the showing. The *Transcript* made no editorial comment on the incident, but its publication of an advertisement for the films made clear its lack of opposition. The advertisement stated: "The surrender of Lee at Appomattox, the assassination of Lincoln, Sherman's march to the sea, the burning of Atlanta, move upon the screen as they never moved in print."[56] That is to say, the alleged documentary value of the film justified showing it regardless of the consequences.

The New York *Times* rarely published news about lynchings unless they were very brutal or contained some unusual element. The *Times* probably provided a public service when in 1903 it published this horrible story of a lynching in Belleville, Illinois:

The mob hanged Wyatt to a telephone pole in the public square. Even while his body was jerking in the throes of death from the strangulation, members of the mob began building a fire at the bottom of the pole. The flames flared up and licked at the feet of the victim, but this did not satisfy the mob, and another and larger fire was started.

When it had begun burning briskly, the negro still half alive, was cut down, and after being covered with coal oil was cast into the fire. Moans of pain were heard from the half dead victim of the mob, and these served further to infuriate his torturers. They fell upon him with clubs and knives and cut and beat the burning body almost to pieces, and not until every sign of life had departed did they desist and permit the flames to devour the body.

The *Times* placed heaviest responsibility for lynchings on the local sheriffs. Its principal suggestion—later proved to have much validity—for the prevention of lynching was a sheriff brave enough to defy cowardly mobs. In 1906, the *Times* opposed federal intervention, but warned that, if conditions became much worse, some such action would have to be taken. The *Times* reported the background of race riots and the spark which inflamed them; it pointed out that the police and troops usually sided with whites by disarming Negroes and allowing whites to roam the streets beating and killing Negroes and burning their homes.[57]

On balance, the newspapers surveyed did not give strong support to Negroes in their struggle for equal rights. One can only conjecture as to the influence on the American mind of this continuing, though lessening, evidence of the violations of the basic principles of American democracy.

NINETEEN

Conclusion

FOR the 1954 edition of this book, I wrote on October, 1953: "The Negro in the United States has achieved today the highest status in his history." I believe in 1965 that, on balance, we American Negroes have edged forward since the end of 1953.

The most significant gains have, of course, resulted from federal intervention. In retrospect, the failure of Congress during World War I to enact laws buttressing segregation and discrimination was a considerable gain. If they had been enacted, the quest for civil rights would have required repeal, or decisions by the United States Supreme Court nullifying them. Repeal is generally more difficult than original passage. There can be little doubt, then, that passage of the World War I bills would have made more difficult the enactment of the 1957, 1960 and 1964 Civil Rights Laws.

In a sense, the defeat of the World War I bills gives the lie to William Graham Sumner's dictum that "Stateways cannot change folkways." This dictum has long been, in part, demonstrably false. Moreover, opponents of the 1957, 1960 and 1964 Civil Rights Laws would not have struggled so hard to prevent their enactment if they had not believed that these laws would effect some changes, as they indeed have. I am not suggesting that defeat of the World War I bills measurably promoted at that time congressional, state, or municipal action in behalf of civil rights. As a contemporary of that period, however, I know that those Negroes who were aware of the defeat acquired new courage. As a historian, I am inclined to believe that this defeat was a greater gain in the quest for equality than was, as I wrote in 1953, the failure of "The New South" to capture the citadels of learning in the North.[1]

Scarcely discernible in 1918, though more evident at the end of 1953, was the crucial and preponderantly positive role that federal courts, especially the United States Supreme Court, would play in supporting the struggle for equal rights. The Supreme Court, in 1911, declared that peonage violated the Thirteenth Amendment, and in 1915, ruled that the

"Grandfather Clauses" violated the Fifteenth Amendment. These were, indeed, small steps but they gathered such momentum that by 1965 the Supreme Court had become the whipping boy of ardent segregationists.

At the end of World War I, none of the seventeen Negro land-grant colleges provided military training as required by the First Morrill Act of 1862. In 1942, however, the first Reserve Officers Training Corps in a Negro land-grant college was established at Prairie View Agricultural and Mechanical College in Texas. By 1950, there were Army or Air Force programs at ten of the seventeen Negro land-grant colleges and at five other institutions of higher learning, exclusively or predominantly for Negroes.[2] Some officers who received their commission from these ROTC units served in the Korean War and continue to hold their commissions. The meritorious career of these officers probably contributed in part to the increase, slow though it was, of the number of Negroes admitted to the Military Academy at West Point and the Naval Academy at Annapolis. Three Negro cadets were enrolled, for the first time, in 1959, at the Air Force Academy, Colorado Springs, Colorado and all of them were commissioned at the end of the regular four years. At the end of 1953, Brigadier General B. O. Davis, Sr. had the highest rank thus far held by a Negro in the regular armed forces of the United States.[3] His son, Benjamin O. Davis, Jr., received his commission as second lieutenant from West Point in 1936. After a distinguished combat career during World War II, he was appointed Brigadier General in the Air Force, and in 1959 Major General in the Air Force, thus exceeding his father's rank. On April 16, 1965, President Lyndon Johnson nominated him for promotion to Lieutenant General, the highest rank held by a Negro officer, and appointed him as chief of staff of United States and United Nations forces in Korea.

The participation of Negroes in all the ceremonies of the funeral of President John F. Kennedy in November, 1963 symbolized not only recognition of services performed by Negroes in all the wars fought by the United States, but to some extent the integration of Negroes in American society.

Notes

Notes

CHAPTER ONE

1. *A. M. E. Review*, VI (October, 1889), 221.
2. See especially U. S. National Commission for UNESCO, XC (50) 65, September 12, 1950, and XC (51) 18, April 5, 1951; Washington *Post*, August 30, 1951, p. 5, news art. (All references to newspapers are to editorials unless otherwise indicated.)
3. See the author's "Some New Interpretations of the Colonization Movement," *Phylon*, IV (Fourth Quarter, 1943), 330–333.
4. Robert Ezra Park, *Race and Culture*, ed. by Everett Cherrington Hughes and others (Glencoe, Illinois, 1950), p. 76.
5. *Congressional Record*, 45th Cong., 3rd sess., p. 1079. Italics as in the original.
6. Francis B. Simkins, *The South Old and New* (New York, 1947), pp. 182–183.
7. Howard K. Beale, "On Rewriting Reconstruction History," *American Historical Review*, XLV (July, 1940), 815.
8. Arthur M. Schlesinger, *Political and Social History of the United States* (New York, 1925), p. 243.
9. See especially W. E. B. Du Bois, *Black Reconstruction in America* (New York, 1935), pp. 381–667, *passim*.

CHAPTER TWO

1. Schlesinger, "Historians Rate U. S. Presidents," *Life*, XXV (November 1, 1948), 65.
2. C. Vann Woodward, *Reunion and Reaction: The Compromise of 1877 and the End of Reconstruction* (Boston, 1951); review by the author in the *Journal of Negro History*, XXXVI (October, 1951), 445–450.
3. Charles Richard Williams, *The Life of Rutherford Birchard Hayes* (Columbus, 1928), I, 318; E. W. Winkler, ed., "The Hayes-Bryan Correspondence," *Southwestern Historical Quarterly*, XXVI (1922–1923), 159.
4. George D. Ellis, comp., *Platforms of the Two Great Political Parties* (Washington, 1932), pp. 43–44; Williams, *Hayes*, I, 462.
5. Williams, *Hayes*, I, 486.
6. *Ibid.*, 488–489, 496; Woodward, *Reunion and Reaction*, p. 25.
7. Woodward, *Reunion and Reaction*, especially pp. 8, 195–196, 201–202.
8. James D. Richardson, comp., *Messages and Papers of the Presidents* (New York, 1917), VI, 4395–4396. Italics as in the original.

9. Williams, *Hayes*, II, 46–48.

10. Boston *Evening Transcript*, March 8, 1877, p. 4; April 2, p. 4; April 11, p. 4; Cincinnati *Enquirer*, April 25, p. 4; Washington *Star*, April 21, p. 2; Chicago *Tribune*, April 2 and 3, p. 4; *Harper's Weekly*, XXI (May 5, 1877), 342; *Nation*, XXIV (April 12, 1877), 216.

11. New York *Times*, March 29, 1877, p. 4; April 1, p. 6; April 5, p. 4; April 7, p. 4.

12. *Ibid.*, April 5, 1877, p. 2, news art.

13. Returns Department of the South, for the Month of April 1877, MSS., National Archives, Endorsed May 21, 1877; Returns Department of the Gulf for the Month of April, 1877, MSS., National Archives, Endorsed May 21, 1877.

14. Williams, *Hayes*, II, 64.

15. Washington *Star*, April 23, 1877, p. 4.

16. *Harper's Weekly*, XXI (July 7, 1877), 518.

17. Cincinnati *Evening Times*, September 8, 1877, p. 1, news art.; Louisville *Commercial*, September 11, p. 1, news art. Italics as in the original.

18. Louisville *Courier-Journal*, September 16, 1877, p. 1, news art.

19. *Ibid.*, September 18, 1877, p. 1, news art.

20. New York *Tribune*, September 19, 1877, p. 1, news art.

21. Louisville *Courier-Journal*, September 19, 1877, p. 1, news art.

22. Nashville *American*, September 19, 1877, p. 1, news art.; September 20, p. 1, news art.; p. 7, news art.

23. Nashville *American*, September 21, 1877, p. 1, news art.

24. *Loc. cit.*

25. *Loc. cit.*

26. Nashville *American*, September 22, 1877, p. 1, news art.; Atlanta *Constitution*, September 22, p. 2; September 23, pp. 1, 2, news arts.; September 27, p. 1, news art.; New York *Tribune*, September 23, p. 4, news art.

27. New York *Herald*, September 25, 1877, p. 4, news art.; Nashville *American*, September 26, p. 1, news art.

28. Nashville *American*, September 27, 1877, p. 1, news art.; New York *Herald*, September 24, p. 4.

29. Richardson, comp., *Messages*, VI, 4411, 4412.

30. *Ibid.*, 4427–4428.

31. New York *Times*, November 14, 1878, p. 4.

32. Richardson, comp., *Messages*, VI, 4445–4446.

33. Senate Report, No. 855, 45th Cong., 3rd sess., pp. XXV, XLIII, XLVI.

34. Williams, ed., *Diary and Letters of Rutherford Birchard Hayes* (Columbus, 1928), III, 552–553.

35. Ellis P. Oberholtzer, *A History of the United States since the Civil War* (New York, 1917–1937), IV, 47–52.

36. Burkes A. Hinsdale, ed., *Works of James Abram Garfield* (Boston, 1882), I, 760–762.

37. San Francisco *Examiner*, November 28, 1878, p. 4.

38. *Congressional Record*, 45th Cong., 3rd sess., p. 54.

39. San Francisco *Examiner*, December 10, 1878, p. 2, news art.; December 11, 20 and 26, p. 2, all news arts.

40. Richardson, comp., *Messages*, VI, 4512–4513.

41. *Ibid.*, VI, 4553–4554.

42. Williams, ed., *Diary*, IV, 58–59.

43. Williams, *Hayes*, II, 68.

CHAPTER THREE

1. Ellis, comp., *Platforms of Great Parties*, pp. 48, 52–53.

2. The discussion of this subject is based on an article by Elvena S. Bage, "President Garfield's Forgotten Pronouncement," *Negro History Bulletin*, XIV (June, 1951), 195–197, 206, 214.

3. Richardson, comp., *Messages*, VIII, 8–9.

4. "The Inaugural Address," *Harper's Weekly*, XXV (March 19, 1881), 179; "The Inaugural Address and the Cabinet," *Nation*, XXXIII (March 10, 1881), 162–163, ed.; Richmond *Dispatch*, March 5, 1881, p. 2; New Orleans *Times*, March 6, p. 6.

5. Louisville *Courier-Journal*, March 7, 1881, p. 2; Mobile *Daily Register*, March 5, p. 2; March 11, p. 2; Atlanta *Constitution*, March 5, p. 2; March 6, p. 2; March 11, p. 2; Charleston *News and Courier*, March 5, p. 2; Memphis *Commercial Appeal*, March 5, p. 1.

6. San Francisco *Examiner*, March 7, 1881, p. 2; New Haven *Evening Register*, March 5, p. 2; Cincinnati *Enquirer*, March 7, p. 4; Indianapolis *Journal*, March 5, p. 4; St. Louis *Globe-Democrat*, March 5, p. 5; Detroit *Post and Tribune*, March 9, p. 2; Boston *Evening Transcript*, March 7, p. 4; Washington *Star*, March 5, p. 4; Pittsburgh *Dispatch*, March 5, p. 4.

7. Chicago *Tribune*, March 5, 1881, p. 4; Philadelphia *North American*, March 5, p. 2; New York *Times*, March 7, p. 4.

8. New Orleans *Weekly Louisianian*, March 12, 1881, p. 2.

9. Mary L. Hinsdale, ed., *Garfield-Hinsdale Letters* (Ann Arbor, 1949), pp. 478–479.

10. James Hugo Johnston, "The Participation of Negroes in the Government of Virginia from 1877 to 1888," *Journal of Negro History*, XIV (July, 1929), 251–271.

11. Vincent De Santis, "Negro Dissatisfaction with Republican Policy in the South, 1882–1884," *ibid.*, XXXVI (April, 1951), 148–159.

12. Cleveland *Gazette*, October 20, 1883; New York *Globe*, October 20 and 27.

13. Richardson, comp., *Messages*, VIII, 55–58, 112–118, 129, 143–144, 175, 184, 188, 198, 237.

14. Ellis, comp., *Platforms of Great Parties*, pp. 54, 57, 61, 65.

15. The paragraphs dealing with Fortune's reactions are based on the M. A. thesis at Howard University by Leinster H. Moseley, "The Negro as Portrayed in the New York *Globe*, New York *Freeman*, and New York *Age*, 1883–1892," pp. 33ff.

16. New York *Globe*, July 26, October 18, November 8, 1884; New York *Freeman*, November 22, 1884.

17. New York *Freeman*, November 29, 1884.

18. Richardson, comp., *Messages*, VIII, 302.

19. New York *Freeman*, March 7 and 21, 1885.

20. For Cleveland's refusal to appoint as minister to Haiti the Negro historian, George Washington Williams, whom Arthur had nominated on March 2, 1885 (!), see the M. A. thesis at Howard University by Pearle Mintz Oxendine, "An Evaluation of Negro Historians during the Period of the Road to Reunion," pp. 28–33.

21. Richardson, comp., *Messages*, VIII, 531; New York *Freeman*, August 14, 1886, news art., August 28 and March 12, 1887, news art.

22. Richardson, comp., *Messages*, VIII, 329, 333, 355–357, 383, 390, 498, 501, 519–521, 528.

23. New York *Times*, June 22, 1885, p. 4; October 1, p. 5, news art.; March 9, 1888, p. 2, news art.

CHAPTER FOUR

1. Ellis, *Platforms of Great Parties*, p. 71.

2. *Ibid.*, p. 68.

3. Richardson, comp., *Messages*, IX, 9.

4. *Ibid.*, 34, 36, 45, 54.

5. Vernon Lane Wharton, *The Negro in Mississippi, 1865–1890* (Chapel Hill, 1947), pp. 202–204.

6. *Congressional Record*, 51st Cong., 1st sess., pp. 691–702

7. *Ibid.*, pp. 771–774.

8. *Ibid.*, pp. 1160, 1210, 1386.

9. Genevieve Swann Brown, "An Analytical and Statistical Study of Higher Education Among Negroes During the Period 1877–1900," M. A. thesis, Howard University.

10. Edgar W. Knight, *Public Education in the South* (Boston, 1922), pp. 420–422.

11. See comment by Philadelphia *North American*, March 21, 1890, p. 2.

12. For a summary of these arguments, see Davis Rich Dewey, *National Problems, 1885–1897* (New York, 1907), p. 90.

13. *Congressional Record*, 51st Cong., 1st sess., especially pp. 1651, 1681, 1682, 1684, 1724, 1935–1938, 2080, 2436; Franklin

L. Burdette, *Filibustering in the Senate* (Princeton, 1940), pp. 51–52.

14. *Congressional Record*, 51st Cong., 1st sess., p. 2436.

15. *Ibid.*, pp. 6537–6543.

16. *Ibid.*, pp. 6549–6554.

17. *Ibid.*, pp. 6560–6611.

18. *Ibid.*, pp. 6672–6689.

19. *Ibid.*, pp. 6700–6735, 6843–6900, 6923–6941.

20. Wharton, *Negro in Mississippi*, pp. 211–212.

21. *Ibid.*, p. 212, quoting the Raymond (Mississippi) *Gazette*, November 1, 1890.

22. *Congressional Record*, 51st Cong., 1st sess., p. 8466; Adelaide F. James, "Legislative Proposals Dealing with the Negro in the Senate, Fifty-first Congress," M. A. thesis, Howard University.

23. Wharton, *Negro in Mississippi*, pp. 199–216.

24. Richardson, comp., *Messages*, IX, 127–129.

25. *Congressional Record*, 51st Cong., 2nd sess., pp. 18–25; Burdette, *Filibustering*, p. 52.

26. John Temple Graves, *The Fighting South* (New York, 1943), pp. 125–126.

27. *Congressional Record*, 51st Cong., 2nd sess., pp. 74–80, 204, 211, 240–294, 324, 365, 407–414, 520, 522, 586, 588, 625–637, 682–683, 713–731, 771, 814, 870–874, 1399, 1416–1419, 1614, 7835.

28. *Ibid.*, 51st Cong., 1st sess., pp. 7836, 7882.

29. *Ibid.*, 51st Cong., 2nd sess., pp. 912–913.

30. *Ibid.*, pp. 1323–1324.

31. *Ibid.*, pp. 1739–1740.

32. New York *Times*, June 19, 1890, p. 4.

33. New York *Age*, November 29, 1890, p. 2; December 20, p. 4; December 27, p. 2; January 3, 1891 (2 items), p. 2; January 10, 17, 31, p. 2.

34. Washington *Bee*, August 2, 1890, p. 2; December 6, p. 2; January 10, 17, 24, 31, 1891, p. 2; Huntsville (Alabama) *Gazette*, December 6, 1890, p. 2; January 24, 1891, p. 1, news art.; January 24, p. 2.

35. Alrutheus A. Taylor, *The Negro in South Carolina during Reconstruction* (Washington, 1924), p. 312; Francis B. Simkins and Robert H. Woody, *South Carolina during Reconstruction* (Chapel Hill, 1932), p. 547.

36. Taylor, *Negro in South Carolina*, pp. 290–297.

37. Simkins, *Pitchfork Ben Tillman* (Baton Rouge, 1944), pp. 171–175, 295 ff.

38. Simkins, *The Tillman Movement in South Carolina* (Durham, 1926), pp. 135–137.

39. *Congressional Record*, 51st Cong., 2nd sess., pp. 297, 360–377.

40. Richardson, comp., *Messages*, IX, 208–211.

41. *Ibid.*, 182–208.

42. Ellis, comp., *Platforms of Great Parties*, pp. 79–80.

43. Richardson, comp., *Messages*, IX, 331–332.

44. Donald Marquand Dozer, "Benjamin Harrison and the Presidential Campaign of 1892," *American Historical Review*, LIV (October, 1948), 49.

CHAPTER FIVE

1. Vernon Louis Parrington, *The Beginnings of Critical Realism in America* (New York, 1930), III, 300.

2. Ellis, comp., *Platforms of Great Parties*, p. 79.

3. Richardson, comp., *Messages*, IX, 31, 436–437, 453, 536–537, 544–545, 633–635, 664, 735.

4. Basil Mathews, *Booker T. Washington* (Cambridge, 1948), p. 91.

5. William Allen White, *The Autobiography of William Allen White* (New York, 1946), pp. 294, 349–350. With the permission of Macmillan and Company.

6. John D. Hicks, *The Populist Revolt, A History of the Farmers' Alliance and the People's Party* (Minneapolis, 1931); Helen G. Edmonds, *The Negro and Fusion Politics in North Carolina* (Chapel Hill, 1951).

7. Ellis, comp., *Platforms of Great Parties*, pp. 92, 102, 103.

8. Richardson, comp., *Messages* (Published by Bureau of National Literature, Washington, 1911), VIII, 6240, 6243.

9. Edmonds, *Negro and Fusion Politics*, Chapters X and XI.

10. "The North Carolina Race Conflict," *The Outlook*, LXIII (November 19, 1898), 709.

11. Richardson, comp., *Messages* (1911 ed.), VIII, 6248, 6277, 6371, 6404, 6430, 6458, 6459, 6465–6469.

12. Edmonds, *Negro and Fusion Politics*, p. 154.

13. The discussion of White's career in Congress is based on Frenise A. Logan, "Influences Which Determined the Race-Consciousness of George H. White, 1897–1901," *Negro History Bulletin*, XIV (December, 1950), 63–65. For White's speech, see *Congressional Record*, 55th Cong., 3rd sess., p. 342.

14. *Ibid.*, 56th Cong., 1st sess., pp. 2150–2151.

15. *Ibid.*, pp. 2242–2245; 2nd sess., pp. 557, 647, 657; Appendix, p. 47.

16. *Ibid.*, pp. 1021, 1022, 2151, 3550; 2nd sess., p. 1637.

17. Samuel Denny Smith, *The Negro in Congress, 1870–1901* (Chapel Hill, 1940), p. 128.

18. *Congressional Record*, 56th Cong., 2nd sess., pp. 1634–1638.

19. *Ibid.*, 56th Cong., 1st sess., p. 1507; Raleigh *News and Observer*, March 5, 1901.

20. Ellis, comp., *Platforms of Great Parties*, pp. 115, 119.

21. *Ibid.*, pp. 105–113.

22. *Congressional Record*, 56th Cong., 2nd sess., pp. 486–748 *passim*; Appendix, pp. 69–75. The author's attention was first called to the Crumpacker amendment by Hattie M. Rice who wrote her master's thesis at Howard University on "The Negro as Portrayed in the Boston *Evening Transcript*, 1901–1907." Complete details were developed by John Moore in his thesis, "The Negro as Portrayed in the Indianapolis *Journal*, 1900–1902."

CHAPTER SIX

1. The list of Justices may be conveniently consulted in Charles Warren, *The Supreme Court in United States History* (new and rev. ed., Boston, 1928), II, 760–762.

2. *Ibid.*, 533–534.

3. John M. Mecklin, *Democracy and Race Friction, A Study in Social Ethics* (New York, 1914), pp. 219–246.

4. 16 Wallace, 36 (1872).

5. For a cogent analysis of Campbell's argument, see Walton H. Hamilton, "The Path of Due Process of Law," in Conyers Read, ed., *The Constitution Reconsidered* (New York, 1938), pp. 170–177.

6. Warren, *Supreme Court*, II, 546.

7. Hamilton, *Due Process*, p. 177.

8. United States *v.* Reese, 92 U. S., 214 (1876).

9. Hamilton, *Due Process*, p. 168.

10. United States *v.* Cruikshank, 92 U. S., 542 (1876).

11. Strauder *v.* West Virginia, 100 U. S., 303 (1880); *Ex parte* Virginia, 100 U. S., 339 (1880).

12. Neal *v.* Delaware, 103 U. S., 370 (1880); Bush *v.* Commonwealth of Kentucky, 107 U. S., 110 (1882); Virginia *v.* Rives, 100 U. S., 313 (1880); Pace *v.* Alabama, 106 U. S., 583 (1882).

13. It is not listed, for example, in W. E. B. Du Bois, ed., *An Appeal to the World!* (New York, 1947), pp. 28–34, since the digest of cases there presented deals with only the post-Civil War amendments.

14. Hall *v.* De Cuir, 95 U. S., 485 (1878). For a full discussion of the Fourteenth Amendment and the commerce clause in this connection, see Sarah Lemmon, "Transportation Segregation in the Federal Courts since 1865," *Journal of Negro History*, XXXVIII (April, 1953), 174–195.

15. Lake Shore and Michigan Southern Railway Company *v.* Ohio, 173 U. S., 285 (1899).

16. Louisville, New Orleans and Texas Railway Company *v.* Mississippi, 133 U. S., 587 (1890); Chesapeake and Ohio Railway Company *v.* Kentucky, 179 U. S., 388 (1900).

17. United States v. Harris, 106 U. S., 629 (1882).

18. Mary Boykin Chesnut, *A Diary from Dixie*, ed. by Ben Ames Williams (Boston, 1950), especially pp. 21–22, 122.

19. Woodward, *Reunion and Reaction*, p. 245.

20. Civil Rights Cases, 109 U. S., 3 (1883).

21. Warren, *Supreme Court*, II, 608.

22. Thelma O. Venable, "Decision of State Courts Involving the Rights of Negroes, 1877–1900," M. A. thesis, Howard University.

23. *Ex parte* Yarbrough, 110 U. S., 651 (1884).

24. Yick Wo v. Hopkins, 118 U. S. 356 (1886).

25. Gray v. Cincinnati and Southern Railroad Company, 11 Fed. 683 (U. S. C. C., Ohio, 1882); Murphy v. Western and Atlantic Railroad, 23 Fed. 137 (U. S. C. C., Tennessee, 1885); Hank v. Southern Pacific Railroad Company, 38 Fed. 226 (U. S. C. C., Texas, 1888); United States v. Buntin, 10 Fed. Rep., 730 (1882).

26. William H. Council v. The Western and Atlantic Railroad Company, *Interstate Commerce Commission Reports* (second series, New York, 1887–), I (1887), 339–347; William H. Heard v. The Georgia Railroad Company, *ibid.*, II (1888), 428–436; William H. Heard v. The Georgia Railroad Company, *ibid.*, III (1889), 111–127.

27. Plessy v. Ferguson, 163 U. S., 537 (1896).

28. Joseph H. Drake, "The Sociological Interpretation of Law," *Michigan Law Review*, XVI (June, 1918), 614.

29. Washington *Post*, October 11, 1949, p. 10.

30. Cummings v. Richmond County Board of Education, 175 U. S., 528 (1900).

31. Andrew v. Swartz, 156 U. S., 272 (1894); Gibson v. Mississippi, 162 U. S., 565 (1895).

32. Carter v. Texas, 177 U. S., 442 (1899); Charley Smith v. Mississippi, 162 U. S., 592 (1895); Murray v. Louisiana, 163 U. S., 101 (1895).

33. Williams v. Mississippi, 170 U. S., 213 (1898).

CHAPTER SEVEN

1. Charles H. Wesley, *Negro Labor in the United States, 1850–1925* (New York, 1927), pp. 1–115; Bell Irvin Wiley, *Southern Negroes, 1861–1865* (New Haven and London, 1938), especially pp. 55–62.

2. Leonard Price Stavisky, "Industrialism in Ante Bellum Charleston," *Journal of Negro History*, XXXVI (July, 1951), 302–321.

3. This paragraph and the following are based largely upon the excellent chapter, "Quasi-Free Negroes" in John Hope Franklin, *From Slavery to Freedom, A History of American Negroes* (New York, 1947).

4. Irving H. Bartlett, "The Free Negro in Providence, Rhode Island," *Negro History Bulletin*, XIV (December, 1950), 51–54, 66–67.

5. Luther P. Jackson, *Free Negro Labor and Property Holding in Virginia, 1830–1860* (New York, 1942); Franklin, *The Free Negro in North Carolina, 1790–1860* (Chapel Hill, 1943); Alice Dunbar-Nelson, "People of Color in Louisiana," *Journal of Negro History*, II (January, 1917), 71.

6. Albon P. Man, Jr., "Labor Competition and the New York Draft Riots of 1863," *Journal of Negro History*, XXXVI (October, 1951), 375–405.

7. Du Bois, *Black Reconstruction*, pp. 241–248.

8. Richardson, comp., *Messages*, VI, 401.

9. Paul S. Peirce, *The Freedmen's Bureau, A Chapter in the History of Reconstruction* (Iowa City, 1904); John William De Forest, *A Union Officer in the Reconstruction*, ed. by James H. Croushore and David M. Potter (New Haven and London, 1948).

10. Du Bois, *The Souls of Black Folk* (Chicago, 1903), p. 39.

11. See especially Du Bois, *Black Reconstruction*, pp. 352–358.

12. Wharton, *Negro in Mississippi*, p. 87; Simkins, *The South Old and New*, p. 183.

13. See especially James S. Russell, "Rural Economic Progress of the Negro in Virginia," *Journal of Negro History*, XI (October, 1926), 557; Franklin, *From Slavery to Freedom*, p. 308.

14. United States Bureau of the Census, *Negro Population in the United States, 1790–1915* (Washington, 1918), p. 460.

15. Simkins, *The South Old and New*, pp. 250–252.

16. Arna Bontemps and Jack Conroy, *They Seek a City* (Garden City, New York, 1945), p. 39.

17. Reports of Committees of Senate of the United States, 46th Cong., 2nd sess., 1879–1880. Report No. 693, Parts I, II and III.

18. Carter G. Woodson, ed., *Negro Orators and Their Orations* (Washington, 1925), pp. 453–487.

19. *Congressional Record*, 45th Cong., 3rd sess., pp. 1077–1082, 1808, 1877–1892; 46th Cong., 2nd sess., pp. 104, 124–125, 150–170.

20. See reference in footnote 17.

21. Corinne Hare Williams, "The Migration of Negroes to the West, 1877–1900, with Special Reference to Kansas," M. A. thesis, Howard University; Woodson, *A Century of Negro Migration* (Washington, 1918), pp. 126–142.

22. *Ibid.*, pp. 143–146.

23. Vicksburg *Daily Commercial*, May 6, 1879.

24. *Congressional Record*, 51st Cong., 1st sess., pp. 419–430, 623–630, 802–807, 966–973, 1046, 1988, 4364.

25. San Francisco *Examiner*, March 3, 1890, p. 1, news art.

26. Mozell Hill, "The All Negro Communities of Oklahoma: The Natural History of a Social Movement," *Journal of Negro History*, XXXI (July, 1946), 254–268.

27. New York *Times*, April 9, 1891, p. 9, news art.

28. *Ibid.*, February 26, 1894, p. 10, news art.

29. J. Fred Rippy, "A Negro Colonization Project in Mexico, 1895," *Journal of Negro History*, VI (January, 1921), 66–73.

30. New York *Times*, August 5, 1897, p. 5, news art.

31. *Ibid.*, February 12, 1878, p. 4, general notes; March 10, 1894, p. 3, news art.; November 15, p. 7, news art.; March 15, 1895, p. 10, news art.; November 8, 1897, p. 1, news art.

CHAPTER EIGHT

1. Du Bois, *Black Reconstruction*, pp. 212–219, 345–379.

2. Wesley, *Negro Labor*, pp. 157–180.

3. Du Bois, *Black Reconstruction*, pp. 684–693.

4. Sidney H. Kessler, "The Organization of Negroes by the Knights of Labor," *Journal of Negro History*, XXXVII (July, 1952), 248–276.

5. Jacob B. Hardman, *American Labor Dynamics* (New York, 1928), pp. 99–101.

6. Lewis L. Lorwin, *Labor and Industrialism* (New York, 1929), p. 23.

7. *Proceedings of the American Federation of Labor, 1889–1902* (Bloomington, Illinois, 1906), pp. 10–13, 31. See Beatrice H. Grevenberg, "A Study of the American Federation of Labor, 1881–1900," M. A. thesis, Howard University.

8. *Ibid., 1893*, p. 56; *1894*, p. 25.

9. F. E. Wolfe, *Admission to American Trade Unions* (Baltimore, 1912), pp. 112–134.

10. Washington *Star*, April 20, 1901, p. 8, news art.

11. Emma L. Fields, "The Women's Club Movement in the United States, 1877–1900," M. A. thesis, Howard University, pp. 59–102.

12. Andrew F. Hilyer, "Report of Committee on Business and Labor," *Proceedings*, Hampton Negro Conference of 1900 (Hampton, 1900), pp. 12–16.

13. Ira DeA. Reid, *Negro Membership in American Labor Unions* (New York, 1930), pp. 101–103.

14. Herbert R. Northrup, *Organized Labor and the Negro* (New York and London, 1944), pp. 17–47.

15. Walter L. Fleming, *Civil War and Reconstruction in Alabama* (New York, 1949), p. 324.

16. Wesley, *Negro Labor*, p. 317.

17. Alma Herbst, *The Negro in the Slaughtering and Meat-Packing Industry in Chicago* (Boston, 1932), pp. 3–20.

18. United States Bureau of the Census, *Occupations, 1890*, p. 19; *Occupations, 1900*, p. cv.

CHAPTER NINE

1. Parrington, *Beginnings of Critical Realism*, pp. 10–13, 54–56.

2. Sterling A. Brown, "Negro Character as Seen By White Authors," *Journal of Negro Education*, II (January, 1933), 180–201; Brown, *The Negro in American Fiction* (Washington, 1937); Brown, *Negro Poetry and Drama* (Washington, 1937).

3. Brown, *Negro in American Fiction*, pp. 67–69.

4. Helen Chesnutt, *Charles Waddell Chesnutt, Pioneer of the Color Line* (Chapel Hill, 1952).

5. The *North American*, June 2, 1900, p. 2, reported that the "Pickaninny Dance from the 'Runaway Girl' is exceedingly well executed."

6. Mary Frances Cowan, "The Negro in the American Drama, 1877–1900," M. A. thesis, Howard University.

7. Harry T. Peters, ed., *Currier & Ives, Printmakers to the American People* (New York, 1942), especially Plates 133, 134, 135.

8. Charles H. Hopkins, *The Rise of the Social Gospel in American Protestantism* (New Haven, 1940), especially pp. 3, 201.

9. Josiah Strong, *Our Country* (New York, 1885), pp. 175–178.

10. Elvena S. Bage, "Social Darwinism in the United States and Its Racial Implications," M. A. thesis, Howard University, especially Chapters III and V.

11. Commager, *The American Mind* (New Haven, 1950), p. 30.

CHAPTER TEN

1. Oberholtzer, *History of the United States*, II, 541.

2. These conclusions are based primarily upon an evaluation of the various papers. See also Joseph E. Chamberlin, *The Boston Evening Transcript* (Cambridge, 1930); Philip Kinsley, *The Chicago Tribune, Its First Hundred Years* (Chicago, 1946); Meyer Berger, *The Story of the New York Times, 1851–1951* (New York, 1951); "Centennial Supplement" of the *Enquirer*, April 10, 1941; *The Fiftieth Anniversary of the Washington Evening Star* (Washington, 1900). The *Evening Register* was selected in preference to the better known Hartford *Courant* because the Library of Congress does not have a complete file of the latter for the period.

3. *Evening Register*, February 17, 1879, p. 2; *Globe-Democrat*, February 7, p. 4; *Examiner*, February 4, p. 2. All references to newspapers are to editorials unless otherwise indicated.

4. *Times*, especially March 27, 1879, p. 1, news art.; March 27, p. 4; April 4, p. 4; April 19, p. 2, news art.; April 26, p. 1, news art.

5. Chicago *Tribune*, February 15, 1879, p. 4.

6. *Enquirer*, April 27, 1877, p. 4; February 11, 1879, p. 4; *Examiner*, February 6, p. 2; *Dispatch*, February 8, p. 2; *North American*, February 8, 1879, p. 2.

7. *Evening Register*, October 16, 1883, p. 2; *Times*, October 16, p. 2; *Enquirer*, October 16, p. 4; Chicago *Tribune*, October 17, p. 4; *Dispatch*, October 16, p. 3; *North American*, October 16, p. 1; *Star*, October 16, p. 1, news art. For the excerpts from the *World*, see the Chicago *Tribune*, October 16, p. 1.

8. *Enquirer*, October 17, 1883, p. 4; *Transcript*, October 16, p. 4; *Evening Register*, October 16, p. 2; *Journal*, October 17, p. 4.

9. *Transcript*, October 16, 1883, p. 4; *Enquirer*, October 17, p. 4; *Examiner*, October 17, p. 1, news art.

10. *Journal*, October 17, 1883, p. 4; *Enquirer*, October 17, p. 4; *North American*, October 17, p. 1; *Globe-Democrat*, October 17, p. 6. For the excerpt from the *Truth*, see the Chicago *Tribune*, October 16, p. 1.

11. *Post and Tribune*, October 17, 1883, p. 4.

12. Raymond B. Nixon, *Henry W. Grady, Spokesman of the New South* (New York, 1943), pp. 108–111, 127, 136.

13. *Times*, December 23, 1886, pp. 1–2, news art.

14. The number of guests has been estimated as high as 400. The actual count of dinner guests listed in the New York *Tribune*, December 23, 1886, p. 1, shows 238 persons at the dinner tables. There may have been others who sat in the audience.

15. See especially the *Journal*, December 28, 1886, p. 7; *Dispatch*, December 31, p. 4.

16. *Times*, December 23, 1886, pp. 1–2, news art. and p. 4; December 25 and 28, p. 1, news articles.

17. *Enquirer*, December 25, 1886, p. 4.

18. *Transcript*, December 24 and 27, 1886, p. 4.

19. *North American*, December 27, 1886, p. 2; *Star*, December 24, p. 6.

20. *Evening Register*, December 27, 28, 30, 1886, p. 2.

21. Detroit *Tribune*, December 27, 29, 31, 1886, p. 2; Chicago *Tribune*, December 24 and 30, p. 4.

22. *Globe-Democrat*, December 31, 1886, p. 6.

23. *Evening Register*, December 29, 1886, p. 3; *Times*, December 20, p. 5; December 25 and 28, p. 1; *North American*, December 21, p. 2; December 23 and 27, p. 1; *Star*, December 22, p. 1; December 23, p. 6; *Enquirer*, December 25, p. 9; *Dispatch*, December 25, p. 1; *Journal*, December 25, p. 1; December 26 and 29, p. 2; Chicago *Tribune*, December 22, p. 2; December 29, p. 9; *Globe-Democrat*, December 29, p. 3; *Examiner*, December 25, pp. 1, 2; December 26, p. 8; December 29, p. 1; all news articles.

24. *Times*, December 23, 1886, p. 3; *Globe-Democrat*, December 29, p. 3; news articles.

25. Woodward, *Origins of the New South* (Baton Rouge, 1952), pp. 130–148.

26. New York *Tribune*, December 20, 1886, p. 2; *Globe-Democrat*, December 23, p. 4; *Dispatch*, December 23, p. 6; Chicago *Tribune*, December 23, p. 10; news articles.

27. *Globe-Democrat*, December 29, 1886, p. 6.

28. *Ibid.*, December 29, p. 8; *Dispatch*, December 22, p. 1; Chicago *Tribune*, December 24, p. 1; *Journal*, December 27, p. 4; all news articles; *Examiner*, December 23, p. 4.

29. David W. Bishop, "The Attitude of the Interstate Commerce Commission towards Discrimination on Public Carriers, 1887–1910," M. A. thesis, Howard University.

30. *Transcript*, December 13, 1889, p. 4, news art.; Detroit *Tribune*, December 13, p. 1, news art.; *Star*, December 13, p. 4; *Enquirer*, December 15, p. 4; *Examiner*, December 13, p. 6; *North American*, December 13 and 18, p. 2; Chicago *Tribune*, December 16, 18, 25, 26, p. 4.

31. *Times*, December 25, 1889, p. 4.

32. *Globe-Democrat*, December 16, 1889, p. 4; December 20, p. 6.

33. *Dispatch*, December 30, 1889, p. 4.

CHAPTER ELEVEN

1. *Transcript*, March 20, 1890, p. 4; Chicago *Tribune*, March 22, p. 4. All newspaper references in this chapter are to editorials unless otherwise indicated.

2. *Evening Register*, March 20, 1890, p. 2; *Times*, March 21, p. 4; *North American*, March 21, p. 2; *Dispatch*, March 21, p. 4; *Enquirer*, March 7, p. 4; *Transcript*, March 20, p. 4; Chicago *Tribune*, March 22, p. 4.

3. *Journal*, July 3, 1890, p. 4; Detroit *Tribune*, July 3, p. 4; Chicago *Tribune*, July 2, p. 4.

4. *Transcript*, July 2, 1890, p. 4; *Star*, July 3, p. 4; *Globe-Democrat*, July 3, p. 6; *Enquirer*, July 3, p. 4.

5. *Evening Register*, July 3, 1890, p. 2; *Dispatch*, July 3, p. 4; *Examiner*, July 4, p. 6.

6. *Times*, July 3, 1890, p. 4.

7. *Transcript*, August 21 and 25, 1890, p. 4; Chicago *Tribune*, August 21, p. 4; *Journal*, August 26, p. 4; *Globe-Democrat*, September 8, p. 4.

8. *Times*, November 5, 1890, p. 4; *Star*, September 15, p. 4; *Globe-Democrat*, September 8, p. 4.

9. *Transcript*, August 25, 1890, p. 4; *Times*, November 5, p. 4; *Dispatch*, August 3, p. 4; Chicago *Tribune*, August 10, p. 12; Detroit *Tribune*, August 17, p. 4; *Globe-Democrat*, August 8, p. 6.

10. *Transcript*, October 3, 1890, p. 4; *Journal*, August 14, 25, 28, October 4, p. 4; Detroit *Tribune*, August 27 and September 13, p. 4.

11. Chicago *Tribune*, August 10, 1890, p. 12; *North American*, August 20, p. 4.

12. *Dispatch*, August 3, 19, 25, 1890; September 3, 19, 22, October 1; all on p. 4.

13. *Times*, August 3, 11, 1890; September 11, October 17, November 5, 13; all on p. 4.

14. *Transcript*, August 8, 16, 21, 25, 30, 1890; September 18, 24; October 3, 18; all on p. 4; Chicago *Tribune*, August 6, p. 4; August 10, p. 12; August 16, 25, September 20, 23, October 24, November 5; all on p. 4.

15. *Journal*, August 1, 8, 9, 14, 15, 16, 18, 20, 22, 23, 25, 26 (2 items), 27, 28 (2 items); September 2, 4, 6, 17 (2 items), 22, 24, 25 (2 items), 26, 27, 29; October 2; November 9, 1890; all on p. 4.

16. Detroit *Tribune*, August 17, 18, 22, 27; September 13 (2 items), 14, 15 (2 items), 22, 25 (3 items), 29 (2 items); October 2, 3 (2 items), 9, 1890; all on p. 4.

17. *Globe-Democrat*, August 5, 8, 18 (p. 4), 19, 22 (2 items), 23, 24, 26 (2 items), 27; September 4, 8, 9, 15 (p. 4), 27 (p. 4); October 7, 15; November 2, 14, 1890; all on p. 6 except where otherwise indicated. The view of Hoffman, which gained wide acceptance, was expressed in his *Race Traits and Tendencies of the American Negro*, American Economic Association Publication, XI, nos. 1–3 (New York, 1896).

18. Chicago *Tribune*, August 21, 1890, p. 4; *Journal*, September 25, p. 4; *North American*, August 21, p. 4; Detroit *Tribune*, September 22, p. 4.

19. *Journal*, January 27, 1891, p. 4; Detroit *Tribune*, January 28, p. 4.

20. Chicago *Tribune*, January 27, 1891, p. 4; *North American*, January 27, p. 4.

21. *Transcript*, January 27, 1891, p. 4; *Evening Register*, January 28, p. 2; *Star*, January 27, p. 4; *Enquirer*, January 25, p. 4; *Dispatch*, January 28, p. 4; *Globe-Democrat*, January 27, p. 4.

22. *Examiner*, January 18, 1891, p. 6; *Times*, January 27 and 29, p. 4.

23. *Examiner*, September 8, 1895, p. 6; *Enquirer*, October 2, 5 and 9, p. 4.

24. *Transcript*, September 19, 1895, p. 4; *Times*, September 13, October 1 and 18, p. 4.

25. *Star*, October 4 and November 2, 1895, p. 4; *Dispatch*, September 14, October 16 and 17, p. 4; Chicago *Tribune*, September 21, p. 12.

26. *Globe-Democrat*, September 23, 1895, p. 4; *North American*, September 30, 1895, p. 4, Editorial; *Journal*, September 19, 1895, p. 9, news art.; Detroit *Tribune*, October 10, p. 2.

27. Washington *Post*, April 14, 1896, p. 6; *Times*, May 19, pp. 1, 3, news articles; *Transcript*, May 19, p. 3, news art.; *Journal*, May 19, p. 5, news art.; *Star*, May 19, p. 8, news art.; *Globe-Democrat*, May 19, p. 7, news art.; May 21, p. 6; Chicago *Tribune*, May 19, p. 10, news art.; *Evening Register*, May 19, p. 6.

28. Booker T. Washington, *Story of My Life and Work* (Toronto and Naperville, Illinois, 1900), pp. 249–257; Mathews, *Washington*, pp. 206–207.

29. *Dispatch*, February 24, 1898, p. 4; *Evening Register*, February 24, p. 6; *Globe-Democrat*, February 10, p. 6, February 12, p. 8, February 23, p. 6, March 23, p. 6.

30. Chicago *Tribune*, February 15, 22, 25; March 1, 1898; all on p. 6; March 27, p. 34, news art.

31. *Journal*, March 2, 21, 24, 25, 28, 31, 1898; all on p. 4.

32. *Transcript*, March 2, 1898, p. 4 and March 26, p. 16.

33. *Evening Register*, August 3, 1900, p. 6.

34. *Times*, August 4, 1900, p. 6; *Star*, August 1, 3, 6, p. 6; *North American*, August 4, p. 6; Detroit *Tribune*, August 3, p. 4.

35. *Journal*, August 2 and 3, 1900, p. 4; Chicago *Tribune*, August 2 and 3, p. 4; *Transcript*, June 4, p. 8, June 5, p. 8, June 8, p. 9, news art.; August 3, p. 6.

CHAPTER TWELVE

1. See especially *Dispatch*, December 24, 1886, p. 2; December 27, p. 1; *North American*, September 21 and 27, 1895, p. 1; *Globe-Democrat*, September 21, p. 15, September 23, p. 10, September 27, p. 9; *Times*, September 19, p. 1. All the newspaper references in this chapter are to news articles unless otherwise indicated.

2. *Globe-Democrat*, especially September 21, 1895, p. 15; September 24, p. 2; September 24, p. 5; September 25, p. 3; September 26, p. 3; September 27, p. 3; September 28, p. 3.

3. *North American*, September 24, 1895, p. 1; *Enquirer*, September 21, p. 9; *Dispatch*, September 21, p. 10; *Star*, September 24, p. 3; *Journal*, September 25, 26 and 27, p. 8; *Times*, September 19, p. 16; *Globe-Democrat*, September 28, p. 3; Chicago *Tribune*, January 2, 1893, p. 10.

4. *Star*, June 4, 1900, p. 12; *Enquirer*, June 4, p. 8; June 6, p. 3; *Evening Register*, June 2, p. 7; Chicago *Tribune*, June 4, p. 1; June 13, p. 1; *North American*, June 2, p. 1, June 5, p. 3, and especially June 5, p. 5.

5. *Enquirer*, December 23, 1886, p. 1; Chicago *Tribune*, December 25, p. 5, December 26, pp. 2, 9; *Dispatch*, December 22, p. 1; *Journal*, December 25, p. 1, December 26, p. 2, December 29, p. 1; Detroit *Tribune*, December 22, p. 2; *Examiner*, December 25, p. 1, December 26, p. 8, December 29, p. 1; *North American*, September 23 and 27, 1895, p. 5; *Globe-Democrat*, December 29,

1886, p. 3, September 24, 1895, p. 1; September 25, p. 3; September 26, p. 6; September 28, p. 3; September 29, pp. 2, 3; September 30, p. 1; Chicago *Tribune*, September 26, p. 4; *Enquirer*, September 21 and 25, p. 1; September 27, p. 9; *North American*, June 1, 1900, p. 16; June 15, p. 4; *Enquirer*, June 2, p. 2; June 6, p. 7.

6. *Enquirer*, November 19, 1883, p. 1; December 23, 1886, p. 1; November 9, 1890, p. 9; February 21, 1892, p. 1; February 2, 1893, p. 1.

7. *Star*, April 19, 20 and 21, 1897, p. 11; April 23, pp. 2, 3; April 24, p. 10; April 27, p. 2; April 28, p. 1; June 4, p. 1.

8. *Transcript*, July 21, 1886, p. 1; *Times*, December 30, p. 3; December 31, p. 2; June 9, 1900, p. 2; *North American*, June 11, p. 3.

9. *Enquirer*, December 26, 1886, p. 2; Detroit *Tribune*, December 22, p. 2; Chicago *Tribune*, September 26, 1895, p. 4; *Transcript*, September 20 and 23, p. 8; *North American*, June 12, p. 5; *Enquirer*, June 6, p. 1; *Examiner*, June 3, p. 20; June 11, p. 7; *Times*, June 11, p. 1; *Evening Register*, June 11, p. 7.

10. *Enquirer*, September 21, 1895, p. 1; *Dispatch*, June 7, 1900, p. 4; *Transcript*, June 12, p. 8; *The New York Times*, June 4th, 1892, p. 4; September 22, 1893, p. 4; October 13, 1895, p. 4; June 5, 1897, p. 4; March 26, 1899, p. 18. All Editorials. Chicago *Tribune*, June 12, p. 6.

11. *Transcript*, September 25, 1895, p. 3.

12. *Dispatch*, September 26, p. 7; *Times*, December 28, 1886, p. 4; *Star*, January 1, March 6, 23, 30, April 1, 3, 5, 8, 1897, p. 3; *Enquirer*, December 23, 1886, p. 1; *Globe-Democrat*, September 24, 1895, p. 2; *Dispatch*, September 18, p. 1.

13. *Evening Register*, December 27, 1886, p. 2.

14. *Transcript*, July 10, 1886, p. 6.

15. *Star*, January 9, 1897, p. 14.

16. *Times*, December 23, 1886, p. 2; *Dispatch*, December 26, p. 15.

17. *Enquirer*, September 29, 1895, p. 20; *Star*, January 2, 1897, p. 24; *North American*, June 8, 1900, p. 11.

18. *Examiner*, December 23, 1886, p. 4; *Globe-Democrat*, December 27, p. 8; June 3, 1900, p. 9; Detroit *Tribune*, June 3, p. 17; *Enquirer*, June 31, p. 16.

19. *Times*, December 25, 1886, p. 4; *Star*, September 18, 1895, p. 4; September 25, pp. 6, 11; *Enquirer*, September 22, p. 4; *Star*, March 6, 23, 30, April 1, 5, 8, 1897, p. 4; June 12, 1900, p. 4; *Dispatch*, September 26, 1895, p. 2.

20. *Enquirer*, September 21, 1895, p. 1; September 22, pp. 26, 28; Chicago *Tribune*, July 28, p. 33; September 29, p. 34; April 22, 1900, p. 66; April 29, p. 62; May 6, p. 66; *Globe-Democrat*, September 29, 1895, p. 32; June 10, 1900, Part 3, p. 13; *Enquirer*, September 29, 1895, p. 28; June 10, 1900, p. 34.

21. *Star*, September 21, 1886, p. 6; *Globe-Democrat*, December

23, p. 4; *North American,* December 29, p. 2; *Times,* December 31, p. 1; *Evening Register,* September 18, 1895, p. 1; *Transcript,* September 19, p. 7; *Globe-Democrat,* September 17, p. 2.

22. For a discussion of the incident, see Edmonds, *Negro and Fusion Politics,* pp. 42–43.

23. *Enquirer,* February 21, 1895, p. 1; February 25 (2 items), p. 4; *Evening Register,* February 21, p. 3; *Globe-Democrat,* February 21, p. 2; February 25, p. 4; Chicago *Tribune,* February 21 and 22, p. 2; February 22, ed., p. 6; Detroit *Tribune,* February 22, pp. 1, 2; February 22, ed., p. 4; February 24 and 25, p. 1; February 26, p. 3; *Transcript,* February 21, ed., p. 4; February 21, p. 10; *Journal,* February 21, pp. 1–2, February 21, p. 4, ed.; February 22 and 27, p. 4; *Star,* February 21, p. 6, ed.; February 21, p. 9; February 25, p. 1, letter; February 25, p. 6, February 26, p. 1; *Times,* February 21, pp. 1, 3; February 22 (2 items), p. 3; February 23, p. 4, ed.

24. *Times,* January 6, 1887, p. 5; July 7, p. 4, ed.; July 1, 1889, p. 1; April 28, p. 9; October 2, 1894, p. 4, ed.; June 16, 1895, p. 16; June 18, p. 4, ed.; June 19, p. 3; July 14, p. 17; October 18, 1896, p. 7; *North American,* June 14, 1900, p. 9; Chicago *Tribune,* June 10 and 11, 1896, p. 6, eds.; October 24, 1896, p. 1; *Enquirer,* November 24, 1897, p. 4, ed.; March 3, 1880, p. 4; March 21, p. 4; May 13, 1882, p. 1; November 22, 1889, p. 4, ed.; August 7, 1891, p. 4, ed.; September 13, 1895, p. 1.

25. *Examiner,* June 12, 1888, p. 5; December 29, p. 1; July 21, 1896, p. 10; November 5, p. 10; *Times,* October 2, 1897, p. 17; *Globe-Democrat,* December 28, 1886, p. 3; *Star,* September 25, 1895, p. 2.

26. *Evening Reigster,* September 16, 1895, p. 2; September 17, p. 1; *Times,* September 20, p. 14; *Transcript,* June 25, p. 6; *Globe-Democrat,* September 25, p. 6; Chicago *Tribune,* September 25, p. 9; October 12, 1897, p. 1; *Enquirer,* February 26 and March 26, 1887, p. 4, eds.; June 1, p. 8; June 21, p. 4; December 13, p. 4, ed.; December 5, 1888 (2 items), p. 2; December 8, p. 9; January 24, 1889, p. 4, ed.; March 16, 1889, p. 1; September 15, 1900, p. 1; June 1, 1900, p. 7.

27. *Examiner,* September 20, 1895, p. 1; Chicago *Tribune,* September 20, p. 1.

28. Emma L. Fields, "The Women's Club Movement in the United States, 1877–1900," M. A. thesis, Howard University.

29. The best coverage was given by the Chicago *Tribune, Globe-Democrat* and *Dispatch,* June 3–13, 1900.

30. See especially the *Dispatch,* June 6, 1900, p. 7; the *Globe-Democrat,* June 5th and 9th, 1900, p. 5; Milwaukee *Journal,* June 8, 1900, p. 8, news art.; *Transcript,* June 11, 1900, p. 6, June 8, p. 12, editorials.

31. *Chicago Tribune,* June 10, 1900, p. 36, letter.

32. *Ibid.,* June 10, 1900, p. 5.

CHAPTER THIRTEEN

1. "One Hundred Years of *Harper's*," *Harper's Magazine* (Centennial Issue, 1850–1950), CCI (October, 1950), 32; Commager, *American Mind*, pp. 74–75.

2. Chesnutt, *Chesnutt*, p. 95.

3. Editor's Drawer, *Harper's*, LXXIV (May, 1887), 993 (italics as in original); Unsigned, "Studies in the South," *Atlantic Monthly*, XLIX (February, 1882), 183.

4. A. Van Cleef, "Barbadoes," *Harper's*, LIV (February, 1877), 387.

5. James D. Corrothers, "A Thanksgiving Turkey," *Century*, LXI (November, 1900), 154; Editor's Drawer, *Harper's*, LXVII (June, 1883), 162; Thomas Nelson Page, "The Story of Charlie Harris," *ibid.*, LXXXVI (April, 1893), 804–805; Ruth McEnery Stuart, "Lamentations of Jeremiah Johnson," *ibid.*, LXXVI (May, 1888), 863–869; A South Carolinian, "The Political Condition of South Carolina," *Atlantic Monthly*, XXXIX (February, 1877), 177–194; A South Carolinian, "South Carolina Society," *ibid.*, (June, 1877), 670–684; Jeremiah S. Black, "The Electoral Conspiracy," *North American Review*, CXXV (July-August, 1877), 1–34.

6. Cartoons, *Century*, LV (January, 1898), 480 and XXXIII (January, 1887), 495; P. Y. P., "Ginger and the Goose," *Harper's*, LXIV (March, 1882), 633–640; Thomas Nelson Page, "The True Story of the Surrender of the Marquis Cornwallis," *ibid.*, LXXXV (November, 1892), 968–969; William W. Archer, "Lazarus Mart'n, de Cullud Lieyer," *Atlantic Monthly*, LIX (April, 1887), 479–491.

7. Charles Battell Loomis, "Bruddeh Isaac's Discourse," *Century*, XLV (April, 1893), 959; Edward Eggleston, "Parsons and Parsons," *Scribner's*, XVII (November, 1878), 139; Merland M. Turner, "The Negro as Portrayed in *Harper's New Monthly Magazine*, 1877–1901," M. A. thesis, Howard University, p. 22.

8. Ruth McEnery Stuart, "A Pulpit Orator," *Harper's*, LXXXVIII (March, 1894), 643–645.

9. Frank R. Stockton, "A Story of Seven Devils," *Century*, XXXI (November, 1885), 99–102; Thomas Nelson Page, "P'laski's Tunaments," *Harper's*, LXXXII (December, 1890), 111–118.

10. Albert Bigelow Paine, "Pointed Arguments," *Century*, LX (June, 1900), 314–318.

11. Editor's Drawer, "Colored Debating Society of Mt. Vernon, Ohio," *Harper's*, LVI (April, 1878), 796–797; see also, Harry Stillwell Edwards, "The Gum Swamp Debate," *Century*, L (September, 1895), 798–800.

12. P. S. M., "Voodooism in Tennessee," *Atlantic Monthly*, LXIV (September, 1889), 376–380; *ibid.*, LXXV (January, 1895),

136–144 and (May, 1895), 714–720. The four stories by Virginia Frazer Boyle in *Harper's* are found in C (December, 1899), 58–68, (January, 1900), 217–223; CI (July, 1900), 416–422 and (September, 1900), 597–602.

13. Unsigned, *op. cit.*, pp. 76–91. For Mrs. Stuart, see, for example: "Apollo Belvedere," *Harper's*, XCVI (December, 1897), 155–158; "Moriah's Mo'nin'," XCII (January, 1896), 321–323.

14. Irwin Russell, "Mahsr John," *Scribner's*, XIV (May, 1877), 127; A. C. Gordon, "De Ole 'Oman an' Me," *ibid.*, XV (March, 1878), 752. See also W. P. Carter, " 'Ole Marster.' ('Fo' de Wah)," *Harper's*, LXIX (September, 1884), 484.

15. Editor's Drawer, "Kentucky Philosophy," *Harper's*, LXV (September, 1882), 645.

16. Harrison Roberts, "Sunday Fishin'," *ibid.* (October, 1882), 806–807.

17. Opie P. Reade, "Cotton is All Dun Picked," *ibid.*, LXXV (November, 1887), 971; S. C. Cromwell, "Corn-Shucking Song," *ibid.*, LXIX (October, 1884), 807.

18. Maurice Thompson, "The Balance of Power," *ibid.*, XC (April, 1895), 796–804.

19. *Century*, XXXI (November, 1885), 159; XXXIII (November, 1886), 159; XXXIV (September, 1887), 799; XXXIII (February, 1887), 655; LX (September, 1900), 648.

20. *Harper's*, LIV (April, 1877), 783; C (April, 1900), 651 and 809.

21. A South Carolinian, "South Carolina Society," *Atlantic Monthly*, XXXIX (June, 1877), p. 684.

22. Thomas Nelson Page, "Relius," *Harper's*, LXXXV (July, 1892), 320–321; Page, "Ole 'Stracted," *ibid.*, LXXIII (October, 1886), 697–703; Page, "Unc' Edinburg's Drowndin'," *ibid.*, LXII (January, 1886), 304–315; Page, "Polly: A Christmas Recollection," *ibid.*, LXXIV (December, 1886), 37–52.

23. Boyle, "A Kingdom for Micajah," *ibid.*, C (March, 1900), 389–393.

24. Book review, "Harris's Uncle Remus: His Songs and Sayings," *Scribner's*, XXI (April, 1881), 961–962; Editor's Drawer, *Harper's*, LXII (February, 1881), 479.

25. Joel Chandler Harris, "Ananias," *Harper's*, LXXVI (April, 1888), 699–708; Harris, "Free Joe and the Rest of the World," *Century*, XXIX (November, 1884), 117–123; Harris, "The Baby's Christmas," *ibid.*, XLVII (December, 1893), 284–292.

26. Constance Fenimore Woolson, "Rodman the Keeper," *Atlantic Monthly*, XXXIX (March, 1887), 261–277; Boyle, "Penny Wise," *ibid.*, LXXV (April, 1900), 518–530; E. M. De Jarnette, "Cream-White and Crow-Black," *ibid.*, LII (October, 1883), 470–474; A. C. Gordon, "A Pinchtown Pauper," *ibid.*, LX (September, 1887), 326–327; "Recent Literature," *ibid.*, XXIX

(March, 1887), 370. Others are briefly mentioned in Mary E. Waters, "The Negro as Portrayed in the *Atlantic Monthly*, 1877–1900," M. A. thesis, Howard University.

27. James Parton, "Antipathy to the Negro," *North American Review*, CXXVII (November-December, 1878), 476–491; J. W. Watson, "With Four Great Men," *ibid.*, CXLVII (November, 1888), 588–591; Edmund Kirke, "How Shall the Negro Be Educated?," *ibid.*, CXLIII (November, 1886), 421–426.

28. Charles Gayarré, "The Southern Question," *ibid.*, CXXV (November-December, 1877), 488; Jefferson Davis, "Robert E. Lee," *ibid.*, CL (January, 1890), 55–66; Parton, *op cit.*, p. 488; Kirke, *op. cit.*, p. 428.

29. Thomas Wentworth Higginson, "Some War Scenes Revisited," *Atlantic Monthly*, XLII (July, 1878), 1–9; A South Carolinian, "South Carolina Society," *Atlantic Monthly*, XXXIX (June, 1877), pp. 670–684; Unsigned, "Presidential Electioneering in the Senate," *ibid.*, XLIII (March, 1879), 369–376; Unsigned, "The Political Attitude of the South," *ibid.*, XLV (June, 1880), 817–823; Unsigned, "A Look Ahead," *ibid.*, XLVII (January, 1881), 103–108.

30. Richard Dana, Jr., "Points in American Politics," *North American Review*, CXXIV (January-February, 1877), 1–30; Black, *op. cit.*, pp. 1–34; Gayarré, *op. cit.*, pp. 472–498; David Dudley Field, "Centralization in the Federal Government," *North American Review*, CXXXII (May, 1881), 407–426; Cassius M. Clay, "Race and the Solid South," *ibid.*, CXLII (February, 1886), 134–138; M. E. Ingalls, "The Duty of the Democrats," *ibid.*, CLXXI (September, 1900), 296–301.

31. See the articles, "Ought the Negro to Be Disfranchised?; Ought He to Have Been Enfranchised?," *ibid.*, CXVIII (March, 1879), 225–283; see also H. H. Chalmers, "The Effects of Negro Suffrage," *ibid.*, CXXXII (March, 1881), 239–248; J. Harris Patton, "Notes and Comments," *ibid.*, CXLII (May, 1886), 516–517.

32. George Washington Cable, "The Freedman's Case in Equity," *Century*, XXIX (January, 1885), 409–418.

33. Henry W. Grady, "In Plain Black and White," *ibid.* (April, 1885), 909–917.

34. "Topics of the Time," *ibid.*, XXX (May, 1885), 164–165; Cable, "The Silent South," *ibid.*, XXX (September, 1885), 674–691.

35. "Topics of the Time," "Marriage and Divorce Again," *ibid.*, XXXII (October, 1886), 958.

36. Wilbur F. Tillett, "The White Man of the New South," *ibid.*, XXXIII (March, 1887), 769–776; "Topics of the Time," *ibid.*, (March, 1887), 807–808.

37. Charles D. Warner, "Impressions of the South," *Harper's*, LXXI (September, 1885), 546–551; Rebecca Harding Davis,

"Some Testimony in the Case," *Atlantic Monthly*, LVI (November, 1885), 602–609; Gail Hamilton, "Race Prejudice," *North American Review*, CXLI (November, 1885), 475–479; Murat Halstead, "The Revival of Sectionalism," *ibid.*, CXL (March, 1885), 237–250; Thomas Nelson Page, "Southerner on the Negro Question," *ibid.*, CLIX (April, 1892), 402–413.

38. The portrayal of the Negro in the *Forum* was investigated by Alexander Woodhouse, a graduate student at Howard University.

39. Thomas B. Reed, "The Federal Control of Elections," *North American Review*, CL (June, 1890), 671–680; Henry Cabot Lodge and Terence V. Powderly, "The Federal Election Bill," *ibid.*, CLI (September, 1890), 257–273; A. W. Shaffer, "A Southern Republican on the Lodge Bill," *ibid.* (November, 1890), 601–609; James McMillan, R. P. Bland, Benton McMillin and others, "Issues of the Presidential Campaign," *ibid.*, CLIV (March, 1892), 257–280; James Bryce, "Thoughts on the Negro Problem," *ibid.*, CLIII (December, 1891), 641–660; J. M. Stone, "The Suppression of Lawlessness," *ibid.*, CLVIII (April, 1894), 500–506; Walter C. Hamm, "The Three Phases of Colored Suffrage," *ibid.*, CLXVIII (March, 1899), 285–296; George F. Hoar, "President M'Kinley or President Bryan?," *ibid.*, CLXXI (October, 1900), 473–486.

40. Among the numerous articles are the following: Booker T. Washington, "Signs of Progress among the Negroes," *Century*, LIX (January, 1900), 472–478; Washington, "Education Will Solve the Race Problem, A Reply," *North American Review*, CLXXI (August, 1900), 221–232; Richard T. Auchumuty, "The Need of Trade Schools," *Century*, XXXIII (November, 1886), 83–92.

41. Washington, "The Awakening of the Negro," *Atlantic Monthly*, LXXVIII (September, 1896), 322–328.

42. E. W. Gilliam, "The African Problem," *North American Review*, CXXXIX (November, 1884), 417–430; Frederick Douglass, "Lynch Law in the South," *ibid.*, CLV (July, 1892), 17–24; W. Cabell Bruce, "Lynch Law in the South," *ibid.* (September, 1892), 379–381; Cesare Lombroso, "Why Homicide Has Increased in the United States," *ibid.*, CLXV (December, 1897), 641–648; Marion L. Dawson, "The South and the Negro," *ibid.*, CLXXII (February, 1901), 279–284; Washington, *A Reply*, pp. 221–232.

43. Thomas Nelson Page, *A Southerner on the Negro Question*, pp. 411–412; Edward W. Blyden, "The African Problem," *North American Review*, CLXI (September, 1895), 327–339; John Roach Straton, "Will Education Solve the Race Problem?," *ibid.*, CLXX (June, 1900), 800–801.

44. Richard Hofstadter, *Social Darwinism in American Thought, 1860–1915* (Philadelphia and London, 1944); Josiah Strong, *Our Country* (New York, 1885).

45. R. W. Wright, "Richmond Since the War," *Scribner's*, XIV

(July, 1877), 311–312; Herbert H. Smith, "The Metropolis of the Amazons," *ibid.*, XVIII (May, 1879), 65–77; Edmund Clarence Stedman, "Christophe," *Century*, XXIII (November, 1881), 34–35.

46. Editor's Drawer, "The Origin of Man by Darwin," *Harper's*, LV (October, 1877), 637–638.

47. Gayarré, *op. cit.*, pp. 494–497.

48. W. Henry Holland, "Heredity," *Atlantic Monthly*, LII (October, 1883), 452; H. H. Chalmers, *op. cit.*, pp. 239–248, italics as in the original; Hofstadter, *Social Darwinism*, p. 153.

49. Bryce, *op. cit.*, pp. 641–660; Thomas Nelson Page, *A Southerner on the Negro Question*, pp. 411–413; Theodore Roosevelt, "Kidd's 'Social Evolution,'" *North American Review*, CLXI (July, 1895), 94–109; Dawson, "Will the South Be Solid Again?," *ibid.*, CLXIV (February, 1897), 193–198; Straton, *op. cit.*, pp. 784–801; Washington, *A Reply*, pp. 221–232.

50. Poultney Bigelow, "White Man's Africa," *Harper's*, XCIV (January, 1897), 775–789; Marquis of Lorne, "The Partition of Africa," *North American Review*, CLI (December, 1890), 701–712; W. Garden Blaikie, "Central Africa Since the Death of Livingstone," *ibid.*, CLXV (September, 1897), 318–322; E. J. Glave, "Glave in the Heart of Africa," *Century*, LII (October, 1896), 918–933; Glave, "New Conditions in Central Africa," *ibid.*, LIII (April, 1897), 900–915; Henry M. Stanley, "The Story of the Development of Africa," *ibid.*, LI (February, 1896), 500–509; Henry Rutgers Marshall, "Rudyard Kipling and Racial Instincts," *ibid.*, LVIII (July, 1899), 375–377.

51. Leonard Wood, "The Existing Conditions and Needs in Cuba," *North American Review*, CLXVIII (May, 1899), 593–601; see other articles listed in Betty R. Jordan, "The Negro as Portrayed in the *North American Review*, 1877–1900," M. A. thesis at Howard University. See also Herbert Pelham Williams, "The Outlook in Cuba," *Atlantic Monthly*, LXXXIII (June, 1899), 827–836 and Queen C. Green, "The Negro as Portrayed in *Scribner's Monthly* and *Century*, 1877–1901," M. A. thesis at Howard University.

52. G. G. Vest, "Objections to Annexing the Philippines," *North American Review*, CLXVIII (January, 1899), 112–120; B. R. Tillman, "Causes of Southern Opposition to Imperialism," *ibid.*, CLXXI (October, 1900), 439–446; Carl Schurz, "Thoughts on American Imperialism," *Century*, LVI (September, 1898), 781–788.

53. Purvis M. Carter, "The Astigmatism of the Social Gospel, 1877–1901," M. A. thesis at Howard University.

54. Ira V. Brown, "Lyman Abbott and Freedmen's Aid, 1865–1869," *Journal of Southern History*, XV (February, 1949), 23–38. Professor Brown generously permitted the author to use relevant parts of his manuscript which was published by the Harvard Uni-

versity Press under the title *Lyman Abbott, Christian Evolutionist: A Study in Religious Liberalism*, 1953.

55. Lyman Abbott, "Our Indian Problem," *North American Review*, CLXVII (December, 1898), 719–728; *Outlook*, LXVII (April, 1901), 948.

56. William Warren Sweet, *Makers of Christianity* (New York, 1937), III, 320.

CHAPTER FOURTEEN

1. Mathews, *Washington*, pp. 3–82.

2. *Ibid.*, pp. 82–93.

3. Not all Negroes had been "ignorant and inexperienced," as even Samuel D. Smith, *Negroes in Congress*, recognizes.

4. This myth has been exploded by Bell Irvin Wiley, *Southern Negroes*, Chapter IV.

5. The address may be conveniently consulted in Woodson, ed., *Negro Orators and Their Orations*, pp. 580–583.

6. *Constitution*, September 19, 1895, p. 1, news art.; *Daily Register*, September 19, p. 1; *Picayune*, September 19, p. 1; *News and Courier*, September 19, p. 1. *Memphis Commercial Appeal*, September 19, 1895, p. 1, news art. All newspaper references in this chapter are to editorials unless otherwise indicated.

7. *World*, September 19, p. 1.

8. *Constitution*, September 20, p. 4.

9. *Ibid.*, October 5, 1895, p. 6.

10. *Daily Register*, September 19–October 19, 1895; *Age-Herald*, same dates; *Picayune*, especially September 25, p. 4.

11. *News and Courier*, September 19–October 19, 1895.

12. *Courier-Journal*, September 22, 1895, p. 6.

13. *Transcript*, September 20, 1895, p. 4.

14. *Evening Register*, September 19, 1895, p. 2.

15. *North American*, September 30, 1895, p. 4; *Dispatch*, September 19, p. 4; *Journal*, September 23, p. 4.

16. Chicago *Tribune*, September 19, 1895, p. 4; *Constitution*, September 20, p. 4.

17. *Constitution*, September 20, p. 4; *Globe-Democrat*, September 24, p. 6.

18. *Examiner*, September 24, 1895, p. 6; *Star*, September 19, p. 4.

19. Detroit *Tribune*, October 6, 1895, p. 2.

20. Horace Mann Bond, *Negro Education in Alabama* (Washington, 1939), pp. 159–163.

21. *Constitution*, September 11, 1895, p. 2, news art.; September 20, p. 4.

22. *Ibid.*, September 15–October 15, 1895.

23. *Loc. cit.*

24. For a sketch of Henson, see *Life*, May 14, 1951, p. 87.

25. *Constitution*, September 15–October 15, 1895.

26. *News and Courier*, September 15–October 15, 1895.

27. *Loc. cit.*

28. *Loc. cit.*

29. *Loc. cit.*

30. *Ibid.*, especially September 22, 1895, p. 6.

31. *Ibid.*, September 15–October 15, 1895.

32. *Daily Register*, especially September 24, 1895, news art.; October 9, p. 3; October 10, p. 1, news art.; October 11, p. 2, news art.; October 13, p. 4; October 15, p. 3, news art.; October 18, p. 1, news art.

33. *Ibid.*, September 27, 1895, p. 1, news art.; October 12, p. 3, news art.

34. *Age-Herald*, September 12, 1895, pp. 1, 2, 5, news articles; September 15, pp. 1, 6, 10; September 16, p. 2; September 17, p. 8; September 18, pp. 1, 2, 3; all news articles.

35. *Ibid.*, September 12, 1895, pp. 1, 5, news articles; September 14, p. 4; September 14, p. 5.

36. *Picayune*, September 11, 1895, p. 4; October 3, p. 4.

37. *Ibid.*, September 11–October 18, 1895.

38. *Loc. cit.*

39. *Loc. cit.*

40. *Loc. cit.*

41. *Loc. cit.*

42. *Commercial Appeal*, especially September 12, 1895, p. 1; September 13, p. 3; September 18, p. 1; September 22, p. 5; September 23, p. 5; September 28, p. 3; September 30, p. 5; October 5, p. 1; October 6, p. 1; all news articles; October 6, p. 4; October 7, p. 1, news art.; October 8, p. 4.

43. *Ibid.*, especially September 14, 1895, p. 3; September 15, p. 5; September 16, p. 4; September 17, p. 5; September 18, p. 2; September 20, p. 5; September 23, p. 2; September 24, p. 2; September 26, pp. 2, 3; September 27, p. 3; September 29, p. 5; September 30, pp. 2, 4; all news articles.

44. *Ibid.*, especially September 12, 1895, p. 2; September 21, p. 2, news articles; September 22, letter; September 24, 30, October 2, all news articles, p. 2.

45. Speer's oration was printed in full in the *Daily Register*, September 19, 1895, pp. 1–2.

46. See also the brief comment in Sterling D. Spero and Abram L. Harris, *The Black Worker* (New York, 1931), p. 50.

47. Washington, *Story of My Life and Work*, pp. 187–191.

48. Washington, "Education and Suffrage for Negroes," *Education*, XIX (September, 1898), 49–50.

50. See especially *North American*, September 30, 1895, p. 4; Detroit *Tribune*, September 19, p. 6, news art.; *Examiner*, Sep-

tember 24, p. 6, news art.; Chicago *Tribune*, September 21, p. 4, news art.

51. *Transcript*, September 21, 1895, p. 14 (italics not in the original); *Evening Register*, September 19, p. 2.

52. *North American*, September 30, 1895, p. 4; *Globe-Democrat*, September 24, p. 6.

53. *Times*, September 19, 1895, p. 5, news art.

54. *Enquirer*, September 1, 1895, p. 1, news art.

55. See especially *Evening Register*, September 24, 1895, p. 2; *Examiner*, September 20, p. 6.

56. *Evening Register*, September 24, 1895, p. 2; *Globe-Democrat*, September 20, p. 6, news art.; September 22, p. 6, news art.

57. See especially *North American*, June 6, 1900, p. 11, news art.; *Enquirer*, June 7, p. 7 and June 8, p. 2, news articles; *Times*, June 7, p. 3, news art.; Chicago *Tribune*, June 4, p. 5, news art.; *Globe-Democrat*, June 8, p. 7, news art.

CHAPTER FIFTEEN

1. Wilhelmina I. Barnett, "The American Negro, 1878–1900, as Portrayed in the San Francisco *Examiner*," M. A. thesis, Howard University, especially pp. 33–47.

2. Shirley M. Smith, "The Negro, 1877–1898, as Portrayed in the Cincinnati *Enquirer*," M. A. thesis, Howard University, especially Chapter V.

3. Kathryn M. Leigh, "The American Negro, 1877–1900, as Portrayed in the New York *Times*," M. A. thesis, Howard University, especially Chapter IV.

4. Ercell I. Watson, "The American Negro, 1890–1899, as Portrayed in the Chicago *Tribune* and in the House of Representatives," M. A. thesis, Howard University, especially Chapter V.

5. Jacqueline L. Jones, "The American Negro, 1877–1900, as Portrayed in the Boston Evening *Transcript*," M. A. thesis, Howard University, especially Chapter V.

6. Romaine F. Scott, "The Negro in American History, 1877–1900, as Portrayed in the Washington *Evening Star*," M. A. thesis, Howard University, especially Chapter V.

7. *Time*, June 11, 1951, p. 93.

8. Leinster H. Moseley, "The Negro as Portrayed in the New York *Globe*, New York *Freeman* and New York *Age*, 1883–1892," M. A. thesis, Howard University, *passim*.

9. I. Garland Penn, *The Afro-American Press and Its Editors* (Springfield, 1891), pp. 280–292.

10. Dorothy H. Cunningham, "An Analysis of the *A. M. E. Church Review*, 1884–1900," M. A. thesis, Howard University.

11. Woodson, *The History of the Negro Church* (2nd ed., Washington, 1921), especially Chapters VIII and IX.

12. Du Bois, *Souls of Black Folk*, p. 37.

13. Abram L. Harris, *The Negro as Capitalist* (Philadelphia, 1936), pp. 194–195.

14. Robert Kinzer and Edward Sagarin, *The Negro in American Business* (New York, 1950), pp. 102–110.

15. J. H. Harmon, A. G. Lindsay and C. G. Woodson, *The Negro as a Business Man* (Washington, 1929).

16. Kinzer and Sagarin, *Negro in American Business*, pp. 92–101.

17. U. S. Bureau of the Census. Abstract Eleventh and Twelfth Censuses.

18. Lawrence J. W. Hayes, *The Negro Federal Government Worker* (Washington, 1941).

19. Genevieve Swann Brown, "An Analytical and Statistical Study of Higher Education for Negroes during the Period 1877–1900," M. A. thesis, Howard University.

20. Ellis O. Knox, "State-Supported Colleges for Negroes," *Negro History Bulletin*, XIV (January, 1951), 75–79, 88–89.

21. Beale, *On Rewriting Reconstruction History*, p. 809.

22. Hugh M. Gloster, *Negro Voices in American Fiction* (Chapel Hill, 1948), pp. 30–34.

23. *Ibid.*, pp. 34–43, 261.

24. Brown, *Negro Poetry and Drama*, pp. 11–12.

25. James A. Porter, *Modern Negro Art* (New York, 1943), pp. 54–77.

26. Wesley, *Negro Labor*, pp. 177–189.

27. See the theses listed in footnotes 1, 2, 3, 4, 5, 6 and 7.

28. Emma L. Fields, "The Women's Club Movement in the United States, 1877–1900," M. A. thesis, Howard University.

29. Mark D. Brown, "The Negro in the United States Army, 1866–1898," M. A. thesis, Howard University.

CHAPTER SIXTEEN

1. Dr. Callis, the author's personal physician, has spent hours discussing with him the "convalescence" of the nation.

2. For additional discussion of the concept, prior to 1925, *see* Rayford W. Logan, "The Historical Setting of *The New Negro*," in Logan *et. al.*, eds., *The New Negro Thirty Years Afterward* (Washington, 1955), p. 18.

3. Dr. Du Bois announced late in 1961 that he had applied for membership in the Communist Party (New York *Times*, November 23, 1961, p. 5). But Du Bois must be judged in terms of his views at any given time.

4. Bishop Alexander Walters, *My Life and Work* (New York, 1917), p. 257.

5. W. E. Burghardt Du Bois, *The Souls of Black Folk: Essays and Sketches* (Chicago, 1903), pp. 13, 53, 59.

6. For the full text of the resolutions, see Du Bois, *Dusk of Dawn: An Essay Toward an Autobiography of a Race Concept* (New York, 1940), pp. 89–92. Many friends of Du Bois, including John Hope, president of Morehouse College and Atlanta University, have spoken of this arrogance. I first met Du Bois at the Second Pan-African Congress in Paris, 1921. If the difficulties which he had with Blaise Diagne, Deputy from Senegal, were typical of his quarrels with Monroe Trotter and others within the Niagara Movement, Du Bois' inability to work harmoniously with them is not surprising.

7. Francis Broderick, *W. E. B. Du Bois, Negro Leader in a Time of Crisis* (Stanford, 1959).

8. Charles H. Wesley, *History of Sigma Pi Phi* (Washington, 1954), p. 52.

9. Wesley, *The History of Alpha Phi Alpha* (Washington, 1935), *passim.*

10. Booker T. Washington Papers, Library of Congress, Container 1095.

11. See above, pp. 276-281.

12. Washington Papers, Library of Congress, Containers 955–958.

13. For an excellent summary, see C. Vann Woodward, *Origins of the New South, 1877–1913* (Baton Rouge, 1951).

14. Kirk H. Porter, comp., *National Party Platforms* (New York, 1924), pp. 232, 263. For earlier platforms, see above, pp. 24, 48–49, 57–58, 61, 63, 86, 89, 95–96, 101–102.

15. *Ibid.*, p. 305.

16. This system, legalized in the Southern states, authorized the employment of imprisoned Negroes by private individuals and corporations for the period of their sentence. See Matthew B. Hammond, *The Cotton Industry: An Essay in American Economic History* (New York, 1897), p. 149, and Fletcher M. Green, ed., "Some Aspects of the Southern Convict Lease System in the Southern States," in *Essays . . . to Joseph Gregoire de Roulhac Hamilton . . .* (Chapel Hill, 1949).

17. Porter, *op. cit.*, p. 281. The role of several minor parties had little influence on the outcome of these elections. Even they rarely spoke in their platforms about the rights of Negroes. *Ibid.*, pp. 217–298, *passim.*

18. It was a dinner and not a luncheon despite the attempt of some Southerners who believed that a luncheon constituted a less grievous assault upon social equality than did a dinner. In addition to contemporary newspaper evidence—e.g., New York *Times*, October 19, 1901—Emmett J. Scott, Washington's close friend who was in Washington at the time, told me that it was a dinner.

19. "A Canvass for Opinion," *Voice of the Negro*, II (1905), 827.

20. See below, pp. 350.

21. William Howard Taft, *Political Issues and Outlooks* (New York, 1909), pp. 231, 237.

22. Jessie P. Guzman, ed., *Negro Year Book* (11th ed., New York, 1952), p. 278; Southern Commission on the Study of Lynching, *Lynchings and What They Mean* (Atlanta, 1931), pp. 8–10.

23. The *Evening Star*, August 17, 1904, p. 13, news art.

24. United States of America v. John F. Shipp *et al.*, *United States Supreme Court Reporter*, 27 (October Term, 1906), 165–167; United States of America v. Joseph H. Shipp *et al.*, *ibid.*, 30 (October Term, 1909), 397; The *Evening Star*, March 20, 1906, p. 17, news art.; November 15, 1909, p. 2, news art., December 31, 1909, news art.; November 16, 1909, p. 6, editorial.

25. Porter, *op. cit.*, pp. 233, 258–265, 299, 305 for the Republican platforms and pp. 210–217, 245, 249, 259, 281 for the Democratic. The minor parties were equally silent, *ibid.*, pp. 217–223, 238–243, 254–256, 286–297, 311–319.

26. *Congressional Record*, 60th Cong., 1st sess., p. 317.

27. Francis B. Simkins, *Pitchfork Ben Tillman* (Baton Rouge, 1944), pp. 394–396.

28. Southern Commission on the Study of Lynching, *op. cit.*, p. 20.

29. A careful analysis of the testimony in the *Congressional Record* (59th Cong., 2nd sess., pp. 1321–1329; 60th Cong., 1st sess., pp. 3124–3127) suggests that the Negro soldiers were goaded into "shooting up the town."

30. Ridgeley Torrence, *The Story of John Hope* (New York, 1948), pp. 154–155; Broderick, *W. E. B. Du Bois*, p. 48; Du Bois, *Dusk of Dawn*, p. 86.

31. The *Washington Star*, June 27, 1904, in Virginia C. Scott, "The American Negro as Portrayed by the *Evening Star*, 1904–1912," M. A. thesis, Howard University, 1952.

32. For a comprehensive treatment, see Audrey A. Walker, "An Experiment in Non-Partisanship by the Negro, 1884–1903," M. A. thesis, Howard University, 1958.

33. M. A. DeWolfe Howe, *Portrait of an Independent, Moorfield Storey, 1845–1849* (Boston and New York, 1932), p. 249.

34. Brown, *Negro Poetry and Drama*, pp. 48–49.

35. This is the title of a poem by Sterling Brown in *United Asia*, V (No. 3, 1953), 150.

36. Brown, *Negro Poetry*, p. 91. Drama by Negroes was less important. *Ibid.*, 112–113.

37. James Weldon Johnson, *Black Manhattan* (New York, 1930), p. 62.

38. Hugh Gloster, *Negro Voices in American Fiction* (Chapel Hill, 1948), pp. 40–67.

CHAPTER SEVENTEEN

1. New York *Age*, July 11, 1912, editorial, p. 4.

2. The myth still persists that J. Ernest Wilkins, whom President Eisenhower appointed Assistant Secretary of Labor, was the first Negro to hold sub-cabinet rank.

3. Porter, *op. cit.*, pp. 320–349, especially p. 337, pp. 351–361, pp. 361–372.

4. Walters, *op. cit.*, pp. 177–191.

5. *Ibid.*, p. 195.

6. *The Crisis*, V (November, 1912), 29.

7. Walters, *op. cit.*, pp. 195–196.

8. Du Bois, *Dusk of Dawn*, p. 235.

9. Sidney S. Tobin made a comprehensive examination of the subject in his "Debates on Negro Problems in Congress, 1907–1921," M. A. thesis, Howard University, 1961. Much of his research was based upon the Grimké Papers in the Negro Collection at Howard University.

10. New York *Times*, November 13, 1914; November 14, 1914, both p. 1.

11. *Congressional Record*, 60th Cong., 2nd sess., pp. 894, 3482–3483.

12. *Ibid.*, 62nd Cong., 3rd sess., pp. 502–507. The section, "History of Bills and Resolutions" in the *Index* for each session shows what disposition was made of them.

13. *Ibid.*, 62nd Cong., 3rd sess., pp. 2929, 2972.

14. *Ibid.*, 63rd Cong., 3rd sess., pp. 1362–1368.

15. U. S. House of Representatives, 64th Cong., 1st sess., Committee on the District of Columbia, . . . *Intermarriage of Whites and Negroes in the District of Columbia, and Separate Accommodations in Street Cars for Whites and Negroes in the District of Columbia*, February 11, 1916 (Washington, 1916), *passim*.

16. Miss May Child Nerney (an employee of the NAACP) to Grimké, March 7, 1914, Grimké Papers.

17. U.S. House of Representatives, 63rd Cong., 2nd sess., Committee on Reform in Civil Service, *Hearings on Segregation of Clerks and Employees in the Civil Service*, March 6, 1914. Washington, 1914.

18. *Congressional Record*, 63rd Cong., 2nd sess., pp. 2929–2933, 3037–3043, 3118–3119, 3130; Tobin, *op. cit.*, pp. 115–121.

19. Tobin, *op. cit.*, pp. 130–163.

20. *Ibid.*, pp. 164–170.

21. *The Crisis*, XVI (July, 1918), p. 111.

22. Emmett J. Scott, *Scott's Official History of the American Negro in the World War* . . . (Chicago, 1919); reminiscences of Negro veterans, including those of the author who was stationed at Newport News and who served in France.

CHAPTER EIGHTEEN

1. This survey analyzed *Century Monthly, Harper's Magazine, Atlantic Monthly* and *North American Review*.

2. These terms were frequently not capitalized.

3. Robert Emmett Ward, "Way Down Souf Once Mo," *Century Monthly*, XCI (January, 1916), 480. For numerous other poems see Daniel D. Simmons, "The Negro as Portrayed in *Century Monthly* and *Forum* and *Century*," M. A. thesis, Howard University, 1951.

4. Owen Wister, "In a State of Sin," *Harper's*, CIV (February, 1902), 457. For numerous other poems see Lawrence Milton Bott, "The Negro as Displayed in *Harper's Magazine*, 1901–1924," M. A. thesis, Howard University, 1951.

5. James Weldon Johnson, "O Black and Unknown Bards," *Century Monthly*, LXXVII (November, 1908), 66.

6. F. Taylor Bower, "Uncle Isiah," *ibid.*, LXIII (September, 1902), 753; J. R. Shaver, "Family Pride," *ibid.*, LXXIV (August, 1907), 650; Bret Harte, "Ward of Colonel Starbottle's," *Harper's*, CIV (December, 1901), 66, 68, 82. For further examples, see Simmons, *op. cit.*, especially footnote 54, p. 67, and Bott, *op. cit.*, *passim*.

7. One scene from the Broadway musical of 1946, "Call Me Mister," still lingers in my memory. The hiring agent ticked off for work several white unemployed men, skipped over a Negro, and resumed the hiring of white applicants.

8. Clifford W. Ashley, "Lancing a Whale," *Century Monthly*, LXXV (November, 1907), 85; R. Shaler, "Bust of Booker T. Washington," *ibid.*, LXVII (September, 1903), 729. For Negroes in whaling and in the salvaging of ships, see Warren Ashley, "The Blubber Hunters," *Harper's*, CXII (April and May, 1906), 676 and 836 and George Harding, "Wreckers of the Florida Keys," *ibid.*, CXXXIII (July, 1911), 275–285. S. H. M. Bylers, "The Last Slave Ship," *ibid.*, CXIII (October, 1906), 742–746; William W. Lord, Jr., "A Child at the Siege of Vicksburg," *ibid.*, CXVIII (December, 1908), 44; Albert Bigelow Paine, "Mark Twain—Some Chapters from an Extraordinary Life," *Harper's*, CXXXIV (December, 1911), 43–44.

9. Richard Watson Gilder, "Our Obligations to Dialect," *Century Monthly*, LXIII (February, 1902), 636.

10. See above page 37.

11. Thomas Nelson Page, "Old Jabe's Marital Experiment," *ibid.*, LXIV (September, 1902), pp. 704–707. It would be tedious to summarize many of these stories, for they varied little from those in the last quarter of the nineteenth century.

12. Henry Stillwell Edwards, "The Little Unpleasantries at New Hope," *ibid.*, LVIV (July, 1902), 433–440; "Isam and the Poll Tax," *ibid.*, LXXIII (April, 1907), 827–829.

13. Arthur McFarlane, "The Piccaninny Band and the Flag of Their Country," *ibid.*, LXXVII (April, 1909), 881–884.

14. Beirne Lay, "Whar My Chrismus?" *Atlantic Monthly*, XC (December, 1902), 749–755.

15. Virginia Baker, "Grandfather Crane Invokes the Aid of Sorcery," *ibid.*, CXIV (October, 1914), 486–496.

16. Patience Pennington, "Rab and Dab: A Woman Rice-Planter's Story," *ibid.* (November and December, 1914), 577–589, 799–808; CXV (January, 1915), 90–98.

17. Woodrow Wilson, "Reconstruction of the Southern States," *ibid.*, LXXXVII (January, 1901), 1–15. The so-called "War Amendments" were the Fourteenth and Fifteenth, promulgated in 1868 and 1870 respectively.

18. William A. Dunning, "The Undoing of Reconstruction," *ibid.*, LXXXVIII (October, 1901), 437–449; Thomas Nelson Page, "The Southern People During Reconstruction," *ibid.* (September, 1901), 289–304; Daniel H. Chamberlain, "Reconstruction in South Carolina," *ibid.*, LXXXVII (April, 1901), 473–484.

19. S. M. McCall, "Washington During Reconstruction," *ibid.*, LXXXVII (January, 1901), 817–826; editorial, *ibid.*, LXXXVIII (October, 1901), 433–437.

20. Emmett O'Neal, "The Power of Congress to Reduce Representation in the House of Representatives and in the Electoral College," *North American Review*, CLXXI (October, 1905), 530–543; Thomas Benton Edgington, "The Repeal of the Fifteenth Amendment," *ibid.*, CLXXXVII (July, 1908), 92–100.

21. Charles Francis Adams, "Reflex Light from Africa," *Century Monthly*, LXXII (May, 1906), 105–107; Robert B. Bean, "Negro Brain," *Century Monthly*, LXXIII (September, 1906), 778–782.

22. Editor, "Editor's Easy Chair," *Harper's*, CXII (January, 1906), 309–312.

23. Ray Stannard Baker, "Negro Suffrage in a Democracy," *Atlantic Monthly*, CVI (November, 1910), 612–619.

24. Booker T. Washington, "Is the Negro Having a Fair Chance?," *Century Monthly*, LXXXV (November, 1912), 46–54; Robert W. Johnson, "If Lincoln Could Return," *ibid.*, 153–154.

25. Daniel D. Simmons, "The Negro as Portrayed in *Century Monthly* and *Forum and Century*, 1901–1932," M. A. thesis, Howard University, 1951.

26. W. D. Howells, "In Charleston," *Harper's*, CXXXI (Sep-

tember, 1915), 749–752; Harrison Rhodes, "Washington the Cosmopolitan," *ibid.*, CXXXIV (January, 1917), 164–165; Howells, "A Confession of St. Augustine," *ibid.* (April and May, 1917), 681–683 and 882–883.

27. Lawrence Milton Bott, "The Negro as Displayed in *Harper's Magazine*, 1901–1924," M. A. thesis, Howard University, 1951.

28. James C. Hemphill, "The South and the Negro Vote," *North American Review*, CCII (August, 1915), 213–219. For a discussion of the "Grandfather Clause," see above, pp. 212–215.

29. Hemphill, "Problems of Negro Education," *ibid.*, CCVI (September, 1917), 436–445. My italics.

30. Thomas Walker Page, "Lynching and Race Relations in the South," *ibid.* (August, 1917), 241–250. Thomas Nelson Page had suggested emasculation of the Negro as an ultimate means of preventing lynching in his article, "The Lynching of Negroes: Its Causes and Its Prevention," *ibid.*, CLXXVIII (January, 1904), 33–48.

31. Booker T. Washington, "The Fruits of Industrial Training," *Atlantic Monthly*, XCII (October, 1903), 453–462; "Heroes in Black Skins," *Century Monthly*, LXIV (September, 1903), 724–726. See also his "Tuskegee: A Retrospect and a Prospect," *North American Review*, CLXXII (April, 1906), pp. 513–523.

32. Washington, "Is the Negro Having a Fair Chance?" *Century Monthly*, LXXXV (November, 1912), 46–54.

33. William Edward Burghardt Du Bois, "Of the Training of Black Men," *Atlantic Monthly*, XC (September, 1902), 289–297; see also "The Freedmen's Bureau," *ibid.*, LXXXVII (March, 1901), 354–365. Du Bois, "The African Roots of War," *ibid.*, CXV (May, 1915), 707–714.

34. Kelly Miller, "The Ultimate Race Problem," *ibid.*, CIII (April, 1909), 536–542.

35. Marion L. Dawson, "The South and the Negro," *North American Review*, CLXXI (February, 1901), 281–282; Anderson Somerville, "Some Cooperating Causes of Negro Lynching," *ibid.*, CLXXVII (October, 1903), 506–512; Thomas Nelson Page, "The Lynching of Negroes: Its Cause and Its Prevention," *ibid.*, CLXXXVII (January, 1904), 33–48. See also Clarence H. Poe, "Lynching: A Southern View," *Atlantic Monthly*, XCIII (February, 1904), 155–165.

36. Mrs. Mary Church Terrell, "Lynching from a Negro's Point of View," *North American Review*, CLXXVIII (June, 1904), 853–868.

37. One sees here a preview of the view, widely accepted in 1965, that violence resulting from desegregation caused many Northern business firms to hesitate about relocating in the South.

38. Archibald H. Grimké, "Why Disfranchisement is Bad," *Atlantic Monthly*, XCIV (July, 1904), 72–81.

39. Cincinnati *Enquirer*, June 18, 1918, p. 1.

40. San Francisco *Examiner*, July 19, 1910, Sunday comics; Chicago *Tribune* weekly Sunday features, New York *Times*.

41. Chicago *Tribune*, June 13, 1908, p. 5, news art.; March 28, 1911, p. 1, news art.; June 9, 1912, editorial, Part II.

42. Cincinnati *Enquirer*, April 20, 1910, p. 5, news art.; June 28, 1916, p. 5, news art.

43. Chicago *Tribune*, January 5, 1908, pp. 1, 4, news art.; January 16, 1908, p. 9, editorial.

44. New York *Times*, January 16, 1905, p. 5, news art.

45. Washington *Evening Star*, December 12, 1904, editorial; November 8, 1905, p. 2; May 2, 1909, p. 16; August 26, 1909, p. 6; September 24, 1909, p. 8; September 28. 1909, p. 8; November 3, 1909, pp. 1, 6, news articles.

46. Washington *Evening Star*, October 25, 1904, p. 8 and November 14, 1904, p. 13, news articles.

47. The Chicago *Tribune* had daily articles about the antics, as the *Tribune* saw them, of the "Black Troops" through most of June, 1908. The quotations are June 8, pp. 2, 3; June 10, p. 2; June 16, p. 12, editorial.

48. *Ibid.*, June 2 and 7, 1912, editorials, pp. 4 and 6, respectively.

49. Boston *Evening Transcript*, June 22, 1915, editorial.

50. New York *Times*, December 18, 1906, p. 5; June 4, 1903, p. 6, news art.; July 1, editorial; December 18, 1906, p. 5, news art. The Chicago *Tribune* quoted the Tennessee *Scimitar* which said that "the most damnable outrage was committed by the President when he invited a 'nigger' to . . . the White House," October 17, 1901, p. 1. Other papers also criticized Roosevelt while some condemned those who criticized the President.

51. Chicago *Tribune*, March 20, 1911, p. 1; March 21, p. 4; March 22, p. 1; March 23, p. 5; March 25, p. 1; March 26, p. 1; all news articles. New York *Times*, March 20, 1911, p. 1; March 21, p. 6; March 22, p. 1; March 23, p. 2; November 7, p. 1; all news articles.

52. New York *Times*, November 16, 1915, editorial.

53. Cincinnati *Enquirer*, July 14, 1903, p. 6, editorial; September 13, 1901, p. 3, news art.; July 27, 1902, p. 1, news art.; December 4, 1912, p. 1, news art.

54. *Ibid.*, July 4, 1917, p. 4, editorial; August 27, 1917, p. 3, news art.; November 3, 1917, p. 1, news art.

55. See the following M. A. theses at Howard University: John E. Brent, "The American Negro, 1901–1907, as Portrayed in the San Francisco *Examiner*"; Howard E. Jernagin, "The American Negro, 1908–1912, as Portrayed in the San Francisco *Examiner*"; Virginia C. Scott, "The American Negro as Portrayed by the *Evening Star*, 1904–1912"; James R. Carroll, "The American Negro as Portrayed in the Chicago *Tribune*, 1901–1907"; Hattie

M. Rice, "The Nergo as Portrayed in the Boston *Evening Transcript*, 1901–1919"; Sebron B. Billingslea, "The Negro, 1901 to 1920, as Portrayed in the Cincinnati *Enquirer.*

56. Rice, *op. cit.*, April 17, 1915, p. 9.

57. Edgar Allan Toppin, "The American Negro, 1901–1921, as Portrayed in the New York *Times*," M. A. thesis, Howard University, 1950.

C H A P T E R   N I N E T E E N

1. See above, pp. 328–329.

2. United States Commission on Civil Rights, *Equal Protection of the Laws in Higher Education, 1960* (Washington, 1961), p. 10; Jesse Parkhurst Guzman, ed., *et. al.*, *1952 Negro Year Book* (New York, 1952), p. 150.

3. See above, p. 335.

Index

Index

71852

21835